"ONE OF THE GREAT POLITICAL, HISTORICAL, GEOGRAPHICAL, AND ARCHAEOLOGICAL ADVENTURES OF ALL TIME."
—*Cleveland Plain Dealer*

"Feiler sets off for some of the world's most dangerous places to follow the key figures and events of the second half of Hebrew scripture. . . . Driven by world events, Feiler looks for seeds of peace at the root of religious conflict. . . . Feiler's careful writing and sweeping histories of the region provide compelling reading." —*Washington Post Book World*

"Engaging. . . . Feiler—accompanied by a wise and wisecracking Israeli archaeologist named Avner Goren—visits biblical sites and rereads the scriptural episodes that took place there. He goes spelunking in the sewers of Jerusalem to discover how David entered the city; he flies over the Western Wall and the Dome of the Rock in an army helicopter; he marvels at Persepolis in Iran and the ziggurat of Ur in Iraq. He bounds through his escapades like Indiana Jones, armed with scriptural exegesis in place of a bullwhip." —*New York Times Book Review*

"At once a riveting journey through contemporary conflict zones in Israel, the West Bank, Iraq, and Iran and a provocative analysis of the Bible considered in the broader context of its times. . . . Dramatic. . . . Feiler bravely goes where most would not tread." —*Christian Science Monitor*

"Hot-wire[s] the ancient biblical texts to facts on the ground in the Middle East." —*Los Angeles Times Book Review*

"A blessing. . . . Enlightening. . . . [Feiler] retrieves the ancient wisdom born in a land now ravaged by modern folly."
—*Fort Worth Star-Telegram* (Grade: A)

"A spiritual trek through history. . . . *Where God Was Born* lets readers learn from the past as they forge their own beliefs in the these turbulent times." —*Chicago Tribune*

"Feiler manages to illuminate ancient texts and modern headlines on the same page. The author chronicles how his journeys have shaped and challenged his own perspectives. And ultimately, he makes religion more approachable. Through it all, his reading is smooth and polished, bringing life to the text."
—*Dallas Morning News*

"A marvelous account. . . . Erudite yet immensely readable, Feiler chronicles a spiritual journey to the roots of Western civilization." —*Booklist*

"Feiler visits . . . places of religious and political significance. What he finds is a deepening belief that the Middle East, scene of so much warfare and destruction, holds the roots and the future of Western faith." —*Sarasota Herald-Tribune*

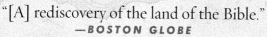

WHERE GOD
WAS BORN

WHERE GOD WAS BORN

A DARING ADVENTURE THROUGH THE BIBLE'S GREATEST STORIES

BRUCE FEILER

HARPER PERENNIAL

NEW YORK • LONDON • TORONTO • SYDNEY

HARPER ● PERENNIAL

A hardcover edition of this book was published in 2005 by William Morrow, an imprint of HarperCollins Publishers.

P.S.™ is a trademark of HarperCollins Publishers.

HarperCollins books may be purchased for educational, business, or sales promotional use. For information please write: Special Markets Department, HarperCollins Publishers, 10 East 53rd Street, New York, NY 10022.

FIRST HARPER PERENNIAL EDITION PUBLISHED 2007.

Border photographs © Michael Storrings / Getty Images

The Library of Congress has catalogued the hardcover edition as follows:

Feiler, Bruce S.
    Where God was born: a journey by land to the roots of religion / Bruce Feiler.— 1st ed.
        p.   cm.
    Includes bibliographical references and index.
    ISBN: 978-0-06-057487-1
    ISBN-10: 0-06-057487-9 (alk. paper)
    1. Palestine—Description and travel.   2. Iraq—Description and travel.   3. Iran—Description and travel.   4. Bible. O.T.—History of Biblical events.   5. Feiler, Bruce S.—Travel—Middle East.   6. Arab-Israeli conflict.   I. Title.

DS49.7.F46 2005
200'.956—dc22   2005043412

ISBN: 978-0-06-057489-5 (pbk.)
ISBN-10: 0-06-057489-5 (pbk.)

07 08 09 10 11 ❖/RRD 10 9 8 7 6 5 4 3 2 1

For Linda

who gives me the courage to go forth

and the reason to come home

He has shown you, O man, what is good,

And what the Lord requires of you:

Only to do justice

And to love goodness,

And to walk humbly with your God.

—MICAH 6:8

CONTENTS

BOOK III
Diaspora

Conclusion

WHERE GOD
WAS BORN

BE STRONG AND VERY COURAGEOUS

I feel the tension before I know its source. My legs begin to quiver, then shake. Soon my whole body is quaking with vibration, or is it fear? Up above, the whir begins to build into a thudding bass beat. Cold air blows through the cracks and up my spine. I'm shivering. My feet are trembling. "Are you ready?" The sound in my ears is crackling, and a bit wicked. I nod. Within seconds the shaking becomes overwhelming, the thumping dense, and the pull so strong it seems ready to suck my head off. I feel as if I'm in a full-body migraine. And then, just as suddenly, quiet. The sound dissolves, my body relaxes. I'm in the air, in a war. I'm at peace.

The helicopter pauses for a second, then accelerates into a gentle glide. Down below, the landing pad disappears, and rows of orange and avocado trees poke up toward the sky. I see the hairs on a donkey's ears. Our nose is tipped, we're flying, yet we're not moving very quickly. Lifting off in a helicopter is like drifting off to sleep: You leave one realm and shift into another; the features seem dreamily unfamiliar; you want to touch what you see, but you can't.

We bank toward the Mediterranean. Voices in my headphones interrupt: *"This is the Air Force. Identify yourself! Do you have permission to be here?"* Boaz, the pilot, smiles. He's anticipated this. He's flown in every war the State of Israel has fought for the previous thirty years. When I asked him what his most dangerous mission was, he thought for a second, then replied, "I once flew seven and a half hours from Israel into enemy territory on a secret mission." I raised my eyebrows; that's halfway to Iran, or Libya.

"Were you part of the mission that destroyed the nuclear plant in Iraq?"

He smiled. "Let's just say I was in the Middle East."

Boaz replied to air traffic control with a mixture of authority and evasion. We did have permission, garnered over the preceding six months, from three government agencies. The night before a suicide bomber had killed seven soldiers in Tel Aviv, and the Israeli Defense Forces (IDF) rescinded its green light. Boaz had to scramble to find a general to overturn the decision. This morning, after we boarded the McDonnell Douglas MD-500, storm clouds descended, limiting visibility above one thousand feet. We were forced to cancel. An hour later, visibility lifted. "There are always risks with flying," Boaz said. We dashed to the landing pad.

Weather was the least of our risks. War was raging—between the Israelis and the Palestinians, between a fragile coalition and Iraq, between the pluralist West and Islamic extremism. Ripples were reverberating around the globe—in Iran, Saudi Arabia, Yemen, Kenya, Morocco, Indonesia, and, yes, the United States. The Cradle of Civilization—the tiny, fertile crescent of land that stretches from Mesopotamia to North Africa—had once more seized control of the world's destiny, and the future of civilization seemed to be at stake.

The bloody clash of faith and politics that filled front pages at the beginning of the new millennium seemed surprising, coming at the end of a century that had appeared to mark the end of God as a force in world affairs. Hadn't Nietzsche declared at the end of the previous century (1882) that God was dead? Hadn't science, capitalism, and the World Wide Web rendered faith a quaint hangover from the past?

As a Jew raised in the American South, I grew up in a world where religion was a regular part of my life but not exactly a central one. Politics mattered more to me than faith; and depending on what I was doing during years as an itinerant journalist, clowning, country music, or Third World travel became my surrogate religion. Who needed to count commandments when you could count countries visited?

Fifteen years into a life on the road, I realized something was missing from my backpack. There were conflicts in the world, and I had questions that my guidebooks couldn't address. To my surprise, the book that kept calling out to me had been sitting by my bed all along. The calling wasn't religious exactly; it was historical, archaeological, cultural. It was a need to explore the world—even the parts of it that seemed scary, like devotion. I had an idea: What if I retraced the Bible through the desert and read the stories along the way?

For a year I trekked across the Middle East, from Turkey to Jordan, and explored the first five books of the Bible. I visited Mount Ararat, crossed the Red Sea, climbed Mount Sinai. That year in the desert changed me forever. I had gone seeking adventure and came back craving meaning. In particular, I came back struggling to understand the uncertain role of God in my life. The world was prosperous and at peace; pulpits were filled with hoorahs of confidence; yet I felt the gnawing tug of doubt.

I didn't know God completely, and I doubted those who did.

And then came the conflagration—planes into buildings, armies into distant countries, security walls around peaceful towns, *genocide, jihad, crusade* in the news. The world that had been at peace was now at war over God. This change seemed startling. Wasn't history supposed to be ending? Wasn't democratic capitalism supposed to lead us all to heaven?

History wasn't ending, of course; it was finally coming home. The collision of politics, geography, and faith has dominated nearly every story in the Middle East since the birth of writing—from the epic of Gilgamesh to the fatwas of Ayatollah Khomeini. It also dominates the greatest story ever told. Jews and Christians who smugly console themselves that Islam is the only violent religion are willfully ignoring their past. Nowhere is the struggle between faith and violence described more vividly, and with more stomach-turning details of ruthlessness, than in the Hebrew Bible.

Yet nowhere is this conflict conveyed with more humanity and hope.

And so, I thought, what better way to confront my doubts about religion and consider the future of faith than to travel to the land where God was born? And, again, what better guide to read along the way than the text that defines identity for half the world's believers?

I would journey to the flash points in the new world war over God—Israel, Iraq, and Iran—and bring along my Bible. And I would begin my quest with the second half of the Hebrew Bible, at the moment when the children of Israel, sprung from Adam and Eve, descended from Abraham, and freed by Moses, face their harshest challenge. "Conquer the Promised Land," God says to Joshua, Moses' successor, at the start of the books of the Prophets. A former spy, Joshua is one of only two Israelites (the other is Caleb) whom God deems righteous enough to survive the forty years in the desert. "Destroy the pagans who live

on the land," God commands. "Seize the future for yourselves—
and for me."

After twenty minutes we approached an isolated landing strip
just north of Ben Gurion International Airport. A silvery
mist hung low over the Mediterranean, a few miles to the west.
Shallow waves unfolded onto the narrow beaches. Palm trees, like
artichokes on sticks, bent in all directions. As we hovered, a man
strode out of a small building onto the black tarmac. He directed
Boaz to his preferred spot, and as the blades spun, he bent and
scampered toward the door.

Yoram Yair is that rare individual known only by his nickname.
For months afterward, when I told Israelis (and Palestinians) I had
gone on a military tour of the Israelite conquest of the Promised
Land with one of the most decorated generals in the history of the
country, a man who had been the first Israeli to penetrate the Sinai
during the Six-Day War, the last to hold the Golan Heights during
the Syrian offensive of the Yom Kippur War, and the one who led
an amphibious landing closest to Beirut during the Lebanon War,
they all said, "*Yaya?* What's he like?"

A rock. As he boarded the helicopter and greeted us all crisply
yet warmly, he evinced an unimpeachable stableness and sureness
of gesture—firm handshake, steady stare, was that a twinkle?—
that made us instantly trust him. My friend and longtime travel
companion Avner Goren, the archaeologist and explorer, who was
nearing sixty and occupied the fourth seat, said Yaya reminded him
of his father, with a set of idioms and associations that belonged to
the generation of epic founders of Israel. "He's part of the fundamental soil of the country."

Yaya was wearing white boaters, navy khakis, and a pink and
green Hawaiian shirt unbuttoned to his chest. He had a silver

Brylcreemed pompadour that, despite the wind, came to a perfect nest above his forehead, causing me to spend the next few hours wondering how he kept it in place in a foxhole. Altogether, with his leathery skin and matte of gray chest hair, he reminded me of my uncle Bubba walking the strip on Miami Beach.

"I will try to be very modest, but maybe there are another five generals in the world today, alive, who have similar combat experience," Yaya said. "Unfortunately for normal human beings, but fortunately for a military person, I fought in four wars, and in each of those wars, I was in a commanding position. You can't see it, but my body is full of shrapnel."

Boaz reminded Yaya that he had once rescued the general on an aborted mission in Lebanon. A soldier had been shot as they evacuated. But Yaya's most difficult episode? Commanding the tank that penetrated the Sinai at the start of the Six-Day War. The unit behind his was hit and destroyed, as was the unit behind that one. "I was about a mile inside the Egyptian stronghold, taking fire from everyone. We were hit by an antitank gun. I asked everybody to jump; luckily I fell outside. My deputy fell inside and was killed. And then we were surrounded by Egyptians, and I thought, This is the end."

"You were held prisoner?"

"No way, are you crazy? I didn't let them capture me. For about thirty minutes I was all alone until our battalion finally reached my place."

Yaya told these stories with no sense of bravado, only duty. This was his job: leading men into war.

"So during these times," I said, "did you ever turn to the Bible for inspiration?"

"Ever since I was a child," he said, "I liked very much the Bible—the story, the heritage, the connection to the land. When I was a young officer, whenever we trained, I always asked one of the soldiers to prepare something about the place. Every Israeli commander will tell you that part of our mission is education. Not just about weapons systems but about values and ethics.

"And I'll tell you," he continued. "The best thing about the Bible is what it teaches about community. Take Moses: When he leads the Israelites out of Egypt, he does what all good leaders should do, first he sets a goal. Then he builds tactics. But before they leave, he asks his people to do a difficult thing: to put blood on the doorposts. Is this for God? Nonsense. God doesn't need signs. Moses does this because he wants the people to develop a strong identity."

I had sought a warrior to take me on my tour. Had I found something more?

"And what about Joshua?" I said. "What does his story tell you about values?"

He raised his eyebrows. "Let's go," he said. "I'll show you."

B oaz moved the collective control shaft up and to his right, and the helicopter again lifted into the air. He leaned on the pedals and pivoted the control stick between his legs. In a moment, we were catamaraning over the central mountains. For such a narrow country (eighty-five miles at its widest), Israel has stunning topographical range, from the flat fertility of the coastal plain, through the rocky isolation of the central hills, to the desert gulch in the east. We were heading toward its most distinctive feature, a geological shelf that runs along the eastern border, dropping with ear-popping alacrity into the lowest gullet in the world, the Syrian-African Rift. To conquer the Promised Land, the Israelites, who end their forty-year trek through the desert bivouacked on Mount Nebo in Jordan, must first cross this lifeless trap.

Avner, Yaya, and I pulled out our Bibles. The biblical narrative has a clear geopolitical arc. The story begins in Mesopotamia, on the imperial shores of the Tigris and Euphrates, with the earliest scenes of Genesis—the Garden of Eden, the Tower of Babel, and the advent of Abraham, four thousand years ago. Leaving his father's house, Abraham travels to the land God promises him, Canaan, the fragile coalition of isolated cities squeezed between superpowers, Mesopotamia to the north and Egypt to the south. But the patriarchs—Abraham, Isaac, and Jacob—are a small family of pastoral nomads in no position to claim their destiny. With Jacob's son Joseph the family decamps to Egypt, where they live for four centuries, quietly growing in stature.

By the thirteenth century B.C.E., the Israelites have multiplied to such numbers that they threaten the pharaoh, who enslaves them and begins killing off newborn males. This precipitates the Exodus, the defining event of the Pentateuch, the Bible's first five books, in which Moses leads millions of Israelites from the most civilized country on earth and parades them into the desert. Instead of heading directly to the Promised Land, a journey of no more than two weeks, Moses first inculcates the Israelites with the values of God. They resist, building idols and demanding a return to slavery. Four decades pass before the Israelites accept their destiny and become a unified nation, ready to fight for the land God promised their forefather eight hundred years earlier.

"So how different was the world that Joshua faced," I asked Avner, "from the one Abraham came to eight centuries earlier?"

He sat forward. Nearly seven years had passed since I first met Avner and the two of us began retracing the Bible, with one eye on archaeology, another on politics, and a third one, unexpectedly, on ourselves. Avner had been bruised by the violence of the intervening years, which ate away at his profession, his pioneering bridge building with Muslims, and his dreams for a greater region in touch with its universal gifts to humanity: frankincense; the alphabet;

civilization; an eternal, invisible God. His gray hair still squiggled from his weatherworn face; his turquoise eyes still stopped time (and women). Newly remarried, with a young daughter, he had more energy than I'd seen in years. But he no longer accepted easy optimism, looking instead for the darker currents and hidden themes in the scorched soil of the region.

"When Abraham came, it was the age of empires," he said. "The world was divided into big powers: Egypt, the biggest, to the south, then the Mesopotamians to the north. It was a bipolar world, and the land in the middle was weak. Canaan wasn't even a state; it was city-states.

"At the start of the thirteenth century B.C.E.," he continued, "the world began to change. Twelve hundred B.C.E. was a land-mark in history." First, Egypt and the reigning Mesopotamians, the Hittites, clashed in Syria, coming to a virtual draw. Soon after, the empires began to decline, leaving a vacuum in Canaan. This social breakdown opened the door to new powers from the West, namely the Myceneans, the Greek-speaking empire that built Thebes and Troy and provided the backdrop for the *Iliad* and the *Odyssey*. Also, a mysterious population called the Sea Peoples be-gan a full assault on the coastal plain. Scholars disagree about whether these Viking-like bands were from the Aegean, Anatolia, or some combination, but the result is the same: a new western front in the struggle for Canaan.

"So if the world before was bipolar," I asked Avner, "would you say this world was nonpolar?"

"I would say it was chaos."

"But why bother? This land is not that big. It's not that fertile."

"If you're in Egypt, it's the only way to get to Syria. If you're in Mesopotamia, it's the only way to get to Africa. If you're in the Mediterranean, it's the only way to get to Asia. It may not be the liv-ing room, but it's a corridor, and a very important corridor at that."

"Israel, the world's greatest hallway."

Learning about this chaos reminded me anew how brilliantly at-tuned the Bible is to the geopolitical realities of its time. It may not be history as we have come to expect it—an objective retelling of events—but it is steeped in rich, historical detail. This richness also highlights an intriguing possibility: If the Sea Peoples are invading a suddenly weakened Canaan from the west, why can't another pre-viously unknown power invade the same land from the east?

The Book of Joshua begins the second major section of biblical books, the Prophets, which follow the five books of the Torah, Genesis through Deuteronomy. The story opens with God address-ing Joshua, Moses' aide who has risen to leader of the tribes. "My servant Moses is dead. Prepare to cross the Jordan, together with all this people, into the land that I am giving to the Israelites." Be "strong and very courageous," God says. Joshua sends two spies to reconnoiter Jericho. A harlot hides them in her home, and they promise to protect her during the invasion if she ties a crimson cord to her window, a vivid echo of the bloody doorposts in Exodus.

The ties between Joshua and Moses are etched even deeper as three days later the former lieutenant leads the Israelites to the shores of the Jordan, the river that extends from Lake Huleh in the north through the Sea of Galilee to the Dead Sea. When the priests bearing the Ark reach the river, the waters divide in the same manner as the Red Sea and "all Israel crosse[s] over on dry land." Once again, the Israelites begin a new phase in their history with God showing his manifest control over nature and his inti-mate involvement in everyday events.

After about fifteen minutes in the air, we reached the Rift Val-ley. From the helicopter, the cleft seemed particularly bar-ren, a frightening gash of charred, chalky sediments, the color of a wasp's nest. The Jordan, depleted from overirrigation, was barely visible, a narrow wrinkle as thin as a pencil line. Not a mile to the west, the Judaean hills begin, gentle slopes covered in gray grooves as if a million earthworms had edged through the sand. From above, the hills look like sleeping armadillos.

"Do you see that?" Yaya shouted. "That's the ancient city." He pointed to the tell, a ten-acre site nestled within the modern city. Human beings have lived here for ten thousand years. The Israelites also stop here first, whereupon God asks Joshua to circumcise all the men, since none has received this holy mark.

"Now why is this the first thing he does?" Yaya asked. "Because he needs to turn his men into fighters. The key to war is making everyone cohesive. In this ceremony, everyone has to commit himself. Remember, they have no antibiotic. And this touches a very sensitive area for every man. Even the Bible says they have to wait a few days for everyone to recover. Yet *every man does it*. This is the fundamental moment of building community."

Afterward, they turn their attention to war. Jericho is blockaded. For six days, forty thousand Israelites march around the walls, led by seven priests, each blowing a trumpet, followed by the Ark. On the seventh day they circle the city seven times. On the final leg, as the priests blow their horns, Joshua cries, "Shout! For the Lord has given you the city." The city and everything in it, especially the silver and gold, are to be reserved for the Lord, Joshua says. With trumpets blaring, the people raise a mighty shout and the walls come tumbling down. The Israelites rush in, killing everything in sight, "man and woman, young and old, ox and sheep and ass." The only people spared are the harlot, her parents, and her brothers.

"So what do you think?" I asked Yaya.

"The first thing you have to see about Joshua is that his background is typical of our way of bringing up leaders. In the Israeli

Army, unlike the American or European ones, you cannot go straight to the academy and become an officer. You have to go through the ranks. First you join as a private, and only if you are a successful foot soldier will you be sent to the squad leader course, and only if you are a successful squad leader will you be sent to officer school. Joshua did the same thing, so when he became a leader, he knew exactly what to do."

"And what about his tactics?"

"Brilliant. In war, you always try to make use of different kinds of tricks. I know everybody talks about miracles—and I don't want to take anything away from God—but capturing Jericho, in my opinion, is the first example in history of psychological warfare."

"Really?"

"Because what they do is surround the city for seven days. Now try to imagine you are defending the city. Everyone in Jericho is nervous; they are expecting attack. They wake up every morning and see the Israelites walking around with their trumpets. And they think any minute they will attack: '*Now* they will! *Now* they will!' But nothing happens. The next morning, the same feeling. People are going crazy!

"Imagine if every day they take you to the hospital. 'Now we are going to operate.' You see the doctors, the nurses, you are scared to death. And suddenly they take you back to your room. No explanation. They don't even say, 'Not today.' The next morning, the same thing. You are going crazy. 'Cut me! Kill me! Do whatever you want, but I can't take this back-and-forth.' That's what happens. Seven days. The Israelites defeat a totally protected city."

We turned north up the valley toward Shechem, a hotbed of contention then as now. To the west, we could see the next target for the Israelites' attack, Ai. After Jericho, Joshua moves northward in an attempt to defeat the weaker towns along the central spine of mountains. Feeling cocky, his spies declare they need only a small garrison to conquer Ai. But the men are quickly routed, which God attributes to the Israelites having kept forbidden booty during the attack on Jericho. Yaya was equally unforgiving: "Don't underestimate your enemy: That's the first rule of war."

Joshua then dispatches thirty thousand men to hide behind Ai. He leads the rest to the city walls, before fleeing in apparent retreat. The men from Ai follow hotly, leaving the city unprotected and easy prey for the waiting troops, who quickly conquer it. Yaya described this as a textbook ambush. It's what follows, though, that is momentous. Joshua marches *all the Israelites*—men, women, and children—north to Shechem, a place of emotional significance because Abraham first stopped here when he came to the Promised Land.

"You see that valley," Yaya called out. We were over the central mountains, where down below a clear boulevard was visible between two ridges. "You can see why Joshua took this path. The people walked in the middle, and he put troops on either ridge to protect them."

Once Shechem is captured, Joshua gathers the Israelites around the Ark, with half facing a mountain of blessing and half a mountain of cursing. Joshua then reads everyone the Laws of Moses. This moment represents the first time in Israelite history when the written Torah plays a central role. "There was not a word of all that Moses had commanded that Joshua failed to read in the presence of the entire assembly of Israel, including the women and children and strangers."

Yaya was awestruck. "Try to imagine how advanced that was," he said. "Women and children were not counted back then. Women got the right to vote only a hundred years ago. This is *three thousand years ago!*"

As he spoke, a burst of shouting interrupted our conversation. The Air Force was furious we were approaching Shechem, modern-day Nablus, one of the bloodiest cities in the region. *"You don't have permission to be here,"* the voice insisted. *"Turn back. Now!"* A small band of ultra-Orthodox Jews had recently blockaded themselves in Joseph's Tomb and been firebombed by Palestinians. "We're not going over the city," Boaz replied, turning to me and winking. The voice did not let up. Directly under us, Yaya pointed out the Balata Refugee Camp, from which dozens of suicide bombers had been dispatched. It looked like an intractable gray maw.

Ignoring the Air Force, Boaz maneuvered the helicopter over the city, which was bracketed by two beautiful peaks: Gerizim, the mount of blessing, and Ebal, the mount of cursing. They were clearly the highest summits in the area. My mind considered how high a rocket-propelled grenade could fly. Boaz seemed unmoved. Earlier, I had asked him if he ever got nervous. "During a situation, you don't have time to feel uncomfortable," he said. "It's like being in a car accident. Afterward, your legs are shaking, but during, you have to guide the steering wheel." And do you feel more peaceful? "From the air, everything looks different. I don't know how to describe it, but when you're up here, you feel better."

He steered us to the center of town, directly between the mountains, and over the monastery of Jacob's Well. And then he stopped. The staccato warnings from the controller continued. The rotor kept spinning, and the sun tried to sieve through the clouds. But we weren't moving. We paused, suspended in midgulp, just beyond the reach of conflict, far from the fullness of calm, motionless, yet hoping for a hint of blessing from the rival hills.

Yaya broke the silence. For the first time all morning, his voice was low, unanimated. It was personal. "Whenever I try to read the Bible," he said, "I try to grab the most significant part. In my opinion, the most significant part of this story is that Joshua didn't read the Laws of Moses only to the heads of the tribes. He read it to everybody. Remember, they had no radios, or loudspeakers. Try to imagine what it means to pass a lesson along the chain so it reaches every man, every woman, every child."

"So why does he do it?"

"Because that's what distinguishes the Israelites from the rest of the world. Moses' rules touch *every little corner of your life*, from the moment you wake up to the moment you sleep. Even hygiene: how to take care of animals, keep your camp clean, what happens when you pee. Even today, how many countries have legislation on how to treat animals? But three thousand years ago, the Israelites built their nation around living a meaningful life. That's why they survived."

The journey south from Shechem became more treacherous. We were covering the most hostile part of the terrain, the central mountains, where for millennia the weaker peoples have been driven to live. What confines the Palestinians to this territory today is exactly what drove the Israelites here in antiquity: because the land is less desirable, the lesser power must accept it. Surviving in the Middle East is elementally a matter of water, not land. The most fertile areas are secured the earliest. In Canaan that means the Galilee, the coastal plain, and what the Bible calls the *shefela*, the foothills. In today's world of long-distance surveillance and projectile weaponry, the tops of mountains might be coveted, but in antiquity they were shunned. None of the strongest cities in Canaan, like Beth-shan and Hazor, or even the second-tier cities, like Jericho or Jerusalem, were built at the summits in their neighborhoods. They were built closest to water.

Joshua's warpath through the Promised Land is brilliantly

designed to capitalize on this. First he threads his population in between Canaanite strongholds and stations them alongside a takable city, Shechem. Then he prepares to attack surrounding cities. But his enemy adjusts. A huge coalition of regional kings, including ones from Jerusalem and Hebron, form an alliance to attack the Israelites. Joshua marches all night to surprise them. The seminal battle takes place a few miles west of Jerusalem, where Boaz steered our craft. The hills below were covered in terraces, desperate attempts to keep rainwater from draining away too quickly.

In the battle, Joshua has the advantage of attacking first. But he has an even greater ally. In the war's most arresting scene, God actually joins the fighting, hailing huge stones from the sky to destroy the fleeing enemy. Desperate for total victory, Joshua pleads for God to stop time. God obliges.

> *And the sun stood still*
> *And the moon halted*
> *While a nation wreaked judgment on its foes.*

Never before, the Bible says, "has there ever been such a day, when the Lord acted on words spoken by a man."

Joshua soon sweeps from north to south and completes his vanquishing of Canaan. "Thus Joshua conquered the whole country," the text says, "with all their kings; he let none escape, but proscribed everything that breathed." In less than ten verses, the dream of the Israelites for over ten centuries has come true.

Or has it? Since I began exploring the Bible, I had been bedeviled by the tantalizing, tender relationship between the details in the text and the facts in the ground. After two centuries of aggressive digging, archaeologists have come to what can be characterized as an awkward accommodation with the Hebrew Bible. For the Torah, there is simply no physical evidence that any of the events described took place. There is, however, plenty of support that the stories fit squarely into the historical reality of the second millennium B.C.E. When Abraham wanders from Mesopotamia to Canaan, for example, he follows a familiar migration pattern. When Moses commits murder and flees to the desert, he travels a well-known trading route. Later, with the rise of the prophets in the middle of the first millennium B.C.E., history arrives in full panoply and the Bible is a much more reliable narrator. Joshua, along with David and Solomon, inhabits a ticklish middle ground.

The primary problem with Joshua's conquest story in the text is that few of the cities described—including Jericho and Ai—show any signs of having been occupied at the time the Israelites appeared in the country. As Avner put it, "The walls could not have come tumbling down around Jericho because the city didn't have walls. Plus, it wasn't inhabited in 1200 B.C.E., when the Israelites arrived. For sure we have a story that was added later." Nevertheless, there is extensive evidence that the social and political landscape of the country changed around this time and irrefutable proof that the Israelites eventually took over. So what happened?

There are four theories. The oldest is the monolithic war theory: the Israelites came en masse, largely as described in the text, with the story receiving some tinkering when it was written down a few centuries later. Avner, like many, was taught this as a child. A more radical idea, introduced in the 1920s, was peaceful infiltration: the Israelites were pastoralists who wandered in with their flocks in seasonal migrations, settled in the sparsely populated highlands, and eventually clashed with the Canaanites.

Later archaeology showed that the Israelite communities were more advanced, unified, and apparently established within a few generations, which gave rise to a third theory, the wave. The Israelites moved in aggressively from outside, but not all at once, and they never really conquered the entire land, only parts of it.

This is what Avner learned in graduate school. A revisionist theory, introduced more recently, suggests the Conquest was an internal rebellion. The Israelites, instead of being outsiders, were Canaanite peasants who broke away from their lords and fled to the highlands, where they adopted the religious ideals of equality gleaned from renegade Egyptians.

"So what do you believe now?" I asked Avner.

"I still believe there is a lot of truth in the biblical story," he said. "Granted, it's much more complicated, but I have difficulties saying they are indigenous people. Archaeologically, I would expect to see much more continuity. The new inhabitants dressed the same, but they had much poorer materials. Even the pottery shows differences. We have a clear break with Canaan. I think we can be confident that the Israelites came from outside and somehow took over the country."

Soon we arrived over the southern hills, our last stop before Jerusalem. Yaya had grown more emotional, pointing out landmarks where he trained as a private. Hearing him tap into that raw passion of youth drew me closer to him, and I said, "The Bible never says men going into war are scared. In your experience, do people get scared?"

"No doubt. One of the things you do as a leader is say, 'All those who are afraid, go back.' Almost everyone will go forward. If you identify with the unit, and your commander, you will overcome your concern. People will do unbelievable things if they believe in the values of the group."

I had been thinking a lot about fear. I wasn't a direct combatant in this conflict. I didn't wear a uniform, live in an occupied town, or face mandatory service, like all young Israelis. Instead I was something odder: a volunteer. The simple fact was that I didn't

have to be in this helicopter. I didn't have to leave my mother crying on the telephone. I didn't have to leave my new apartment and
the mementos I'd just bought on my honeymoon. I didn't have to
leave my new wife.

Yet I did.

And I was afraid. Afraid that I was doing the wrong thing, that
I was taking my life into my hands, that I was bringing pain to the
people I loved. And I was concerned that the idea that motivated
me—thinking about the past as a way to understand the present—
was wrong.

Still, my motivation seemed clear. After decades of traveling
around the world, thinking about religion and God had brought
me more stability than I had ever experienced. Exploring the world
through the prism of the Bible had allowed me to understand my
surroundings in a way I never thought possible. Interfaith problems are rooted in Abraham; the first war in Iraq was between
Cain and Abel. For years I ran decisions through the part of me
rooted in my hometown in Georgia and the part grounded in my
Ivy League education. Now I also ran them through the Bible and
the lens of meaning provided by the ancient stories.

But nagging questions remained. The hardest one I was asked
about my earlier journeys through the Bible was how they had affected my faith. I was raised as a fifth-generation Jew in the South
in one of the oldest synagogues in the United States. Religion was
a matter of rote and pride, not a matter of conviction. But my
journey grounded me, I often said. I discovered in myself a molec-
ular attachment to the land. My bond with the Bible moved from
my head to my feet.

I felt safe.

But there was something I felt that I rarely said: Traveling in the
desert drew me closer to God but further away from organized religion. I love the text, but not necessarily what human institutions

have done in its name. Manipulation, exclusivism, hatred, and violence are undeniable outgrowths of biblical monotheism. Perhaps I had no need for religion and could cultivate a personal, nonsectarian relationship with the Bible, with other seekers, and with God.

September 11 at first deepened that conviction. My animosity toward religion seemed bolstered by the new reality, as violence in the name of faith now imperiled the world. Turn on a news broadcast anywhere. Fundamentalists had seized control of faith and slammed the door on tolerance. There was only one route to salvation, and Osama bin Laden, or Mullah Omar, or Jerry Falwell, or any number of radical Jewish settlers I had met over the years held the key. To me this extremism held an alarmingly real prospect for religious war.

But the alternative—radical secularism—seemed equally dangerous and unappealing. The bloodiest wars of the twentieth century were fought for secular ideologies, including socialism, fascism, and communism. When I was growing up, the world had seemed to be disengaging from religion; it turned on the axis of the Cold War and worshiped the twin gods of science and pleasure. In the West, the biggest alternative to faith was capitalism and the promise that the global marketplace held for heaven on earth. People were just too busy getting ahead and enjoying the moment to worry about profiting from the past or preparing for the afterlife. The result left what Jean-Paul Sartre called a God-shaped hole in human consciousness, where the divine once was but had disappeared.

So is there a middle ground? I wondered. Is there a place where faith and tolerance can live side by side? In short, is religion just a source of war, or can it help bring about peace?

As I tried to answer those questions, the Bible took on new meaning—and new urgency—for me. In particular, I became fascinated by the underappreciated second half of the Hebrew Bible, in which the birth of religion is described in dramatic, contentious detail. For the first thousand years of Israelite history, the patriarchs have a personal relationship with God and their descendants receive the 613 Laws of Moses. But their ways of worship—building altars, making burnt sacrifices—bear little resemblance to what organized religion would become. Nowhere in the Torah, for instance, does it say how to conduct a wedding or a funeral. Not until the first millennium B.C.E. do the Israelites begin to refine the basic tenets of biblical monotheism—worshiping in the Temple, reading the Bible, celebrating Shabbat. The Dead Sea Scrolls, dating from the late first millennium B.C.E., contain extensive details on how to plan nuptials.

The latter parts of the Bible portray this evolution as messy at best. Here, in a glorious sweep that heralds God's kingdom on earth, Joshua parades the Ark into Israel, David unites the tribes in Jerusalem, and Solomon builds the House of the Lord. But here also, in a vivid portrait of the moral decay that shadows that kingdom, Jeremiah decries the ethical rot of the people, Isaiah weeps over their exile to Babylon, and Ezekiel dreams of their return to Zion. In this graphic interplay, the Bible seems to be saying that godliness and godlessness are in perpetual tension.

For years I deflected questions about religion by pointing out that organized faith didn't exist during the time of the patriarchs. The second half of the Hebrew Bible puts that vacancy to an end, as Israel develops Judaism, the foundation faith for Christianity, Islam, and half the world's believers today. And Israel was not alone. Around the globe, from Japan to India to Iran to Greece, organized religion was invented in the first millennium B.C.E. The German philosopher Karl Jaspers termed these years (800 to 200 B.C.E.) the Axial Age, because they gave rise to Shintoism, Confucianism, Hinduism, Zoroastrianism, Judaism, and Platonism. The central challenges of our time—the relationship between individuals and God, faith and reason, theocracy and democracy, church and state—were born in the centuries between Moses and Jesus. For that reason, some scholars believe we are in a new Axial Age. Regardless, the need to understand the birth pangs of religion is more pressing than ever.

At the close of my first journey, as I climbed down from Mount Nebo, I had turned to Avner and said, "We're not done yet." Finally I understood why. I had to return to the scene of my desert transformation. I would travel through the tinderbox of Israel, exploring the prickly relationship between God and the first kings of Israel. I would try to penetrate Iraq, the birthplace of the Bible and the scene of the most traumatic—and least understood—revolution in the history of religion, the Babylonian Exile. And I would attempt to pierce the religious iron curtain surrounding Iran, home to the unexpected savior of the Israelites, Cyrus the Great, the first interfaith leader in history.

"Great, the Axis of Upheaval," my wife cracked.

Still one more reason drew me back to the Bible. The comfort I took from my earlier travels had been undermined by a series of crises. My mother got cancer; my father, too, had been touched by illness. I had arrived in a new phase of life. On a personal level, one relationship ended, and another began. That, too, failed, which sent me back to the woman whose strength, wisdom, and fire mirrored the feelings I had in the desert. One thing love and faith have in common is that they grow from the same human amalgam of unease, desire, passion, and need.

We were married on a June evening under the stained-glass light of Noah and by the words of Moses in my childhood synagogue. Two rabbis, each invoking Abraham and Sarah, wove the present to the past with an ineffable flax. It was the part of religion that seemed most appealing: the comfort and import of repetition, something totally familiar that became, through its sheer ordinariness, something fresh and uplifting.

Two months later, I kissed my wife good-bye and set out to undermine everything we had built. The world was filled with terror, fear, and death. War, so long prosecuted in the name of states, was now being rendered most commonly in the name of God. The Bible, which for so long had seemed the refuge of the past, suddenly seemed the most vital route for making sense of the tumult of the hour.

I had wanted to go on my first journeys back to the Bible.

I needed to go on this one.

I arrived in Jerusalem on the most gorgeous day I could remember, drinking in the clean air. Wind tussled the palm fronds, a *kippah* blew down the street, a huff of clouds chugged by as if from a storybook train. On a passing bus, a pudgy elderly couple, Eastern Europeans who no doubt had survived World War II, gripped each other in a tight embrace, as if granting and taking life. There is no uncomplicated emotion here. No day is purely beautiful; no tragedy is merely tragic.

Avner and I drove to the fashionable German Colony to have dinner. It seemed safe. No bombing had ever occurred on this block. "Are you armed?" the guard said at the gate of an open-air restaurant. Earlier, a soldier across the street had foiled an attack, holding up the arms of a heavily perspiring man to prevent him from detonating the explosives around his neck.

After dinner we walked back to the car. Most of the shops were closed, except one. It was crowded, bright, with a square red sign that said COFFEE. "That's new," I said. "I hear it's wonderful," Avner said. "We should go there sometime." He paused as if to say, "Should we?" Nah, it was late, our helicopter tour was scheduled for the morning. I was asleep by 11:00 P.M.

Twenty minutes later the telephone woke me from a dead

sleep. "There's been a bombing in Jerusalem," Avner said. "I think you should call home." I had done so earlier, after a bombing in Tel Aviv. I telephoned my wife, who was more shaken this time. "Please, no more outdoor restaurants," she said. My mother started pleading. My father was grim.

I got off the phone and turned on the television. The familiar chaos was on the screen—people crying, running, splattered blood on a young girl's face, a darkened arm in the street. And then they showed where it had happened. A bright red sign. Square. COFFEE.

Never before in my years of traversing the Middle East and confronting the reality of religious violence had I felt such a trembling of raw emotion. "Oh, my God," I cried out, alone. I grabbed at my face. I felt the imminence of death, as if I had touched a place in my body I didn't know was there. I watched the endless loop on television, the faces of people I almost knew. I muted the sound and for a few minutes, groggy from half sleep, watched over and over and over again. I turned the sound up and heard how the bomber had been stopped, someone had shouted *"Terror!"* and still no one was safe.

My wife called back, and I started babbling, trying to be soothing, yet a little out of control. By the end I was just hugging the phone in silence. Finally I turned off the television and tried to sleep, half waiting for another call. The room was cold. It was late. Tomorrow was the anniversary of September 11.

We were climbing again, approaching Jerusalem from the south, gliding over the bank of pines that rings the city. "Get ready!" Yaya said. We drifted above the ridge, and suddenly the city burst before us, like a platter of treats being served up by a waiter. My heart leapt as my eye scurried to orient itself, looking first for the bell tower on the Mount of Olives, then the Tower of

David, and finally the large plaza with the golden dome at its heart. "Pray for the well-being of Jerusalem," wrote the Psalmist.

> *"May those who love you be at peace.*
> *May there be well-being within your ramparts,*
> *peace in your citadels."*
> *For the sake of my kin and friends,*
> *I pray for your well-being;*
> *for the sake of the house of the Lord our God,*
> *I seek your good.*

Yaya was bursting with pride, a little boy with a train set he had built himself. "Look! That's the hill we captured in '48." "That's where David eyed Bathsheba." "Wait! Do you see that . . ." The windows nearly fogged with the intensity. After a while I stopped looking at the landmarks and stared at him.

"You're part of one of the most efficient, lethal fighting forces in the world," I said. "And yet you're passionate about the Bible? What would your soldiers say?"

"Can I tell you a secret?" he said. "For years I chaired the committee that wrote the code of ethics for the IDF. It was one of the most enjoyable assignments I had. In the introduction we wrote that all our ethics are based on the values that come from our Bible. I once taught at the War College outside Washington, and they said no other military in the world has such a code."

"But the Bible is so brutal," I said. "Joshua kills women and children."

"That was the custom of the time," he said. "Today, the battlefield is the place where real human character is displayed. I have seen people ready to make the ultimate sacrifice. I have seen people turn into animals. The difference is their values. Do you know that during the whole Yom Kippur War and the Lebanese War there was not even one case that an Israeli soldier raped a woman? You won't find any army in the world with such a record."

We arrived over the Old City. For the first time all day, the clouds dissolved and a clear, white sun washed over the honey-colored stones. A rainbow appeared over the gilded onion domes of the Russian Orthodox church in Gethsemane. "Wanna go for a ride?" Boaz said.

I held on. He pushed down on the control shaft, and suddenly we began to dive. We were forbidden from flying below five thousand feet. Soon we were at four thousand, then three. Our nose was headed at the heart of the Temple Mount, the Haram al-Sharif, the legendary Mount Moriah, where Ariel Sharon inflamed the second Intifada, Yitzhak Rabin led the capture during the Six-Day War, King Hussein watched as his grandfather was assassinated and he received a bullet to his own chest. Mohammed ascended to heaven from here; Jesus made a Passover pilgrimage here; Solomon built the Temple here.

Two thousand feet. Fifteen hundred.

None of us was speaking. My eye was drawn to the crescent on the top of the golden dome. The guard towers on the four corners. The black-capped worshipers at the Western Wall. We were blasting through the cornea of what the Talmud calls the Eye of the World. Our tail swung left, then right, but our head never wavered, locked onto the glint of infinity that has lured people to this spot since God was born. It was like being pulled backward through a vortex of time, an ineluctable wave of legend on top of custom, hatred on top of hope.

The dial said 1,000 feet. We were close enough to hear the prayers. We were near enough to get shot. We were poised in a nameless breach between heaven and earth.

When I first came to Israel, I was drawn by the country's physicality, the dripping sense that past *and* future lived closer to the surface of every life. In Jerusalem I was more alive. Here I could engage the smorgasbord of history and politics, war and peace, that had absorbed me since I was a teenager arguing current events around the breakfast table. I had walked down the steps to the Western Wall, placed my hands on the stones, and wept. I had reached the bedrock of my identity. I had come home.

But now, suspended above that plaza, I wondered. The stones seemed so unmoving, and the history in them so inflexible. The dimensions of that holy mountain had become the battle lines of holy war. Maybe the only way to reach peace was to peer beyond the tangible structures and reclaim the original sacred space. The Temple was never supposed to be merely a place; it was supposed to be the embodiment of an idea: Humans can live in consort with God.

This tension, I realized, forms the undercurrent of the Bible: trying to balance a life on earth with a life that meets the standards of God. When Moses gathers the tribes at the end of his life, he warns them that conquering the land will not end their challenges; it will begin them. And he cautions them that God will punish failure to obey his laws by ripping them from the land. "The Lord will scatter you among all the peoples from one end of the earth to the other."

When Joshua gathers the tribes at the end of his life, he delivers a similar message. Do not mingle with the foreigners that surround you and worship their pagan gods. "You will not be able to serve the Lord," Joshua says. "He is a jealous God; he will not forgive your transgressions and your sins." This is the painful message at the heart of the Conquest: For centuries the Israelites had dreamed of setting foot in the Promised Land, but once they arrive there is little celebration. There is doom. Instead of being a land of milk and honey, it is a land of blood and tears.

This reality sets up the question that defines the rest of the Hebrew Bible: Which is more important, living on the land or living a life of God? For me, this question was acute. So much of my rediscovery of the Bible was about reconnecting to the land. But for the Israelites, occupying the land involves a vicious slaughter of men, women, and children. One overlooked legacy of Israel's God is the beastly violence he continually demands. If you love the lessons of the Bible—particularly its legacy of ethics and morality— it's sometimes hard to love the stories of the Bible. The life of God is not always a life of peace and light.

And neither is life on the land. Jews often claim that, according to the Bible, God promised this land to Abraham; we were here first, and our claims should have precedence. The land is vital to Judaism. But the Bible delivers a very different message. It says living on the land is not the most important thing; living on the land *while obeying God* is the most important thing. The land is secondary to living a virtuous life. Faced with a choice, the people of Israel should chose the values of heaven over the virtues of earth.

"So you fought for this land," I said to Yaya, gesturing to Jerusalem and beyond. "Would you give it back?"

"It depends on what you want to achieve," he said. "War is just a tool to achieve your national goals. Land is important to a nation, but so is language, and ideology. The Jewish people have always wanted to come back to Jerusalem. But more important than this city, or any city, are the rules, the beliefs, the way to treat yourself, your wife, your neighbors. The key to Judaism is the principle that everyone is responsible for the well-being of the people."

"At the end of the story, Joshua gathers all the Israelites at Shechem," I said. "He tells them they must choose the God of Abraham or the gods of Canaan. If you were talking to the Jewish people today, what would you say?"

"As I told you, the most important thing for any leader is to define the goal. For me, the goal is to live in this place, in peaceful conditions with our neighbors, according to our values and beliefs—and not to sacrifice our values and beliefs because of a piece of land, or a question of pride. You have to compromise. All our history we have compromised. But there is one thing we cannot compromise: our values."

The helicopter started to rise. I felt the now familiar vibration from above, the swell of air from below, the gentle lift.

"Can that goal be achieved?"

"No doubt," he said. "No doubt."

Back in Jerusalem a few hours later, the air was still electrified, sad. I went to visit Bikur Holim Hospital, the cramped Dickensian building in the heart of the city that serves as ground zero for many of the victims of suicide bombings. A pall of emptiness still hung over the seventy-five-year-old building, as a guard slowly inspected my bag. Inside a long, dimly lit hallway, a few family members huddled along the stone walls; patients with wounds on their faces sat in wheelchairs.

Seven people were killed in the blast at the coffee shop; fifty-seven were wounded. Craig Nelson, a reporter eating at a pizza parlor across the street from the café, described seeing a man turn away from his restaurant, run into the shop, utter *"Allah Akbar,"* "God is great," then blow himself up. His severed head landed in the middle of the street. The neck is the weakest part of the body, the police explained. Nelson found a twenty-year-old woman curled on her side, gasping for breath, her arm twisted grotesquely. Her hair was singed gray. Nava Applebaum died in his arms. Eight feet away lay the corpse of her father.

Dr. David Applebaum, a native of Cleveland, was one of Israel's most famous emergency room physicians. He had flown back that evening from a conference in Manhattan, where he was asked to speak about his pioneering efforts to treat victims of suicide bombings. He had taken Nava to the café for a father-daughter chat to impart some last-minute advice. Today was to be her wedding day. She was buried instead. As Nava's body was lowered into her grave, her fiancé placed a farewell gift on her shrouded body. It was her wedding ring.

"In the last three years, we've had more than twenty-four suicide bombings," explained Alex Farkas, a friend of Avner's who worked as the hospital's spokesman. Alex was a forty-something Hasidic Jew, with a beard and white shirt; he was disheveled from a night of no sleep. "We got information yesterday morning from the police that a bomber was on his way to Jerusalem. We even knew the color of his shoes. And they caught him a few meters from here; the hospital was his target. But we didn't have warning about the man at the café."

With so much experience, the hospital had become adept at crises. "People come from all over the world to learn how we do it. You hear the doors banging, then—it's a miracle—in two minutes you wouldn't recognize the place. It's like a new dimension of smell, light."

First come light victims, often strapped to chairs. Next are more serious victims, brought by professionals. Ambulances use a special code to get through the barriers, after the IDF warned that bombers might usurp medical vehicles. Then come people in shock, screaming. "Last night we had a serious case, a man who saw his friend lose two legs. He was hyperventilating so severely it took four hours before he came out of it."

I asked Alex how he would explain to someone, like my mother, why there was so much violence in a place of such faith. Was religion to blame?

"I will tell her that one thing is for sure: There is one God, and God controls the world. God controls the bomb, and the bomber. God chooses the doctor who takes my wife's three eggs and, through IVF, turns one of them into my son. And God decides that Dr. Applebaum and his daughter, on the day of her marriage, will go into heaven.

"And I will tell her," he continued, "that as a religious person, I believe the world is going to get better. There will be a messiah. It is written in the Bible that the sheep will live together with the wolf."

"But when you read Joshua," I said, "the story suggests you can't have God's kingdom without violence."

"Why does a baby, when it's born, have to go through such drastic bloodshed? I don't know. I didn't create the world, but I know that good things come from stress. Through that war, the land of Israel was created. Through this war, we created many methods of saving lives."

He told me a story. A woman had come into the hospital the night before. She had shrapnel in her back and was covered in blood. She was hysterical. They got her during the Golden Hour, the first sixty minutes after a crisis. They saved her life. "Do you want to meet her?"

Before I could think I was ushered down the hall, through the emergency ward, into a dimly lit room. Tzippy Cohen was sitting against the pillows in a loose-fitting hospital gown, her bangs hanging limply around her expressionless face. The twenty-five-year-old Australian was more alert than I would have expected, but her eyes were still vacant. She was vacationing from New York, where she works at the National Society of Hebrew Day Schools, just blocks from Ground Zero.

"We decided kind of late, Let's go out for coffee," she said. "We chose the German Colony, because it's not the center of town. We took a cab, because you're not supposed to take buses. I had wanted to go to Café Hillel. I had heard it was good."

"It looked very inviting last night," I said.

"It was full, we noticed that. We decided not to sit outside, safety-wise. We also made a decision to sit in the back, safety-wise. I had a salad, nothing major. We were just picking at our food.

"And then, in the middle of nowhere . . ." Her eyes blinked. "And you knew what it was. There was no question it was a bomb. The place just jumped, like an electric shock went through us. I can't separate anything, except to say: Bang. A shock. Black. Smoke. Shattered. And then a split second of darkness and silence. Followed by screaming. And running. And pandemonium."

Her voice trailed off.

"I knew immediately I had to get out of there," she continued. "I felt I was cut. I was bleeding. Instinct told us to go out the back. We climbed through the glass walls, which were blown out, and went running through the alley, just screaming. 'Call an ambulance! Someone call an ambulance!' A lady said, 'Come with me,' and drove me to the hospital. When I got here I realized there was blood on my body that was not my blood. My hair had pieces in it. . . . It was other people."

Again there was a pause.

"So why were you saved?" I asked.

"I believe in higher powers," Tzippy said. "If you ask me, it's a miracle. I was in New York on September 11 and watched the second tower fall. I was covered in dust. My faith does not let me believe that if I'm going to a land—my *holy* land—that something will happen to me. If I would have died here, I would have died in New York."

"But in the face of what you've seen, some people might say that religion is the problem. You have come face-to-face with one of the worst things a human being can do."

"I have to say, on the contrary, it makes me do a turnaround. I need to turn closer to religion. I am lying here for a reason. You can't attribute something like this to coincidence every time it happens. Luck doesn't come your way so much. If I have learned anything from this experience it is that, despite the evil in this world, there is still goodness in each human being. When I walk out of here, I owe it to God to do something good for his allowing me to survive such hell." She attempted a wan smile.

"And I will."

BOOK ONE

LAND

. 1 .

MAN OF BLOOD

R azor wire is made up of thin metal twine with small sharp barbs every few inches that is twirled into coils about two feet in diameter, then bundled outside fences, roofs, and doorways like a lethal scarf. Razor wire is so ubiquitous in Israel it could almost be the national flower. It even looks like a shrub, the way it twists and turns, catches plastic bags and soda bottles in its web, and rubs against civilization like poison ivy on a playground. Whenever I see a bundle, I imagine myself making a daring escape through its coils. Then I see myself slipping, my leg catching in the tangle, tearing, then blood, and the disappointment of failure. Razor wire is barbed wire with a greater power to intimidate.

It does have one unexpected benefit, though. The airiness of its coils allows just enough light to get through so that if you leave it for a while, at, say, the checkpoint between Jerusalem and Bethlehem, a sprout of yellow daisies can take root in the desert and pop up through the fear.

Razor fences are not the only impediment to traveling the six miles from Jerusalem to Bethlehem. There is also, on this chilly morning, the Israeli Army, the Palestinian security forces, and a border so volatile that Avner couldn't traverse it. He left me at a long line of cars to walk along a cliff with a few Italian tourists in wheel-chairs, through a checkpoint armed with Israeli teenagers, into a gamut of taxi drivers so desperate for business one actually looked hurt when I passed him by. "Why are you angry?" he shouted.

Moments later Arlet Odeh sped up in a white Mercedes. She was thirty years old, with dangling curls, a hawk nose, and deep bags under her eyes that came more from lack of hope than from lack of sleep. Arlet was also a tour guide with no tours to guide. For three years she hadn't worked. Her father is old, she said, her mother ill. They are one of only one hundred Palestinian Chris-tian families left in town. "We are living in a cage," she said. "But living means having a life. I have no life. Would you like to see where Jesus was born?"

"Actually, on this trip, I'm interested in King David."

She brightened. "He was born here, too!"

We headed toward the center of town. The cobblestone streets, repaved when Pope John Paul II visited for the bimillennium of Jesus' birth, were deserted, shops boarded up, few people in sight. Though Christmas was still months away, a pale plastic wreath and faded star dangled from the side of the road.

Bethlehem is one of the few cities that appears across the entire two-thousand-year arc of the Hebrew Bible, from the patriarchs to the prophets. The city is first mentioned in Genesis as the place where Jacob's wife Rachel died after giving birth to Benjamin. A tomb marks the spot, which we passed on our way into town, fenced in, empty. Joshua later assigns the area to the tribe of Judah, and it's frequently mentioned during the period of the kings, most prominently as the birthplace of King David. The story of the boy warrior who becomes the king of Israel lords over the early books of the Prophets and introduces what will become a major theme of the second half of the Hebrew Bible: the Israelites' quest to find proper balance between their spiritual identity as an ethically minded people of God and their political identity as a nation strong enough to survive in a region of superpowers.

After the lightning conquest described in the Book of Joshua, the biblical story quickly becomes diffuse, even chaotic. The Book of Judges describes an awkward transition as the people settle the land and try to determine their political leadership. The preeminent fact of the Israelites' existence is that, unlike their neighbors, they don't have a monarch. Four times the text says, "In those days there was no king in Israel," adding, "every man did what was right in his own eyes." For two hundred years, their leaders are judges, including Ehud, Gideon, and Samson, from the Hebrew word *sopet*, which adds the theological element of divination to the more legalistic English term. The authority of the judges comes from God, the ultimate *sopet*, and their principal task is to ensure that the people uphold the Laws of Moses.

But the people are not satisfied, especially as they are repeatedly trounced by the Philistines, the new power along the coastal plain. Samuel, the reigning judge at the time, gathers the Israelites and leads a comeback. But the people still feel insecure and, around 1020 B.C.E., parade en masse to an aging Samuel: "Appoint a king for us, to govern us like all other nations." In a classic case of "Throw the bums out!" they declare they are not happy being ruled exclusively by God; they want more competent, secular leadership based on sound economics and a strong military.

We have reached a familiar moment, when the crabby wandering people of the desert become the surly settled people of the land. The Israelites are never happy. In the Sinai they gripe about the lack of food and poor leadership and demand to be sent back into slavery; in the Promised Land they gripe about their lack of power and poor leadership and demand to be subjected to a king. In both cases, Israel lives up to its namesake, *Ysra'el*, one who wrestles with God.

And God, as he has done before, lashes out: "Me they have rejected as their king." Still, he grants the request but asks Samuel to warn them of their mistake. Samuel's speech is one of the most prophetic in the Bible. A king, he says, will take your sons and sacrifice them in battle, take your daughters and make them perfumers, cooks, and bakers. He will seize your choice fields, take a tenth of your grain, claim your slaves and beasts of burden, and put them to work for himself. "The day will come when you cry out because of the king whom you yourselves have chosen; and the Lord will not answer you that day."

There are many dangers in discussing the Bible in contemporary terms; so much about the ancient world bears little resemblance to our democratic, post-Enlightenment world. In antiquity, all leaders used the gods to bolster their authority. But Samuel is clearly skeptical of having a king over Israel because he believes a monarch will not uphold the values of God. By granting the Israelites' request for a monarch, God acknowledges that they must form a state. The judges, with their ambiguous power, just won't do anymore. But if the Israelites do get their state, God wants their leader to have limited power. The king can rule the country, but God must still have dominion over the spiritual life of the people. In contemporary parlance, state and church should be separate; morality is too important to be entrusted to humans.

Our first stop was a small Catholic school, covered in lemony Jerusalem stone, where three cisterns discovered in 1895 are known as David's Wells, after a passage in Samuel in which David, as a young commander, muses out loud, "If only I could get a drink of water from the cistern which is by the gate of Bethlehem!" Three warriors promptly battle the Philistines to produce the water, only to have David callously reject the drink.

Arlet and I continued toward the town center. The birth of David in the first Book of Samuel marks a milestone in the narrative. Scholars generally regard the Bible's first four books—Genesis, Exodus, Leviticus, Numbers—as a single unit. Deuteronomy is linguistically and stylistically linked with the subsequent books—Joshua, Judges, I and II Samuel, I and II Kings—into a second unit, known as the Deuteronomistic History. These books describe the five hundred years that include Joshua, the united monarchies of David and Solomon, the split kingdoms of Israel and Judah, and their ultimate destruction, ending with the population's exile to Babylon in 586 B.C.E.

Just as Moses is the dominant character in the first section, David is by far the seminal figure in the second. His name appears more than one thousand times in the Hebrew Bible. Some scholars have even suggested that Israel's faith should have been called not Judaism (from the kingdom of Judah, which David headed) but Davidism. By receiving the blessing of eternal kingship, he also becomes the messianic forefather of Christianity. Even the Koran honors him as a prophet. David, the Bible says, is clearly "a man after God's heart."

But he's also "a man of blood."

David's story begins with Saul, the first king of Israel. After the Israelite tribes enter the Promised Land, each one is assigned a region, where they quickly begin setting up rival spheres of influence. Saul controls the central region, but he is too weak to forge a unified state, so God goes looking for a worthier man. "I am sending you to Jesse the Bethlehemite," God tells Samuel, "for I have decided on one of his sons to be king." In a charade prescient of Cinderella, Jesse marches seven sons before Samuel, who rejects them all. "Are these all the boys you have?" Samuel says. "There is still the youngest," says Jesse, who is tending flock. A "ruddy-cheeked, bright-eyed, handsome" boy appears. He's also a stalwart fellow, the text says, is sensible in speech, and plays the lyre with such skill that when King Saul hears it, he feels better and evil spirits leave him. The boy's name, in all likelihood, means "beloved."

The Bible, in other words, protests too much. Even from these early verses, the portrait of David is too good to be true; he's more heart tugging than Abraham or Moses, more dreamy than a love-struck first date. Also, certain patterns reappear. David is the younger son who claims power over his elders, as were Isaac, Jacob, and Joseph. He's also a shepherd, a familiar metaphor for a king that began with the pharaohs and continued through Jesus.

But amid this hagiography, the text sends a hidden message that all might not be well. David's lineage can be traced through several women: Ruth, who was from Moab, not Israel, and seems to have been sexually promiscuous; and Tamar, who seduced her father-in-law and bore him twins. David's family tree has roots in tainted, foreign soil, which, in an age when land is central to identity, places his loyalty to Israel at least somewhat in doubt.

We arrived at Bethlehem's heart, Manger Square, which had recently been replanted with palm trees in an effort to gussy it up. Today, the only people around to appreciate it were several hundred Palestinian mourners who emerged from the church carrying a simple black coffin on their shoulders and an enormous crucifix in their arms. Waiting by the door for their exit were a bride and groom in full regalia. "A funeral and a wedding on the same day!" I said to Arlet.

"The funeral was in the Catholic part," she said. "The wedding in the Greek Orthodox."

Ah, the ecumenical age.

Unlike their siblings in Europe, churches in the Middle East often appear bulky and sullen—pale brown, Escher-like patch jobs that appear to have been constructed by feuding committees, from the inside out. Bethlehem's Church of the Nativity is a sterling example of this architecture by time line: this door from the Byzantines, that arch from the Middle Ages, never mind that a lintel conceals the arch. Constantine's mother, Helena, identified this site as Jesus' grotto and ordered a church built in 326 C.E.; it has been rebuilt every few hundred years since. Stepping through the low Crusader door—built four feet high to prevent nonbelievers from entering on horseback—I emerged in a dark, spacious sanctuary. Four rows of Corinthian columns line the hall, which has a stone floor with occasional trapdoors revealing mosaics.

The space soon unfolds into a complex maze: To the right is a Greek Orthodox chapel, to the left an Armenian one. Nearby is a small Franciscan patio with four plucky lemon trees. In 2001, the Israeli Army surrounded the church after Palestinian gunmen barricaded themselves inside, along with 160 hostages. For a symbolic forty days, the prisoners slept in corners, losing thirty pounds each. "A priest made soup for the people," Arlet said. "He used the leaves of the lemon trees and the oil from the lamps. They ate it every three days."

I asked if the church had any symbols recognizing David's importance to Bethlehem, and she led me down a narrow set of stairs to an underground chapel. A small marble altar is tucked into the wall, with eighteen wooden icons dangling from its mantel. Embedded in the marble hearth is a fourteen-point silver star that marks the spot of Jesus' birth. A Latin inscription reads HERE JESUS CHRIST WAS BORN TO THE VIRGIN MARY.

"The star has fourteen points," Arlet explained, "because there are fourteen generations between Jesus and David—"

"And fourteen more between David and Abraham."

We smiled at this shared bit of knowledge. The holiest spot in Bethlehem shows the deep roots between Judaism and Christianity: both believe the blood of David runs through the messiah.

As it happens, the interfaith roots of David extend even deeper. The most iconic symbol of Judaism today is the six-pointed star, or hexagram, made from two interlocking equilateral triangles and known as the Magen David, or Star of David. This motif, however, is not Jewish in origin. In the Hellenistic world, hexagrams were used by all religions, and in the Middle Ages, Jews, Christians, and Muslims alike used them to ward off demons and fires. In the fourteenth century, Jewish mystical texts began associating the image with the shield of God used to protect King David, and it first appeared on a Jewish flag in Prague in 1527. Enlightenment Jews needed a symbol equivalent to the cross to indicate that Judaism was a religion, not a race, which led to the Magen David being adopted by Zionists as a symbol of strength and by Nazis as a brand of hate. The Star of David adopted for the Israeli flag was blue to evoke the Jewish prayer shawl, which harkens back to the tradition that the Ten Commandments were carved on blue stone from God's sapphire throne.

"So when you bring people here," I asked, "do they think it's the *actual* place where Jesus was born, or do they think it's just a story?"

"It's a difficult question," she said. "Most of the time I explain that, as a Christian, I *believe* this is the place. None of us knows the actual place, but for generations we have believed it was here."

"There are many scholars who say that the reason Jesus was born in Bethlehem is because the Hebrew Bible says the messiah must come from the House of David. Otherwise, why would a pregnant woman have left Nazareth and walked three days to get here?"

"The Bible says there was a census that required people to re-turn to their hometown," she said matter-of-factly, "and Joseph came from Bethlehem. So there's the reason!" She scratched her head for a second. "You have to understand, for us believers, we don't care about these questions. If you find an answer for this question, you'll just find another question, so in the end, it's better not to question."

We retreated outside and proceeded back to the border. As we drove, I noticed that Arlet was wearing an image of the Virgin Mary around her neck. She's one of an estimated thirty thousand Palestinian Christians living in the Palestinian territories, or 2 per-cent of the population. Once as high as 13 percent, the population has dwindled in recent years as Christians sought better opportuni-ties abroad. "So let me ask you," I said. "You're a Christian, you live surrounded by Jews and Muslims. Can the religions get along?"

"They have to get along, otherwise we all will suffer. As a Christian, I prefer the Jewish people; you can deal with them as humans. I will never allow myself the mistake of marrying a Mus-lim. But I'm still a Palestinian; I just don't care about a state. Re-ally, all I want is to live in peace."

"So do you belong to a country?"

"No, I belong to a city. Bethlehem."

I met Avner at the border, and we drove east toward one of the most overlooked regions of Israel, the Elah Valley. Tucked in the foothills between the central highlands and the Negev, the Jordan Valley and the coastal plain, the Elah, named for the pistachio trees that line its cascading slopes, is a hidden breadbasket, filled with vineyards, orchards, and one of the largest eggplant farms in the Middle East. It's also home to one of the more famous showdowns in history, between David the Bethlehemite and Goliath the Philistine.

As the David story begins, the biblical story is concentrated in the southern half of the Promised Land. "There are a number of reasons for this," Avner explained. "First, this is a better area to cultivate than up north around Shechem. There are fewer rocks and more rain. The second is geopolitical. The Philistines, a powerful, rival kingdom from the Aegean, occupy the nicest land, along the Mediterranean coast of Canaan."

"People think of Israel today as being so tiny," I said. "But ancient Israel was even tinier, *half* of what it is today."

This sets up the central tension of the story: if the Israelites want to grow, they must acquire better land. They can't go east; there's a desert. They can't go south; there's a desert. They can't go north; they will bump into the Mesopotamians. The only way to expand is to go west, but the Philistines are in the west. The underlying reality of David's life is that the only way for Israel to fulfill its destiny is to confront the Philistines. But this isn't easy. The Philistines, whose name comes from the Hebrew root for *Palestine*, brought a highly sophisticated society from the Aegean. For starters, they had a monopoly on forging iron, which gave them better weaponry, even chariots. To them, the Israelites were bumpkins.

"Remember, the Philistines are repressing the Israelites," Avner said. "That means conscription; it means taxes. It means they can do whatever they want. They come from a highly urban, extremely civilized society. The Israelites come from the desert. The Philistines are building *huge* cities. Ekron is eighty acres, compared with two to three acres for the biggest settlement of Israel."

One irony of this story is too rich to ignore. The Philistines have been much maligned in history, largely because the Bible presents them in such negative light. Long after they disappeared, their name endured—as an insult. The word *Philistine* first entered nonbiblical usage in seventeenth-century Germany, when literary critics used it to mean "enemy." Soon German students began labeling nonstudents or other venal people *Philister*. This usage entered English, where a philistine came to be any person who has no sophistication or knowledge of culture. But the original Philistines were very sophisticated. Indeed, in the battle between the Israelites and the Philistines, the *Israelites* were the philistines.

"So the Philistines have better land," I said. "They've got bigger cities. They've got greater technology. Why should the Israelites risk defeat?"

"This is the Promised Land," Avner said, "and it needs to be settled. But in order to do that, the Israelites need a leader."

We rounded a bend and suddenly were there: the verdant site of David's showdown with Goliath. Part of me expected we would have to trek to some isolated spot far from the highway, but the duel took place on the main crossroad through the valley—then, as now, the easiest way to get from the mountains to the coast. We pulled into a grove of squatty olive trees with sage-colored leaves and gnarled trunks that looked like creatures out of Tolkien. On either side of the half-mile-wide valley were grassy tells, remains of the two cities mentioned in the story. Running along one side was a dry riverbed carpeted with small white stones.

In I Samuel 17, the Israelites and Philistines mass on opposing hills. A Philistine representative, Goliath of Gath, steps into the plain. He is six cubits and a span, around nine and a half feet, tall and is wearing a bronze helmet, greaves, and a breastplate, which together weigh 5,000 shekels, or 125 pounds. He carries a spear with a shaft like a weaver's bar, meaning it has a roped handle, and an iron head that weighs 600 shekels, or fifteen pounds. "Choose one of your best men and let him come down against me," Goliath cries. "If he bests me in combat and kills me, we will become your slaves; but if I best him and kill him, you shall be our slaves."

Three of Jesse's sons are encamped with the Israelites, and David is dispatched from Bethlehem to take them a care package of parched corn, bread, and cheese. David arrives at the barricades just as Goliath speaks. The boy is rapt: "Who is that uncircumcised Philistine that he dares defy the ranks of the living God?" David's brother scolds the lad: "I know your impudence and impertinence; you came down to watch the fighting!" David marches straight to Saul anyway and volunteers to be his proxy. Saul dismisses him: "You are only a boy." But I have "killed both lion and bear," David counters. Finally Saul relents. "May God be with you."

Saul places his armor on David, but the boy can't move. He chucks the protection, grabs a stick and a few smooth stones, and totes along his sling. Goliath scoffs at the boy. "Am I a dog that you come against me with sticks?" David's reply is one of the more memorable in the Bible: "You come against me with sword and spear and javelin; but I come against you in the name of the Lord." The Philistine advances, but David, shockingly, runs *toward* him. He reaches into his bag, loads a stone into his sling, and hurls it at his enemy. The stone strikes Goliath in the forehead and sinks into his skull, killing him instantly. David lunges for the warrior's mighty sword and slices off his head. The boy then parades his severed trophy to Jerusalem. The Bible has a new savior prince.

The story is certainly memorable, and everyone from Michelangelo to Mark Twain has taken a spin on it; on playing cards, the sword on the king of spades commemorates this battle. But even the Bible suggests the story may be hyped. For starters, II Samuel 21 relates that it was actually Elhanan of Bethlehem who killed Goliath the Gittite, a giant who had six fingers on each hand, six toes on each foot, and a spear like a weaver's bar. The version that appears in the Dead Sea Scrolls and the Septuagint, the original Greek translation that predates the text we read today, suggests Goliath wasn't even that tall, four cubits and a span, which is less than six and a half feet.

The logical conclusion is that the story is a romantic gloss designed to make David into the boy hero devoted to God. Usually this is the sort of conclusion that archaeologists come to, but in the case of David, history may actually bolster the tale. The description of Goliath fits squarely into the model of mercenary warfare in the Mediterranean at the time. He has iron, which is consistent with the Philistines. His outfit is what Avner called a "greatest hits" of the region: Egyptian armor, an Asiatic sword, an Assyrian helmet. Even the method of sending a single emissary into combat mirrors the battle of Hector and Achilles in the *Iliad*, which takes place around this time.

More striking, because David *was* unburdened with armor, he may have had the tactical advantage. Josephus, writing in the first century C.E., was one of the earliest to suggest that Goliath's substantial armor may have "impeded a more rapid advance." In antiquity, warriors came in three categories: heavy infantry (Goliath), cavalry, and light infantry (David). Light infantry often had the advantage in hilly terrains like the Elah. Thucydides stresses in his *History of the Peloponnesian War* that the heavy infantry of Athens was destroyed by the light infantry of Sicily, often by using the sling. Sling stones, carved flint about the size of tennis balls, are frequent finds around the Mediterranean. From a military point of view, it is plausible that David defeated Goliath.

Could I? Avner hopped from our Jeep and started rummaging through the back until he emerged with a piece of cardboard about the size of my hand. He bored a hole in each side and threaded a piece of rope through one side, then the other, until the contraption hung down about a foot from his hand. "This is a sling," he said.

I was shocked. I had always assumed David used a Y-shaped stick with stretchable bands. This device had only a single rope with a piece of fabric. "You mean it's not a slingshot?"

"That requires rubber. David didn't have rubber. Shepherds today still use this type of sling to chase predators."

Avner walked over to the riverbed and picked up a handful of pebbles.

"They look like camel dung," I said.

He loaded the stone into the belly of the sling, pulled back his arm to begin swinging, and the stone fell feebly to the ground. We laughed. He tried again, and the stone shot backward, strafing my leg. We laughed again, but this time I stepped behind a tree. "This could get dangerous." He tried a third time, and the rock flew forward, about three feet, and tinkled to the ground. "I have a better idea," he said.

Avner returned to the car and came back with bandage from a first-aid kit. He unfurled the gauze, revealing a soft cotton patch in the middle, more flexible than the cardboard. I put a stone on the cotton and swung my arm a few times, as if pitching a baseball. I quickly realized that the hard part is not swinging but releasing only one of the two ends of the rope, so the stone comes out clean. I let go, the stone launched forward, but not very far. By this point, Goliath would have skewered me with his spear.

Finally I had an inspiration. Instead of pitching my entire arm forward, as if tossing a lasso, I rotated just my wrist, and did it backward, as if jumping rope in reverse. Suddenly I built up a head of steam—you could hear the sling whipping through the air—I released one of the handles, the stone came shooting out like an underhanded strike in softball, and it took off, whizzing by my leg, avoiding Avner altogether (point!), crossing the riverbed in a single whir, and just for a second causing a shocked lump in my throat as I heard the anticipation of the crowd, the collective dreams of a life of freedom, the hope that a single, smooth white stone could change the course of time. "Do you believe in miracles?"

The stone hit the cliff about thirty yards away with a faint, pale ping.

"Oh, well," I said. "I could have killed David, but I don't think Goliath."

A few minutes later we turned down a dirt road overrun with organic vegetables and brimming with grapevines. A burst of bougainvilleas and geraniums lined the steps to a small terra-cotta-tiled restaurant and winery. The name was carved in wood, KELA DAVID, "David's Sling." The logo showed two sticks in a Y formation: a slingshot, not a sling. Half an hour earlier I wouldn't have known the difference.

Smadar Kaplinski greeted us warmly, a hint of gray peeking through her mopped red hair. We ordered plates of eggplant ragout, pickled olives, hummus, and home-baked bread, along with a glass of her Cabernet. Joan Osborne was singing "What If God Was One of Us" on the radio. Smadar was something of a Davidic figure in the land of David. A former bureaucrat with the Department of Education, she had been living with her husband and children in Tel Aviv when she decided she needed to flee her marriage. She decided to overturn her life as well.

"I looked from village to village for a place to buy for me and my children," she said. "I knew I could make money from food. All my friends told me not to go, I wouldn't survive. I told them I would, with good weather, open air, and hard work. I hate to say it, but Israeli people don't like to work."

"So why did you choose this place?"

"The weather. The soil. The people. The relationship between Israelis and Arabs is better here than elsewhere. We work together. We trust each other. We are friends."

She opened a restaurant, began tilling the fields, and now produces ten thousand bottles of wine a year, as well as the best garlic soup and pineapple cake in the region. All she needed was a name.

"We wanted a name with meaning," she said. "We feel that we

are part of our past. We are continuing the life of the Jewish people from the Bible. David's sling is close to us. Three kilometers
from here is where the fight took place."

"David is the story of an underdog," I said. "Are you an underdog?"

"I feel that I have made a good life for my children. I had family problems before I arrived here. I had no money. I came where
there was nobody. Yet this place makes you feel strong. Now I
have a restaurant, a winery, a farm. It's the area of dreams."

I asked her if she felt some spirit was looking over her.

"I don't know, but I do feel God helped me make good things
for my family. I know that we appreciate our lives more than before. We need to serve our land in this country, not just our cities.
We have to make agriculture, take care of our water, make sure
that our air is clean. My children will know how to do this now."

"And where is David in this story?"

"When I go to pick up my workers in the morning, and I see a
young shepherd walking along the top of the ridge, I can see him.
I can see him when I close my eyes, as a little boy, not tall, with orange hair, and curls."

"But when he grows up," I said, "he's not so innocent. He's a
bandit; he's cruel to women."

"I'm not going to criticize him," she said. "Their life was complicated. Biblical heroes weren't always good, but neither am I. I
try to be good, but I feel that a lot of time people use me, and lie
to me. I'm not as good as when I arrived here. Maybe that's the
way I'm most like David. Living here can make you believe in
God, but it will also make you tough."

W e drove a few miles away, to a hill in the center of the Elah
Valley, to set up camp for the night. We found a grove of
Jerusalem pines, planted by the Jewish National Fund to reforest

the country after the Ottomans chopped down most of the trees to build a highway from Syria to Saudi Arabia. Parks like this, with picnic areas, outdoor cafés, and military lookouts, are commonplace in Israel and sometimes make camping in the country akin to hiking in Switzerland.

Except the peaks are lower. We laid our gear near the top of the hill and within a few steps could see all the way to the Hebron Mountains in the east and the Mediterranean in the west. In the fifty miles between us and the coast, few lights were visible, and we could barely see Gath, home base of Goliath. By contrast, the swath along the shore was lit up like an amusement park. Today, three thousand years after David, the basic population structure of the land is unchanged: sparse in the middle, dense along the coast.

Soon we were growing nostalgic. A flash of fireworks went off on the coast, and I was surprised Israelis could still celebrate with explosions. "When you and I first started traveling years ago," Avner said, "we were in the bubble of peace. Everybody, and especially I, was full of great hope that we could reach a peaceful solution. I was working closely with people in the West Bank, Gaza, Jordan, Egypt. Those connections are still valid, and on a people-to-people level we still relate as human beings. But there is a lot of sadness now—and big questions."

He was lying on his sleeping bag, propped on his elbow. The desert-worn lines on his face were accentuated by a candle. Naturally gnomic, his mind seemed to have paused on the edge of a groove, as if rubbing endlessly on a mourner's bead.

"I started looking around," he continued, "and asking, 'Why are we not succeeding?' All our problems are not Palestinian problems. There are concerns with Israeli society. We have no constitution, no long-term plan. One of the problems with Israel is that our leadership is mostly people from the Army who are used to solving immediate problems. We have a deep lack of identity. I'm sure one of the reasons people cling so strongly to the land, and don't want to give up this or that piece, is that they have nothing else to hang on to. They've forgotten what the land stands for."

This idea was similar to the one I had heard from Yaya, and I was surprised to hear it again from such a different political viewpoint. One of the central themes of the Pentateuch is the longing for land and the promise it holds for living in peace and freedom with God. But no sooner do the Israelites conquer the land than they squander the peace and destabilize their relationship with God. Is being on the land incompatible with being in accord with God?

"Many of the first Zionists who came here," Avner continued, "turned their backs on the diaspora and Judaism. They said, 'We are new people, we are connected to the land, why pray all the time?' So much so that among many young people today, like my children, there is a feeling of hostility toward religion. Seventy percent are secular. There is no country on earth where young people travel so much looking for meaning—to India, South America, doing drugs."

"So where should their meaning come from?"

"From their culture. From their heritage." He paused. "From the Bible."

Avner had always loved the Bible, but he always loved the land even more. The notion that the Bible may be more important than geography in building identity was a new idea, and I was struck by how his own agitation had brought us to a similar place. After our first journey, I felt a primeval connection to the desert. But when the bubble of peace from those years ruptured, I, too, went looking for new meaning. I turned first to religion, in particular to the shared ancestor, Abraham. All three monotheistic faiths claim him as their father; surely his story could provide common ground. In a new journey through the region, I discovered that while the biblical story of Abraham has a message of unity, each of the religions that grew from his line had reinterpreted the story for its own exclusive purposes. Abraham became as much a source of war as he was a seed of peace.

Faced with this malleability, I sought refuge in the story itself. If every generation could reinterpret the narrative for its own purposes, why not us? Maybe we could find in it a message for our time. After my book on Abraham was published, I initiated a series of grassroots, interfaith conversations; within months, thousands of people around the world had taken part. And suddenly I noticed that people of all faiths were seeking wisdom in the past.

This reaching back was the new face of religion in the West. While attendance at churches and synagogues may have declined, Americans in particular took their freedom from institutional religion and set out on their own to reengage traditional texts. This back-to-the-Bible movement included surging adult-ed courses, the pop Kabbalah fad, Bill Moyers's popular *Genesis* series, novels such as *The Red Tent* and *The Da Vinci Code*, and dozens of best-selling nonfiction books by Karen Armstrong, Thomas Cahill, Elaine Pagels, and in a small way, my own.

A new movement was afoot: Make Your Own Faith. And maybe I shouldn't have been surprised. In the same way we no longer blindly accept what our politicians tell us, our journalists, or our parents, we no longer fully accept what our religious leaders tell us. In the age of limitless information, the endless bookshelf, the Internet, we are all journalists. We are all historians. And now we are all theologians. Rather than merely accepting the past, each of us sifts through the past. We must make our own culture, our own heritage.

Our own Bible.

And here was my convergence with Avner. "I'm interested in strengthening our connection to the Bible," he said, "because it's deeper than land and will help us make peace with our neighbors."

"I'm interested in strengthening my connection to the Bible,"

I countered, "because it's deeper than religion and may hold clues for making peace among the faiths."

"Maybe after 9/11, we are forced by bigger powers to do that," Avner said.

I looked at him. "You never would have spoken that way before."

He looked at me. "Neither would you."

We were heading south, into a flatter, more isolated region where the foothills begin to melt into the wilderness and vineyards give way to chalky flats. The desert encroaches. This is also the area where the gentle prince David begins to morph into a wild man.

After David's victory over Goliath, the real battle of his early life—his showdown with King Saul—is squared. David has one advantage in this seemingly insurmountable challenge. Everyone he meets falls in love with him. This includes the men of Saul's kingdom; the women ("Saul has slain his thousands," they swoon, "David, his tens of thousands"); even Saul's own son Jonathan, who "loves David as himself." Faced with David's growing popularity, Saul grows mad with jealousy and tries to spear his young rival. When that fails, Saul tries drawing David closer by offering first one daughter, then another in marriage. Marrying the king's daughter was tantamount to staking a claim on the throne, and David seems to have this motivation in mind. The text says Saul's daughter Michal "had fallen in love with David"; Michal, in fact, is the only woman in the entire Hebrew Bible who is said to love a man. David, meanwhile, refers to their nuptials as merely "becoming Your Majesty's son-in-law."

But Saul lays a trap: he sets his bride's price impossibly high, at one hundred Philistine foreskins, hoping David will be killed in the process of penis scalping. But David outmaneuvers the king again, bringing back two hundred. Finally Saul tries to slay his new son-in-law, but Michal and Jonathan arrange his escape. Jonathan's role in protecting David is most remarkable because, as Saul's eldest son, he has the most to lose from David's ambition. One lesson of these early stories is that David is masterful at using the love of others to advance his own career.

What follows is a darker, more unexpected period in David's life. He becomes an outlaw, a traitor, and a murderer. One claim sometimes heard from biblical critics, and frequently from broader skeptics of religion, is that the Bible is simply made up, invented by the Israelites to aggrandize their history by claiming sanctification from a previously unknown god. But a close look reveals a deep strain of weakness, even criminality in the Bible's heroes that seems contrary to what a propagandist would invent. Abraham permits his wife to philander with the pharaoh and tries to kill both of his sons; Jacob outright deceives his father to swipe the inheritance of his brother, Esau; Moses commits murder and flees to the desert.

Even in this context, David's behavior is shocking. In a sketchy, episodic series of events, David flees from Saul and begins to roam the untamed southern quadrant of Israel, deftly shifting alliances among city-states controlled by the Philistines, those commanded by the Judaeans, and even some leftover strongholds from Canaan. Three ongoing struggles dominate this area in the tenth century B.C.E.: between the Philistines and the Israelites; between the Northern Kingdom of Israel and the Southern Kingdom of Judah; and between the settled cities and bandits from the desert. David cleverly takes advantage of this chaos by presenting himself as the savior of each group. Fortunately for him, each group willingly accepts him because they are desperate to capitalize on his reputation as a man with extraordinary martial gifts.

First he tricks the king of Nob (an Israelite) into thinking he's still allied with Saul. Next he feigns madness before the king of

Gath (a Philistine), letting saliva drool down his beard in a bid for asylum. Finally he bolts to the southern hills, raises a corps of four hundred bandits, and begins terrorizing the area, including his fellow tribesmen. His most significant act is a face-off with Nabal, the leader of one of the most powerful tribes in Judah. Unable to extort money from Nabal, David threatens to obliterate his town. Nabal's wife, Abigail, holds David back, saying the Lord will serve him. Sure enough, Nabal soon drops dead and David weds Abigail, making him the most powerful layman in Judah, a short step to the king.

Positive, perfectly timed, supposedly coincidental events like this occur frequently to David in his lightning rise to power. David may not be the most pious man in the Bible, but he's certainly the luckiest. His ultimate act of cunning is to *join forces* with the Philistines in their battle with Saul. The Philistine king figures David has terrorized his own people so much that they will never accept him as a leader. "He will be my vassal forever." This line marks a stunning admission. The authorized account of the first king of Greater Israel concedes that he collaborated with the enemy. As opposed to earlier biblical stories, like those of the patriarchs, which took place thousands of years before the Bible was recorded in the mid–first millennium B.C.E., the story of David happened in recent historical memory, so biblical writers clearly feel they can't airbrush out all the distasteful details. All they can do is try to spin them to the hero's advantage.

And boy do they spin. David stands alongside the Philistines and prepares to join the people of Goliath in a war against his father-in-law Saul. On the eve of battle, the Philistine generals recall David's reputation ("Hey, isn't he the one who slew those tens of thousands?") and announce they don't trust him. At the last moment, the king sends David south to Ziklag to wait out the battle. Even this works in David's favor, as it gives him a convenient alibi when Saul and his three sons, including Jonathan, take their own lives in the face of overwhelming force from the Philistines, yet another well-timed happenstance that advances David's career.

As someone raised on the sugary milk of David, the boy king of Israel, brave, valiant, and free, I was horrified to read how blood-curdlingly ambitious he was. His portrait reads more like that of a tin-pot dictator leading a bloody coup than that of a humble servant of God building the family of the future messiah. He's a cross between Attila the Hun and Genghis Khan, the first Machiavellian prince. Even a cursory examination of the scholarly literature produces eye-popping assessments. The biographer Jonathan Kirsch says David is a "Robin Hood with bloodstained hands." The scholar Steven McKenzie, in his book *King David*, calls him a "terrorist." Baruch Halpern, perhaps the leading archaeologist of his generation, likens David to Hannibal Lecter and extrapolates from the evidence that he was probably a Philistine who appropriated Israel's iconography for his advancement.

Before I could make peace with the Bible, I had to confront a question: Was David really Goliath, an outsize mercenary bent on taking advantage of everyone and serving only himself?

We were staring at cows. We had driven a few hours to the western edge of the Negev and a rocky, pale green cattle pasture, a rare respite of irrigation in Israel's southern wasteland. Avner put our Jeep into four-wheel drive, plunged into a ravine, crossed a brook, then accelerated to the top of Tel Sera. Sites like this are one treat of traveling in the Middle East, grassed-over barnacles in otherwise humdrum fields and containing trapdoors into the past. With grass so rare in the region, this five-acre tell, about three stories tall, was the first I had visited that smelled like cow dung.

Tel Sera is thought to be the biblical Ziklag, where David was sent to wait out the battle. On his arrival, the city has been sacked and all the women and children, including David's wives, who had been living there, carted off by desert tribesmen. David and his men quickly hunt down the enemy, reclaim the women, and destroy the tribe. But instead of merely distributing the loot of battle to his soldiers, David sends some to the guards back in Ziklag, and even more to the elders of Judah all across the region. Suddenly the bandit has become a politician. By the time he marches to Hebron, the men of Judah gleefully anoint him king. The fox finally has his crown.

I asked Avner if the type of banditry David uses during his roaming years was common.

"Yes, especially in marginal areas like this. Notice, we're on the border between the foothills of Judah, the coastal plain, the Negev, and the Sinai. From here you can raid all the rich areas, then retreat to the edge. This is the biblical equivalent of the Wild West."

"Moses is enslaved and commits murder," I said. "David is a bandit for a time and a mass murderer. The Bible seems to portray its leaders not simply as glowing figures."

"We have said several times that the Bible shows David in a very human way. For believers, this means it was reality. But as a scholar, I think one reason is that the written text reflects the living tradition about these figures. You can try to portray David in the most favorable light, but everyone already knows he was a bandit, so you have to include that element in your version."

"There is a more revisionist view," I said, "that the story is an elaborate apology for David. By shielding him from the murders of rivals and giving him plausible deniability over the timely dispatch of his enemies, the text is simply making excuses that are too good to be true. So that just after his exile to Ziklag, when Saul is killed by the Philistines and David sets out for Hebron to become king of Judah, this was his diabolical plan all along. Some even suggest that he was a renegade Philistine, who broke away from his own people and moved inland from the Mediterranean coast to set up his own fiefdom."

Avner hesitated for a moment.

"I do agree, of course, that there are a few voices in this story and that everything was edited. So we are not talking about a solid biography of David. But I think to identify him as a Philistine is a bit too far. The Philistines were the power here, so the fact that David might spend time with them after his rupture with Saul is not unheard of. As we have seen, this was a period of shifting powers.

"And I don't know if it's my own background and education," he continued, "but I recoil at the idea that David was a Philistine. I don't see why someone would alter the story that greatly."

"So whether or not you accept the idea that David is a Philistine," I said, "you do agree that David, in the formative period of his character, is a man who will use violence, deceit, charm, murder—anything at his disposal—to gather political power around him."

"Absolutely. But I want to refer to what we've heard from a few people, including Yaya, that his behavior goes better with the values of his own time than with the values of ours. We may not like these values, we may find them immoral, but they were very common."

"So from the point when he kills Goliath," I said, "to the moment he takes over in Hebron two decades later, he's a canny, tactical, ruthless leader. We can respect his skill, but we don't have to admire his character. You can study him, but you don't want to have him over to dinner."

"Yes. I would even go so far as to say that he wouldn't have very nice table manners."

· 2 ·

YOUR THRONE SHALL BE
ESTABLISHED FOREVER

The water pulsed. It bubbled up from underneath the stone floor in clear, green gurgles. The gentle belches from the underground spring—the source of life for biblical Jerusalem—cascaded into a small square pool, where they dissipated briefly before overflowing down a narrow staircase into the darkness. The rush of water in the tunnel below was so loud I felt as if I was staring into the gape of the Styx.

And it smelled. The sewers of modern Jerusalem had seeped into this tunnel, merging the effluvium of present-day toilet waste with the purity of the richest spring in the Judaean hills.

I took off my boots. I peeled off my socks, unhooked my belt, and began slipping my safari trousers to the ground. The stone felt cold beneath my feet, and I dipped my toes into the water. Whoa! Freezing. I quickly withdrew my foot as a shiver went up my calf. I was standing half naked at the mouth of a grotto few people had entered in four thousand years. Hidden for millennia beneath layers of rubble, this passageway from the Gihon spring, through dense limestone bedrock, directly into the heart of the City of David, had been reopened for a matter of only months.

And it had already ignited a geyser of controversy.

I was here to parse that scandal, and to consider a question that has bedeviled Bible lovers for thousands of years: How did David, a devilish renegade from the southern hills, manage to conquer the impregnable town of Jerusalem, merge within it the forces of God and state, transform it into the holiest city in the world, and morph himself into the progenitor of the messiah? As real estate speculation, few gestures have had more lasting impact than David's conquering of Jerusalem. As an act of strategic warfare, it was masterful. As politics, it was brilliant.

But as an act of tactics, it's a four-millennium-old mystery. How did he do it?

Avner handed me an orange hard hat, which I strapped on my head. I stretched a clip-on light around my forehead and turned on the beam. Side by side, Avner and I looked like a pair of Laurel and Hardy coal miners auditioning for a road show of *The Full Monty*. Since we would need our clothes later, Avner suggested we tuck them into my knapsack.

"Whatever you do, don't drink the water," he said.

We stepped into the current.

In almost every way imaginable, Jerusalem is a city on the edge. It's on the eastern edge of the central mountains. It's on the western edge of the Syrian-African Rift. It's on the perpetual edge of sectarian war. Though the city sits atop a series of low-rising hills, both the Galilee, to the north, and Hebron, to the south, have higher mountains, which means Jerusalem rests like a saddle between the two. It's a wet city, with an impressive thirty-two inches of rain a year, but the desert starts just on its doorstep. An hour away is the Dead Sea, where the annual rainfall is two inches.

Modern Jerusalem is built in concentric circles. At the heart is the Old City, a three-thousand-year-old walled enclave that is less than one square mile. It contains many of the city's most sacred sites: the Temple Mount, the Western Wall, the Dome of the Rock, the Church of the Holy Sepulcher. Only 40,000 inhabitants live in the four quarters of the Old City—Armenian, Jewish, Muslim, and Christian. Most of Jerusalem's 600,000 residents live outside these walls in neighborhoods built over the last century. Two-thirds of those residents are Jews, who live largely to the west and south of the Old City; one-third are Arabs, who live largely to the north and east, though those distinctions are weakening.

The Temple Mount occupies the far eastern edge of the Old City, on the lip of the Kidron Valley, just opposite the Mount of Olives. Immediately south of the Temple Mount, outside the medieval walls, a small promontory juts southward about half a mile. This cliff-top hamlet, about twelve acres in size, is easily overlooked, because it's surrounded by higher peaks and more electrifying sites, but this hill is where Jerusalem began. It is called the City of David.

Hours before plunging into the sewers, Avner and I met at the entrance to David's city. Our plan was to explore the hillside ruins, then enter the secret web of underground water tunnels that burrow through the cliff like passageways through an ant farm. At the bottom of the cliff was the cesspool and perhaps an answer to the mystery of David's triumph of Jerusalem. Did he sneak up through the sewer?

We were met by an old friend. Gabi Barkay is an archaeologist who looks like the vintage newspaper editor from *Spider-Man*, with a stringy black comb-over, nicotine-stained fingers, and an air of seen-it-all-before. In 1979 he made what one magazine called one of the ten greatest finds of the twentieth century, a tiny silver roll engraved with the oldest piece of biblical writing ever found. I asked him why Jerusalem began on this hill, when the Temple Mount and the Mount of Olives were so much higher.

"Because it's the only one of these hills with a natural supply of water," he said. "The Almighty springs low to the ground. And the Gihon, which means 'gusher,' is the most plentiful one around. We definitely may say that if this spring didn't exist, there wouldn't be a Jerusalem."

We descended a set of stairs and entered the excavation. Remains have been found here dating from the third millennium B.C.E., long before Abraham would have passed by. As early as the eighteenth century B.C.E., residents began building elaborate underground tunnels to transport water from the Gihon to the surface. By the tenth century B.C.E., Jerusalem was a city controlled by a Canaanite clan, the Jebusites, who surrounded it with walls and built intricate houses and a citadel.

This is the city David coveted. The second Book of Samuel opens with Saul dead and David swaggering into Hebron to become king of Judah, the southern half of the bifurcated Promised Land. He promptly has six sons by six different women. The Northern Kingdom, Israel, quakes before David's growing prowess. Saul's son Ishbaal is king of Israel, but the power behind the throne is Abner, a David-like Svengali. Abner secretly reaches out to David to form an alliance, but David demands that Abner turn over David's first wife, Michal, who has remained in her father's kingdom. Abner fulfills his end of the bargain, but David has him assassinated anyway, and follows by beheading Ishbaal. This is how David finally seizes control of Israel and forges the first unified monarchy. It takes a tyrant, but the land of Israel is finally united.

Though not really. Israel never fully capitulates to this carpetbagger from the south. David, recognizing his crisis of legitimacy, designs a guileful response. He moves the capital of the new united monarchy out of the southern stronghold of Hebron but stops short of taking it to the north. He finds a tactical middle ground, a city in the previously untamed midsection of the country. Millennia later the United States underwent a similar process when it moved its capital from New York into the neutral swamp of Washington, D.C. David's city would not be in Judah and not be in Israel.

It would be in Jerusalem.

"The whole thing is politics," Gabi said. "David was born in Bethlehem, on the doorstep of Jerusalem. He had the dream of forming a dynasty, but he needed a clean slate. David's plan all along was to create an Israelite trinity: one dynasty, one god, one city. The dynasty can be seated only on one throne; only one God can be worshiped by that people; and only one city can be home to both. That is the holy trinity concept of the tenth century, and it was centered on this spot."

We continued our downward path. Gabi pointed out various highlights, including the famous Area G, a royal compound with tombs that some scholars believe may have been David's home. Halfway down the hill was a small stone door. We stepped inside and found ourselves at the threshold of a tunnel, one of a series of interlocking passageways that connect the city above with the spring below. The tunnels were designed so that residents could descend through bedrock and retrieve the water without leaving the city walls. Already we could hear the echo of the flow rushing hundreds of feet below us. I felt a sort of boyish excitement, as if I was entering some forbidden part of the basement.

The tunnel had been outfitted with a staircase. We proceeded into the abyss. The walls were illuminated by a few lightbulbs strung along the vaulted ceiling. Stone niches, about shoulder high, indicated where ancient oil lamps had illuminated the work of burrowing into the limestone. Scrape marks were still visible. "You should regard yourself very lucky," Gabi said. "Where do you have another place that has hardly been touched in four thousand years?"

"So what did they use to carve the tunnels?" I asked.

"Stone," Gabi said. "Iron was not yet in use. This was the Middle Bronze Age. They knew copper, they knew bronze, but these materials were too soft. The bronze they had was hard enough to stab your foe but not hard enough to cut through the hard rock of Jerusalem."

These tunnels were so unusual that for thousands of years they went unknown. The Bible alludes to them in II Kings 20, which lists the exploits of King Hezekiah in the eighth century B.C.E.: "He made the pool and the conduit and brought the water into the city." Some medieval travelers ventured inside, looking for evidence of the lost treasures of Solomon. But the tunnels were introduced to the West by Edward Robinson, the American antiquities specialist, son of a Congregationalist preacher, who came to the Holy Land in 1838 as part of the West's new quest to prove that the events in the Bible truly happened.

Setting out from Egypt, Robinson retraced biblical sites through the Sinai and Negev. He hired camels to tote along his supplies: rice, biscuits, and dried apricots, as well as three compasses, a thermometer, telescopes, two muskets, and copies of the Bible in English. Muslim residents in Jerusalem had assumed several stones projecting from the Western Wall of the Temple Mount were the result of an earthquake. Robinson's familiarity with ancient writings allowed him to identify them as remnants of the Second Temple compound. Today they are called Robinson's Arch.

Robinson also made his way into the tunnels, where he hoped to find evidence of the Temple. "He was crawling on his belly," Gabi said, "with the help of his elbows, in mud and filth that had accumulated here for generations. He didn't know there was an outlet on the other side, so he stopped before he found the water."

The real breakthrough came three decades later, with Charles Warren, a twenty-seven-year-old lieutenant in the British Army. Warren had begun his career scaling Gibraltar and arrived in Jerusalem in 1867 to search for the Temple. Arrested by local Turkish officials for appearing too bellicose, Warren eventually garnered permission to scale the southern wall of the Haram. One day his sledgehammers disturbed daily prayers at the Al Aqsa mosque and worshipers pelted him with stones. Not to be stymied, he moved to the Church of the Holy Sepulcher and searched for the real tomb of Jesus, only to be shut down again. Finally he turned his attention to the City of David.

"Warren was a very talented man," Gabi said. "To think that he was only in his twenties. It was written that for every day he would have been in battle he would have earned the Victoria Cross. For every day he was in Jerusalem, you can't imagine what he suffered. He got malaria, he got arrested, his workmen staged violent uprisings. Shakespeare writes in *Macbeth* about the forest of Birnam Wood moving toward Dunsinane; in this case the forest moved toward Charles Warren in the form of a mudslide. As he was digging in the tunnels, he triggered an avalanche that nearly buried him alive; he survived by dangling from a rope. In another case he dug a pit and disturbed the equilibrium of some underground sewage, which broke through and nearly drowned him. He quickly dismantled some doors and floated to safety in liquid waste. Every day was such an adventure that Indiana Jones was nothing in comparison to the truth of Charles Warren."

"So why did he do it?"

"I don't believe his motivation was religious. He had a scientific, human curiosity. He had an interest in the past. And he was naturally brave. Later he was knighted and became head of Scotland Yard, before being forced to resign because of not catching Jack the Ripper. He was the only true victim of Jack the Ripper, in fact, because there was no Jack the Ripper. The whole story was blown up by the public as a result of fear."

I started to question his theory but stopped short: If we can't even agree on what happened in London a century ago, how are we ever going to agree on what happened in Jerusalem *thirty* centuries ago?

Warren was the first to pierce the length of these tunnels, in March 1867. Crawling on his stomach, he carried a notebook in his left hand, a pencil in his right, and a candle in his mouth. He was his own canary in the shaft, wondering what would happen if his oxygen disappeared. The most famous outlet in the system, a thirty-foot vertical shaft, still bears his name. Warren thought he had discovered the base of the Temple. Fearing the building would collapse, and finding no wood in tree-starved Israel, he bought up beams from as far away as Egypt to buttress his discovery. He eventually ran out of money and had to close down.

Warren's aborted mission meant the full triumph of discovering the secret underside of David's conquest of Jerusalem had to wait forty years for yet another eccentric Brit, Montague Parker. As a thirty-year-old captain in the Boer War, Parker held a séance and claimed to have made contact with Solomon, who revealed the location of his buried treasures. Joining with a Finnish soothsayer who claimed he could decode the Bible, Parker raised hundreds of thousands of pounds from titillated investors. With a staff of London subway engineers, they pitched up in Jerusalem in 1909. They met near universal resistance, from the Turks and the Jews. The latter were led by Baron Edmond de Rothschild, the French philanthropist, who resented this interloper mucking around holy sites.

"Parker was a lunatic," Gabi said. But he did manage to enlist one pivotal booster, Father Hughes Vincent, a Catholic priest and the town's leading authority in antiquities. While Parker may have thought his excavations were leading to a hidden trove of jewels, Vincent went along and studied the masonry and water flow. Noting the presence of Bronze Age burial caves and ancient fortifications, he concluded that the water system belonged to the pre-tenth-century B.C.E. Canaanite city. Hallelujah! Montague Parker (er, Father Vincent) had discovered the City of David and perhaps unlocked the three-millennium mystery of how the wily prince had managed to breach the inviolable city walls.

But how reliable was this information? Surely these men were daring and colorful. For me, one of the joys of trekking around Jerusalem is learning the stories of these adventurers and trying to step in their shadows. The Bible surely has provided grist for the greatest scavenger hunts in history. Where else can a morning stroll bring one into contact with Baron de Rothschild, Jack the Ripper, and Birnam Wood comes to Dunsinane? But given a century of improvements in archaeology, were they scholars?

"They were pioneers," said Gabi. "They were brave. They were crazy enough to go on adventures that nobody today would dare. They were creative enough to use whatever techniques were available to them at the time. Even if we disagree with some of their conclusions, we have to admire them. But mostly, we have to thank them. They invented archaeology."

By midmorning we had arrived at the bottom of the tunnels. We stopped walking *down* and began walking on level ground, turning sideways to squeeze through a sliver in the walls. The ground was muddy, the ceilings caked with cobwebs. Our faces were covered in dust.

We turned a corner and suddenly stared down into a vast cavern. Our voices bellowed into an echo. Below us was a huge stone pool of water, twenty feet in diameter and deep enough to dive into. The chamber was pitch-black, except for the beams from our headlamps. It looked like the inside of a stone igloo.

Parker discovered this pool at the termination of Tunnel 3 and labeled it the Round Chamber. The boulders used to construct this pool were the largest ever employed in Jerusalem until Herod the Great remodeled the Temple Mount at least eight hundred years later. The importance of this pool, the massiveness of its walls, and the sheer effort that went into tunneling so extensively through solid limestone raise the question that has tantalized Bible lovers since Warren first dug here.

"So," I said, turning to Gabi for what he knew was coming, "is there any evidence that these tunnels were used for anything *other* than water?"

"These are waterworks, first and foremost," Gabi said. "But as they exist, they could have been used for anything else, for storage, for quarrying the stone for construction, and yes, for penetrating the city. The enduring question surrounds how David conquered Jerusalem and whether he came this way. That, I'm afraid, is a linguistic question."

Near the start of II Samuel 5, the thirty-seven-year-old King David leads an assault against the Jebusite city of Jerusalem. "You will never get in here!" the residents shout. "Even the blind and lame will turn you back." But David handily captures the stronghold. He then announces what the Revised Standard Version translates as "Whoever would smite the Jebusites, let him get up the water shaft to attack the lame and the blind." The term *water shaft* in this sentence comes from the Hebrew word *tsinor.* The

King James Version renders the same word as *gutter*, and others translate it as *water channel* or *conduit*. Does this term mean David *climbed up* the water system and took the city by surprise? Maybe that's why no one had taken Jerusalem before: They hadn't thought of this route.

"*Tsinor* is translated in all English Bibles as *gutter*," Gabi explained, "following the translation that first appeared in the Latin Vulgate. The reason is the Hebrew term was never understood, and translators couldn't do what we do today, which is to say, 'Well, it's Hebrew, but we don't understand it.' So the English makes sense, but it has nothing to do with the original Hebrew, which doesn't make sense. It's a defective text. We know today, from the Dead Sea Scrolls, that the full text of second Samuel did not survive."

"Does the word appear elsewhere in the text?"

"*Tsinor* is a hapax legomenon," Gabi said, "meaning it occurs only once in the Bible. Is it a gutter? Is it a sexual organ? Is it a statue of the Jebusite defenders that had to be touched to signal the takeover of the city? We don't know."

"Then how did this whole idea of David climbing up the water shaft get started?"

"Ah."

When Warren published his findings of the waterworks in 1871, some people immediately suggested the waterworks might be connected to the David story. These speculations caught the imagination of Father Vincent, who during Parker's excavation suggested that the general Joab climbed through the tunnels, snuck into the city, and flung open the gates for David and his men. This would explain the lack of extensive destruction at the time of the supposed conquering. Father Vincent was also a close friend of Eliezer Ben-Yehuda, the inventor of modern Hebrew, who wrote the first dictionary of the language in Vincent's monastery. Vincent persuaded Ben-Yehuda to accept the term *tsinor* as "windpipe," which is how the word is used in spoken Hebrew today.

So is this what happened?

Most scholars have said no. For decades the great archaeologists of Jerusalem lined up against the theory. They received confirmation in 1981, when Yigal Shiloh reexcavated the tunnels and concluded that none dated before the ninth century B.C.E., meaning David couldn't have climbed up through them because they hadn't been built at the time. The theory was dead, at least until 1999, when Roni Reich reexcavated the tunnels yet again and made a startling discovery. In order to see what he found, Avner had concocted a plan. Gabi would stay on dry ground and aid us from above. Avner and I would remove our shoes, take off our trousers, and wade into a stretch of tunnel that seemed impenetrable.

The water around our ankles was cold and the bottom filled with pebbles. As we slogged forward, we had to lean against the limestone walls, which were covered in crust and cobwebs and felt like the inside of a cocoon. At times the space was barely broader than my shoulders.

The water began only a few inches high but gradually deepened, and quickened. In no time it reached the middle of my thighs, and I had to bend my knees to avoid being toppled by the current. I felt reptilian. The tunnel smelled like the inside of the tank I used as a boy to grow tadpoles into frogs—a fetid, muddy grog that gave off the disquieting odor of evolution.

Soon the water neared my waist, and I had to pull my T-shirt up to prevent it from getting drenched. I was wading waist deep in the freezing, raw sewage of Jerusalem in some quixotic attempt to discover how King David had captured his capital. I thought back to one of my mother's mantras: "The best way to learn is by being hands-on."

Thanks.

After about twenty minutes, we reached a fork in the tunnel. One passage veered to the left. The other continued straight ahead, where it quickly dead-ended into a stone wall. The wall had a round opening about three feet off the ground that was the size of a ship's porthole. "We're going through it," Avner said.

"There?" I said. "We'll never fit!"

Avner rolled over a small boulder from the middle of the stream and placed it underneath the hole. I stuck my head through the porthole and saw dryish land. I dropped my belongings on the other side and figured that the fastest way through was feetfirst. Avner gave me a boost. I stepped up on the rock, put one foot through the cubbyhole, and leaned back against the wall of the tunnel. My calves began to strain. My underwear ripped. And suddenly I couldn't move. I'd always gotten a kick out of saying that Avner, with his round belly and jolly face, looked like Winnie-the-Pooh. Now I was the one stuck in a hole.

We pushed and pulled, tugged and aarghed, and eventually I squeezed through the opening, collapsing into the muddy glop on the other side. Avner, learning his lesson, went headfirst and came through in a matter of seconds. We were standing in the mud, our belongings in a heap. My light was extinguished. His beam provided the only glimmer. Avner broke the silence. "Look up."

Turning, I stared at a thirty-foot vertical chute that looked no wider than a backyard well. With its mottled lining and brown color, it looked like a classroom model of a piece of large intestine. This was Warren's Shaft. When Roni Reich reexamined this site, he discovered Jebusite pottery where we were standing that clearly contradicted earlier theories and proved this shaft *did* predate David. It has been here since the middle of the second millennium

B.C.E. Even more, Reich discovered that the shaft wasn't *carved* at all; it was a natural sinkhole. "This is not Warren's Shaft at all," Avner said. "It is the Almighty's Shaft."

So David could have gone up it. But did he?

I heard a slithering through the heart of the shaft, and a curl of rope landed at my feet. It was followed by a metal clang as a harness and ascenders splashed in the mud. There was only one way out: up. We were going to touch the *tsinor* ourselves. Gabi, I now realized, was standing at the top of the shaft in the part of the tunnel we had passed by earlier. Warren's Shaft turned out to be a vertical shortcut, as in a game of Chutes and Ladders. As Gabi affixed the rope to a bar at the top, I stepped into an orange harness, tightened it around my waist, and clamped myself onto the rope. With virtually no experience in rock climbing, I wasn't quite sure how to proceed. I refastened my hard hat and took a tentative step toward the mouth of the shaft. Avner gave me a boost. With a few steps, jerks, and strained pull-ups from rock crevices, I managed to make it about a third of the way up the shaft. Look out, Jebusites, here I come.

This venture was particularly satisfying to me because, as a child, I was not blessed with physical strength. My deepest fears were of being wrestled, wrangled, beaten up. I am haunted by a memory of visiting a friend at age six when his much older brother answered the door. I was terrified he would punch me. "I've already had a broken leg," I said wimpily. As an adult, I have wondered whether my sense of adventure is in part an attempt to purge this childhood fear, pushing myself to extremes but ones that can be navigated by wit, not strength. I've never been engrossed by acts of pure force. I like sports; I'm naturally athletic. But unlike my older brother, I was never particularly interested in the military. My father was in the Navy, but like so many things in my family, that interest seemed to pass to the firstborn son. I'm more like my mother; I'm attuned to pain in others and inclined to offer comfort.

This may be one reason David seems so unappealing to me. He clearly is steeped in the insecurities of being younger, weaker. But instead of responding with humility and the sensitivities that might come from being aggrieved, he overcompensates with the most brutal use of violence to consume power. He's not Franklin Delano Roosevelt, he's Napoleon. And if one appeal of the Bible is to contemplate *oneself* in the great historical moments of the Israelites, as readers are expressly commanded to do at Passover, then I do not find myself reflected all that much in the story of David. Unlike Abraham, Moses, or any number of biblical figures I might wish to be like, David seems repugnant. I don't want to be him; I want to flee from him.

And I got my chance. About halfway up the sheer face of Warren's Shaft, my foot slipped and my left hand sprang free from the rock. My right hand burned as it strained to hold the rope. My head cracked against the jagged stone. I howled. A chunk of flesh flew off my palm, and my hard hat fell to the ground. My legs sagged. I was left hanging limp on the rope, the eensy-weensy spider halfway up the waterspout. As the Bible declares upon David's triumph of Jerusalem, "No one who is blind or lame may enter the House." I was clearly not David.

A few minutes later, after I'd eased myself back down, Avner took his turn and got no farther than I had. It's possible David snuck into Jerusalem through these tunnels; he, or his deputy, could have brought a ladder. Surely either one of them was stronger than either one of us. But given David's history of distancing himself from the dirty handiwork of state building, the idea that he would have gone to these lengths, especially given the ease with which such an ascent could have been repulsed, including after they entered the city and went to open the gates, seems improbable. He would have wanted to march into the city only after others had done the killing, and then only with trumpets blaring.

On first glance the question of how David took Jerusalem may not seem to matter. As Avner said, "After he takes the city, everything changes. Jerusalem evolves into something much more than a geographical entity. It becomes a theological emblem. It becomes the chosen place of the Almighty. It becomes the holiest city on earth."

Yet precisely because Jerusalem does become so important, the fact that the text is vague on how David conquered it seems emblematic. Similar moments of creation and re-creation in the Bible—those periodic new beginnings that propel the Israelites into fresh phases of history—are among the most dramatic in the text. The conception of Adam and Eve in the Garden of Eden gets seventeen verses, plus twenty-four for their expulsion. God's call to Abraham and his departure for the Promised Land get eight verses, including a passionate, direct plea from the divine. Moses' heart-stopping cleaving of the Red Sea and the Israelites' escape to the wilderness takes thirty verses, an entire chapter.

David's capture of Jerusalem is brushed over in three curt verses. What should be a heart-pounding climax is instead cryptic and obscure, shielded by a linguistic pall. The message the text is sending is piercing: David does not deserve credit for conquering Jerusalem. His character is too base to profane the elevation of God's glittering city on a hill. Three thousand years later, it seems only fitting that leading experts speculate that he captured the place by coming up through the sewer. The Bible, as ever, gets the last laugh.

Certainly from us.

We had no choice. We had to turn back through the sullage.

Back at ground level, the bandage that had once been our Goliath's sling now served to wrap my hand. We said good-bye to Gabi and went to a Palestinian kebab house to salve our wounds and to confront the most surprising twist in David's life. His rise to power does not end in triumph; it ends in loneliness. The main reasons for his collapse: arrogance, divine providence, and women.

After he secures Jerusalem, David's first act is to summon the Ark of the Covenant, which has been residing in the Northern Kingdom of Israel. This is another tactically brilliant maneuver to help secure the loyalty of the north, which is honored that its treasure has been elevated to national icon. David dances before the Ark to the tune of lyres, harps, timbrels, and cymbals. The text says he leaps and whirls before the Lord, which prompts Michal to accuse him of exposing his genitals before the multitudes—in effect, he flashes the Ark. "The Lord chose me instead of your father," David says, "and appointed me ruler over the Lord's people Israel." His message: I will dance before the Lord and dishonor myself all day if I want to.

The act of bringing the Ark to Jerusalem has great symbolic power. The Ark and the Ten Commandments are the physical manifestation of the Laws of Moses handed down by God on Mount Sinai. They represent the covenant between God and the people of Israel—God promises to protect the people; they promise to uphold his code of conduct. It is the locus of Israelite religion. In the several hundred years between the promulgation of these laws and the rise of David, the Ark has been trapped in the feuding among the tribes, its influence diminished. By uniting the tribes and bringing the Ark to Jerusalem, David for the first time marries the political fortunes of the Israelites with their religious tradition. Again, putting it in contemporary terms, he fuses church and state.

Symbolically, David's move brings the legacy of Mount Sinai to Mount Zion, one of the biblical names for Jerusalem. In some ways, this act is the culmination of the Conquest because the tribes are finally united with a single capital. But David is concerned his act is incomplete: He lives in a house of cedar, a sign of wealth for a wandering people, while the Ark abides in a tent. Shouldn't he build a temple for it?

In a stunning rebuke, God says no: "From the day that I brought the people of Israel out of Egypt to this day I have not dwelt in a house, but have moved about in Tent and Tabernacle." In effect God puts David in his place: "Who do you think you are building a house for me? I am still king of the world; you are merely king of a few territories." God, whose relationship with humans has always been something of a courtship, stops short of consummating his relationship with David. They can move in together, but they're not ready to build a house together.

But then God does something even more surprising. He promises to give everything he just denied to David, to David's children: "When your days are done and you lie with your father, I will raise up your offspring after you, one of your own issue, and I will establish his kingship. He shall build a house for my name, and I will establish his royal throne forever." God says that when the offspring does wrong, he will chastise him, but he insists he will never withdraw his favor. "Your throne shall be established forever." God, whose earlier commitment to protect the Israelites is conditional on their upholding his laws, now makes an unconditional promise to protect the House of David. The covenant is now one-way. No matter what happens, David's house will reign forever.

As is often the case, God offers no explanation for this gesture, which will have huge consequences for Jewish and especially Christian history. Some scholars suggest this covenant may be the work of biblical redactors, Jerusalem scribes who edited the story centuries later and were interested in promoting David's ties to their city. Others suggest that kingship had become the norm in the Ancient Near East, prompting God to uphold this tradition. Either way, one irresistible conclusion is that God is clearly trying to have it both ways: keep his association with the shining new capital but distance himself from its cavalier king.

No matter the reason, the promise predictably emboldens David, who proceeds to expand aggressively across the region, marching south into the Negev, north to Damascus, and even east across the Jordan into Moab, Ammon, and Edom. The Israelites, the tiny family that began with Abraham wandering sonless from Mesopotamia, have suddenly become a mini-empire. The Fertile Crescent, which has long been marked by empires on either end, now has one in the middle. Most historians doubt that David ever enjoyed this kind of reach; the tiny kingdoms of Israel and Judah almost assuredly could not have provided the soldiers and resources required. But the notion that a united monarchy could have asserted some regional influence is tantalizing considering that in the tenth century B.C.E. both Egypt and Mesopotamia were in decline. History does not endorse the biblical story, but it does suggest its backdrop is accurate.

As for the morals of the story, they, too, are mixed. One reason for David's popularity today, especially among Jews, is his extraordinary assertion of brute power. Many Jews see themselves collectively as that vulnerable child I was, afraid of getting beaten up. This view is understandable. Jews have been beaten up for centuries—and not by their older brothers but by their younger ones, Christians and Muslims. David is an appealing corrective. He beats others up first, and seems to do so not just with impunity but with God's express blessing of eternal salvation. Even the savior of Christians claims descent through the King of Israel.

But the story of David also holds an important reality check for Jews, which I, for one, was uncomfortable to learn. The upside of being a small people—today, there are 12 million Jews, 2 billion Christians, and 1 billion Muslims—is that Jews have long considered themselves more tolerant than their fellow monotheists. Others may claim to be universal faiths; Jews are content with being a leading-edge minority. Yet David proves that Israelite religion was not always satisfied with being small. In its frisky, adolescent years, before being slapped back to size by the Assyrians and Babylonians, the Israelite nation, too, wanted to assert its power, and its way of life, on its neighbors. Even in the Jews' own story—the Bible—David is the first king to impose his religion on others. Jews must be careful before accusing others of tyrannical behavior when their story blazes the trail. Long before Constantine, David makes the first play to establish monotheism as the universal faith of the Near East.

And he fails. After all, how can he control the entire region when he can't control his own family?

T he thing about David is he loved women."

Yael Lotan was taking a sip of lemonade and speaking about the subject of her recent novel. A fiery-haired time bomb of a woman, Yael had been frequently under arrest for supporting Palestinians during her fifty-plus years as a British-born Israeli intellectual. In many ways, she was a classic radical. She didn't much care for Zionism. She didn't much care for men.

But she did care for David.

"David intrigued me enormously, because he's so rich and complicated we feel he's real. He's got terrific strengths but also terrific weaknesses. My goal was to eliminate the mythology around him and write about him as an abandoned child who rose to become a very romantic king."

"Romantic?"

One afternoon David rises from his couch and strolls to the roof of the palace, where he eyes a woman bathing outdoors. David summons the woman, who is identified as Bathsheba, daughter of Eliam and wife of Uriah. Bathsheba, who has just purified herself after her menstruation, lies with David and returns home, only to send word, "I'm pregnant." David responds by sending not for Bathsheba but for her husband, who is away in the army. David bribes Uriah, then sends him home to sleep with his wife and provide cover for the king. Uriah refuses to visit his wife and sleeps at the entrance to the palace. "What's the matter with you?" David asks. Uriah says that having sex would make him ritually impure for battle. "The Ark is at the palace," he says. "Our men are at war. How can I sleep with my wife?" Flabbergasted, David gets Uriah drunk and once more sends him home, but the king is rebuffed a second time. Finally, in an act tantamount to usurping the life-and-death powers of God, David sends Uriah to the front line to be killed, making him yet another unfortunate cog in the king's way disposed of at a convenient time. David then invites Bathsheba into the palace, where she delivers a son.

"I'm inclined to believe Bathsheba engineered the whole story," Yael said. "In this kind of topography, anyone who takes a bath on top of a roof knows very well that others are looking. And David has the highest vantage point of all. She knows he's a lecherous old thing, and she deliberately exposes herself to him."

"If so, what's her motive?"

Yael looked at me, pityingly. "To get into the king's bed! It's a damn good motive. It's a whole lot better than being just the wife of a general. Such things happen. Look at Henry VIII and Anne Boleyn. Her older sister was his mistress, but she wanted a king for herself."

"So are we supposed to be impressed that she's as manipulative as the king?"

"In matters of women and children, David can be very naïve. And he probably thinks, Why not? She's good looking. Why not take her to bed? But he doesn't realize he's met his match."

To begin, God gets furious and sends the prophet Nathan to deliver a parable about a rich man who is too cheap to offer hospitality to a traveler, and a poor man who gives the traveler his only lamb. "The rich man who did this deserves to die," David wails. "That man is you!" Nathan replies. God then delivers a curse on David for his behavior toward Uriah: Your house will always be at war. More immediately, "I will make a calamity rise against you," God says. "You acted in secret, but I will make this happen in the sight of all Israel." Soon Bathsheba's son falls critically ill and, on the seventh day, dies. David ignores the customary postdeath fast, consoles Bathsheba, and she delivers him another son.

His name is Solomon, which means "the replacement."

"This is where Bathsheba shines," Yael said. "She's wonderfully manipulative, and when she becomes the number one wife, she does everything in her power to make sure Solomon inherits the throne."

David, meanwhile, is distracted by the fulfillment of God's curse. Turmoil arises among his earlier sons, Amnon, who rapes his sister Tamar, and Absalom, who avenges the rape by murdering his half brother Amnon. Absalom is exiled by David and soon goes on to lead a coup against his father. David is forced to flee to Jordan on his bare feet, weeping. Absalom chases his father across the river, where David and his remaining loyalists strike back, killing twenty thousand of Absalom's troops. David then looks the other way as Absalom gallops through the woods, gets his locks caught in a tree, and is murdered by David's deputy. The defrocked king returns to Jerusalem to reclaim his tarnished throne.

But David is old. He lies around the palace in his pajamas, disoriented, senile. His attendants search for a young virgin to perk him up. A beautiful girl, Abishag, is brought to the palace, but the king is impotent. Abishag stays around anyway. Bathsheba, concerned that she has been supplanted by Abishag and that Solomon won't inherit the throne, sidles up to David and reminds him, "Dear, remember how you promised that *Solomon* would replace you?" Clearly David made no such promise, but Bathsheba executes a deft bedroom coup. Solomon is named sole heir.

"So where's the romance in *this* story?" I said to Yael.

"Oh, my goodness, it's very romantic," she said. "First of all, Abishag is this girl from the north brought to this old king; she starts out as a foot warmer and rises to become majoress domo. Second, she's the one person totally devoted to him in the midst of the power struggles within his family. Thus she's the one person he trusts implicitly."

"A lot of women have told me over the years that they don't have a way into the Bible. The men have all the power. As a woman, do you think David offers you a way in?"

"No. The Bible is clearly patriarchal; women in that society played a very minor role. The Bible deals with a period in which women really were ciphers."

"So given this, can we take lessons from these stories? Their legacy is supposed to be morality."

"That's bunk. It's three thousand years ago. Europeans were still living in caves. Rome hadn't been built. Athens hadn't arisen. Why apply modern ideas to these guys? Especially since, in modern times, people don't seem to be much better."

"So you seem to have plenty of reasons not to like the Bible. It's patriarchal. It's used by moralists of all religions. And yet you're passionate about it."

"Because we are probably the only people in the world who can read with the greatest of ease a text written thousands of years ago. Modern Greeks can't easily read Homer. Today's Chinese can't read Confucius. In India, a Hindi scholar must study Sanskrit. Europeans can't simply read Latin. The one achievement of Zionism that didn't come at anyone's expense was the revival of the Hebrew language. I dedicated my book to my daughter, because she can read this story and realize that, as romantic as these women are, she *doesn't* have to be like them. She's not a cipher.

"She can even be like David."

O ur final act in confronting David was to visit his tomb. Avner and I climbed from the hillside perch of the City of David, into the walls of the Old City, up endless crisscrossing staircases, until we reached the summit of Mount Zion. What today is called Zion is the highest peak in the Old City, in the southwest corner, just across from the King David Hotel. It is not to be confused with what the Bible calls Mount Zion, though that is confusing, too.

The term *Zion* has at least four usages in the Bible. The first is the name for the Jebusite stronghold that David conquers and renames the City of David. Solomon builds the Temple on the ridge above this—today's Temple Mount—which the Psalms refer to as Zion. During the Exile, this hill came to be associated with the entire city of Jerusalem and later the entire people of Israel. I "have said to Zion: You are my people!" God declares in Isaiah. After the destruction of the Second Temple in 70 C.E., Jews continued to pray for the restoration of Zion, a further metonymy that associates the people with its sacred homeland. This usage was picked up by the nineteenth-century movement of Jewish renewal and return to the land, which called itself Zionism.

The hill that is today called Zion represents still another usage, introduced by medieval travelers who wrongly believed this summit once held the City of David. Today it houses an elaborate complex containing a school, a synagogue, and the room in which Jesus is said to have held the Last Supper. At the back of the small synagogue is a darkened niche containing the Tomb of David, an eight-foot-long cenotaph draped in royal blue velvet. It is embroidered with one Star of David for each year of Israel's independence and an inscription from Psalm 137 that reads "If I forget you, O Jerusalem, let my right hand wither."

Is this really where David was buried?

"For sure the first tomb was not here," said Avner. "It's too far from David's city. But there is a hint in Josephus that his tomb might have been moved, maybe as far as here."

The building itself may date from the time of Josephus, in the first century C.E. In 1948 the Israeli archaeologist Jacob Pinkerfeld removed the marble floors and discovered three additional floors below: the first belonging to a Crusader church, the next to a Byzantine church, and the final one to a Roman church from the late first century C.E. Inscriptions suggest this synagogue was built not by Jews but by early Christian Jews, who believed Jesus was the messiah. The interfaith roots of David run deep in this soil.

And even deeper in the architecture. Up a flight of stairs is the kind of room one finds only in Jerusalem. It's a large hall, lined with Jerusalem stone and vaulted Gothic ceilings. In the corner is a *mihrab*, a Muslim prayer niche. The Gospel of Luke says Jesus held a Passover seder with his disciples on the night before his crucifixion in what the Greek calls an *anogeon* and the Latin terms a *cenaculum*, the kind of second-floor dining room in Greco-Roman homes. In English this term is rendered as *cenacle*, or Upper Room. So here is a room of Muslim prayer, holy for Christians as the site of a Jewish holy meal.

"So was the Last Supper held here?"

"It was held in a house," Avner said. "But in the New Testament, Peter says they know where the Tomb of David was located. So it's at least possible the two were in the same place."

We climbed a few more stories to the roof. The view was spectacular. We could see all the way from the Al Aqsa mosque to the terraced neighborhoods of West Jerusalem. The sky had its first hint of afternoon marigold-colored light and the air smelled of orange trees.

We pulled out our Bibles. In I Kings 2, as David's life is drawing to a close, he summons Solomon for a final blessing: "I am going the way of all the earth; be strong and show yourself a man." Keep the charge of the Lord, David continues, walk in his ways, follow his commandments. If your descendants are scrupulous in their conduct, David quotes God as saying, "your line on the throne of Israel shall never end." Suddenly the covenant that had been unconditional has become conditional: The Israelites must again uphold God's laws in order to earn his blessing. "So David slept with his fathers, and he was buried in the City of David." The length of David's reign over Israel was forty years, including thirty-three in Jerusalem, yet another link later echoed with Jesus, who died at thirty-three.

But unlike Jesus, David seems to end his life surrounded by few disciples, and even fewer loved ones. He is lonely and weak. He is pitiable. What lessons should we learn from his rapid rise and devastating fall?

Avner and I were joined by Yair Zakovitch, dean of humanities at Hebrew University and a biographer of David. "The thing you have to remember about the Bible," he said, "is that the events and characters are just vehicles to convey messages. The biblical narrative was written to educate our young nation, not so much to tell us what really happened."

Dr. Zakovitch is a gentle, mesmerizing scholar who looks like a shaman, with a brown plaid shirt, an entirely bald head, and large ears that point out from his pate in the manner of Yoda's. I wanted to curl up at his feet and listen to him talk forever.

"Biblical historiography is unique in many ways because it goes from one character to another, presenting our history through people. And that history is the story of the failure of our leaders. God is our blessing; our leaders are our punishment."

At this point I actually did sit down.

At the time of Genesis, in the second millennium B.C.E., all nations have their kings, he continued. "And we are still a young, dysfunctional family. It is as if God were kind enough to give us a chance to learn from the mistakes of others. We see the failure of Adam and Eve, of Noah, of the Tower of Babel. Then we get Abraham, who makes mistakes as well—and we are still paying for those mistakes.

"The Bible never presents us with *perfect*," he went on. "Because what can I learn from a perfect person? Perfect people stand on a pedestal just looking at me. The Bible wants us to learn from our leaders."

"And what should we learn from them?"

"That they won't solve all our problems. Moses is presented as the ultimate leader, but he makes mistakes. Then comes Joshua, who makes mistakes, too. But God saves them. He gives land to the people of Israel, yet they are not grateful. They turn to worship idols. All through Judges we have the same pattern: the people sin, they are punished, they cry, God sends them a savior. Again and again. But God loses his patience, and the quality of the saviors deteriorates throughout the book.

"And then you hear the voice of the people," he continued, "'Send us a king!' But already in Deuteronomy 17 the Bible tells us what it thinks of kings. The monarchy is an institution initiated not by God but by the people. It's a bad idea, a very bad idea. And we know that kingship won't lead us anywhere. It will lead us to exile."

"Then why have so many kings?" I asked. "For four hundred years the Bible presents us with kings."

"Because the Bible has its sense of humor. If any leader gets onstage for a moment, you are optimistic and have some hopes that it will work. King Saul: 'Wow! This tall, handsome guy looks like he's really going to save us.' Two chapters later he is already failing. Same thing with David: 'Wow! Such a nice guy, this little boy, like a male Cinderella. He kills Goliath, he gives this great speech about God.' But then he becomes a tyrant. And you have this tension between David's success—he gave us Jerusalem, he conquered an empire with us—and his failures as a family man. So kingship is not the answer. The same thing happens with Solomon. Soon enough, we get to the point God warned us about in the Torah. That's why I say our leaders are our punishment."

"So what is the message the Bible is trying to send by highlighting this tension between David's public success and his private failure?"

"That morality matters. If you fail as a person, even your success as a king won't help. If your character is weak, your whole nation will pay for it."

"So this leads me to the big and obvious question," I said. The sun had begun to set behind us, leaving a silvery purple sheen to the sky. "If David's character is so weak, why does God give eternal blessing to his family?"

Dr. Zakovitch dropped his voice to a near whisper, causing me to draw closer to him.

"Because we got used to having a king. Even though the individuals may not have been stellar, the royal line was quite strong. It lasted four hundred years. That's why all the prophets, who come later, say we will have a king in the future. But if you read these visions carefully, particularly the ones that play an important role in the New Testament, like Isaiah 11, 'A shoot shall grow out of the stump of Jesse,' or Micah 5,

And you, O Bethlehem of Ephrath,
Least among the clans of Judah,
From you one shall come forth
To rule Israel for me.

"Many of them don't mention the name of David. They talk about his father, Jesse, or his hometown, Bethlehem, but not David specifically, because David was already considered far from perfection.

"They seem to be saying, 'We'll go back to the woods, we'll try again, who knows, maybe this time we may succeed.' They present a compromise between those who want a king and those who don't. And the compromise is: There will be a king, but his powers will be limited. He'll be God's deputy on earth. It will be clear that he doesn't have the authority to be the one who saves."

In other words, the legacy of David's life is as a warning *against* having again the likes of David, one who attempts to husband profane and sacred power in his own hands. This may be his most startling legacy of all: the first biblical figure who effectively merges church and state becomes the reason that the Bible all but endorses separating church and state. Secular leaders must be strictly curtailed and kept out of spiritual terrain.

"The best example of this is the prophet Zechariah, chapter 9," Dr. Zakovitch said.

> *Your king is coming to you.*
> *He is victorious, triumphant,*
> *Yet humble, riding on an ass.*

"The new idea of a king is one who is gentle. He's not riding a horse. Kings ride horses. A horse is associated with military power. If you compare this prophecy with the one in Deuteronomy, you will see the limits now put on the king. He shouldn't be rich. He shouldn't have lots of gold and silver. He shouldn't even have a horse. He should have only a donkey. He should understand that God has the real power, not him."

"But if David's legacy is so tarnished, why do the Gospels want to link Jesus to David at all?"

"Look, the Gospels are a very good piece of Jewish literature, and they understand that one cannot have a messianic leader who is not Davidic. If you want to convince the Jews that Jesus is the one, he has to be linked with David. He has to fulfill the prophecies. A messiah king has to be born in Bethlehem, he has to come to Jerusalem. Sure enough, when Jesus enters Jerusalem he enters on a donkey, because that's what we read in Zechariah 9."

The afternoon had become evening now, the time of day when the air has a chill but the stones still emit a memory of warmth. Few people were entering the Old City at this hour; most were departing. I was left with a feeling of emptiness. I remember the first day I came to Jerusalem, a friend greeted me with a hug and the words "Welcome to the City of David." I felt a boyish pride. Yes, this is a place of triumph, I thought, even for a people with few triumphs in our history. Now I felt no such pride.

What surprised me most about the portrait of David I now had was that it appears at all in the Bible, which by all accounts was heavily edited by his apologists. If this is the authorized version of David's life, one can only imagine what a good critic might have done with the unvarnished truth. But to me, the story delivers a powerful message. David is an experiment. The people wanted to wrest control from God and invest it in a secular leader. That David turns out to be so flawed suggests that God wants us to accept the limitations of political leadership and return at least our spiritual allegiance to him. No matter how powerful we become, we still need God. No matter how much we accomplish, our moral conduct still determines our fate.

But how do we achieve a personal relationship with God? That question remains unanswered in the books of Samuel, which offer few clues for how people should interact with the divine. Prayer, worship, communal gathering, even reading the Torah are all alien concepts in the tenth century B.C.E. For this reason, David is ultimately a transitional figure, the bridge between Moses and the prophets. David brings the Israelites the geopolitical power they must have to survive in the region, but he stops short of bringing them the moral clarity they need to become a shining example to the world. To achieve that, the children of Israel must generate a national identity grounded not in the behavior of their leaders but in the conduct of their people.

They must form a religion.

THE HOUSE OF THE LORD

I had an idea. What if I tried to walk around the most contentious real estate in the Middle East? I wanted to draw closer to Solomon. I wanted to touch ground zero in the battle for God. But mostly I wanted to challenge my growing ambivalence over the fact that the most sacred icon of my religion is a *wall*. Was it time to replace this icon?

"What if we try to circumnavigate the Temple Mount?" I said to Avner.

"It can't be done," he said. "It's too dangerous."

"So where do we start?"

The southwest corner of the Temple Mount is my favorite spot in Jerusalem. It's a peaceful, rarely visited harbor of antiquity that manages to seem serene, even divine, although it's just a few steps south of the Western Wall, a few steps north of a Palestinian slum, and a few feet under the Al Aqsa mosque. The area consists of an extensive excavation that has been turned into a park. Dozens of stone blocks, the size of refrigerator-freezers, lie toppled on one another like alphabet blocks spilled from a toy chest. These blocks once formed the upper part of the wall King Herod erected around the Second Temple. Burned and pitched overboard by the Romans in 70 C.E., they remain untouched since being exhumed in the 1970s. For me, they are the best place to experience the raw presence of the Temple without the pressure to conform to the aggressive proselytizers at the Wall.

"The thing about Herod's Temple Mount," Avner said, "is that it's not square. It's a trapezoid. The eastern wall is shorter than the western wall, so the other walls actually slant." The compound covers thirty-five acres, the size of an average Roman city at the time.

"But this was only *part* of the city," Avner added, "which shows you how big the complex was, and even more how big Jerusalem was. This was the largest complex ever built on earth—at the time of Herod and for many centuries later."

"And how did it compare with Solomon's Temple?"

Herod's Temple was actually the third Israelite temple constructed on this hill. The first was built by Solomon around 964 B.C.E. and destroyed by the Babylonians in 586 B.C.E. The second was begun in 520 B.C.E., after the Israelites returned from exile. This building was remodeled but fell into disrepair. Herod, the reviled Roman governor who ruled Palestine in the decades before Jesus, initiated a major rebuilding in 20 B.C.E.

"Herod's temple was the same size as Solomon's," Avner said, "but his complex was *much* bigger—and Solomon's included a palace."

I ran my fingers down the corner of the wall, a rough edge that felt like the crust of stale bread. The retaining wall here is the height of seventeen limestone blocks, almost sixty feet. The stone was cold, even in the sunshine. I noticed a slightly recessed, beveled edge around the perimeter of each block that reminded me of a picture frame. And then the biggest shock of all: There was no mortar between the blocks, no cement. Nothing.

"The stones were so immense they held themselves in place," Avner said. "I was part of the team that excavated here with Benjamin Mazar beginning in 1968, and we were amazed that the stones are completely level. You cannot put a piece of paper in between them, and not only because there wasn't paper then." He gestured for me to follow. "And Mazar made an impressive discovery." He led me toward a broken stone on the ground. It bore a Hebrew inscription: "To the place of trumpeting."

"Josephus explains that the beginning and end of every Sabbath were announced by the priest blowing a trumpet. This stone would have stood at the corner of the Temple complex. It fell here during the destruction." I looked up: I could almost hear the rocks tumbling, the Temple collapsing, a culture crumbling, the people running. "Flee for refuge," cries the prophet Jeremiah.

Blow the trumpet of Tekoa.
For evil is appearing from the north,
And great disaster.

We walked around the corner to the start of the southern wall. We were now directly in between the Temple Mount and the City of David. Pigeon droppings cover the blocks here. The centerpiece of the southern wall is a monumental staircase that served as the main entrance to Herod's Temple. The grayish steps, alternating between narrow and broad, are carved directly into bedrock in places. To the left is a group of rock-hewn ritual baths where worshipers cleansed themselves before entering the holiest site in Judaism. People passed into the compound through two arches that are visible on the wall.

"If you were participating in a sacrifice, you would enter one gate, walk in one direction around the plaza, then exit through the other. People in mourning would walk the other way, so everyone would know something was wrong." He paused. "That was during the Second Temple."

"But what about Solomon's Temple?" I said. "Why is it so mysterious?"

"Because the remains are under the Temple Mount, and we can't dig there. We must rely on the text."

We pulled out our Bibles. Immediately after David's death, Solomon faces trouble. Adonijah, David's son by an earlier wife, tries to execute a coup. "You know the kingship was rightly mine," he says to Bathsheba. He asks her help in allowing him to marry Abishag, David's former consort, a gesture tantamount to claiming the throne. Solomon responds swiftly, by having his half brother killed. The echoes haven't dimmed on the trumpets of Solomon's coronation, and already he is assassinating his siblings. Like father, like son.

But the story is sending other messages, too. Earlier heroes of the Bible have a distant, mythic air to them: Adam lives to be 930 years old; Noah, 950; Abraham, 175; Isaac, 140; Jacob, 147. With Joshua and David, history comes skidding into the picture, and the characters suddenly seem, well, mortal. David reigns for a downright earthly 40 years, as does Solomon. Solomon doesn't even get a honeymoon before his profane character is put on display. The one area where Solomon is allowed to be larger than life is women. The Bible tells us he has seven hundred wives and three hundred concubines. Even if he spent merely one night with each (on their anniversary?), it would take him nearly two years to see them all—and almost another year for his mistresses.

The obvious conclusion is that these numbers are typological, designed to show his epic powers in love. Actually what they show is his epic powers in international politics. "Marriages in the ancient world were expressions of power," Avner said. "The fact that he had so many wives indicates he had broad-reaching power." The best example occurs in I Kings 3, which says, "Solomon allied himself by marriage with the Pharaoh king of Egypt. He married Pharaoh's daughter and brought her to the City of David."

"Before Solomon, Near Eastern kings would send their daughters to Egypt to marry," Avner said. "Hearing about the daughter of Pharaoh coming to Jerusalem to marry is quite a change. The Bible says Solomon ruled from the Euphrates to the Nile. We have no evidence of his having such a large territory, but at least we can conclude he had a well-established one."

To cement this power, Solomon decides he needs the one mark of authority that everyone in the region can understand. He needs a temple. "It's the culmination of a long process," Avner said, "that begins when the Israelites leave the desert and start becoming an urban society. Becoming an urban society means adopting a completely new language, and that vocabulary includes a capital, an army, and a temple. And the bigger your temple, the stronger your god."

To understand the meaning of Solomon's Temple is to understand three things. The first is the message of its location, which superimposes Solomon's religion over the Canaanite faith that preceded it. When David first dreams of building a temple, he selects a location, "the threshing floor of Araunah the Jebusite." The Hebrew word for "threshing floor" is *goren*, Avner's surname. "My grandfather's name was Galperin," Avner said. "He emigrated from Romania in 1910. At the time Israel was becoming a state, lots of people adopted Hebrew names. I was born Galperin, but my father changed our name right before I went to first grade. On my first day, the teacher called out, 'Galperin.' I said, 'No, no. It's Goren!'"

In antiquity, a threshing floor was generally located in a high place, where bedrock was exposed and wind could blow the chaff from the wheat as it was winnowed. Because food was believed to come from the gods, Canaanites often built prayer niches at such sites to honor the spirits of fertility. A *goren*, in other words, was a holy place. David's decision to erect God's Temple on a Canaanite holy place is consistent with the ancient practice of co-opting pre-existing sanctified spaces. The message they hoped to send was "My god is stronger than yours." Though Jews and Christians would later complain that Muslims co-opted *their* sacred spot by building the Dome of the Rock over the ruins of the Temple, the truth is, David did the same thing first. The first lesson of the Temple Mount is that religious rights and wrongs cannot be refereed by claiming first dibs. If they could, Jerusalemites today would be worshiping the god of bread.

The second message is that sanctuaries cost money, and to raise money leaders often burden their subjects. Solomon pays for his Temple in a variety of ways. The first is levies on international trade. Solomon's most famous wife, the Queen of Sheba, meets him as part of a trade delegation. Living in Arabia, she hears of Solomon's fame and travels to Jerusalem "with a very large retinue, camels bearing spices, a great quantity of gold, and precious stones." He answers her queries, shows off his palace, and even wows her with his table manners; she is left breathless, hands over her wealth, receives a few gifts, and returns home his wife.

The spices in this story are almost certainly frankincense, the mysterious resin prized around the region for its role in concealing malodors at sacrifices. Frankincense trees grow naturally only in southern Arabia, in modern-day Yemen, and the resin was transported via camel caravans across the desert to Gaza, where it was distributed around the Mediterranean. The fact that Sheba treks months through the sand to scope out Solomon, then leaves him with levies, suggests the vastness of his influence as a trader.

But the real source of wealth used for the Temple comes from taxes and slaves. Solomon forces the provinces to up their monthly contribution; then he imposes hard labor. He sends thirty thousand slaves to Lebanon to harvest cedar and conscripts another seventy thousand porters and eighty thousand quarriers. Even if these numbers are inflated, as seems likely, the irony is too rich to ignore: The Israelites, whose suffering at the hands of Egypt inspires God to free them from bondage, have now become slaveholders and taskmasters themselves. The northern tribes, who suffer most, actually seek alliance with Egypt. What a turnabout. A new pharaoh has arisen over the region, one who enslaves the Israelites, forces them to build a monument to his god, and drives them into rebellion. It sounds like the pharaoh of Exodus. Only this pharaoh's name is Solomon.

The final lesson of the Temple is that no religion in the Ancient Near East is unique. The English word *temple* is the most common translation for the Hebrew word *hekal*, which is related to Akkadian, Ugaritic, and Canaanite words meaning "great house." While the English word connotes a public structure, the Hebrew connotes a residence, as in a dwelling place for the deity on earth. The same connotation applies to another word commonly used to describe the Temple, *bet elohim*, House of God.

As detailed in the text, the basic ground plan of the Temple is a rectangle—165 feet long, 85 feet wide—the precise dimensions of the White House. The building is 52 feet high, just shy of the White House. The Temple is relatively simple on the exterior, save two enormous bronze pillars flanking the entrance. Inside are three successive chambers: a small entrance hall, a large main room illuminated by tiny windows, and a holy inner sanctum, called the Holy of Holies, hidden by olivewood doors. Only priests were allowed to enter the Temple, and they could enter the Holy of Holies only once a year, on Yom Kippur.

Both the central space and the inner sanctum are lined with

cedar panels, which were carved with cherubim, palm trees, and flowers, then covered with gold. Since the Temple is designed to be God's residence, the two inner chambers have furnishings—wooden furniture plated with gold leaf—as well as numerous altars, lamps, tables, and other ritual objects for sacrifices and offerings. Inside the Holy of Holies, two cherubim with wingspans of 15 feet protect the prized possession, the Ark of the Covenant, the portable wooden altar that is the representation of God's presence on earth.

The Temple is such a transcendent and elusive icon of antiquity—the architectural equivalent of the Lost City of Atlantis—that one can easily imagine it as the singular achievement of Israelite culture. But in fact, it is commonplace. The idea of a temple to house one's deity was well known across West Asia, and Solomon's Temple drew heavily from its neighbors. The exterior was similar to that of Phoenician temples from the time; the three inner sections were similar to those of Canaanite temples and ones from North Syria. The entire structure was nearly identical to the Egyptian temple at Karnak, which was 45 feet high and 65 feet long, with a forest of internal pillars, and a windowless inner sanctum. The bottom line is this: The size of the Temple may have been impressive, but few viewing it during its lifetime would have thought it proclaimed that the God of the Bible was manifestly different from or superior to other gods.

The wandering God of Abraham may finally have found his mountaintop home, but his power still lay more in his wilderness narrative and less in his house of stones.

Avner and I walked down Herod's steps to the extensive excavation in front of the southern wall. Flat ground gave way to the familiar crosshatch grid of modern archaeological sites. Archaeologists don't remove all of one layer in order to get to the one below; they dig in squares, like a three-dimensional checker-board in which all the white squares are at ground level and all the black are, say, three thousand years old. This method enables future generations to excavate alongside today's work with more sophisticated equipment and revised theories.

Avner led me to the edge of a narrow walkway, where we jumped down into a hole and, hugging a small tree, shimmied into a pit nearly ten feet below. At the bottom were the remains of an old stone tower, discovered by Charles Warren in 1886. "When Mazar excavated here in the 1960s," Avner said, "he found remains from the time of Solomon, the only remains we have in the area of the Temple Mount." The stones were covered in ash, which Avner said was likely from the sacking of the compound in 70 C.E. I rubbed my fingers across the soot and brushed some on my cheeks.

As I did, I heard rustling on the ground above us. The tree began to shake. A voice started barking, in Hebrew: "Who is that? What are you doing here?" It was a woman. "Come out, now!" Avner looked at me. "You might want to use more of that ash," he said dryly. He started answering, "Don't shoot," and climbed out the pit. By the time I got to the top, Avner and the woman were hugging.

Eilat Mazar looks like a fireplug; she's squat, colorful, and has red hair. At rest, she is quiet and sturdy, but angry, she can positively gush. The granddaughter of Benjamin Mazar, Israel's digger in chief, Eilat grew up skipping around these stones, dreaming of the past, and ogling the celebrities who came to pay homage to her grandfather. "Everyone came in those days," she said. "Ariel Sharon, Golda Meir, Ben-Gurion. You have to understand, this dig was something unique—*ten continuous years*, a monster thing for archaeology."

When Mazar died in 1996 at age ninety, his granddaughter assumed his legacy.

"So let me ask you a question," I said. We sat down on the stones. "It seems that the Second Temple gets all the press, and the First Temple is overlooked."

"The reason is connected with politics," she said. "I got my Ph.D. at Hebrew University, and we grew up believing that Solomon built the Temple. I dug here in 1989 and found lots of pottery that we could date from the tenth or ninth century B.C.E. We don't know precisely which one. I was young and quite stupid, so I thought that to be careful I should date it to the later time. Suddenly Israel Finkelstein and his cohorts at Tel Aviv University began to suggest that Solomon didn't build the Temple. It was built later, they said. But I disagree."

"So what's the most concrete thing you found from Solomon's time?"

"It's where you just were," she said.

"You mean the wall?"

"It's not just a wall. It's a city gate, it's a tower, it's part of a whole complex. The Bible says Jerusalem reached its apex under Solomon, and I believe it."

"But do you believe it was an empire? Finkelstein has written that the city of Jerusalem at the time was not large enough to be the center of a regional power."

She laughed. "He's such a troublemaker." Then she turned serious. "If you really look at the construction from the time of Solomon, it shows power. The stones are too big, the buildings are too strong. Just look at the size of the stones you were just touching. Do you realize they are nearly twice as big as the Byzantine ones right next to them—and the Byzantine stones come from fifteen hundred years *later*! No weak ruler could ever build such an enterprise."

While Jewish archaeologists claim that their inability to excavate under the Temple Mount has hindered them in these debates, some Muslims have pounced on the lack of evidence of Solomon's Temple as an opportunity. After Israel recaptured the Temple Mount in 1967, Defense Minister Moshe Dayan, seeking peace, quickly returned control of the plaza atop the complex to the Muslim religious authority, the *Wakf*. Jews were forbidden from worshiping on the plaza. Some rabbis even urged Jews not to set foot on the hilltop, because they could not know for sure where the Temple actually stood. Israeli soldiers kept Jews away, in part to keep out fanatical groups who wanted to build a Third Temple to make way for the messiah.

But the *Wakf* had other ideas. It refused to recognize Israel's sovereignty over the exterior walls of the compound and over time began to question whether a Temple had ever been constructed. The Haram was the site of a mosque from the time of Adam, the *Wakf* maintained. As the chief Palestinian Muslim, Mufti Ikrima Sabri, said days before my visit: "There is not even the smallest indication of the existence of a Jewish temple on this place in the past. In the whole city, there is not even a single stone indicating Jewish history." On the ground, this policy led to ruinous results, like a 1986 Palestinian building project that tore through a Herodian wall. Israel's Supreme Court ruled that it violated Israeli law but did nothing to halt the work. The issue was simply too explosive.

In 1999, the conflict finally erupted. The *Wakf* commenced its most extensive renovation, creating an emergency exit for a little-known prayer area underneath the Al Aqsa mosque. Crusader Christians had worshiped here and erroneously labeled the rooms Solomon's Stables. The *Wakf* explained that contemporary Muslim worshipers needed a place to pray when it rained. It drove bulldozers onto the Haram and opened an entrance that was two hundred feet long and seventy-five feet wide. Using hundreds of dump trucks, many in the middle of the night, the authority then hauled twenty thousand tons of debris to the Kidron Valley and dumped them over the hill.

Soon a bulge appeared on the southern wall of the Temple compound, which Jewish critics claimed was caused by the renovations. The bulge protruded more than two feet and stretched one hundred feet long. "The wall could collapse," said Jerusalem mayor Ehud Olmert. "It *will* collapse," said Eilat at the time. But the Palestinians refused to let Jewish officials examine the damage up close. "This bulge has been under our monitoring since the seventies and has neither grown nor shifted in thirty years," said the director of the *Wakf*. "We don't feel there is a dangerous situation." The shouting escalated; tempers flared; and finally Jordanian engineers were summoned to replace some stones. Years later, the work had not been completed.

"For most of the last century, the Temple Mount has been a political battlefield," I said to Eilat. "Is the struggle getting worse, or has it always been this bad?"

"No question it is getting worse. Since the beginning of the last century, the only people who were ruling the Temple Mount were Muslims. And the place suffered. There was the earthquake of 1927. There were wars. And the only buildings that were reconstructed were the Muslim ones. The whole mound is an ancient site, three thousand years ancient, that nobody really took care of. It's just a matter of time before a crack appears in one of the walls and something collapses."

"So you're saying the compound is so unstable that one of the buildings will actually fall?"

"It's obvious. Because it's so neglected. No treatment has been done, ever, on this ancient compound."

"But that's World War III."

"Well, I'm waiting for it. It's not going to be small, that's for sure."

"Do you think the Muslims are trying to wipe out Christian and Jewish history?"

"I think we're dealing with people who don't give a damn about anything other than their religion. Period. And it's not like they're really battling to destroy other religions, it's like other faiths don't even exist. And they say it."

"But what about fanatics on the Jewish and Christian sides?" I said. "Do you think they should build a Third Temple?"

She squirmed at bit at this question. "Well, you know, it's my nature that I don't like extremes. I don't think violence brings a better life to anybody. So, no, I don't think so. But I don't think that letting the Islamic fundamentalists do whatever they wish is the right thing, either. First of all, an ancient archaeological site should be preserved and taken care of. And then, of course, freedom of religion should be permitted. Not everybody should be satisfied, but the mainstream should be satisfied. The Muslims can have their mosques and pray, but it's not only theirs. It's ours, too."

We said good-bye and continued our journey. The eastern wall of the Temple Mount is by far the most treacherous. As the eastern border of the Old City, this stretch of Herod's compound sits on a narrow ledge, about fifty feet wide, which drops off precipitously into the Kidron Valley. On the far side is the Mount of Olives. The valley takes its name from the brook of Kidron, which means "turbid," after the amount of sediment in its water. In antiquity, the valley was considerably deeper, but centuries of destruction in the Old City have filled it with debris. Today it's a tense passageway linking two Palestinian neighborhoods. Jews are not permitted to walk here.

"Join me for an adventure?" Avner said.

"We haven't broken the law all day," I said.

We walked around the corner, hopped up on a low stone guardrail, and prepared to climb to the base of the wall. Instantly a shout came from above. An Israeli officer bolted from his guard post, gripped his machine gun at the ready, and ordered us to stop. Avner told him we were on an academic mission. The soldier was unimpressed. We nodded and returned to street level but continued walking forward. Within fifty yards, we spotted a small grove of olive trees. We ducked into the trees, checked to make sure we were out of eyeshot of the guard, then tiptoed to the base of the wall.

The scene was eerily quiet. I could hear worshipers milling about on the esplanade above. The air smelled of citrus, evergreen, and charcoal embers. A bell tower on the Mount of Olives sounded once, then quieted. Thousands of tombstones lined the face of the hill.

"There have been tombs on the Mount of Olives since the time of David," Avner said. "Near the street is a mausoleum that once had a pyramid on top; it's called the Tomb of the Daughter of the Pharaoh. Another is a memorial to Absalom. Pilgrims used to throw rocks at Absalom's shrine to show that leading a revolt against your father is not the way to behave."

"So if this was a cemetery, why did Jesus come here the night before he died?"

"It was a haven, outside the city walls, away from the people and religious institutions he did not agree with. The Kidron had always been the end of the city. The Mount of Olives was filled with orchards, and one of them was Gethsemane, which means 'oil press.'"

"So if the Mount of Olives was known as a place of death, would his coming here indicate that he had some foreknowledge that he was going to die?"

"The story suggests that, but there were cemeteries all around the city, 360 degrees. I think it's more because he wanted peace for his soul—and because the prophets say the messiah will come from the east."

We were walking along the stone path at the base of the wall. Some Palestinian workers were chiseling stones. A woman in a head scarf walked by, looking down to avoid eye contact. "You're being watched from the top of the wall," Avner said. "They have guns."

"Israelis?"

"No, Palestinians."

"I'm not going to look."

Soon we came upon a double-vaulted stone gateway. The top of the gate sticks up beyond the top of the retaining wall. The entrances are stoned in—and have been for a thousand years. The effect was grand but empty, like someone offering you a gift, then pulling back his hands. This is the Golden Gate, perhaps the most famous portal in Jerusalem. The gate has two archways: the Gate of Repentance and the Gate of Mercy. The prophet Zechariah suggests that the messiah would enter Jerusalem from the east. As the Golden Gate is the only entrance to the Temple Mount from the east, many Jews consider it the messiah's entrance point. The Gospels suggest Jesus fulfilled this prophecy and entered the city on Palm Sunday through this gate.

The side-by-side gates rest on stone pillars that are said to have been a gift to Solomon from the Queen of Sheba. But wasn't Solomon's Temple destroyed? Maybe not entirely. Josephus writes that the eastern wall was the only one not rebuilt by Herod. In 1969 the American archaeologist Jim Fleming was investigating the wall following a heavy rainstorm. In front of the Golden Gate the ground opened up, and he fell into a hole about eight feet deep. He found himself knee-deep in bones. "Then I noticed with astonishment," he said later, "that on the eastern face of the wall, directly beneath the Golden Gate, were five wedge-shaped stones neatly set in a massive arch. Here were the remains of an earlier gate to Jerusalem, one that apparently had never been fully documented."

The *Wakf* quickly cemented the hole and placed an iron fence around the Golden Gate.

The reason Fleming landed in a puddle of bones is that death is everywhere around the Golden Gate. Hundreds of graves crowd the eastern wall. Muslims believe that on judgment day, a knife's edge will stretch over a valley from a mountain to heaven's gate. If that mountain is the Mount of Olives, as legend suggests, then the Golden Gate would be the entrance to eternity, and anyone buried here would have a presumed advantage. Jewish legend, however, holds that the messiah is forbidden from traversing a cemetery, which means those buried here would be hindering *everyone's* salvation. Jews and Muslims can't even agree on whether it's good or bad to be buried near heaven's door.

Whoever is right, the image of a perilous ravine serving as the final frontier between life on earth and life ever after has become one of the most haunting images to emerge from these hills. Like so many other ideas from the Bible, what once was physical has become metaphoric. The Kidron is the Valley of Death.

"The Lord is my shepherd," reads the King James rendition of Psalm 23.

> *I shall not want.*
> *He maketh me to lie down in green pastures: he leadeth me beside the still waters.*
> *He restoreth my soul: he leadeth me in the paths of righteousness for his name's sake.*
> *Yea, though I walk through the valley of the shadow of death, I will fear no evil: for thou art with me; thy rod and thy staff they comfort me.*

A few steps beyond the Golden Gate, we reached an even larger gate with medieval doors. The doors were open. Arab vendors were selling fruits and vegetables. Little boys were kicking soccer balls. This is Lion's Gate, also called St. Stephen's Gate, one of seven active gates into the Old City. The Israeli Army used this entrance to capture the city in 1967. The doors are still broken from that encounter. It's the same direction the Romans used to capture the city nineteen centuries earlier.

"Why is it so much easier for everyone to take the city from the north?" I asked.

"It's flat," Avner said. "There's no Kidron. And you don't have to fight up a hill. It's the same reason Herod built his cistern here. It's the highest point in the Old City."

Avner led us through the gate, back into the Old City. We were now in the Muslim Quarter, at the northern entrance to the Temple Mount plaza. Washing stations with stone basins lined the inside of the wall. Vendors hawked postcards and prayer beads. Worshipers streamed through a portal onto the plaza, which was guarded by Israeli police. We had a spectacular view of the hexagonal Dome of the Rock, with its cobalt, turquoise, and mustard-colored arches, intricate sixteenth-century tile work, and bold, golden dome. The dome, often photographed in pink dawn light, has become so associated with Jerusalem, even in Jewish iconography, that it seems emblematic of the larger holiness of the place. Whenever I see it pictured behind Palestinian spokesmen—photographed from this angle, which is its view from the Arab-dominated neighborhoods—I am jolted into remembering its political potency.

We continued along the outside of the northern wall, which is largely hidden by modern buildings, until we reached the heart of the Muslim souk, a warren of clothing stalls, religious schools, spice vendors, and trinket shops. We ducked down a deserted alley, stepped through a doorway, and climbed a dark set of stairs. Inside a bare, whitewashed room, we waited to meet an old friend, the chief archaeologist for the *Wakf*, and Eilat Mazar's doppelgänger during the brushup over the southern wall.

Yusef Natsheh is as moderate a Muslim as one can find in Jerusalem. He's short in the manner of an overgrown schoolboy, bespectacled, and was dressed this morning in a green plaid sport jacket that seemed fresh off the rack from High Street in Oxford. His eyes brightened as he welcomed us back. He ordered tea. After a while, I asked about the idea some Jews have of building a Third Temple on the Haram.

"In my opinion, it's a small idea so far," he said. "But this idea is like a piece of snow, whenever it starts rolling it becomes bigger."

"There is another small idea," I said, "on the Palestinian side, which is that the Temple was never there. Do you believe that?"

"Let me speak for myself," Dr. Natsheh said. "From an archaeological point of view, I believe there are many remains which could be identified with developments that took place before Islam. And I think, surely, one of these developments could be what you talk about."

"Could be?" I said. "Or was?"

"Could be. I am not expert in this field. But this is my knowledge as a person who reads and hears and sees. So I am not going to tell you *was*, because I'm not an expert."

I was surprised to hear this coming from someone so openminded. "So that part of the wall where Jews pray now," I said, "the Western Wall—"

"Or, according to our views, the El-Buraq," he said, using the Arabic name for Mohammed's horse, who is said to have been tethered there during the Prophet's nighttime ascension to heaven.

"The El-Buraq," I said. "If there was no Temple, why do Jews pray in this spot?"

"According to research, this only began in the sixteenth century," he said. "Before that, Jews prayed on the Mount of Olives. And allowing the Jews to pray at El-Buraq was an act of Muslim tolerance."

"Jews think this wall was connected to Herod's Temple. Do you agree?"

"As I told you before, exactly, yes. Most people think this was built by Herod. But that doesn't indicate that it is Jewish. It's Roman. It could be for our tribe. But even if it is Herod's Temple, does that give people the right to diminish, destroy, or extinguish other cultures, which are still living and have been for fourteen hundred years?"

"So when I, as a peace-loving Jew, come to this wall, and touch it, what do you think I should feel?"

"You have to feel what is in your heart," he said. "You feel your culture, your past. And you have the right to feel that, as long as you don't threaten other people. This also applies to Muslims. I don't think it's a big issue for Muslims to admit that there was an old culture here."

"So if you don't think it's a big deal, then why do most Palestinians disagree?"

"Because they are feeling threatened. I'm sorry, but it's what we feel when a group of Jews approach the Haram with arms. If you are in my position, what is your reaction? You ask my feeling when a peaceful Jew wants to pray. He wants to reach God. There are different paths to God. So what about a Palestinian who is living here for generations and generations and seeing his path neglected, deserted, destroyed?"

The tea came, and we took a second to enjoy a break. I've never been a fan of Arab tea, which I find too bitter without sugar and too sweet with it. But the rules of hospitality often compel me to sample it, as I did this morning. Eventually I asked Dr. Natsheh if he believed we were in a religious war.

"No, I don't think so," he said. "But religion is used to serve the people. If we were true religious people, we would sit together and reach an agreement that was different from a political one."

"But aren't religious people part of the problem?" I said. "Wasn't it religious people who built the new mosque on top of the Haram?"

"Never," he said. "We expanded, maybe, an area that already existed. We, what we called, rehabilitated some place. We have needs, you know, just as you do. Now it's cold. If people come this Friday and it's raining, how will they perform their prayers in open spaces?"

"But what about the destruction?" I said.

"They accused us of using bulldozers. Give me one Israeli excavation in the early 1960s and '70s in the country that did not use bulldozers. What happened in 1967 when the Israelis leveled the plaza in front of the Wailing Wall? Why do you have the right to do certain things and we don't? Sure, if the situation were different, we would like to do it in a different way. But do you want religious people to wait for three seasons while we excavate? Religious people are not so happy with archaeology. And I understand them."

He sat back in his chair.

"May I speak as a friend?" I said.

He nodded silently.

"You seem sad," I said. "Do you feel the voices of hate are overwhelming now, and the voices of moderation are drowned out?"

"Unfortunately, I do. It really makes me feel that hope is so far for any of us."

"Have you lost hope?"

"Not yet. If I lost hope, I would lose life."

"But why don't you start crying, throw your arms up, and say, 'It's too much! God, I can't do it.'"

"Because I belong here," he said. "I was born in Jerusalem. When I was seven years old, I used to cross the Haram every day on my way to school. I would have a sack of books, and I used to play here for ten minutes before going to school. We have a difficult situation, but that is no excuse to leave."

"And do you feel that God is looking out for what you are doing?"

"God created us, and I believe that we have to do as much good as we can. In the Koran there is a verse which I repeat sometimes with friends. 'For a human being, there is nothing but his work.' I believe in that. After all the politics, God will come and judge Yusef Natsheh, whether I was serious."

"And what will he say?"

"I don't know. I myself am never satisfied. I am a human being, and I have my deficiencies."

We had one more wall to traverse. Around the corner from Yusef Natsheh's office, a small doorway opens onto the Via Dolorosa. Two Israeli guards sat protecting it. We stepped inside, descended a staircase, and found ourselves at the start of what may be the bloodiest stretch of the Wall. The Western Wall Tunnels comprise an intricate network of underground caverns, passageways, and secret excavations that run the entire fifteen-hundred-foot length of the western perimeter of Herod's compound. Covered by debris for centuries, this stretch of wall was excavated following the Six-Day War.

The northern end of the tunnel, where we were standing, consists of a subterranean channel, carved into bedrock, that once supplied water to Herod's complex. First discovered by Warren, it was reexcavated in the 1980s and opened to tourists. The *Wakf* would not allow visitors to exit into the Muslim Quarter, so tourists were obliged to retrace their steps, thus limiting the number of guests. Fed up, Prime Minister Benjamin Netanyahu hastily ordered an exit opened without permission after midnight on September 25, 1996. Yasser Arafat went ballistic, accused the Israelis of destabilizing the Haram, and set off riots that killed at least a dozen Israelis and five dozen Palestinians. The Jordanians and Egyptians threatened to join the scuffle before the Clinton administration brokered a cooling off.

Today the passageway was nearly empty, victim to the larger degradation of the region. The tunnel has a dank, timeless quality to it that reminded me of climbing into the pyramids in Giza. After a few hundred yards the channel ends, and we arrived in a vaulted chamber the size of a Romanesque church. Dramatic lighting shimmered up the walls. A handful of worshipers, mostly women, sat inches from the wall, which looks exactly like the Western Wall, only unbleached by the sun.

"For religious Jews, this spot is even holier than the Western Wall," Avner said, "because it's closer to where the Holy of Holies would have been."

"Why is the Western Wall more famous than the Eastern," I said, "considering that if you were standing here during Solomon's time you'd have been facing the back of the building?"

"All temples in the ancient world faced east," he said, "because they wanted to front the rising sun. But the Holy of Holies was in the *rear* of the building, so it's holier than the façade."

Next to the wall a section of Herod's masonry was missing, and the gap was filled by a concrete slab. This patch was nearly the trip wire of World War III. In 1981, Yehuda Meir Getz, the rabbi of the Western Wall, led an unauthorized mission to burrow eastward from this spot, underneath the Haram, to find the Holy of Holies. Getz was a mystic who prayed every morning in the Tunnels dressed in a black robe and white headdress, with a Bible in his pocket and a pistol on his hip. He was joined in his brinkman-ship by Rafi Eitan, an adviser on terrorism to three Israeli prime ministers, who later recruited the American Jonathan Pollard to spy against the United States.

Breaking through the sacred barrier, Getz and Eitan discovered a cavernous tunnel, which they believed was a spring used by priests before entering the Temple. "We were of the view that without heavy tools," Eitan said, "using a delicate chisel, we could chip away at the soft limestone walls. We thought we could ad-vance quietly and secretly to discover the hiding place where the priests had concealed the Temple artifacts and arrive at the spot, just under the Holy of Holies, where the Ark of the Covenant was hidden."

Getz and Eitan believed that finding the Ark, which has been missing since the death of Solomon, would herald the return of the messiah. Instead, their chiseling raised the hackles of wor-shipers on the Temple Mount, who sent youths on ropes into the excavation. A conflagration ensued: the Muslims prepared water cannons to shoo away the diggers; Getz's wife summoned students from the nearby Jewish school; both sides scuffled until the police arrived. Prime Minister Menachem Begin promptly ordered the illegal passageway filled with concrete.

"I will now retire from the project with a bitter taste in my mouth," Rabbi Getz confided in his diary. "I have never felt the humiliation of Judaism that I felt today in our own sovereign country. I pray that this is the end of exile."

We reached the end of the tunnel and burst back into the sun. Before us now was the familiar face of the Western Wall, the eighty-five-foot-long limestone façade, no longer than a basket-ball court, that for centuries has served as the steadfast core of

Jewish identity. The twenty-four layers of stones, each a different size, reach a height of fifty feet and stand as an indomitable patchwork quilt of pain and perseverance. Each row of stones is set back a few millimeters from the layer beneath it, meaning the entire wall slopes slightly eastward, contributing to its stability. When Jews began tucking notes into crevices, the absence of mortar, once a mark of Herod's mastery, became a physical manifestation of Jewish spirituality: squeezed out by larger forces, with no space left to thrive, Jews nuzzled their prayers into the forgotten recesses of history. Just out of reach, the notes give way to carob bushes that drip between the seams like icing between layers of a birthday cake. What allows plants to survive in stone with no soil and little water, yet produce tender fruit? What allows a people to endure through affliction with no land and little sustenance, yet produce a thriving seed?

We walked down the ramp, placed cardboard *kippot* on our heads, and made our way to the benches in the back of the male-only worshiping area. Hundreds of dark-coated men strolled about, opening books and nodding quietly. Across a small divide, an even greater number of women crowded into a much smaller area. I checked to see if any Palestinians were preparing to throw stones from the Haram.

Our walk had left me exhausted yet riled up. None of the scars we encountered, none of the gestures of self-appointed probing, saving, erasing, or rewriting seemed in the least bit related to how most people I know experience God. What has always appealed to me about the Temple Mount is how many of the holiest spots in the Abrahamic faiths are all gathered on the same piece of earth. Geography, so central to the roots of monotheism, seems to bond practitioners into some forced accommodation.

Now I wasn't so sure. The Temple was dreamed up by David and built by Solomon as a way for a king, whose hold on power was insecure, to honor God but also to secure his own control over a wobbly united monarchy. Herod, whose family were converts to Judaism, used the Temple for a similar political purpose. This legacy seemed to be repeating itself. Far from being a purely religious place, the Temple seemed to me to be more and more like a largely political place. Given this history, why base my religious identity on its remains?

We pulled out our Bibles. Solomon takes twenty years to construct the Lord's House and his royal palace, an event that comes to a close in I Kings 9. Only a few verses later, God has already turned against the king. Solomon's many wives lure his attention to other gods, and he even builds shrines to two, the god of the Moabites and the one of the Ammonites. This is a stunning admission: the man who builds the Temple to the one God of Israel also builds monuments to honor the gods of lands David had supposedly vanquished. As a gesture promoting coexistence and interreligious harmony, Solomon's act is foresighted.

But the Bible hates it. "The Lord was angry with Solomon, because his heart turned away from the Lord." God berates him: "Because you are guilty of this, I will tear the kingdom away from you and give it to one of your servants." God raises up adversary after adversary and rips the united tribes asunder. By the time Solomon dies, Israel is once again a splintered nation, the dream of imperial dominance shattered. The Temple would stand for another 350 years, be destroyed, and rise for 500 years more, but the land God promised to Abraham would never be whole again.

In its place, Jews would eventually begin to worship in synagogues—miniature, surrogate temples of a sort—and they would save their highest prayers for a remnant of the Temple. Invoking this sacred rampart, they would wail at the memory of God's lost house and plead for its reconstruction. At least that's the story I was taught as a Jew growing up in the last decades of the twentieth century.

Only it's not true. After the destruction of the Second Temple, the entire compound fell into disuse. Jews were forbidden from entering Jerusalem and, with the exception of a few isolated uprisings, mostly stayed away. Jews believed God's presence never left the Temple area, but for centuries the traditional place for mourning the loss was the Mount of Olives. Not until the Turks overran Jerusalem in 1516 did Suleiman the Magnificent issue an edict permitting the Jews to pray before the Temple's remains. The Western Wall soon became a center of Jewish life, and the belief that God's spirit had never departed from the area now became associated with this particular spot. Jews removed their shoes before praying, kissed the stones, and wrote petitions to God, which they inserted into the cracks. The Wall became a symbol of the divine, and an emblem of the Jewish people.

Non-Jewish observers began to notice the particular aural praying style of the Jews and nicknamed the site the "wailing place." As the British cleric Samuel Manning wrote in 1873, "Here the Jews assemble every Friday to mourn over their fallen state. Some press their lips against crevices in the masonry as though imploring an answer from some unseen presence, others utter loud cries of anguish." When the British took over Jerusalem in 1917, the popular term for the area became the "Wailing Wall," which is the phrase I learned as a child. But after the Israelis liberated the area on June 7, 1967, Jewish leaders renamed the sacred spot the *Western* Wall, claiming that Jews need no longer weep, as their state had been renewed and their freedom of worship returned.

The question for me, after our circumnavigation, was whether the wall had become too fetishized. Has the bickering over every speck of limestone detracted from the larger spiritual meaning of the Temple, which is a spot where God dwells close to humans and humans strive to be closer to God? By focusing so intently on the physical structure of the Temple, rather than on the covenant with

God it was meant to embody, Jews risk equating their faith with a totem, which is the essence of the paganism they tried to transcend.

"For me, the Temple is such an abstract thing," I said to Avner. "It's this strange place, only a priest can enter it, then only once a year. There are sacrifices. It seems unlike everything modern Judaism represents."

"On the other hand, religious Jews study these practices daily," Avner said. "How you prepare the frankincense, how you prepare the animals. They anchor themselves to the physical details. I agree that the Temple has become an icon and not a sign of the obligations that God and humans make to each other."

"But what about you? As a person who loves the Bible, and grew up in Jerusalem, do you feel attachment to the Temple?"

"As a symbol only. I have big problems with the idea that a Third Temple should be built. For me it's withdrawing back into a nonspiritual land of Judaism. Most of Judaism was developed after the Temple was destroyed. During the First Temple, the Israelites believed that God lived here. What happened during the Exile in Babylon is that those who believed God has a territory were forced to change. God had to be everywhere. This is the great vision of monotheism that allows Judaism to reach a quite impressive level of spirituality."

"But I'm confused. The first time I came to Jerusalem, I walked down this plaza, put my hand on the Wall, and cried. But now that I think about it, I wasn't crying for the Temple. I was crying for having arrived here, for the history of suffering in Judaism, for the love my mother taught us about God. I was crying for the Jewish people."

"Same with me. In 1967 I was in the Army, listening on the radio, hearing the soldiers coming to the Wall. And I cried like crazy."

"But now what I believe is that those tears were not to have the Temple rebuilt," I said. "I'm not crying because the Temple was destroyed. If anything, I'm *here* because the Temple was destroyed. That's what allowed Judaism to survive. It became portable."

"I agree. Personally, I don't need the Wall anymore. It was a symbol of everything the Jewish people were longing for, and we've fulfilled that longing. But I have understood since I was four years old that the Temple was something beyond our reach. Judaism doesn't need the physical structure. We have something higher: an understanding of the nonphysical dimensions of God."

"But why, if you have devoted your whole life to archaeology, do you want to be in a position where the physical places don't matter? Wasn't the entire theme of our first journey together the importance of land?"

"Because I see the land as only a part of the culture that came out of this time. I can take the essence of the land with me into a higher, more spiritual plane."

"Then why does God promise land to Abraham at the very beginning?"

"Because God relates to us on two levels: the level of faith and belief, and the level of nationality and being a people. As a nation, you need land. But as a religion, you do not. That's the essence of what we've learned so far on this journey. Moses is the most central figure of the religion, even though he never sets foot on the land. David and Solomon are the greatest leaders of the nation, but they are moral degenerates and disappointments to God. The lesson of the second half of the Bible is that physical land, political power, even the Temple, are not the ends for God's people. Following God's law is the goal."

I said good-bye to Avner and stayed behind. As the sun slowly set behind me, the town's shadow inched up the stones until the face of the Wall was in darkness and the sky behind it deep blue. The plaza got more crowded as the sun receded. Dusk is a time of prayer.

I got up and started walking toward the Wall. I had made this walk many times, but today was different. For the first time I was approaching the stones not with reverence but with ambivalence. I was overcome with the feeling that I wanted to tear down the Wall as a way to liberate Jews from their obsession with stones and wipe out the fanaticism it had come to represent. Surely Judaism is more resilient than any symbol. Surely faith in God does not depend on who controls a few feet of masonry.

I could hardly believe my emotions. My journey retracing the Pentateuch had been a paean to land. In the Torah, God repeatedly pushes his chosen people into the wilderness so they will develop a closer relationship with him. For me, going into the desert achieved a similar end. And I was hardly alone. From Moses to Buddha to Jesus to Mohammed, the history of religion shows that venturing away from the civilized world and into isolated landscape is one way to become more intimate with the divine.

But my current journey was teaching me something deeper. Land is not the destination. Being in a sacred space does not guarantee that one will act more nobly. History is also replete with examples—the rebellious Israelites at Mount Sinai, the marauding armies of the Crusades, the suicide bombers of today—that show you can be in a holy place and still not be holy. Proximity to God cannot be confused with intimacy with God. And if one goal of my travels was to confront my own doubts about faith, I was learning that I could no longer rely on the once familiar pillars of my religious identity: King David, the Temple, the Western Wall.

I had to find my own route to God. I had to tear down the icons I once blindly accepted, go back to the source, and construct a new religious identity. And I felt this way not because I wanted to— who wants the burden?—but because I felt forced by the religious battles around me, by the petty sectarian violence, and most of all, by the Bible.

One would think the first books of the Hebrew Bible after the Torah would be the story's crowning achievement. The Israelites have endured generations of humiliation in Canaan, centuries of enslavement in Egypt, and decades of isolation in the desert. They are finally ready to conquer the Promised Land and fulfill their destiny as God's people. Moments of triumph do fill the text—the lightning sweep through the land, the new capital in Jerusalem, a brief blazing empire across the Fertile Crescent. But the overall feeling of these books is disillusionment: The judges fail, the kings fail, the people fail, even the Temple fails. And the Bible responds to these failures by making a bold and unexpected shift.

God flushes the people from the land he promised them. He sends them back into the wilderness. He exiles them.

It's a pattern we've seen before. From the beginning, the Bible follows a narrative cycle of creation, destruction, and re-creation. God creates the world, fills it with plants and animals, then adds humans to the mix. Humans disappoint, God wipes out the earth with a flood, then starts again with Noah. Noah disappoints, God withdraws his favor, then starts again with Abraham. The patriarchs disappoint, God sends their descendants into slavery, then starts again with Moses. The Israelites disappoint, God banishes them to forty years in the desert, then starts again with Joshua.

This pattern continues apace once the Israelites reach the Promised Land. Joshua disappoints, Saul disappoints, David disappoints, Solomon disappoints. So yet again God goes looking for a new set of leaders to be his partners on earth, a new group of men to fulfill his promise to spread his blessing to "all the families of the earth."

There are monarchs who follow Solomon. Kings I and II contain

an endless litany of the divided leaders of Israel and Judah—
Rehoboam, Jeroboam, Abijam, Asa, Baasha, Nadab, Ahab, Je-
hoshaphat, Ahaziah, Joram. But find even the greatest lay lover of
the Bible today and ask him to name three kings who ruled in the
centuries after Solomon. Some might manage Hezekiah, the great
eighth-century B.C.E. leader who expanded Jerusalem; a few might
muster Josiah, the enlightened seventh-century ruler in whose
court many scholars believe the Bible was first recorded. But who
could come up with much more than that?

The truth is: Even Bible lovers don't know these leaders, and
there's a reason. The Bible turns against them. The experiment in
investing God's authority with earthly rulers has come up short.
And so God shifts his favor toward a different kind of partner, one
who won't husband his authority into brutal leadership. The new
hero won't be God's arm, he will be God's voice. He won't rule
with power, he will speak for the powerless. He won't embody the
state, he will speak for the people. And look whom God chooses:
Elijah, Isaiah, Jeremiah, Ezekiel, Amos, Jonah, Daniel. Some of
the most enduring figures in the Bible.

We may no longer be able to name the kings.

But we can name the prophets.

And so the Bible reinvents itself yet again. It no longer is the
chronicle of the ruler; it becomes the poetry of the outsider. It no
longer is the tale of the king; it's the portrait of the people. The
most powerful portion of the Hebrew Bible following the forty
years in the wilderness is not the forgettable narrative of the kings;
it's the stirring story of the Exile, and the prophets who give it
meaning.

And for me, as I reached the Wall, the lessons were clear. I must
sever my attachment to the land. I must end my devotion to a
physical symbol. I must look beyond stones. In elevating the
prophets, the Bible speaks directly to the challenges of our time,

and what it says is surprising. God cares more about how we behave than about how much territory we control. God believes that
secular leaders cannot provide moral deliverance. God directs us
to turn away from power and embrace the part of our community—
and ourselves—that is vulnerable. We should listen instead for
what the prophet Elijah experiences as the "still, small voice" of
God, the soft, murmuring sound in our most wounded places that
yearns for goodness and aches for forgiveness. We should be open
to pain, and dedicated to assuaging it.

For some reason this message of tenderness is rarely taken
from the Bible anymore. More take confidence, arrogance, and
the authority to impose their faith on others. Yet most people in
the text who do that, like David and Solomon, do not end as noble
figures. Even dramatic victories, like Joshua's, are quickly followed
by periods of moral murkiness. The heroes are the ones—like
Abraham, Moses, or the newly minted prophets—who look critically at power, and even at God, and keep their gaze on the moral
foundation of life on earth.

I take humility from this story. I take self-restraint from the
narrative. And most freeing of all, as I stop short of touching the
Wall, I realize I must look beyond the outward remains of God's
glory in order to construct my own private relationship with God.
I must turn, instead, to where the prophets point. I must turn to
loss. I must turn to exile. I must turn to the source of salvation I
would have least imagined.

I must turn to Babylon.

BOOK TWO

EXILE

IN THE GARDEN OF EDEN

Kejo Level III Rapid Response body armor is made in South Africa to manufacturing standards set by the U.S. Department of Justice. The ballistic material that composes the vest is Kevlar HT 1100 d'tex. The garment contains two ceramic plates capable of stopping 7.62-by-39-millimeter ammunition from an AK47 assault rifle, as well as protecting against 7.62-by-51-millimeter projectiles fired from a G3 assault rifle and 5.56-by-45-millimeter rounds fired by an M16 assault rifle. Weighing six pounds, the made-to-measure vest is covered in a polycotton, sixty-five-to-thirty-five mix, along with textured nylon 6.6, stitched together with polyfill thread SABS 1362. It can be washed with warm water and pressed with a warm iron but should not be bleached. It is dry cleanable.

And surprisingly fashionable. Black and form-fitting, with an optional Kevlar groin protector that hangs over the waist like a miniskirt, the entire getup reminded me of an outfit some Mad

Max–like postapocalyptic warrior would wear. Basically it feels like a sandwich board with really, really stale bread.

At 4:15 on a cool desert morning, I stuffed my rented XL armor into a duffel bag, along with a ballistic combat helmet designed for the Israeli Army, a satellite telephone, a dozen PowerBars, and a Bible, threw the bag into the backseat of a taxi, and headed toward Camp Doha outside Kuwait City. Home to the Third United States Army—"Always First—Always Ready"—Camp Doha is the forward headquarters of U.S. Central Command and, months after the fall of Saddam Hussein, the jumping-off point for anyone hoping to fly into Baghdad.

Ever since I'd come up with the idea of retracing the Bible, I had longed to visit Iraq. The land between the Tigris and Euphrates rivers, the Cradle of Civilization, has been known since antiquity as Mesopotamia and gave birth to the earliest empires in history, from Sumer to Babylon. The Garden of Eden was rooted here, the Tower of Babel was conceived here, the first alphabet was scripted here, the day was carved into twenty-four hours here, and some of the greatest stories ever told were first uttered here, from the epic of Gilgamesh to the saga of Abraham.

But for thirty-five years, these sites were mostly closed to the West, eventually sealed off from outside scholars, and, in the case of Babylon, crudely reconstructed as a propagandist playground to promote the idea that Saddam Hussein was the new Nebuchad-nezzar, the great emperor of antiquity. I dreamed of seeing where the Tigris and Euphrates merge. I yearned to walk where Abraham first pined for God. Mostly I hoped to penetrate the black hole of the Middle East and see for myself if the provenance of so many Western values could elucidate the struggle for those values today.

But I was rebuffed. My first attempt, in the late 1990s, was quickly shot down by the U.S. State Department. Later Pope John Paul II tried to visit these sites, but Washington deterred him, too. I received a break in 2001, during a chance meeting with Bob Simon of CBS News, who offered to show me how to sneak across the border. Three days later came September 11.

Eighteen months later came Operation Iraqi Freedom. The fall of Saddam seemed to fling open the door to the past. I knew I must go now.

But how? Commercial flights into Baghdad had yet to resume. Overland from Turkey involved a day through the mountains. Overland from Jordan involved ten hours through the desert, the last three through the flinty Sunni triangle. Overland from Kuwait involved traversing a wicked no-man's-land. The photographer Gwendolen Cates and I, working with the editors of *Parade* magazine, who commissioned a story from us, managed to persuade U.S. Central Command to offer us coveted seats on a military shuttle. "But once you land, you don't want to stay with us," one sergeant advised me. "We are the targets." Avner, as an Israeli, was not allowed to go.

The closer the trip came, the more my stomach sickened, and the more my friends and family tried to dissuade me from going. "Why do you have to go *now*?" my mother said. A close friend and former spy wrote that he could no longer keep his mouth closed: the risks were simply too high. For weeks I didn't sleep. I wandered from room to room at night, inevitably drawn back to the Internet, desperately reading news from the front: three U.S. civilians are murdered, a roadside bomb kills five, two journalists are taken hostage, a suicide bomb flattens a hotel. I took out additional insurance but told no one the category: "accidental death and dismemberment."

One person was unwavering in her support. While others said, "Go later, it will only get better," my wife said, "Go now, it will only get worse." An experienced traveler, she understood the risks, but she also understood the importance of this journey to me. "It's who you are," she said. "It's why I love you." As each day ticked by, I found myself tightening my focus on her, growing nostalgic, grasping at nascent rituals, like attempting the Sunday crossword puzzle . . . and falling pitifully short. Then one day I recognized these acts—family, history, tradition—as the building blocks of religion. We were reliving a timeless return. The gnawing pain had stripped away the slick independencies of urban life and drawn us closer. When, hours before my departure, two CNN employees were gunned down near Babylon, we lay on the floor, clinging to each other, weeping.

But the emotion I felt was not just fear; it was also gratitude. Returning to the cradle of faith had reminded us of our own.

"I know you will come back to me," she said.

"I promise."

Later, without telling her, I sat at her desk and wrote my wife a farewell note. "If you are reading this, then I have not come home to you," it began. "I have not fulfilled my promise to you. I have left you, alone." I wrote of our commitment to each other, and to engage the world. I wrote of my dreams for her. And I invoked words only she would understand: "Make life, my love."

Then I signed the note, hid it in a secret place, and told only one person where it was.

The streets of Kuwait City were deserted before dawn but lit up like Las Vegas. Huge multilane highways sweep through gilded towers and shiny marble malls like grand prix lanes through Monaco. Save for the lack of liquor (and slots), Kuwait City seems like an overgrown casino, with amenities that startle and attendants who smile but deep down know that everything's a gamble. Hurry, hurry, get what you can before your protector—Saddam, America, the royal family—collapses like a house of cards.

Past the billboards hawking Levi's and Cinnabon, the sky begins to widen, the palms stretch their fronds, and an amusement park rises. Behind Entertainment City is the entrance to Camp Doha, with a guard shack, a generator, and a line of garbage trucks.

Captain Duke Duecker greeted us in a white SUV. Most of Camp Doha seems designed to minimize the tension of being so far from home while reducing the stress of being so close to war. We ate pancakes, sausage, and Kellogg's cereal in a mess tent festooned with greenery, fresh pastry carts, and carved watermelon fruit baskets. The camp boasts high-speed Internet access, a Subway sandwich shop, and a 24/7 gym. "It's like being in a really nice jail," Captain Duecker said.

A short drive away is the 721st Air Mobility Operations Group. Dozens of men were crowded into a windowless waiting area: Spanish soldiers in uniform, American missionaries in sweat suits, British contractors in jeans watching John Wayne movies on DVD, Aussie oilmen in tank tops reading *Hot Biker* magazine, and one man in a blue blazer and pressed white shirt studying *America's Role in Nation-Building from Germany to Iraq*. The weatherworn faces, tattoos, and buzz cuts made the fraternity look like a field trip to a Soldier of Fortune convention. The twenty-three-year-old next to me, from rural Oregon, was going to Kirkuk to help drill a pipeline. "We were going to be in a military convoy, but every time the trucks cross the border they are bombed," he said. He was staying for nine months.

Finally, at 2:30 P.M., Captain Duecker reappeared. "Flight 51, gather your belongings. Let's go!" He paraded us onto the tarmac and asked each of us to claim a pair of Sound Guard nonallergenic, green-and-orange earplugs, MADE IN USA. "Now I'm serious as a heart attack," he said. "These things are packed by blind people. Sometimes there are only one in a box. Sometimes none." Sure enough, my box had only one, and I was given a replacement.

We walked to the aircraft, a stone gray C-130 with a U.S. flag on the tail, USAF painted under the wings, and serial number 01270 on its side. The back was open skyward, and a ramp banked toward the ground; it looked like the mouth of a giant steel alligator. Inside, the plane was dark and disorienting, like the interior of a submarine. Four rows of benches stretched back to front; ladders and red mesh dangled everywhere. Two fire extinguishers and an ax hung just over my seat. The plane had only a few windows, and those were concealed behind gear. It's the only plane I've ever been in where the flight attendant wore a pistol.

"Who's on their first flight to Baghdad?" the attendant asked.

A few of us raised our hands.

"Hopefully it will be interesting but not sporty going in there," he said. He paused for a second. "Sporty means we're being shot at."

At 3:45 P.M. we taxied to the runway, a frightening vibration welled up under my feet, and minutes later we lifted into the air. The first time I flew in an airplane, my dad explained that nervous fliers either get sweaty palms from perspiration or white knuckles from gripping the seat too hard. On this trip I had both. I stared ahead and ticked away the miles. The flight was scheduled to last an hour and a half; I checked my watch three times in the first eight minutes. After a while I peered past the passenger across from me, through the sand-splattered glass, and caught a glimpse of a muddy line in the sand.

The Tigris.

The reason to go.

Y ou can't understand religion today without understanding the prophets. Abraham may have been the first to realize there is only one God. Moses may have delivered God's blueprint for social conduct to his chosen people. David may have unified those people into a singular political entity in God's chosen land. But the prophets—divinely elected spokespersons who enraptured the Ancient Near East in the middle of the first millennium B.C.E.—were the first to unite the strands of monotheism in Israelite history with hints of social justice in Mesopotamian history to create a comprehensive belief system that offered the bounty of a single, universal God to all the people of the earth, no matter their class, region, or background.

The triumph of monotheism in Western history owes more to the prophets than to any figure in the Pentateuch. The hope for reconciliation among feuding monotheists today may also hinge on these stirring, sometimes opaque, but unfailingly invigorating figures.

The idea of prophecy has deep roots in the Bible. Abraham is labeled a prophet, as is Moses' brother, Aaron. Their sister, Miriam, is called a prophetess. Moses himself is exalted in Deuteronomy as "the greatest prophet who ever lived." But while these figures interact with God and sometimes intervene with him on behalf of the Israelites, they don't embody what the word comes to mean later: They aren't full-time messengers deciphering God's views, no matter how cryptic, and conveying his feelings, no matter how harsh. God specifically says of Moses in Numbers that he is *not* a prophet: "With him I speak mouth to mouth, plainly and not in riddles."

Other proto-prophets appear after the Conquest. Some, like Samuel, are called "seers." Others, like Nathan, are God's functionaries. The first full-scale prophets are Elijah and his disciple, Elisha, who serve as miracle workers in the battle between God and the pagan deities. Elijah eventually flees to Jordan, where he is whisked away in a fiery chariot. He is transported to heaven but does not die, which sets up his later role as the precursor to the messiah and the prototypical "Wandering Jew" of folklore, a position memorialized to this day by Jews who set a place for him at the Passover table.

The most famous prophets arise in the centuries after Solomon in direct response to the decline in moral authority of the kings. The Hebrew name for these figures, *nabi*, likely comes from one of Israel's northern neighbors, suggesting the phenomenon was well known in the region. The Hebrew word connotes not a mere predictor of the future but a proclaimer of God's will. The prophet does not suggest what *will* happen; he or she dictates what *must* happen if the people don't alter their ways. He is not a prognosticator; he is a poet, a social critic, a moralist. He is a man of God, with all the power, moral vision, and contradiction that implies.

So why were prophets suddenly necessary in the first millennium B.C.E. when they hadn't been needed earlier? One reason is the dramatic shift in the lives of the Israelites. As the wandering tribes of the desert became the settled people of the land, society became more polarized. Landowners and nobility amassed great wealth, often by oppressing the needy and forcing the lower classes into harsh labor. In contemporary parlance, the rich got richer and the poor got poorer. Also, everyone was having a bit too much fun. Faced with their new urban lives, the Israelites responded as many country-come-to-towners have done, by indulging in the licentiousness of the big city—fornication, adultery, gluttony, callousness. The prophets' history-altering breakthrough was to suggest that this carefree, heartless social condition violated God's vision for humanity. The proper worship of God involves the proper treatment of fellow human beings. "Why should I forgive you?" Jeremiah quotes God as saying.

> *Your children have forsaken me.*
> *They committed adultery*

And went trooping to the harlot's house.
They were well-fed, lusty stallions,
Each neighing at another's wife . . .
As a cage is full of birds,
So their houses are full of guile;
That is why they have become fat and sleek;
They pass beyond the bounds of wickedness,
And they prosper.
They will not judge the case of the orphan,
Nor give a hearing to the plea of the needy.
Shall I not punish such deed,
Says the Lord.
Shall I not bring retribution
On a nation such as this?

The fifteen prophets who have biblical books named after them come in all guises, and from all corners of society. Isaiah is an influential member of the court, Micah is a rural layman. Ezekiel is married, Jeremiah is unmarried. Haggai is old, Zechariah is young. They share hostility to wealth, iniquity, and might, and hold a deep fellowship with God. Their arrival marks a fundamental shift in the biblical narrative: away from the mighty and toward the meek. "The nations are but a drop in a bucket," Isaiah proclaims, downplaying the idea of an Israelite state that David, Solomon, and others spent centuries trying to achieve. By diminishing the importance of monarchs, the prophets return the attention of the Bible to where it was in the first chapter of Genesis, on all humanity, rendered in God's image.

Prophecy reached its peak during two calamitous periods in Israelite history: the eighth century B.C.E., around the fall of the Northern Kingdom; and the late seventh century B.C.E., during the destruction of the Southern Kingdom. The first period is captured by Amos, a shepherd who linked Israel's moral collapse with the rise of the Assyrians to the north. "I scourged you with blight and mildew," God says through Amos. I withheld your food, I refused you rain, I sent you pestilence, yet you did not turn back to me. "Prepare to meet your God, O Israel." Your sons and daughters shall fall by the sword, and Israel shall be exiled from its soil.

The theme of exile permeates the most prominent prophets—Ezekiel, Isaiah, and Jeremiah. Jeremiah was born during the reign of Josiah, the reformist king who discovers a copy of Moses' Law in 622 B.C.E. and tries to return the country to its godly roots. Mesopotamia is in turmoil; the Babylonians are vanquishing Assyria. The Egyptians take advantage of the power vacuum to storm the Euphrates, but the Babylonian prince, Nebuchadnezzar II, routs them at Carchemish and chases them back to the Nile. He would have conquered Egypt if his father hadn't died in 605 B.C.E., propelling him to the throne. A new warrior prince stands astride the Fertile Crescent.

But the new king of Judah, Jehoiakim, in an incalculable blunder, sides with Egypt. Nebuchadnezzar II shows up in person to punish Jerusalem in March 597. Jehoiakim is deported to Babylon, along with his mother, the entire court, and seven thousand men in chains. Jeremiah, meanwhile, adopts the revolutionary position that Judah had brought defeat on itself and it was God's idea that the people lose their land. He struts around Jerusalem, a yoke about his neck, quoting God: "I herewith deliver all these lands to my servant, King Nebuchadnezzar." *My servant?* God is so committed to the idea that Israel shall abide by his laws or not inhabit his land that he actually commandeers a foreign leader to *destroy his holy city*. Not since God wiped out thousands in Sinai has his vengeance been so unforgiving.

Judah's replacement king, Zedekiah, brushes off Jeremiah's warnings and sides again with Egypt. A flabbergasted Nebuchadnezzar II attacks even harder. Jerusalem holds out for over a year, but famine prevails. This time Nebuchadnezzar leaves nothing standing. He breaches the walls, ransacks the houses, and burns the Temple. Zedekiah's eyes are plucked out, his children are slaughtered before him, and he's hauled in bronze fetters to the river capital of Mesopotamia. The prophet Joel, working at the same time as Jeremiah, captures the forlornness. "Numberless are those that do the Lord's bidding," he says, referring to the Babylonians. They rush in like warriors, scale a wall like fighters, enter windows like thieves. Before them the earth trembles and heaven shakes, sun and moon are darkened, and stars withdraw their brightness. "Joy has dried up."

The Bible has a surprising reaction to these events. Instead of seeing them as signs of doom, it sees them as precursors to salvation. The ability to see historical events as theological allegory is one essence of the religious mind. The Greeks may have invented history, but the Israelites popularized the idea of looking at history not as the mere playpen of the gods but as a place where the actions of every human being help direct the future. *Your* philandering contributed to the fall of Israel, the prophets insist; *your* greed helped cause the sacking of the Temple. Like most aspects of religion, this notion can be used for harm, as when some religious leaders blamed social deviance in the United States for causing September 11, but it can also be used for great solace, as it is in Babylon. Exile, the prophets proclaim, will save Israel.

One difference between the prophets and earlier biblical heroes like Moses or Joshua is that they don't really do anything. There is no splitting of the Red Sea, no conquering of Jericho. What they *do* is speak. Their power comes from words. The most common literary trope in the Prophets is the line "Thus says the Lord." The effect of this repetition is to echo the most transformative use of language in the Bible, the story of Creation. In the opening line of Genesis, God uses words to create the universe. "When God began to create heaven and earth—the earth being unformed and void, with darkness over the surface of the deep and wind from God sweeping over the water—God said, 'Let there be light.'" "God said" is the line that creates the world in Genesis. "God says" is the line that re-creates it in the Prophets. The pattern returns: creation, destruction, re-creation.

And in this vision of redemption, the prophets refer frequently to one biblical story as their fantasy of the type of world they will re-create: the Garden of Eden. In the prophets' worldview, God equals fertility; the absence of God equals desolation. Israel is the garden of God's eye; exile is desert. "Before them the land was like the Garden of Eden," Joel says as the conquerors approach. "Behind them, a desolate waste." The prophet's greatest gift is that he offers comfort at this moment of desolation. Out of desperation, he tenders hope. "Have no fear, my servant Jacob," the Lord declares through Jeremiah, invoking the name of the patriarch as the unified father of all the tribes.

> *Be not dismayed, O Israel!*
> *I will deliver you from far away,*
> *Your folk from the land of captivity.*
> *And Jacob shall again have calm.*

Words again prove central to salvation: God will *write* the solution on the Israelites' hearts. "I will make a new covenant with the House of Israel. I will put my teaching into their inmost being and inscribe it upon their hearts."

The prophets' message here is stunning. Not only will salvation come from destruction but it *depends on* destruction. The people need pain to appreciate their blessings. "I will single out for good the Judean exiles whom I have driven out from this place," God says in Jeremiah. "I will look upon them favorably, and I will bring them back to this land." Exile, God says, is *good*, echoing once more the word he uses repeatedly during Creation: "And God saw that it was good." God never forgets. Though he kicked man and woman out of Eden, he never deserted them. Though he cast the Israelites into slavery, he never forgot them. Though he dispatched the Israelites into Babylon, he never forsook them. He did each of these for the Israelites' *good*.

And to prove his commitment, God offers his exiled people the ultimate reward: He will send them back to Creation. He will return them to Eden. "You were the seal of perfection," God says in Ezekiel,

> *Full of wisdom and flawless of beauty.*
> *You were in Eden, the garden of God.*
> *Every precious stone was your adornment:*
> *Carnelian, chrysolite, and amethyst;*
> *Beryl, lapis lazuli, and jasper;*
> *Sapphire, turquoise, and emerald;*
> *And God beautifully wrought for you . . .*
> *You walked among stones of fire.*
> *You were blameless in your ways,*
> *From the day you were created*
> *Until wrongdoing was found in you.*

Now I have struck you down, God says. I have destroyed you. But I will not surrender you.

I will save you. "When I have cleansed you of all your iniquities," God continues, "I will people your settlements, and the ruined palaces shall be rebuilt, and the desolate land, after lying wasted in the sight of every passerby, shall again be tilled. And men shall say, 'That land, once desolate, has become like the Garden of

Eden.'" This is the unforeseen goodness of going into exile. Babylon will not be the end of Israel. It will be its redemption.

The surest route to salvation is traveling through the pit of desolation.

About twenty minutes from Baghdad, Flight 51 began its descent. My ears popped. The passengers shifted edgily. The plane started to bank from side to side, and the wings fluttered, like those of an agitated pelican preparing to dive for a kill. We were descending more rapidly than a commercial craft, and the extra G's were tangible. The corkscrew landing was designed to avoid being hit by shoulder-launched missiles. At the back window, a spotter bobbed rapidly up and down, struggling to eye any ordnance harpooning our way.

The last few seconds were like a frightening elevator plunge, and we hit the ground with a loud crunch. I expected a sigh of relief, or applause. Instead the landing was greeted with grim-faced resolve. The plane ride was over. Now the real test began.

On the tarmac we were surrounded by huge ground-moving equipment, attack helicopters, and F-16s. The air was moist and slightly chilly; it smelled of diesel and spoiling fruit. The sun had set, leaving the sky a dishwater lavender. This timing created a problem. Our takeoff had been delayed so long we risked breaking the first rule of survival in Iraq: never go out at night. "Act with haste," said Captain Monica Walden, a cheery African American who had offered to drive us into town.

A forklift arrived with the crate containing our luggage, and the passengers swarmed over the mound like ants over a cake at a picnic, tearing at the camouflage, yanking out bags in mild hysteria. "Put on your armor," Captain Walden ordered. I reached into my duffel to retrieve my helmet and promptly dropped my vest into a huge puddle of mud, splashing my clothes and dousing my vest. Dry cleanable? My armor was sopping wet.

We piled into an SUV and headed into town: a Hummer in front, a Hummer behind, exactly the kind of convoy I had seen attacked nightly on television. "Sorry, this is going to be a chilly ride," Captain Walden said, as she and her colleague, another African American woman, rolled down their windows and stuck their M16s outside, pointed skyward.

Our pace began to quicken as we left Baghdad International Airport, passed through five checkpoints, and eventually reached the highway. It took me a minute to realize we weren't driving on the proper side. We were speeding at ninety miles per hour the wrong way down a major highway, with cars whipping past in the opposite direction. A truck approached us from behind. Don't you know we have guns? I thought. And the power? The truck passed us effortlessly. Wait, who does have the power anymore? I wondered.

"My friend in North Carolina just had a baby," Captain Walden said to no one in particular.

"Mine, too!" her friend said. They started talking about the merits of breast feeding and the best way to burp a baby. I was dumbfounded. It was as if we were on a picnic.

"Aren't you afraid?" I asked Captain Walden.

"Personally, I am not fearful," she said.

"Why not?"

"I'm a Christian. I don't have the spirit of fear. I don't believe I'm going anywhere until it's time to go."

The Flowers Land Hotel in the upscale Karada district is shielded behind concrete barriers, where guards used mirrors to examine the underside of vehicles. A mix of journalists, aid workers, and fashionable do-gooders were hanging around the lobby, which is decorated with surreal ceiling paintings depicting twisted vines and overeager bougainvilleas that reminded me of the canni- balistic flytrap in *Little Shop of Horrors*. The teenage desk attendant was watching television. "My uncle was just killed in a suicide bombing," he said by way of introduction. "I just saw his face on Al Jazeera."

I reached to comfort him. As I did, a burly South African named Casper appeared at my side and noticed my dumbstruck gaze. "You look like you have Baghdad Head," he said. "Don't worry, in forty-eight hours this will all seem normal."

By the time I crawled into bed at 12:30 A.M., I was wobbly with exhaustion. Peace is a room with tape on the windows, only one blackout per hour, and the rat-tat-tat of machine-gun fire to keep one's dreams on edge. I lay awake, wondering what would happen if a bomb exploded through the picture window at the foot of my bed. Would a mortar in the lobby collapse my room? My legs started trembling. I felt the urge to cry—not tears of pain but those of a boy, alone. Twice in my life I had felt homesick: as a seven-year-old on my first night at sleepaway camp, as an eighteen-year-old on my first night out of the country.

And now. I called out for my wife, by name. "*Linda.*" I needed comfort, security, solid ground.

I needed sleep.

The road south from Baghdad is cluttered with the detritus of war: bombed-out bridges, scorched tanks, looted oil tankers. Every few feet is a fruit stand selling the spoils of lifted sanctions: apples, oranges, and bunches and *bunches* of bananas. Under the embargo, bananas were scarce; now they were hawked on every corner and thrust into our window at every stop, like squeegees.

Casper was right. After forty-eight hours, Iraq began to seem, if not normal, then at least manageable. We were greeted with a bewildering blizzard of advice: Don't drive in a GMC, they're used only by the military; don't drive in an SUV, they're used only by the Coalition; put tinting on your windows, no one will notice you're a foreigner; don't use tinting, people will think you're CIA; always wear your body armor; never wear your body armor; sleep in the front of the hotel; sleep in the back; carry a gun; don't carry a gun; never drive over dead carcasses, it's where they place road-side bombs; never wear khakis, only military wear khakis; never wear blue jeans, only Americans wear blue jeans.

Be safe.

By the second day we had assembled a team, a plan, and an un-marked car. Our driver was Bijar, a quiet, fearsome former Iraqi Air Force officer who hid on his base when the war began, then fled to his wife and three children as U.S. Marines approached Baghdad. He dreamed of opening a meatpacking company. Our fixer/bodyguard/guide was Hikmat, a jolly university English pro-fessor with a dense, Saddam-like mustache and several grown chil-dren. Our plan was to drive all the way south to near the border with Kuwait, then work our way north, visiting biblical sites, re-turn to Baghdad, and exit north through Turkey. By going back to the deepest roots of civilization, and the earliest stories of the Bible, I hoped to better understand the connections between hu-mans, religion, and religious war. Is the confidence to kill in the name of God the natural outcome of having faith? Or can religion coexist with tolerance?

Within half an hour of leaving Baghdad, we had reached bar-ren countryside. The wheat was scraggly in the mostly brown fields, the cows were thin, and the herds of sheep threadbare. We passed an imposing brick wall. "That was the nuclear plant the Is-raelis bombed in 1981," Hikmat said. I smiled in honor of Boaz.

We were traveling over 110 miles an hour when suddenly a black-and-white dog wandered across the highway. Bijar swerved, cursed, but hit the animal head-on, killing it instantly. He kept driving. The one situation we most wanted to avoid was stopping. Looters were known to sit by the highways with shotguns, picking out foreigners. But soon parts of our car—the light, a piece of the bumper, a swath of hood—began flying into the windshield. We had no choice. Bijar pulled over, Gwendolen wrapped a black scarf around her head, and I slid on the hood of my windbreaker. The two Iraqi men jerry-rigged the hood into place, bent back the bumper, and within seconds we were off. "Safety first," Hikmat said.

After several hours the scenery began to change: concrete farmhouses were replaced with mud huts, women in black chadors swarmed the fields, giant portraits of Shia ayatollahs arose. And water—rivers, puddles, canals—appeared everywhere. We had reached the womb of the world.

The term *Mesopotomia* has always been an uneasy fit with the upper arm of the Fertile Crescent. A combination of the Greek words *mesos*, meaning "middle," and *potamos*, meaning "rivers," Mesopotamia suggests that the most vital part of the land is between the rivers. In fact, more habitable land occurs outside the streams. But the larger point still holds: Unlike more temperate climates, say that of Europe or the United States, where the bulk of territory is well watered with rain, the Middle East is far more dependent on rivers.

The Tigris and Euphrates are not long, as rivers go. The Euphrates, whose name means "sweet water," covers 1,740 miles, making it the twenty-eighth longest river in the world. The Tigris, whose name means "fast as an arrow," stretches 1,180 miles, the fifty-fourth-longest river in the world. But they are strategically placed. They begin in eastern Turkey, 50 miles from each other, not far from Mount Ararat. When they emerge from the Taurus Mountains, they are 160 miles apart; they converge near Baghdad, where they are 20 miles apart. They diverge again before meeting in Qurnah, 200 miles southeast of Baghdad, whereupon they flow together into the Persian Gulf.

Geologists suggest the two rivers probably never met in biblical times. In antiquity, the Persian Gulf was a broad valley, which slowly filled with seawater as the ice caps melted twelve thousand years ago. Around 4000 B.C.E. the gulf was six or seven feet above its present height, meaning its shoreline reached all the way to Basra in southern Iraq. A combination of regressing sea levels and accumulating silt has added around 150 miles of land in the last few thousand years, including all of Kuwait.

Key to Mesopotamia's rise was the regular supply of freshwater, especially in the south, where the temperature can often reach 120 degrees Fahrenheit. But the rivers are not unalloyed gifts. Unlike the Nile, which floods in late summer, the Tigris and Euphrates overflow in spring, too late for winter crops and too early for fall ones. Also unlike the Nile, which flooded reliably for millennia, the Tigris and Euphrates are more erratic. Dependent on snowfall, they sometimes flood too little and sometimes too much. Mesopotamia hovers between desert and swamp.

But in one crucial way, the Tigris and Euphrates are like the Nile: They have a legacy of tensions between the highlands and the low. Ethiopia and Egypt still battle over which should be the beneficiary of the Nile. The same with Turkey and Iraq over the Tigris and Euphrates. In antiquity, the chief rivalry was between the Assyrians, who lived in the highlands, and the Sumerians and Babylonians, who lived in the low. In this competition, one place has been consistently overlooked: the southern marshlands. It's here that the Tigris and Euphrates meld to create a vast network of saline wetlands. It's also here that Saddam executed his most destructive environmental catastrophe. And it's here, Genesis suggests, that Adam and Eve first walked.

The egress of Mesopotamia, the Bible implies, is the entrance to the Garden of Eden.

Nasiriyah is a riverside town where it's not safe to walk by the river. Two hundred and fifty miles south of Baghdad, the strategic heart of the south, Nasiriyah was the site of a brutal battle during the British defeat of the Ottomans in 1916, center of the failed Shia uprising in 1991, and home to some of the bloodiest fighting in Operation Iraqi Freedom in 2003. Not long after the end of the war, eighteen Italian troops stationed along the Euphrates were killed by a suicide bomber. We drove by the building, its roof collapsed and concrete walls dust on the ground.

A few blocks away, the Irrigation Department was hidden behind layers of security, its floors flooded under several inches of water. The water seemed amusing, until we followed it into the building, up a small incline, and into the office of the director. How could Iraqis reconstruct their country, I thought, when the department charged with regulating water could not even control its own bathroom? Dreams spring eternal, however, and one man was dreaming big.

Azzam Alwash has good teeth. He has good skin. He has a nice smile. He also has a trim white beard cut close to his face in the manner made popular by American television actors in the 1980s. An engineer by training and activist by default, he looks like a cop from *Miami Vice*. And fresh from twenty-seven years in exile in California, he was on a mission made for Hollywood: he wanted to reflood the Garden of Eden. Five minutes after meeting him, I wouldn't have bet against him.

"Shall we go see the marshes?" he said. "The best sun for pictures is in the afternoon."

He even understood lighting.

Azzam and a colleague squeezed into our car, and we turned

west. Azzam was born in nearby Kut; his father had been the head of the water department. "The irrigation engineer rules the south," he said. As a boy, Azzam traveled the marshes with his dad. "It's the most beautiful place on earth," he said, "except Yosemite." Driven into exile by Saddam, he settled in California and became an avid kayaker. "When I first started dating my wife, I told her, 'Wait until Iraq gets liberated. I will take you kayaking in the most beautiful wetlands.'" He paused. "Then I became aware that the marshes were disappearing."

The marshlands at the confluence of the Tigris and the Euphrates were one of the most abundant ecosystems in Mesopotamia, filled with fish, shrimp, and a population of Marsh Arabs. Ninety percent of seafood eaten in Iraq in 1990 was caught in the marshes. In 1991 the Shias revolted against Saddam and were brutally crushed. Massacres bled the region red. "And the people in the south did what they did for eternity," Azzam said. "They fled to the marshes to escape the wrath of the central government." In retaliation, Saddam drained the marshes. In three years 8,000 square miles—the size of Massachusetts—were reduced to 800. An ecosystem that had thrived for more than ten thousand years vanished overnight.

"From an engineering point of view, it's admirable," Azzam said. "But this is one instance when engineering was used as a weapon of mass destruction. Three hundred and fifty thousand people were dislocated."

For centuries, the mentality of humans was to conquer nature, he continued. "We built dams, rerouted rivers. But since the 1960s we have begun to understand that wetlands play a vital role in biodiversity. They are the liver of water. Iraq has been using its rivers as open sewers, but the marshes cleaned out the impurities. Since the drying of the marshes, the coral reefs of the gulf have been decimated. The fisheries have been cut in half. Shrimp are no longer caught."

In the mid-1990s Azzam began traveling to conferences to

spotlight Saddam's crime. His goal was to reflood the marshes. "The sanctions were on," he said. "Nobody wanted to listen. By 1998, I gave up." After September 11, however, Washington took note. With money from the State Department, Azzam and his wife started a foundation out of their bedroom. Its name: Eden Again. "As an engineer, I never really believed in Paradise," he said. "Engineers believe they can improve on God's design. But the older I get, the more I disbelieve that theory." He winked. "Also, having lived in the U.S. for twenty-seven years, I know a little about marketing."

Azzam moved back to Iraq after the war but was hamstrung by security. It was too unsafe for his family. The marshes were a breeding ground for thieves. A colleague drove to meet some Marsh Arabs, who promptly shot him in the leg and took his car. Uneasiness still hung over the area. Indeed, the farther we got out of Nasiriyah, the more uncomfortable I became. The scenery was stirring—bushy marshes that reminded me of Georgia's low country, stately birds soaring over the water—but the roads were empty, and the sun vibrated ominously off the asphalt.

We needed a bathroom break and pulled into a store. As I waited, Hikmat approached me nervously. "Where's your money?" he said. "In a pouch," I said. "I think you should give it to me," he said. I handed it to him immediately. He hiked up his trousers and wrapped the pouch around his calf. "I think you should give me your camera as well."

My throat clenched. "What's going on?" I said.

"I must be honest," he said. "We are being followed."

"What?"

"A red Toyota has been trailing us since we left Nasiriyah. I think they intend to rob us."

"That's it," I said. "We're going back."

"But, Mr. Bruce, you want to see the marshes."

"Safety first," I said.

Within seconds we had piled into the car and turned back toward Nasiriyah. Azzam's colleague, who had been quiet, now spoke up, in dialect. The day before he had made a similar drive, and some looters had attacked his car, stripped off his clothes and shoes, and left him standing in his socks by the side of the road. "Then why did he come with us?" I whispered to Hikmat. "He wants the twenty-dollar tip we will give him at the end of the day."

We drove home in silence. "Maybe I should hire security," Azzam mused. As we said good-bye later, I asked him, "So why are you doing this?"

"Because I could not live with myself if I don't," he said. "As it is, I hardly sleep. Here I am, seventeen thousand miles away from the two most precious things in my life, my two little girls, eight and eleven. I'm missing the best part of their lives. But God bless my wife. She said, 'Look at yourself in two years' time. If you don't do this, are you going to be happy? Because if you're not happy, I don't want to be living with you.'"

"Are you going to be happy?"

"No man deserves to be as happy as I am doing my job. But I'll be truly happy the day that I can take a trip with my wife and my two girls through the marshes. And that day is coming. I believe at least 30 percent of these wetlands can be reclaimed. I see communities of Marsh Arabs in green houses, with potable water and solar energy. If I could make that happen, and have my family here, I would be living the perfect life."

"In Paradise," I said.

"In Paradise. Well, working on Paradise."

The next morning we set out in a southeasterly direction for Qurnah. The road was so rife with hooligans we could travel only between 9:00 A.M. and 2:00 P.M. Few portions were paved, and there was no shoulder. "Saddam wasted his money making problems with Iran and Kuwait," Hikmat said. "So you see the roads."

Still, this was the first stretch of countryside that struck me as genuinely beautiful. The sky was a brilliant cerulean blue. Some date palms had been decapitated (part of Saddam's effort to flush out deserters from his many wars), but more bent in appealingly odd directions, like a prickly dance floor. Noah would have been busy here with all the cows, ducks, donkeys, sheep, goats, water buffalo, and black cattle. "It seems very biblical," Gwendolen said. More like a desert oasis than a plush English garden, the scenery reminded me how much my image of Eden had been filtered through European art.

I pulled out my Bible. From the opening sentence of Genesis, water is everywhere. Water is the one thing God does not create; it's just there, on day one, covered in darkness, when God begins creating heaven and earth. On day two, God creates an expanse in the midst of this water, separating water from water. Out of this water he draws land, a stunning reflection of what I now understood was the way lower Mesopotamia was born—earth emerging from rivers. Over the next three days, God creates time, then living creatures and birds. On the sixth day, he spawns human beings. "Let us make man in our image, after our likeness," God says, in a startling use of the plural. "They shall rule the fish of the sea, the birds of the sky, the cattle, the whole earth."

When Creation ends, God plants a garden in Eden, to the east, and places man within it. The garden brims with trees, with the tree of life in the middle, along with the tree of knowledge of good and bad.

A river issues from Eden to water the garden, and it then divides and becomes four branches. The name of the first is Pishon, the one that winds through the whole land of Havilah, where the gold is. The name of the second river is Gihon, the one that winds through the whole land of Cush. The name of the third river is Tigris, the one that flows east of Ashur. And the fourth river is the Euphrates.

The first two rivers are unknown today, while the last two suggest Eden was meant to be in Mesopotamia.

With man in place, God commands him to eat from any tree except the tree of knowledge of good and bad. He then creates a woman. A serpent tells the woman that if she eats from the forbidden tree she will be divine. The woman eats, then feeds her husband. For the first time the two perceive they are naked and sew fig leaves to cover their bodies.

God, who is moving about the garden, soon discovers the disobedience. He curses the serpent to a lifetime of crawling, scourges the woman with painful childbirth and an eternity of being ruled by her husband, and sentences the man to a lifetime of toiling the soil and an afterlife of being buried in it. "From dust you are," God says, "and to dust you shall return." God then clothes the man and woman in skins, banishes them from the garden, and stations cherubim and an ever-turning fiery sword to the east of Eden to guard the entrance.

From antiquity, people have wondered about the location of Eden. A few prophets suggest the garden was on a mountain, which would make sense with the river flowing from it. "You resided on God's holy mountain," God says to the Israelites in Ezekiel. Some linked the garden with the Temple, which was also on a mountain and had water flowing eastward from it. The identification with Jerusalem was enhanced by the name of the second river, Gihon. Though its location seems to have been a mystery even in the first millennium B.C.E., the link with the spring underneath the City of David was not lost on biblical ears.

While some tried to identify the physical place, more understood that the garden would never be found—and maybe wasn't intended to be. The Jewish philosopher Philo, a contemporary of Jesus, insisted the story was an allegory. "To think that it meant that God planted vines, or olive trees, or apple trees, or pomegranates, and any trees of such kinds, is mere incurable folly."

Yet even as the story's authenticity was being debunked, the power of the Garden of Eden as a story to influence world events was growing, exponentially. The prophets may have redefined history as religious allegory, but more striking is how religious allegory came to redefine history. Nowhere is that more true than with the Garden of Eden.

Just as early Jews—the prophets—looked to Eden for inspiration to help them withstand the power of Nebuchadnezzar II, early Christians looked to Eden for inspiration to help them withstand the power of the emperors. Abused by Rome, Christian commentators latched onto the line in Genesis that says every human was created by God in his image as a way to counter the abuse of the emperor. "I would ask you," wrote Clement of Alexandria, "does it not seem to you monstrous that human beings who are God's own handiwork should be subjected to another master, and, even worse, serve a tyrant instead of God, the true king?" At a time when three-quarters of Romans were either slaves or descendants of slaves, this argument held great appeal.

Over time, Christians echoed the biblical prophets and used the Garden of Eden to construct an entirely new vision of social order, one founded no longer on the divine claims of rulers but on the inherent rights of every human being. Gone was the kingdom of David; in its place was the kingdom of Adam. The divine gift does not appear "in any single person," wrote Gregory of Nyssa in the fourth century, "but this power extends equally to the whole race." Bishop John Chrysostom, nicknamed "golden mouth," took this argument even further in a direct rebuke of imperial authority. "In the beginning, God honored our race with sovereignty," he wrote in the fourth century. "The image of government is what is meant; as there is no one in the heavens superior to God, so there is no one on earth superior to humankind." Since equality exists in all people, imperial rule is sin. Humans should rule themselves by "free choice and liberty."

But Chrysostom was on the wrong side of his time. When Constantine converted to Christianity in 312, the church shifted from being a persecuted community to being a hegemonic force. The most influential thinker of his age, Augustine, endorsed imperial rule, saying Eden proved humans were incapable of self-government. Freedom, he argued, was the basis of evil, because Adam, when faced with the choice of obeying God or following Eve, succumbed to his sexual instincts. He chose sin. "The soul, then, delighting in its own freedom to do wickedness, and scorning even to serve God, willfully deserted its higher master." Adam's sin was so grave, Augustine concluded, that humans should be subjected to tyrants to shield their lust for passion. Augustine's reading became the foundation of Christianity's suspicion of human sexuality and the basis for the church's alliance with state power.

The Garden of Eden had become the dominant narrative at the heart of Western history.

Centuries later, when the American colonists went searching for a metaphor to express their frustration with British imperial rule, they looked back to the Bible, too. First they used the story of David to argue against the kind of tyranny that Augustine had supported. In *Common Sense*, Thomas Paine, the great poet of liberty, quotes Samuel's rousing assault on kingship in I Samuel 8 and concludes, the Almighty "hath here entered his protest against monarchial government." The colonists seized on an earlier biblical passage as divine justification for total equality. The stirring words of American Creation—"We hold these truths to be self-evident, that all men are created equal, that they are endowed by their Creator with certain unalienable Rights"—are a direct echo of the words of biblical Creation, "Let us make man in our image."

The importance of the biblical Creation story only grew in American life. George Washington was fond of quoting a poignant evocation of Eden found in I Kings 5 and Micah 4. "May the children of the stock of Abraham who dwell in this land continue to merit and enjoy the good will of other inhabitants," he wrote to the Jews of Rhode Island, "while everyone *shall sit in safety under his own vine and fig tree, and there shall be none to make him afraid.*" Presidents from Franklin Roosevelt to George H. W. Bush quoted this same verse. The preceding verse contains an even more famous vision of Paradise: "And they shall beat their swords into plowshares / And their spears into pruning hooks." This line is carved into the entrance of the United Nations. What began as Paradise had become a utopian model for world peace.

The legacy of the Garden of Eden is so long it stretches back to, well, the Garden of Eden. When George W. Bush cited, as one reason to invade Iraq, the dream of spreading liberty—"I believe freedom is not America's gift to the world; I believe freedom is the almighty God's gift to each man and woman in this world"— he echoed, intentionally or not, an idea that came from Iraq. Freedom is not alien to Mesopotamia. It is not new to this place.

It was born here.

Qurnah was a parking lot. We drove over a bridge and stared, disbelieving, at an endless morass of automobiles, trucks, and motorcycles. Three realities of Iraqi towns had converged to create the quagmire: the vegetable market, the looting market (where stolen goods were offered for sale), and a daylong line for petrol.

We navigated through the congestion, turned toward the one green neighborhood in town, and soon arrived at a majestic crossing—two wide, shimmering boulevards of water, vivid silver, like twin chrome fins from a 1959 Cadillac Coupe DeVille reflecting a cloud-blanched sky. The rivers approached each other at an eighty-degree angle, chugging at the stately pace of locomotives. Years earlier I had stood by the Euphrates near its fountainhead in eastern Turkey, where the turquoise rapids raced with glee. Here the darker waters seem grayed by their travels and slowed somewhat by age. A handful of fishermen paddled by in a wooden boat. The Tigris and the Euphrates, in their last lengths of independence, were emblems of a bygone time.

But in union they were infinite. At the spot on the horizon where the currents merged, the color seemed to vanish from the waters and the sky, as these two eternal gifts of creation gathered into each other's arms. At the terminus of Mesopotamia, water *un*separated from water, and the heavens rose from the deep. I had reached the earliest day. No more land was between the rivers.

Not far from the conflux, we approached a neighborhood. No people were around, no cars, only a few mud-brick houses. On the riverbank, a boy in a brown robe led a small huddle of goats. He was holding a staff and smoking a cigarette. Just above him was a small public park, about the size of a basketball court, surrounded by a shoulder-high stone fence. This was Janat Adan, the Garden of Eden. The park contained two live olive trees and one dead one, and was covered in concrete. Joni Mitchell was right: They paved Paradise. To one side was a shrine marking the spot where, according to a Muslim legend, Abraham met Sarah. The space was lifeless and devoid of color.

Within seconds, a gaggle of children arrived. They swarmed

us, tugged at my clothes, and climbed Adam's Tree, a leafless trunk with three blond branches reaching into the sky like twisted driftwood trumpets. The boys had bright blue sweatshirts, the girls pink and red dresses. For a moment the park glistened with joy, and for the first time since I arrived in Iraq, I felt the air well with hope.

It didn't last. We were in the heart of concentric waves: the children, some curious teenagers behind them, and just beyond the walls, a few gruff men. Hikmat approached. "Those men are *ali baba*," he said, using the Arabic term for "bandit." "They flashed guns. They told me they intend to rob you." I peered at him, distressed. "I must be honest," he said. "I told them we would protect you, and they offered me a percentage of whatever they stole from you. I think we must go now."

We gathered our belongings and hurried to the car. Events were unfolding so quickly, my head was spinning—a mix of awe, fear, and dark humor. *We were being kicked out of the Garden of Eden!* Not since Adam and Eve, I thought. Hah!

Of course this wasn't the actual garden. A biblical flood in 1954 rerouted the Euphrates, so the two rivers have met in Qurnah for only half a century, not the fifty-eight centuries of Jewish tradition. Still, the experience of touching this garden left me oddly uplifted. The legacy of Genesis 1:26—"Let us make man in our image"—links each of us to God and empowers us to read the story for ourselves.

And at the moment, I read Eden as a story of longing, loss, and renewal. At the start of Genesis, God yearns for a human partner as much as humans long for God. *God* has the idea to create humans in his image and to bid them to rule the world in his stead. He gives Adam the right to name the animals, an act of using words as a form of creation that suggests God is re-creating himself in man. Eve, meanwhile, uses her God-given freedoms to try to become like God. She eats the fruit so she and Adam "can be like divine beings." Each side—humans *and* God—aches to be the other.

That's where Eden comes in. From the moment it appears, the Garden of Eden represents a physical place where the created and the creator can find spiritual union. Adam and Eve wander the garden without shame; God moves about the garden "at the breezy time of day." They are one. The problem with this fragile harmony is that humans don't know the difference between good and bad. Later, when the fruit provides this knowledge, God promptly boots them from Paradise. "Now that the man has become like one of us," God says, "knowing good and bad, what if he should stretch out his hand and take also from the tree of life and eat, and live forever!" God hides himself behind protective leaves, just as humans earlier did.

For generations to come, humans continue to drift away from God. But God, through beneficence, loneliness, or both, refuses to abandon them. He still longs for humans, and they still long for him. By the time of the prophets, God finally realizes that humans are no threat to usurping his power. They clearly have difficulty decoding the difference between right and wrong. And so he re-opens the gates to Paradise that have been closed since Adam and Eve. He removes his leafy protection and makes himself vulnerable again.

He invites us back to Eden.

Standing in this seemingly godforsaken place, I felt God's beckoning more than ever. I felt it in Azzam and his irrational desire to overturn the degradation and reclaim the natural flow of these rivers. I felt it in the text. "For the Lord shall comfort Zion," extols the King James Version of Isaiah 51:3. "He will comfort all her waste places, and he will make her wilderness like Eden, and her desert like the garden of the Lord." I felt it in my heart. Never had I appreciated the awesome challenge of freedom more than I had since coming to Iraq.

And I felt it in the place. Just as we began piling into the car, a young girl pushed through the crowd of onlookers and handed me a gift, a token that seemed to embody the ability of life to poke up through the ruins and offer a vision of hope: an olive branch.

Humans might blight the garden, but Eden never dies.

. 2 .

COME, LET US
BUILD US A CITY

U r leaps from the pages of history. It winds through the an-
nals of archaeology with legends of golden jewelry and
a gilded harp. It hosts the palace intrigue of some of
the more colorful autocrats of antiquity—Sargon, Ur-Nammu,
A-anniepadda. It lingers in the background of some of the most
enduring tales of Mesopotamia: the epic of Gilgamesh, the deluge
of Noah, the birth of Abraham. It is the setting of an Agatha
Christie murder mystery.

And not long after the fall of Saddam, it welcomed Iraq's first
Pizza Hut, built for the U.S. Air Force 407th Air Expeditionary
Group at Tallil Air Base. The franchise caused an uproar because
Army bases, unlike Air Force ones, are barred from having fast-
food restaurants, and soldiers stationed nearby said the exclusion
caused morale problems.

Late one morning we approached Tell Muqayyar, the ruined
city of Ur, capital of ancient Sumer, just outside of modern-day
Nasiriyah. The site lies on the grounds of Tallil Air Base, which

Saddam built here hoping his enemies would not attack and risk having a stray bomb destroy one of the more famous archaeological sites in the world. Dozens of tractor-trailers, armored personnel carriers, and tanks lined the road. At the guard booth, a U.S. airman was surprised to see us. "We don't usually get civilians here," he said.

Down a narrow road, brown grass spread from the pavement in an open expanse. The ground was sandy and flat, part of the floodplain of the Euphrates. The perimeter was lined with coiled barbed wire. A camel strolled by.

As we approached the tell, I began to notice a hulking structure emerging on the horizon, a cross between a giant sand castle and a UFO. The 150-foot-wide building was the color of mud and seemed to grow ineffably out of the soil, civilization emerging from the sands. The building was made from two tiers of mud bricks, each tier about 30 feet high. The tiers were stacked one on top of the other, with the upper story set inward from the bottom. In front, a giant staircase invited visitors to the summit. On the sides, two ramps did the same. On top, where a third tier should have been, was nothing. Time had decapitated the signature of Mesopotamia. It had erased the summit of the ziggurat of Ur.

But it did little to diminish its power.

I stepped from the car and for a second couldn't breathe. When I had dreamed of Iraq, I had dreamed of standing here. My eyes welled. The building emitted a raw, primordial power, like a giant footprint of the gods. The tension that had gripped my chest for days suddenly lifted, replaced by a surge of blood to my head like a rush of sugar after a day of fasting. I was struck that a structure so heavy could make me feel so light-headed. I threw off my body armor and began racing up the huge stairway, counting the steps aloud like a little boy.

The decision to visit Ur was easy, even though the city appears by name only in Genesis. For one, Ur is central to the story of Abraham. But more, Sumer serves as an important link between the birth of humanity and the humane vision of the prophets. The notion that Abraham began his journey toward the Promised Land near the same place the Israelites were later banished from the Promised Land suggests the stories share an underlying connection. The importance of exile in Israelite life began long before Babylon.

Buildings like this actually predate Abraham. Enormous mud-brick platforms were constructed in Mesopotamia as early as six thousand years ago. Beginning in the mid–third millennium B.C.E., some of these buildings were erected with receding tiers, ranging from two to seven levels. The tops, accessible through ramps or stairways, housed temples or shrines. Remains of at least twenty-five ziggurats still speckle this area.

Around 2100 B.C.E., southern Mesopotamia came under the control of King Ur-Nammu, who built ziggurats in numerous cities, including Eridu, Uruk, and Nippur. He built the one in Ur to draw closer to Nanna, the god of the moon. The lowest platform comprised 7 million mud bricks, strengthened every six layers with reed matting and sand. These layers of silt functioned as shock absorbers, giving the building flexibility in the event that a flood destabilized the soil. The building was faced with more than 700,000 fire-baked bricks, stamped with Ur-Nammu's name and glazed in bright colors. Numerous holes in the outer layer allowed the mud bricks to expand and contract as they got wet, then dried.

The Sumerian name for these buildings was Etemennigur, or the Foundation of Heaven and Earth. Akkadian, the extinct Semitic language from southern Mesopotamia, refers to these structures as *ziqquratu*, from the root word *zaqaru*, meaning "to build high." This word was introduced into Europe in the eighteenth century by caravan traders and eventually made its way into

English as *ziggurat*. The Etruscans took the same root to form *ekzakkera*, or "breast of God," as ziggurats have large, mammary-like shapes. From *ekzakkera* travelers created a jargon term for women's breasts and the Latin *exaggerat*. This etymology seems only fitting: The grandest ecclesiastic structures of their time have inspired untold generations of hyperbole.

One legacy of the architecture of the ziggurat, in other words, is the art of *exaggeration*.

At 122 steps I reached the top. The surface was uneven and covered in small pebbles. Dozens of terra-cotta shards, some decorated with insignias, sprinkled the ground. I approached the edge tentatively. Down below were the partially excavated remains of a huge city—royal palaces, a cemetery, neighborhood housing. The surrounding scenery was depressing: low mudflats as brown as a paper lunch bag, occasional date palms, very little water. I looked in vain for the Euphrates but remembered it had been diverted by a flood in 1954. Today Ur is a ghost town on the banks of a ghost river.

As I surveyed the landscape, a small group of U.S. soldiers arrived on the summit. Sergeant First Class Robert Sasser was giving a tour. "Genesis 11 says Abraham lived in Ur of the Chaldeans," he said. "That's this spot, men. Abraham married Sarah and together they moved up to Harran." Dressed in desert camouflage fatigues, Sergeant Sasser is a huge man, with looming shoulders. He would need no pads to play linebacker in the NFL. In his mid-forties, he has pale skin and green, intense eyes. When he finished I went over to see him.

"My mother read me stories about this place years ago," he explained. "And I love it here. I'm an elder in a church, so this is where I belong."

"Which church?"

"It's a peculiar story, really," he said. "My father was in the military, so we lived all over. We tried many different churches, but none really stuck. Then in my teens I learned about the Church of Latter-Day Saints. My mother sought it out. We were all baptized, and from then on, it's been my life."

"Is your mother alive today?"

"No, sir," he said. "But she's patting me on the back right now. She guided me here."

"What would you tell her it feels like?"

"I'd say uplifting. Really, that's the word to describe it—and not just because I'm standing on top of the biggest building around. I came here to do a military mission, but I plan to do much more." He explained that he was helping local Iraqis build schools and work on water distribution. His uncle had already raised some private funds to help.

"For me, that's the reason to be here," he continued. "It's religious. It's biblical. Not all the folks that are here understand the significance."

"So what *is* the significance?"

He reached into the pocket of his shirt and pulled out a Bible. I reached into my bag and pulled out mine. He stared at me, and for a second I thought he would cry. But he didn't seem all that surprised. It seemed natural to him somehow that I would be here, Bible in hand, in the middle of a war zone. He embraced me, and we sat down on the stones.

After Adam and Eve are kicked out of the Garden of Eden, the great primeval events of Genesis unfold with thundering quickness: the births of Cain and Abel, the Flood, the Tower of Babel. At the start of Genesis 11, everyone on earth speaks the same language. "And as they migrated from the east, they came upon a valley in the land of Shinar and settled there." Shinar refers to ancient Sumer. "Come, let us make bricks and burn them hard," the people say.

> Brick served them as stone, and bitumen served them as mortar. "Come, let us build us a city, and a tower with its top in the sky, to make a name for ourselves; else we shall be scattered over the world."

The idea of a tower that men could use to climb up to heaven sounds eerily like the stepped pyramids of Mesopotamia, and ever since these buildings were unearthed in the nineteenth century, the popular image of the Tower of Babel has been a ziggurat. The bitumen in the description refers to a black, pitchlike compound of carbon and hydrogen that seeps from underground oil sources and was used to seal these buildings and others. The Arabic term for this site, Tell Muqayyar, means "built of bitumen."

The only figure who doesn't celebrate the building of the tower is God. "If, as one people with one language for all, this is how they have begun to act," he says of humans, "then nothing that they may propose to do will be out of their reach." He scatters the people and confounds their speech. And he names their construct Babel, a clear reference to the nearby capital of Babylon—one hundred miles to the north—though *not* the root for the English word *babble*, which is thought to be imitative of baby talk and more likely comes from the Latin *babulus*.

Following this story, the Bible outlines a detailed list of human generations, its fifth genealogical chain in six chapters. The earlier lists describe the ten generations that lead from Adam and Eve to Noah; this list describes the ten generations that run from Noah to Abraham. The overwhelming implication is that all humans come from the same biological source. Near the end of the recitation, Genesis 11:26 says, "When Terah had lived seventy years, he begot Abram, Nahor, and Haran." The story continues, "Haran died in the lifetime of his father Terah, in his native land, Ur of the Chaldeans." Later, Terah takes "his son Abram, his grandson Lot, the son of Haran, and his daughter-in-law Sarai, the wife of his son Abram, and they set out together from Ur of the Chaldeans for the land of Canaan."

One curious detail in this careful litany is that the Bible does not say Abraham was born in Ur, as millions believe. It merely says that his brother was born there and that Abraham left there with his wife. (Abraham is still called Abram at this point, his wife, Sarai; God would change their names later.) This seemingly minor lapse has generated great dispute. Some Muslims believe Abraham was born hundreds of miles to the north, in the southern Turkish town of Sanliurfa, just north of Harran, which is the family's first stop after leaving Ur. This location would seem to make some geographic sense, though it's far afield from the preceding story, the Tower of Babel, which appears to take place in southern Iraq.

Jewish and Christian tradition puts the birthplace here, the site of ancient Ur. But that identification has problems, too, as the term *Chaldeans* refers to a population that did not inhabit the area until the ninth century B.C.E. Abraham, by contrast, would have been born at least a thousand years earlier. A mention of Abraham in Deuteronomy 26 suggests he was an Aramean, which refers to a different Mesopotamian tribe, from hundreds of years after Ur faded. With such diverging clues, scholars believe the Bible conflates different traditions into a single narrative. Either way, all traditions agree that Abraham has Mesopotamian roots.

For me, Abraham's connection to this soil suggests that biblical writers wanted to root the Israelites in the birthplace of civilization, both to plant their origins in the earliest moments of human history and to suggest that Abraham's one God supplanted the multiple gods of Mesopotamia. Also, Abraham appears to have been an alien during his time in Ur, with a belief system different from that of his neighbors. When God calls Abraham to leave Mesopotamia in Genesis 12, Abraham doesn't question him. He acts as if he already knows God. The idea that the forefather of the Israelites was an outsider reinforces the idea that the Israelites are always apart from their surroundings. In Genesis, Abraham is described as a "stranger and a sojourner"; in Exodus, Moses is described as a "stranger in a strange land"; in Jeremiah, the Israelites are described as living among strangers. The message of this repetition transcends time: Wandering is a natural state for Israel. Being in exile is positive.

God's children should not become overconfident and start imposing their will on others. Instead, descendants of Abraham have an obligation to be more sensitive to others in their midst because they themselves are perpetually other. They are at home in the unfamiliar.

"For me," Sergeant Sasser said, "the significance of this story is that if you go through Scripture, you realize that all three monotheistic faiths trace our roots back to Abraham. The Islamic faith, through his son Ishmael. The Jewish and Christian faiths, through his son Isaac. A lot of people do their genealogy work, and some can trace their families back to right here."

I asked Sergeant Sasser why genealogy is such a rich tradition in the Church of Latter-Day Saints.

"Because we are a huge family," he said. "In order for all God's people to come together in the hereafter, and be with our Heavenly Father, everyone must have the same blessing. We trace our genealogical roots back as far as we can to give baptism to those people who have passed before us, so they may go where we are going."

I mentioned that ever since 9/11, many people believed the world was in religious war. Did he agree?

"Yes, sir," he said. "But we can get past this."

"How?"

"Strangely enough, it's not done with weapons. It's done with love and consideration for each other. We're not here to tear up stuff, we're here to rebuild. We want places like Ur to be here, just like this, forever and ever."

Sergeant Sasser was married with five kids—"age twenty all the way down to ten." In the event that his children could not visit here, I said, what would he want them to know?

"I'm not a writer or a poet," he said, "but I will share the message that the world is all about people. It's neighbors. It's friends. We're all family, no matter where we're from. We're all connected. And sooner or later, we're all going to be in the same place, right back with the Heavenly Father, where we all belong."

A fter our conversation I walked down the grand staircase at the front of the ziggurat. The steps, which had been restored along with the rest of the building in the 1970s, were shallower than those of modern staircases, which forced me to walk more slowly. On either side, bricks had been formed into wide banisters, not unlike the areas between escalators that children sometimes use as slides. Altogether, being on the ziggurat was like climbing around one of the monuments on the Mall in Washington, D.C.—grand, quasi-civic, quasi-religious architecture, completely out of scale with anything familiar, giving one a feeling of awe, insignificance, and pride.

Back on the ground, I was met by a short, toothless man with sunbaked skin carrying a stack of maps and drawings. We were the first tourists in more than a year, he said, and he was eager to give us a tour. He launched into a spiel: "The name of this city, Ur. Ur the capital of the Sumerians. Sumerians lived four thousand years before Christ."

"Hold on a second," I said. "Who are you?"

Dhief Muhsen was one of a multigenerational line of attendants who live alongside the ziggurat—his grandfather had dug
with Leonard Woolley in the 1920s; his grandson had just been
born. He never leaves the site, he said, even during war. Were you
in peril during the latest conflict? I asked. "The tanks came," he
said. "One time a shot landed thirty meters from my house. Maybe
they thought I was dangerous." He paused for a second. "Now can
I give you a tour?" We proceeded toward the ruins.

The roots of civilization in Iraq go back at least seven thousand
years, when humans stopped wandering from place to place, hunting and gathering, and began to settle on small pieces of land and
cultivate more regular supplies of food. In the mid–fourth millennium B.C.E., the region underwent a climate change, turning
cooler and drier, which allowed agricultural techniques born in
the mountainous upper regions to stretch into the flatter areas in
the south. Irrigation was so successful that early farmers grew
chickpeas, lentils, millet, wheat, turnips, onions, garlic, and mus-
tard. Burgeoning populations hurried to exploit this newfound
wealth, developing the plow for faster farming, the sled for drag-
ging grain, the cart for carrying goods, and the sail for ferrying
products as far away as Egypt, India, and the Far East.

By 3000 B.C.E. a flourishing civilization existed in southern Iraq
that called itself "the place of civilized lords" and its population
"the black-headed people." Sumer, as this land was later named,
comprised an area of around ten thousand square miles, stretching
from Baghdad to the gulf, and made up of city-states separated by
open steppe. Sumer rose and fell numerous times but reached a
peak with the reign of Ur-Nammu, lasting for around a century,
from 2112 to 2004 B.C.E. This was the period of the ziggurat and
around the time the Bible suggests Abraham was born. Flush with
technology, elite Sumerians invented the potter's wheel, the arch,
the dome, and other amenities of civilized life, including beer.

Sumerians were the first to use barley and other cereals to brew sweetened malt, called *bappir*. This fermented brew was mentioned in the Code of Hammurabi and even had its own goddess, Ninkasi, "the lady who fills the mouth." "When you pour out the filtered beer of the collector's vat," read one ode to Ninkasi, "it is like the onrush of the Tigris and Euphrates."

Sumer's reputation as the provenance of Western civilization rests primarily on two innovations: its breakthrough use of the written word and its vision of a god-centered world. Both have deep echoes in the Bible and profound implications for the religious conflicts of today. The earliest writing in Mesopotamia probably occurred on animal skins or paper, though both are easily destroyed and no remnants exist today. Instead, almost everything we know about the history of western Asia comes from writing on baked clay tablets. As early as the fourth millennium B.C.E., scribes began taking lumps of fine clay and molding them into smooth, cushion-shaped tablets an inch or two long and three-quarters of an inch thick. Using the end of a reed stalk cut on an angle, the scribe would draw pictograms, which were later replaced with horizontal and vertical lines that look like elongated triangles. This writing, the first evolved system in history, is called "cuneiform," from the Latin *cuneus*, or "wedge."

During our tour, I asked Dhief Muhsen whom of all the people who had ever lived in Ur he would most want to meet. "The person who invented writing," he said. And what would he tell this person? "You served the world. Anytime anyone anywhere sits down to write a letter, they are a baby of Ur. They are a child of Iraq."

Much of Mesopotamian writing was used to record economic transactions, but numerous epic poems survive that paint a detailed portrait of the population's religious worldview. The Sumerians may not have been a people of the Book, but they were a people of the tablet, making them forebears of the biblical tradition of using written narrative as a basis for collective identity. Sumerians believed that the universe consisted of a flat disk, sitting on primordial waters and covered with a dome. Heaven and earth were populated by gods, who looked human, had human defects and passions, and were endowed with supernatural powers that filled humans with awe and fear. The narrative pinnacles of Sumerian religion bear striking resemblance to the Bible. In Sumerian creation, earth emerges from a watery chaos, and the gods planted a watered garden where humans lived in Paradise (the word *Eden* is derived from the Sumerian *edin*, meaning "a plain" or "open country"). Sumerian epics describe a time when all humans shared a single language until the gods intervened to create a confusion of tongues.

The most stunning parallels occur in twelve tablets that relate the epic of Gilgamesh, the likely fictitious king of the Sumerian city of Uruk. Gilgamesh is an oppressive ruler, so his constituents appeal to the gods, who create a nemesis, Enkidu. Born naked in the wilderness, Enkidu is tempted by a harlot, who educates him about sin and teaches him to wear clothes. The similarities to Adam and Eve are striking. After Enkidu dies, Gilgamesh, still fearing the gods, seeks out Utnapishtim, the only man granted eternal life. During his journey, Gilgamesh tussles with an unknown supernatural figure in a scene that prefigures the biblical moment when Abraham's grandson Jacob wrestles with God. When Gilgamesh finds Utnapishtim, he is residing in a secret garden covered in precious stones. The gods had been planning to destroy the earth with a flood, Utnapishtim reveals, though one god took pity and advised Utnapishtim to abandon his possessions, build a seven-tiered ship, and take with him the seed of all creatures. Utnapishtim did so, and after seven days, the ark landed on a mountain and he sent forth a dove. Humanity was saved. The path for Noah was set.

When I first visited the Tigris and Euphrates, at the outset of my first journey exploring the Bible, I was shocked to learn of the

Mesopotamian parallels to Genesis. I was also disturbed. If the stories were lifted from Sumerian sources, then touched up by biblical editors to serve their own purpose, perhaps that undermined the singularity of the Bible, and my faith. Avner pointed out that while the similarities are profound, one difference sets the biblical stories apart: The Sumerian tales have many gods; the Bible has one. His answer put my mind at ease.

Today, I have a different view. I still believe that the Bible's one invisible, universal God is a qualitative difference and one primary reason why biblical religion survives and Mesopotamian does not. But I no longer fear that exploring the connection undermines the Bible, or my attachment to it. Instead, I see the diverse roots of the Bible as a strength, not a weakness. One recurring problem with the religions that grew out of the Hebrew Bible is that each has a tendency to believe its faith is unique, its interpretation of the text absolute, and its relationship with God so exclusive it has the right to harm those who disagree. The idea that the writers of the Bible were influenced by sources that predate their own suggests the Bible should be seen not as sui generis but as being in dialogue with other texts. And if scriptures can be in dialogue, surely the faiths that grow out of those scriptures can be in dialogue as well.

In that interplay, what the Bible chose to adapt from Mesopotamia is telling. Both traditions, for example, view water as primary, land as emerging out of water, and humans as emerging from land. Geography is primal. More important, even the idea that many believe began with the biblical prophets—social justice— shows glimmers in Sumer. One Mesopotamian epic advises people to worship their god every day, but also

To the feeble show kindness,
Do not insult the downtrodden,
Do charitable deeds, render service all your days.

Do not utter libel, speak what is of good report,
Do not say evil things, speak well of people.

These words could easily have been written by any of the Hebrew prophets.

The greatest concept the Bible shares with its Sumerian forebears is not Creation, the Tower of Babel, or the Flood; it is the understanding that humans yearn to make contact with their gods and need those gods to help them improve their lives on earth. That yearning for the divine cannot be excised from civilized society, as some skeptics suggest today; it is one of the primary expressions of civilized human society. To live in peace does not require the removal of religion from our lives; it requires the discovery of the beneficent elements within religion that have lived alongside the hateful ones since humans first began to make sense of their environment.

We arrived at the royal compound not far from the ziggurat, site of one of the most famous overreaches in archaeological history and backdrop to one of that discipline's least likely love stories. The mounds are mostly covered over now and show little sign of the fanfare they created when they were unearthed in the 1920s. The limp feeling they invoke was best captured by Agatha Christie in her novel *Murder in Mesopotamia*, based on her visits to Ur during Woolley's excavation. "I wondered what sort of palaces they had in those days, and if it would be like the pictures I'd seen of Tutankhamen's tomb," writes the narrator, Nurse Amy Leatheran.

But would you believe it, there was nothing to see but *mud*! Dirty mud walls about two feet high—and that's all there was to it. Mr. Carey took me here and there telling me things—how this was the great court, and there were some chambers here and an upper storey and various other rooms that opened off the central court. And all I thought was, "But how does he *know*?" though, of course, I was too polite to say so. I can tell you it *was* a disappointment! The whole excavation looked like nothing but mud to me—no marble or gold or anything handsome—my aunt's house in Cricklewood would have made a much more inspiring ruin!

Discovered in 1625, Tell Muqayyar was first associated with the Bible in the mid-1800s. Round-the-clock excavations begun by Sir C. L. Woolley in 1922 lorded over the field of archaeology for more than a decade. Woolley was a man of "slight build and no commanding appearance," a colleague commented. "But presence, yes!" Braving shootings and looting, he pulled up lavish jewelry, silver weapons, and a four-thousand-year-old golden harp, an enlarged re-creation of which greets visitors to Nasiriyah today. When gold beads that Woolley discovered went missing, he announced that local workers would be paid a bonus every time one was found in the ground. Workers who had been selling them to local dealers quickly went and retrieved them; Woolley's price was three times the market rate.

But Woolley's greatest flair was public relations. He had what Christie called "the eye of imagination." "While he was speaking I felt in my mind no doubt whatever that the house on the corner had been Abraham's," she wrote in her autobiography. "It was his reconstruction of the past and he believed in it, and anyone who listened to him believed in it also." In 1929 he dug a one-yard-square pit, at the bottom of which he found extensive water destruction. His staff was underwhelmed; river overflows were common in Mesopotamia. But Woolley had other ideas, writing, "I was quite convinced what it all meant." He asked his wife, Katherine, a former volunteer, who announced, "Well, of course, it's the Flood!" She was referring to *Noah's* flood, something hardly provable by a three-foot-wide hole. But the next year they expanded the dig to seventy-five yards wide, and Woolley announced that the Flood had covered an area three hundred miles long. "It was not a universal deluge," he wrote, but it *was* the inspiration of the biblical story. Though he had no proof whatsoever for this connection, gullible newspaper reporters gushed over his discovery.

While Woolley and his wife were stealing the international spotlight from Ur, a more curious couple was stealing secret glances. In 1928, following the breakup of her first marriage and with nine novels already to her credit, Agatha Christie traveled to Iraq, alone and on a whim. She took the Orient Express from London to Damascus, then rode forty-eight hours on a six-wheel bus across the desert to Baghdad. After visiting friends, she traveled by train to Ur junction, where she was welcomed by Katherine Woolley, who had everyone on the dig read *The Murder of Roger Ackroyd*. "I fell in love with Ur," Christie wrote, "with its beauty in the evening, the ziggurat standing up, faintly shadowed, and that wide sea of sand with its lovely pale colours of apricot, rose, blue and mauve changing every minute."

The following year she returned, and this time Leonard Woolley asked his deputy, the shy, twenty-six-year-old Max Mallowan, to chaperon Christie, fifteen years his senior. In her autobiography, Christie recalled their first meeting, in verse:

> *I'll tell you everything I can*
> *If you listen well:*
> *I met an erudite young man*
> *A-sitting on a tell.*
> *He said: "I look for aged pots*
> *Of prehistoric days,*
> *And then I measure them in lots*

And lots of different ways.
And then (like you) I start to write,
My words were twice as long
As yours, and far more erudite.
They prove my colleagues wrong!"

Mallowan accompanied Christie back to Baghdad, and along the way their car broke down in the desert. Impressed by her lack of panic, he followed her all the way to England and, with flowers in hand and a diamond in pocket, proposed. "Five thousand years ago is the choicest age I know," he said.

And once you learn to scorn A.D.
And you have got the knack,
Then you could come and dig with me
And never wander back.

The two were married the following year, an unlikely desert romance that thrilled everyone who heard about it—except Katherine Woolley. The prima donna of Tell Muqayyar, whom Mallowan described as "dominating and powerful," declared: "There is room for only one woman at Ur." Christie was banned from the dig, forcing her husband to return alone. Sitting at home, the writer quickly wrought her revenge: the murder victim in *Murder in Mesopotamia*, who is described as a "queer woman," "a mass of affectation," and "a champion liar," is based on Katherine Woolley. She is felled by a falling millstone.

Back at the base of the ziggurat, another group of U.S. soldiers had arrived. They were milling around, snapping photographs, and joking. Part of the 607th MP Battalion based in Grand Prairie, Texas, the men were serving their last day at Tallil following more than a year in the region. The next morning they would fly to Camp Doha, then home.

The leader was fifty-year-old Chaplain Steve Munson, a soft-spoken man with a small brown cross on his floppy desert hat. Like all chaplains, he carried no weapon. Instead he was shadowed by a burly sergeant, Adrian Buruma, who had a machine gun large enough for both of them. Chaplain Munson had a broad, welcoming face, covered in sunspots, that exuded a secure, serene confidence and all-Americanness that reminded me of Arnold Palmer.

Chaplain Munson entered military service in the 1970s, then left a decade later after being called into ministry with the Southern Baptist Church. He returned to uniform around the time of the first Gulf War and was now in the reserves. On a chain around his neck, next to his dog tag, he wore a medallion with a verse from Joshua. "I will be strong and courageous. I will not be terrified or discouraged, because the Lord God is with me wherever I go." I asked him if it was true that there are no atheists in foxholes.

"When people go through a difficult experience," he said, "they come to realize that there has to be more to life than what they think there is. A lot of times they find they can't handle their stress. They can't survive on their own. Then the door opens to be able to discuss with them how to develop a relationship with Christ."

"You're Southern Baptist," I said. "Does that mean you're evangelical?"

"We're not allowed as chaplains to proselytize," he said. "Instead you ask leading questions: 'Why do you think you're having stress?' 'Where do you think you might get hope?' 'Why did you come to me and not a friend?' Usually they will give you the permission, which you need to be able to lead them into a relationship with God through Christ."

I asked him if he had performed any baptisms in Iraq.

"We had a baptism overlooking the ziggurat," he said. The

soldiers took an ammo crate, lined it with plastic, then filled it with water. A half dozen men from different denominations received holy rites while a sergeant played "Amazing Grace" on the saxophone, black gospel style. "You just felt this overwhelming presence of the Lord," Chaplain Munson said. "To overlook this site and think that somewhere in this area Abram may have walked."

He paused. A twinkle leapt into his eye. "Now we hadn't had a shower or bath in three weeks," he said. "So afterwards we all looked at that crate and said, 'Why let that water go to waste?' So three or four of us jumped in, and we did rub-a-dub-dub three men in a tub." He chuckled at the memory.

"I'd like to ask you about a difficult topic," I said. "One difference between the first Gulf War and now is that 9/11 happened. The world has taken on an aura of religious conflict. Has there been any anti-Muslim feeling you've perceived among soldiers?"

"There has been a mixture," he said. "For the most part, there's not an anti-Muslim feeling, there's an antiterrorist feeling. And there's an understanding that there's a difference between the common Muslim we meet every day and the right-wing fanatics. I've found over the years that soldiers are usually a little more educated on those things than civilians. They are here, experiencing this, and they know who is threatening and who is not."

"So do you think in the same way the military was racially integrated before the rest of American society that the military is more sensitized to interfaith awareness than the regular population?"

"I think the tendency is yes," he said. "Chaplains make it a point to make sure people understand and tolerate other faiths. Look at our worship services on Sunday mornings. We don't have a Baptist worship service. We have a worship service. Since we've been here, our core group includes Episcopalians, Baptists, Lutherans, and Disciples of Christ."

"So does denomination not matter anymore?"

"Oh, no. It matters, but we talk about it. And we never violate our core beliefs. We all believe in the Virgin Birth, we believe in the death, the burial, and the resurrection of Jesus Christ. We believe he died on the cross for our sins. We believe in the Second Coming. We would disagree on how to conduct a baptism, for example, but we all agree that baptism is an essential part of our faith."

The afternoon was moving toward that hour when it was unsafe to be outdoors. The colors were warming toward the Agatha Christie palette: apricot, rose, blue, and mauve. I asked Chaplain Munson if he would offer us a farewell reading. He directed us toward the base of the stairs that lead to the top of the ziggurat.

We pulled out our Bibles. One curious aspect of Judaism and Christianity is that, for all the importance of the earliest biblical books to each faith, the actual religious worship of each tradition focuses more on the latter books of the Hebrew Bible—namely, the Prophets and the Psalms. Jewish Shabbat services include a reading from the Torah; the holiest prayer in Judaism, the *Shema*, comes from Deuteronomy and Numbers. But Jewish services also include a weekly reading from the Prophets, known as the *haftarah*, a custom that is believed to have originated when Syrian rulers in the late first millennium B.C.E. forbade the study of the Torah. The heart of the weekday morning service, the *Amidah*, comes from the Prophets and the Psalms; the same with the afternoon service. Nearly every service includes a reading of Psalm 20, which promises that God answers those in distress. "Now I know that the Lord will give victory to his anointed."

The same emphasis applies to Protestant and Catholic liturgies. The New Testament is filled with references to the Prophets and replete with evidence that Jesus prayed using the Psalms. As recorded in the Gospel of Luke, the last words of Jesus, "Into your hands I commit my spirit," echo a line from Psalm 31, "My fate is in your hand." Eastern Orthodox, Roman Catholic, and Anglican church services all make systematic use of the Prophets and Psalms. One of the most famous prayers in Christian liturgy, the Sanctus, is built on a quotation from Isaiah 6: "Holy, holy, holy is the Lord of hosts: the whole earth is full of his glory." Many of the Psalms were set to music and have become the most memorable hymns in Christianity.

The reasons for this focus have largely to do with literary form. Beginning with the Prophets, the writing in the Bible becomes less dependent on narrative, which largely defines the Pentateuch, and more interested in poetry, oracle, and lamentation. The prophets take declarations from God and make transcendent proclamations about human behavior and the Lord's magnanimity. Isaiah 6, for example, is actually set "in the year that King Uzziah died," 742 B.C.E., when the prophet witnesses the Lord on his throne, surrounded by seraphim. But the seraphim's exclamation, "Holy, holy, holy is the Lord of hosts," can easily be turned into a timeless prayer, as it was with the Sanctus, which has nothing to do with Uzziah.

The 150 psalms, which appear in the Hebrew Bible following the Prophets, take this literary evolution even further. They are direct prayers to God. Unlike the rest of the Hebrew Bible, in which God involves himself in life on earth and speaks, prods, cajoles, and reaches out to human beings, in the Psalms human beings reach out to God. The human yearning for contact with the creator, implied since the Garden of Eden, finally becomes overt. "Answer me when I call, O God," pleads Psalm 4. "O Lord, my God, in you I seek refuge," says Psalm 7.

Though the Bible attributes many of the Psalms to early Israelite figures, notably David, scholars agree that the writing of the Psalms likely began in the Babylonian Exile and continued for several centuries. This timing is significant. The Psalms reflect a time when the Israelites, removed from their land, become less interested in physical manifestations of worship, like the Temple, and more interested in nonphysical worship, like prayer. Unlike sacrifices, which could be offered only in the Temple, and only by a priest, a psalm can be recited anywhere by anyone. While the bulk of the biblical narrative focuses on the Israelites as a nation, the Psalms speak for the raw, individual human heart. The Bible, which begins with the grandest act of all, creating the universe, has finally arrived at the most intimate act, an invitation for each person to speak directly to the divine. The essence of the biblical story—contact between humans and God—no longer happens exclusively to the people in the narrative; it can now happen for all of us. The Bible has ceased being merely the backstory of religion; it has become a central part of religion.

Which is one reason its influence still holds. When I asked Chaplain Munson what passages from the Bible spoke to him most while he was serving in Iraq, he mentioned Jeremiah 29:11, "For I am mindful of the plans I have concerning you, declares the Lord"; and two psalms, 16, "Protect me, O God, for I seek refuge in you," and 91, which he called the soldiers' psalm.

He flipped through his government-issue, desert camouflage Bible to Psalm 91 and prepared to read aloud. Before he did, I noticed a small notation on the top of the page, "3-09-03, Arifjan." I asked him what it meant.

"We were stationed in Camp Arifjan on the night the war was supposed to begin," he said. "We had been given the mission to secure the border where the Iraqis were expected to attack. The XO came to me," he said, using the military abbreviation for executive officer, "and he was greatly concerned that if we were attacked, we would probably lose some soldiers. He asked me to lead a prayer with all the men, and I chose this psalm." He began to read:

O you who dwell in the shelter of the Most High
And abide in the protection of Shaddai—
I say of the Lord, my refuge and stronghold,
My God in whom I trust,
that he will save you from the fowler's trap,
from the destructive plague.
He will cover you with his pinions;
you will find refuge under his wings;
His fidelity is an encircling shield.
You need not fear the terror by night,
or the arrow that flies by day,
the plague that stalks in the darkness,
or the scourge that ravages at noon.
A thousand may fall at your left side,
ten thousand at your right,
but it shall not reach you.

The psalm ends with the following passage:

Because he is devoted to me I will deliver him;
I will keep him safe, for he knows my name.
When he calls on me, I will answer him;
I will be with him in distress;
I will rescue him and make him honored;
I will let him live to a ripe old age,
and show him my salvation.

"There are at least three dozen books of the Bible," I said, "and 150 psalms. Why did you choose this one?"

"I believe God leads through his word," he said. "When you are in stressful situations, he will lead you to specific parts of his word that will have meaning and will give you encouragement to make it through. In this instance, I couldn't have asked for anything better. When we heard that first night lightning, lightning, lightning, and Scud missiles were flying at us from all directions, we had the comfort of knowing that, as it says here, the plague will not overcome us, God will cover us in wings, the terror of the night will not destroy us.

"And I'm not sure if this will make any sense to you, but as we were praying together that night, we received a promise that we would have no loss of life in our battalion. I believe the Lord gave us that promise on March 9, 2003." He paused and looked out over the landscape. His eyes were dark, impenetrable. The only sound was the crinkly paper of our Bibles flapping in the wind.

Then he looked back at me. "Tomorrow we will leave the country after nearly a year, the only battalion in our brigade with no loss of life."

BY THE RIVERS OF BABYLON

"Are you scared?" Linda asked.

I was standing in front of the Al-Janoub hotel in Nasiriyah, a drab concrete building with balconies that look like airport security barriers glued to the side of a jail. Every evening, forced to confine ourselves to Soviet-style hotels as Hikmat and Bijar gathered roasted chicken, white beans in tomato sauce, and flat bread for dinner, I tried to use my Thuraya satellite telephone to reach home. Priced at an exorbitant rate, minutes were precious; but service was even rarer: satellite telephones, chunky devices like early cell phones, work only when the thick antenna is pointed, unobstructed, toward the heavens. That meant the only way I could assure my family I was safe was to do the most dangerous thing imaginable: stand alone in the middle of the street.

"I'm wearing my body armor," I said. "It's unbelievably heavy. I pulled my back out. And it's impossible to take a nap in the car, the armor is so boxy. But no, I wouldn't say scared is the feeling. The feeling is one of concentration: Do I go down that street? Do I walk through that crowd? Do I trust that man?"

"You sound better."

"It's odd, but in some ways it was much more stressful worrying about coming here than actually being here, once you get over the sound of gunfire all the time."

"I wish you didn't tell me that. And your e-mail about the guy from the water department getting shot. Oooh. I didn't like that very much."

"Yeah, maybe that was too much information. I was just trying to be honest."

"What about all the suicide bombings?"

"Twenty people were killed this morning at a police station. But the strangest thing about life here is how differently you process the information. Unless the attack is immediately in front of us, or where we might be in a few days, it's amazing how quickly the mind tunes it out. The survival instinct is a powerful thing."

"Where are you going next?"

"Babylon."

" 'By the rivers of Babylon . . .' Wow. I can't believe you'll actually be there."

"I miss you, baby. See you soon."

"I'm proud of you. I can't wait."

By far the most dangerous thing we did on any given day was drive. One doesn't quite realize how fragile law and order is until one tries to get from one place to another in a vigilante nation. We got up early for the 150-mile drive north to Babylon so we could beat the traffic, which clogs all arteries through the country by early afternoon. Also, highway pirates sleep late, we were told, which meant morning commutes were supposed to be less stressful.

Setting out along the banks of the Euphrates, we encountered the familiar mix of jalopy tractors, random military caravans, and brightly colored semi trucks with matinee-style portraits of Shia saints taped to their windshields and silhouettes of women painted on their mud flaps. About an hour north of town, the traffic slowed, and we were directed to the side of the road by an American soldier on the roof of a Humvee wielding a machine gun. As we waited, a five-mile-long convoy of oil trucks inched by. The civilian drivers were some of the fiercest-looking men we'd seen, with bodies like wrestlers' and faces like prison guards'. Some wore ski masks, others goggles. Most slung Kalashnikov rifles over their shoulders. "They look scared," Hikmat said.

Half an hour later we were allowed to resume, but our progress continued to be stalled because we were trapped behind the convoy on a single-lane road. On several occasions, Bijar attempted to maneuver onto the shoulder to pass, but the soldiers protecting the convoy's rear aimed their guns at us. We eased back into formation. Finally we arrived at a double-lane highway and were allowed to drive along the right of the convoy. At one point Bijar, attempting to pass a civilian car, dipped briefly in between two trucks. Without warning, the truck from behind accelerated rapidly and smashed into our rear bumper, swerving us out of control and threatening to pin us between the tankers. The trunk began to crinkle. The tanker backed off, then reared forward like an angry elephant about to hit us again. At the last second Bijar jerked back into the adjacent lane. We would be late to Babylon.

Around 11:00 A.M. we arrived on the outskirts of what looked like a Disney-style theme park. Picnic tables lined the shores of manicured canals with hyper-blue water, like the artificial waterways in It's a Small World. A giant concrete statue of Hammurabi, his arms crossed like those of a stern elementary-school teacher, lorded over the park. Nearby was a stone billboard with the face of

Saddam Hussein. It was pockmarked with bullet fire, a bad case of revenge acne.

Saddam rebuilt parts of Babylon and erected a palace on its highest hill in order to claim that he was the inheritor of the ancient empire. He then opened the park to the public as a sort of Six Flags over Hammurabi. The park had been turned into a coalition base at the start of the war and was now guarded by Polish troops. We approached the two-lane road leading up to the entrance. A sign read, in English and Arabic: "Military vehicles to the right; civilian vehicles to the left." We started down the wrong lane but caught ourselves. Seconds later, as we approached the actual entrance, a taxi made the same mistake and drove down the wrong lane. The guards shouted at the car, but it didn't stop, and the soldiers opened fire, blowing out the taxi's tires and splintering the windshield. Smoke spiraled from the engine. An Iraqi driver leapt from the car with his arms in the air. I had never been so close to bullets fired in anger.

We were met by Major Dezso Kiss of Hungary, a rotund figure with spectacles and a trim beard. He drove us through a buzz of satellite trucks, mess tents, and troops from twenty countries. Noting that the Tower of Babel was erected nearby, Major Kiss said soldiers here communicate in one language, English. "The Tower has finally been built," he said.

We neared a blocky, deep blue gate, like the Arc de Triomphe painted the color of blueberry pie. This was Saddam's version of the famed Ishtar Gate. Huddled at the bottom was a gaggle of military personnel, a few private security guards with bulging body armor and M16s, and one man who was running his nose along the stones, seemingly oblivious to the chaos around him. He was dressed in rumpled khakis, a starched white shirt, a blue blazer, and Reebok tennis shoes. He wore thick calico glasses and was carrying a briefcase and a Burberry trench coat. He looked like a character from an Agatha Christie novel who'd pitched up suddenly on the wrong movie set.

I leapt from the car and ran to greet him. "Dr. Russell," I said. "I'm so happy to see you."

Sumer may have been the first grand civilization of Mesopotamia, but Babylon was the first great empire—the younger sibling that pushed aside its elder, like Jacob purloining the birthright from Esau. While Sumer was at its peak in the late second millennium B.C.E., wandering tribes from Arabia began to move north into the heart of the Tigris-Euphrates Valley. Initially they maintained their pastoral ways and settled on the outskirts of Sumerian cities, but over time they began to infiltrate urban areas and set up a rival political force. In 1781 the German scholar August Ludwig Scholzer coined the term *Semitic* to describe the languages spoken by these tribes. Later, *Semite* came to refer to the people. Both terms derive from the name of Noah's son Shem, who was said to be the ancestor of the Assyrians, Aramaeans, Israelites, and Arabs. Semites, in other words, are the ancestors of today's Muslims, Christians, and Jews.

The first triumph of the Semites was to set up the kingdom of Babylon, just south of modern-day Baghdad, about halfway between the mountains of the north and the lowlands of the south. The name comes from the Akkadian word *Bab-ilu*, meaning "the gate of the god"; it appears in the Bible as Babel and was later Hellenized into Babylon. Babylon was by far the most famous city of the Ancient Near East, more influential than Ur, Damascus, or Jerusalem, the last of which was a mere hilltop afterthought when Babylon first seized the world stage around 1800 B.C.E.

The initial golden age of Babylon arose with Hammurabi, a fearsome leader who reigned from 1792 to 1750 B.C.E. Some cuneiform tablets link Hammurabi with King Amraphel of Shinar, who appears in Genesis 14, a contemporary of Abraham. Sumer had been mostly a haphazard conglomeration of city-states, many with their own calendars, which never coalesced into a force strong enough to assert control over their neighbors. Hammurabi, by contrast, was one of the great administrators of ancient history, who centralized economic control and used the resulting bevy of resources to expand his authority across the region.

Hammurabi's greatest legacy was the promulgating of an intricate set of 281 laws governing everything from what happens to someone who steals another's slave (put to death) to what happens when someone takes over another's farm but is too lazy to till the fields (return the farm to the owner). Some penalties seem particularly expressive of Mesopotamia: If one man brings an accusation against another, the accused must jump into the river. If he sinks, the accuser gets possession of his house; if he floats, the accuser gets put to death and the accused gets the house.

The Code of Hammurabi was reproduced many times, but the only surviving example was inscribed on an eight-foot-tall slab of black diorite, whose permanently recorded laws gave birth to the expression *written in stone*. The number 13 was left off the enumerated list, considered unlucky even then. Contrary to reputation, the Code was not the first legal code in history; other examples predate it. Its legacy comes from its sometimes surprising humanity and advanced sense of social justice. Women had fewer rights than men, for example, but the protections afforded them were still revolutionary. A woman could lend money, buy or lease property, and initiate legal proceedings. And unless unfaithfulness could be proved against her, she could not be summarily divorced.

Hammurabi's preamble contains one of the earliest and most forward-looking declarations of human rights. Marduk, the ruling god of Babylon, calls Hammurabi "to bring about the rule of righteousness in the land, to destroy the wicked and the evil-doers; so that the strong should not harm the weak; so that I should rule over the black-headed people, and enlighten the land, to further the well-being of mankind." The roots of Western humanity show their earliest glimmers in the writings of Mesopotamia.

Viewed from these riverbanks, two of the most lasting innovations of the Bible—the 613 laws of Moses and the moral paeans of the prophets—appear less as unprecedented creations and more as evolutions of ideas emerging in the region over thousands of years. That these notions reach their fullest expression in biblical writings that date from the Exile, when the Israelites *return* to Mesopotamia, makes the influence of the earlier ideas even harder to ignore. The Bible, too, is a child of Iraq. Its true innovation was to take beliefs first carved in stone and, as Jeremiah says, inscribe them on human hearts.

John Malcolm Russell is an unlikely activist. With his big nose and bookish nervousness, he bears a striking resemblance to Woody Allen. He stammers. But the fifty-year-old Assyriologist from the Massachusetts College of Art in Boston moved to Iraq after the war to serve as chief archaeologist. At great personal peril, he helicoptered into looting zones, wrangled with complacent security forces, hunted down organized thieves, and attempted to wrest control over the most aggressive threat to ancient history in a generation. "I've never been just an archaeologist," said the Missouri native. "I've always been a bit of an activist. There are a lot of archaeologists who want to make a difference. The difference is: I get to do it."

Saddam's Ishtar Gate is actually two-thirds the size of the original. The replica has two forty-five-foot towers with an arched entrance and is covered with hundreds of glazed reliefs of dragons and bulls, which march in alternating rows like beasts on their way to slaughter. Built in honor of the goddess of love, the original gate was one of eight entrances to the city erected by Nebuchadnezzar II. After Hammurabi, Babylon underwent several centuries of decline; it returned to prominence around 1100 B.C.E. under Nebuchadnezzar I but was quickly eclipsed by the Assyrians, who established a vast regional empire in the mountains north of Baghdad. After sacking the kingdom of Israel, the Assyrians turned to Babylon, razing the city in 689 B.C.E. and tossing the remains of its temples, walls, and palaces into the water. The Babylonians fought back sixty years later, under King Nabopolassar, but it was his son, Nebuchadnezzar II, who ruled for forty-three years beginning in 605 B.C.E., executed the destruction of Jerusalem, and elevated Babylon to the most prominent city in the world.

"Nebuchadnezzar rebuilt the Ishtar Gate three times," Dr. Russell explained, "probably within a fairly short period. Each time, instead of tearing it down, he just covered the old one with earth, then built another on top. Would you like to see the real gate?"

We walked through the archway onto the broad central avenue of the city known to the Babylonians as "May the enemy not cross it." This mile-long processional, once lined with shops, was the Champs-Elysées of Mesopotamia. To our left was the rebuilt royal palace, with tan brick walls soaring forty feet high, topped with crenellations. To the right stood a temple to the goddess of the dead, one of an estimated twelve hundred religious sites within the city walls. Behind us, outside the city walls, were the remains of a ziggurat.

As a child growing up in Savannah, Georgia, I was taught that my hometown was the first planned city in North America, with a meticulous grid of streets and parks stretching away from the river. Savannah, historians believe, modeled itself after the planned city of Peking (now Beijing), dating from the fifteenth century C.E. Babylon was a planned city twenty centuries before that. One of the biggest cities in the ancient world, Babylon was roughly square, bisected by the Euphrates and surrounded by an eleven-mile wall wide enough on top for two four-horse carriages to pass each other without touching. Its mix of straight streets stretching from the river bears striking similarities to Peking and Savannah. Even Herodotus, who visited in the fifth century B.C.E., was struck by the order: "The houses are mostly three and four stories high; the streets all run in straight lines, not only those parallel to the river, but also the cross streets which lead down to the waterside."

"Why is it that civilization began south of here, in Sumer," I asked Dr. Russell, "but Babylon became much more powerful?"

"Agriculture actually began in northern Mesopotamia," he said. "The north was an extraordinarily lush and wealthy area. Because of all the snow and rain, you could farm anywhere. So it was a good place to develop settled societies. But you can't irrigate the rivers in the north. The riverbeds were too low, and it was impossible for ancient societies to raise the water high enough to reach the fields.

"In the south, the riverbanks are not as high," he continued, "the rivers flood naturally, and it's much easier to build irrigation canals because the landscape is flatter. The reason civilization began in the south is that it takes a significant population to maintain those canals, carry the water long distances, and allocate the water to different farms. That process stimulated the people to get organized."

"So societies in the south were more complex."

"Exactly. But as the irrigation systems became more sophisticated, they could carry water longer distances. Once you can do that, it makes more sense to tap the rivers farther upstream, so you can maintain the canals at a higher level and reach more fields. But you also have to be able to control lots of territory and have the cooperation of a lot of people. Babylon represents the next evolution in the development of intricate urban societies."

"So what was the practical difference between Sumer and Babylon?"

"Sumer I think of as city-states," he said. "Babylon as a nation-state. Sumer was where civilization began, but Babylon was how it spread into the world."

The real Ishtar Gate appears at the bottom of a twenty-foot-deep trench in the center of the city. The remains on display here, over thirty feet long, represent the lowest portion from one of the early gates that Nebuchadnezzar II built over. The final gate left standing was carted off to Berlin following excavations in 1902. The blue has long since disappeared from these bricks, and the surface is the color of cardboard. But the most striking feature is the vast number of bas-relief lions and dragons that cover the surface, like emblems on an Hermès tie. With their scaly pelts and curlicue tails, the creatures jut from the wall like three-dimensional tattoos. "With all these decorations, this is clearly a ceremonial gate," Dr. Russell said. "Also, it was designed to intimidate visitors to the palace."

I actually felt that the otherworldly quality of the beasts made Babylon seem more alluring than I had expected. In fact, I was struck by how much baggage I had brought to the site, expecting to find clues of some twisted, dark regime. Babylon must be evil, I thought; the Bible says it's so. But the more I saw of the remains, and the more I read of its history, the more I realized I had to re-calibrate my view of the defining episode of the second half of the

Hebrew Bible. Babylon was not the evil empire; it may even have been Israel's redeemer.

We pulled out our Bibles. The idea that Jerusalem was totally destroyed by Nebuchadnezzar II, the kingdom of Judah wiped off the world stage, and the Israelites plunged into unconsolable despair is, in many ways, the creation of the Bible. One of the most evocative turns of phrase in the entire text, the opening verses of Psalm 137, is a searing portrait of sadness.

By the rivers of Babylon,
there we sat,
sat and wept,
as we thought of Zion.
There on the poplars
we hung up our lyres,
for our captors asked us there for songs,
our tormentors, for amusement,
"Sing us one of the songs of Zion."
How can we sing a song of the Lord
on alien soil?
If I forget you, O Jerusalem,
let my right hand wither;
let my tongue stick to my palate
if I cease to think of you,
if I do not keep Jerusalem in memory
even at my happiest hour.

Psalm 137 was popular from the earliest years of Jewish liturgy and is still sung by devout Jews before the grace after meals. The Renaissance composer Salomone Rossi turned it into a lament for Jewish nationalism, and the nineteenth-century English composer Isaac Nathan wrote the melody popular in Jewish worship today.

Some have tried to turn the verse that begins "If I forget you, O Jerusalem" into an Israeli pledge of allegiance. Psalm 137 is also one of the most popular psalms in Christian hymnals, used often during Vespers, or evening services, and put to plaintive melody in the musical *Godspell*.

Yet the impression this psalm leaves of the Exile is misleading at best. For starters, the Exile should be seen not as an isolated example of Israelite misfortune but as part of a sweeping period of global transformation. In the same way that the Israelites' conquest of the Promised Land occurred amid large-scale upheaval in the twelfth century B.C.E., their exile to Babylon occurred amid a similar period in the sixth century B.C.E. Societies had grown far more complex since Sumer, which now allowed domineering nation-states to accrue more disposable income and, among other things, gave rise to a more influential intellectual class. The prophets in Israel reached their apogee at the same time Siddhartha Buddha was preaching in India and Nepal, Confucius was teaching in China, Zoroaster was gaining influence in Iran, and the Pythagorean philosophers were writing in Greece. Scholars have been unable to draw direct, causal relationships among these thinkers, but their confluence suggests broad social change was causing humans to reach for new sources of meaning in their lives.

Second, not that many Judaeans appear to have been shipped off to Babylon. Jeremiah puts the number at 4,600, though that probably refers only to men and, like all biblical numbers, is hardly reliable. More telling, Jeremiah talks of a "remnant" who stayed behind in Judah and reports that after the conflagration of 586 subsided, Judaeans returned from surrounding areas. In all likelihood only the most landed, the most learned, and the most monied of Israelites were deported, which means the turmoil to the society may have been great but so would that elite population's ability to regroup in Mesopotamia have been.

Which leads to the third and most significant point: Babylon wasn't that bad for the Israelites who lived there. Details are impossible to come by, and plenty of mournful remembrances survive in the Bible, such as Ezekiel's famous plaint that Israel in exile had become "dry bones." But far more clues suggest that the Israelites lived a full and fruitful existence in Babylon. Jeremiah 29 reproduces a remarkable letter that the prophet sent to "the priests, the prophets, the rest of the elders of the exile community, and to all the people whom Nebuchadnezzar had exiled from Jerusalem to Babylon." Jeremiah quotes God as commanding the Israelites:

> Build houses and live in them, plant gardens and eat their fruit. Take wives and beget sons and daughters; and take wives for your sons, and give your daughters to husbands, that they may bear sons and daughters. Multiply there, do not decrease. And seek the welfare of the city to which I have exiled you and pray to the Lord in its behalf; for in its prosperity you shall prosper.

Babylon is not anathema to Israelite prosperity, God suggests; in fact, Israelite prosperity *depends* on Babylon's success. The defeated must strive to make their conquerors excel, for in so doing they ensure their own success. Exile, God reiterates, can be *good*. "I will single out for good the Judaean exiles whom I have driven out from this place to the land of the Chaldeans," God says in Jeremiah 24, using the word *Chaldean* to suggest the deportees have returned to the birthplace of Abraham. "I will look upon them favorably, and I will bring them back to this land."

The biggest challenge the Israelites faced in the Exile was answering the question Where is God? During the monarchy, the Israelites had believed that God dwelled in his house in Jerusalem and promised that the House of David would reign forever. If so, what happened to God when his house was sacked and David's heir deported? Did God exist anymore? Here the prophets made their most profound contribution to Western religion. Ezekiel, writing during the Exile, declared that God's real presence was not to be confused with his temporary presence on earth. Ezekiel speaks of watching God's spirit leave the Temple Mount, then visit him in Babylon. Ezekiel relates the Israelites' experience in exile to their experience in the Exodus: Just as God showed dominion over Israel *no matter where they were*, including Egypt, so God shows dominion in Babylon: "As I entered into judgment with your fathers in the wilderness in the land of Egypt, so I will enter into judgment with you."

The importance of this message to the future of religion cannot be overstated. From the moment God promises land to Abraham until Moses' death on Mount Nebo, the underlying theme of the biblical story is that wandering is only a temporary state for the Israelites. Their destiny lies on the land, where they will fulfill God's vision and create a holy community on earth. This idea is consistent with Ancient Near Eastern religion at the time, in which gods were affixed to different locations. But the Israelites' experience of living on the land goes horribly wrong, of course, and the prophets must deliver a different message: Wandering is holy, too. God is not exclusively a figure of the land; he's also a figure of the wilderness. He's a figure of *all lands*.

God is everywhere.

This simple idea changed the world because it meant the god of the Israelites did not reside just on a mountaintop in Jerusalem—he could live along the banks of the Euphrates, on the shores of the Nile, or alongside any river or mountain, anyplace in the world. This notion could have been a mere platitudinous response to the crisis, but it took hold because of how the Israelites responded to their national trauma. The towering significance of what happened by the rivers of Babylon is that the Israelites did not merely weep; they set about redefining what it meant to worship God. They invented Judaism.

The exact details of this birthing are not clear. Some of the exiled Judaeans clearly began to worship other gods; some seem to have suggested rebuilding the Temple in Babylon. But the majority seem to have understood that the bulk of their practices from Jerusalem were dead and that they needed new ways to honor, debate, and interact with God. One idea they adopted was to gather in small groups and discuss the words of the Lord. These congregations, "by the walls and in the doorways of their houses," as Ezekiel puts it, were temporary human sanctuaries that could replace the displaced holy sanctuary. These congregations were also more populist than the Temple in Jerusalem, which was limited to the priests. Later these sanctuaries would mature into synagogues.

Another custom that rose to prominence was celebrating the Sabbath. The idea of taking one day a week to rest, renew, and honor God goes back to the first wilderness experience in the Sinai. But as Jeremiah notes, the tradition never stuck: "They would not listen or turn their ear; they stiffened their necks and would not pay heed or accept discipline." So the prophets trot out the idea again and this time raise the stakes. As Isaiah notes, redemption now depends on obedience.

If you call the sabbath "delight,"
The Lord's holy day "honored";
And if you honor it and go not your ways
Nor look to your affairs, nor strike bargains—
Then you can seek the favor of the Lord.

With the loss of holy space, holy time becomes important.

A further notion that grew out of the Exile involved distinguishing the Israelites from their neighbors. Among so many different conquered people walking the streets of Babylon, the Judaeans were deeply concerned with maintaining their sacred identity. Ideas such as ritual purity, circumcision, and marrying only within their own community took on heightened, ritualistic meaning. We are witnessing the emergence of a religion.

But the sine qua non of this evolution was the elevation of text to the core of the faith. The importance of narrative and written law to Israelite religion had been emerging for many centuries, going back to the Ten Commandments, the first thing written down in the biblical story. This appreciation of recorded words continued to evolve through the monarchy, when portions of the written Bible began to enter Israelite public life. But the Exile accelerated this tendency. With no access to sacred sites, sacred text became Israel's lifeline to its past. As Jeremiah's letter to the exiles indicates, priests were becoming more important—and more focused on directly serving the population, not just worshiping God in the Temple. They began to edit the myriad of oral and written traditions of Israelite history and combined them into a unified canon. The Bible may not have been born in Babylon, but it certainly came of age here.

This maturation may be one reason why the final version of the Hebrew Bible contains so many references to Mesopotamia. "Here we are sitting by the Ishtar Gate," Dr. Russell said. We had settled at the base of the ruin in one of the sharp shadows created by the midday sun. Dr. Russell spoke slowly, searching for each word carefully, but his thoughts came out as fully formed paragraphs.

"The Judaean population was here," he continued. "It's interesting that when they wrote down their early history, the stories have a very local flavor. The Garden of Eden got placed here. The Flood sounds indigenous. The same with the Tower of Babel. If you look past the palace"—he gestured to his left—"just down that street was the ziggurat. Traditionally, big imperial constructions were built by populations subjected by a king. So figure in 586, Nebuchadnezzar had captured Jerusalem and brought the Judaean population into southern Mesopotamia and employed them to help with the ziggurat. And it must have been a struggle for those folks to maintain their identity, because you walk the streets of Babylon, and how many languages would you hear? Languages from Iran, from Turkey, from Arabia, from Egypt. You would have heard languages from everywhere. And it must have been interesting for the Israelites to speculate how it got that way. Here's the greatest city in the world, with so many languages spoken, and this huge tower nearby. Maybe one of them started telling a story. . . ."

A minority of biblical scholars, cognizant of these influences, suggest the Israelite intelligentsia invented the early stories of Genesis during the Exile. More propose, as I have come to believe, that the stories have deep oral roots that stretch back to an earlier time, perhaps as early as the patriarchs, and the stories were just edited and written down during this period. But that option raises prickly questions as well.

"Setting these stories in Mesopotamia may make sense because the Israelites were here," I said to Dr. Russell, "but it seems to contradict one goal of the Bible, which is to glorify the Promised Land. Part of me thinks the Bible prefers the Israelites when they're not on the land to when they are."

"The challenge for any exile population is not to assimilate," Dr. Russell said. "To me, the biblical epic is a model for a people in exile. It gives the people a Mesopotamian origin, then describes one member of their family, Abraham, traveling west toward Israel. He becomes a role model to follow. 'Here we are. Our ancestors started here. After some troubles, they ended up in the Promised Land. We should do the same thing as soon as we can.' If you're stuck here and you want to go back there, you start constructing your narrative so that people will see that as a desirable goal."

"So given the fact that Babylon was the superpower of the day," I said, "and the Israelites the vanquished minority, why is it that Babylonian culture did not survive and Israelite culture did?"

"There is something very compelling about the narrative of a people who are always in trouble, who are always facing adversity, but who have a common identity and a common God. You don't find that in Babylonian religion. There's not a single-minded devotion to a single theological figure. They've got a multitude of gods. You move from one city to another and different gods have authority.

"The Israelites, in Babylon, begin to develop a universal religion," he continued. "When you begin to think you can practice a religion without it being tied to a single place, without God being in the Temple but being in other places, too, that's a revolutionary idea. And it allows the religion, the god, to survive anywhere."

I don't really remember dreaming of Babylon as a child. The city doesn't have an iconic building, like the pyramids or the Parthenon. It doesn't have a huggable hero, like Sinbad or Aladdin. It doesn't have a defining postcard image, like the Dome of the Rock or the carved temples of Petra. The only things readily associated with Babylon are its hanging gardens, but no one knows what they looked like. Thirty-five years behind Saddam's iron curtain just made the situation worse. Virtually no pictures of Babylon appear in photo books. For all practical purposes, Babylon is anonymous. Even after years of studying the Bible, I had no idea what to expect when I entered its walls.

I was stunned. Babylon was a huge city, with evidence of power at every turn—thick walls, intricate carvings, elaborate canals, sophisticated architectural details. The Ishtar Gate, for example, is built with interlocking joints so it will not collapse if the ground softens during a flood. Most of all, I was struck by how the city reflects a mastery of advanced mathematics. Math has deep roots in Mesopotamia; the Sumerians were the first to parcel the day into twenty-four hours and the circle into 360 parts. The Babylonians went further, perfecting the use of the sundial, the water clock, and the lunar calendar, in which the year consisted of twelve months of either twenty-nine or thirty days with an extra month inserted regularly. The ziggurat of Babylon was oriented to the four cardinal points of the compass.

This sophistication surprised me, I think, because I still viewed the city through Bible-colored glasses. Despite years of studying ancient societies, part of me still instinctively looked down on Mesopotamian cultures as having a god of the sun, for example, and a god of the moon. These ideas may have helped them invent civilization, but they are so outmoded today that they seem emblematic of a young society, still clinging to its agrarian roots.

But walking around Babylon, I could no longer sustain my knee-jerk superiority. The elaborate temple of Ninmakh, for example, the god of the underworld, and another to the god of the moon, Sin, reinforce the deep parallels between religion and science in the ancient world. Adoration of the moon and stars inspired the Babylonians to devise the most advanced astrology in the Fertile Crescent. Some scholars suggest ziggurats were built, in part, as observatories to assist priests in making astrological calculations.

Moreover, on rereading the Bible, I realized that the text doesn't condescend to the accomplishment of the Mesopotamians at all. In fact, the Bible openly honors them. At the height of their power, in the sixth century B.C.E., the Babylonians were known across the region as *Chaldeans*. This name was taken from the Arabian tribe that settled in central Mesopotamia in the ninth century B.C.E. and

eventually seized control over the kingdom. Both King Nabopolassar and his son, Nebuchadnezzar II, were from the Chaldean,
tribe. *Chaldeans*, the term Genesis affixes to Abraham's compatri-
ots, is the name that Jeremiah, Isaiah, Ezekiel, and other prophets
assign to the Babylonians. Herodotus, the Greek historian who
described Babylon in the mid–fifth century B.C.E. as "surpassing in
splendor any city of the known world," also called its residents
Chaldeans.

Far from an insult, *Chaldeans* was a term of respect. The Babylonians were so associated with cutting-edge scientific thinking that
the word *Chaldean* came to mean "astronomer" across the Fertile
Crescent and into Greece. That the editors of Genesis appear to
have retroactively applied this term to Abraham nearly fifteen hundred years earlier suggests the Israelites, far from condescending to
their captors, wanted to show they were *de*scended from them. The
Babylonians were not barbarians. They were not philistines. They
were the Oxonians of their day. And since the Israelites could not
defeat them, they decided to join them.

But how smart were the Babylonians? Did they rewrite the laws
of gravity? On the northern limits of the city is a mound where
Nebuchadnezzar erected his summer palace. Few remains are visible today. After years of excavations beginning in 1899, the German archaeologist Robert Koldewey uncovered here a citadel,
built on stone arches. Stone was rare in Babylon, which relied
mostly on mud bricks. Koldewey plowed through ancient sources
until he found a mention of an unusual construction. "Ta da!" he
declared. He had discovered the Hanging Gardens.

The Hanging Gardens of Babylon are like the Lost City of Atlantis: Everything we know about them comes from people who
never saw them. Accounts suggest the gardens were built by Nebuchadnezzar II to comfort his homesick wife Amyitis, who came
from Medes, in modern-day Iran. Medes was mountainous and

green, as compared with the baked flatland of Babylon. This story is certainly romantic, but no evidence exists to support it. In fact, no contemporaneous descriptions of the gardens have been found. Herodotus, who arrived a century and a half later, didn't mention them, which suggests they were gone by the time he got there.

The first discussion of hanging gardens comes from the Greek geographer Strabo, who in the first century B.C.E. (five hundred years after Nebuchadnezzar II) described gardens consisting of "vaulted terraces raised one above another, and resting upon cube-shaped pillars. These pillars are hollow and filled with earth to allow trees of the largest size to be planted." One reached the highest story by stairs, Strabo said, along which ran something akin to water elevators, "which are continually employed in raising water from the Euphrates to the garden." The entire construction was said to be four hundred feet square and eighty feet high, more than twice the footprint of the ziggurat but around the same height. But even the gardens described do not hang in the sense of being suspended from anything; the name comes from an inexact translation of the Greek *kremastos*, which means not "hanging" but "overhanging," as in dripping over a balcony or terrace, like ivy cascading from a window box.

Despite the lack of evidence, the gardens were famous enough to be included in the original list of seven wonders (literally "must-sees") of the ancient world, compiled by the Greek poet Antipater of Sidon around 140 B.C.E. The list included, in chronological order: (1) the pyramids of Giza; (2) the walls of Babylon; (3) the hanging gardens of Babylon; (4) the statue of Zeus at Olympus; (5) the temple of Artemis in Ephesus, Turkey; (6) the mausoleum of Governor Mausolus in Bodrum, Turkey; and (7) the colossus of Rhodes. By most accounts, one of the more famous items considered to be one of the original seven wonders, the lighthouse at Alexandria, seems to have been added centuries later in lieu of the walls of Babylon.

So why has something mythical endured as the most famous legacy of Babylon?

"I think the Hanging Gardens are like a mirror," Dr. Russell said. We were strolling up the central processional on our way to Nebuchadnezzar II's palace. The sun was beating on the sidewalk. Babylon was empty, except for us. "Look at the Hanging Gardens and you see yourself. It's pretty clear that nobody who wrote about them had ever seen them, and the descriptions that survive would have been technically impossible at the time."

"If that's so, then why was it so mythologized, and why were people so eager to believe the myth?"

"Gardens were not mere playgrounds in the Ancient Near East," he said. "They were important political statements. We have Assyrian accounts that describe how after the kings campaigned across the region, they came back home and built a garden that was evocative of the land they had just conquered. You built a model in your capital of the place you'd annexed. Gardens were not designed to please your wife; they were to remind the people of the extent of your realm and to bring examples of the flora and fauna from all over the realm into one place. They're a kind of zoological and botanical microcosm of the empire."

"Does the Garden of Eden evoke the same idea?"

"Absolutely. It's a kind of center of the world, isn't it? With one giant river, which divides into four rivers, which then flow around the world. Plus all sorts of different animals and trees. It's very much like a Mesopotamian royal garden. Only in its case, the ruler is God."

"What's interesting about Babylon," I said, "is that while the sun and the moon gods have long since disappeared, the gardens are the one idea that has endured."

"People love gardens," Dr. Russell said. "They can suggest power, they can suggest beauty. But above all they're a way for humans to mold something into the image they choose. They're not like the stars, which we can't control. Gardens are humans exercising control over nature. They are our Creation. They are a way for us to play God."

We entered Nebuchadnezzar II's palace. Reconstructed walls of caramel-colored bricks climbed forty feet high, topped with hundreds of small pyramidal merlons. The walls were interrupted with elongated arches, more than two stories tall, that allowed vistas from room to room in the multichambered complex. The concrete floor was empty in each room, and there was no roof. Altogether the feeling was like standing in a half-completed mock-up of Buckingham Palace—only there was no grandeur, just quiet strength.

But this palace was no longer alone. Standing at the entrance to Nebuchadnezzar II's headquarters, one looks over a lawn of ruins, stumps of foundations and hints of walls that have not been reconstructed. Above this yard, on the highest hill in Babylon, is a totally new palace, two stories tall, built of red and white marble in receding tiers in a direct echo of a ziggurat. This palace had belonged to Saddam Hussein.

Saddam's interest in Babylon had largely to do with bolstering Iraqi pride during the country's decade-long quagmire with Iran, and burnishing his claim to be leader of a pan-Arab resurgence. He touted Nebuchadnezzar II's destruction of Jerusalem as a herald of the Arabs' impending defeat of Israel. "Nebuchadnezzar was the one who brought the bound Jewish slaves from Palestine," he said. "That is why, whenever I remember Nebuchadnezzar, I like to remind the Arabs—Iraqis in particular—of their historical responsibilities. It is a burden that should not stop them from action but rather spur them into action because of their history."

Saddam's efforts had curious effects. On the one hand, by turning the ruins into his backyard, he guaranteed that Babylon was
one of Iraq's few ancient sites to receive money for preservation
and was not open to widespread looting during his tenure. On the
other hand, his lording over the complex sent a number of apoca-
lyptic Christians into a frenzy of doomsday prognostication.

Some Christians believe the reconstruction of Babylon is a crucial step that will precede the Second Coming of Jesus Christ. This
idea is hinted at in Revelation, the sometimes cryptic final book of
the New Testament, which forecasts the end of time. In Revelation, Babylon is described as the "mother of whores and of earth's
abominations," the Antichrist, whom God will soon destroy.

Fallen, fallen is Babylon the Great!
It has become a dwelling place of demons.
For all the nations have drunk
of the wine of the wrath of her fornication
and the kings of the earth have committed fornication with her,
and the merchants of the earth have grown rich
from the power of her luxury.

These references to Babylon in the New Testament, not the
citations in the Hebrew Prophets, are the source of the contemporary usage of *Babylon* as a place of sin and debauchery.

As long as Babylon lay in ruins, however, which was most of the
last two thousand years, the apocalypse could not happen. When
word of Saddam's rebuilding spread, a wave of pamphlets and books
flooded the evangelical community in the United States, suggesting
that the end of time was one step closer. "Here was another thrilling
proof that Bible prophecies are infallible," writes Charles Dyer in
The Rise of Babylon: Is Iraq at the Center of the Final Drama? And what
do those prophecies show? "Babylon is destined for devastation,"

Dyer explains, "but Jerusalem is destined for deliverance." Babylon is the great prostitute; Jerusalem is the bride, the wife of the Lamb. "When God's final curtain falls on the world stage, only one of these cities will remain, and she will remain forever."

Once again, the Middle East had produced a rich religious snare: Saddam rebuilt Babylon as a way to prophesy the fall of Israel, while his rebuilding was seen by some lovers of Israel as a way to prophesy the fall of Babylon. Babylon had become like the Temple Mount, another battleground in the struggle over God.

S o may I ask you a question?" I said to Dr. Russell. "Why did you come here?"

We were standing before a reconstructed cement proscenium stage in a long, narrow room of Nebuchadnezzar II's palace. On the wall was an arch with three perimeter pipings of brick that gave the niche a quiet regality. The king would sit here to receive visitors, Dr. Russell said, and the wall behind him would have been decorated with lions marching toward him from either side. Dr. Russell asked me to snap his picture on the platform, a reminder of how privileged we both felt to be here.

"Because I was willing to come," he said.

"What has been the best part of your job?"

"Repairing the Iraq Museum in Baghdad. Undoing twenty-four years of deferred maintenance and neglect under Saddam, plus some rather nasty looting at the end of the war. Putting a roof over Sennacherib's palace in Nineveh. Arranging for Iraqi scholars to travel to the United States. What I hope I'll be leaving is a community that got back on its feet, when Iraqi scholarship, the Iraqi museum, and Iraqi archaeology rejoined the world."

"And what's the worst thing you discovered, archaeologically?"

"The real disaster has been the looting," he said. "I flew in a helicopter recently over a few of the country's ten thousand sites. Major sites that would have taken centuries to excavate, every one of which would have rewritten our history books countless times over, are just gone. Ruined. The damage in only a few months is incalculable. We've gotten a few of the sites under protection, but most are still being stripped as we speak. It's the single worst disaster to our Mesopotamian heritage that's ever happened. Substantial parts of our past in Sumer and Babylon have been destroyed, and we'll never know what we lost."

"Is it possible that some remains exist because the looters don't have the sophistication to dig deep enough?"

"Oh, they're really sophisticated. They're organized into gangs, and they go *very* deep. They're digging through houses, temples, palaces, city walls, neighborhoods, cemeteries."

"So even if those objects show up in private collections in Tokyo, London, or Chicago, they will still be worthless?"

"There are only two values to an artifact," Dr. Russell said. "One is its commodity value, which appeals to certain selfish collectors. The other is as part of our human past, which collectors don't care about but most people do. Objects mean nothing unless you find them in context. They're just pretty pieces of stone. The only thing that gives an object value is if you find it in the grave of the person it was buried with, or in the palace where it was used. It doesn't matter how many pieces are out, the only ones that count are the ones that are still in the ground."

"So give me an example of a question we're not going to know the answer to, because this stuff is gone," I said.

"The great thing about archaeology," he said, "is that every excavation raises questions you didn't even think to ask. Every excavation that I've ever been involved with causes fundamental changes in what we think. Now, we'll never know what we're missing."

"So how do you feel about this?"

He raised his voice. "It's awful! I mean, what kind of people are we that we can neglect our past and that part of ourselves that is so fundamental for us as civilized beings? I worry because we call this the Cradle of Civilization. If we destroy this, what does that make us?"

"One of the most famous lines in the Bible," I said, "is 'By the rivers of Babylon, there we sat, sat and wept—'"

He cut me off. "You can't fly over completely ruined sites, hundreds of square miles of our past that's been destroyed, and not weep."

A shadow crossed his face. I looked up at the sun. We had reached the end of our day. And somehow it seemed fitting that we would end on this note. Most of the writing about exile in the Bible ends with hope. God will redeem the Israelites. He will send them back to the land. He will restore them to Eden.

Yet the most famous passage about Babylon ends on a darker note. Psalm 137, the one that begins "By the rivers of Babylon," goes on to describe how the Babylonians mock the Israelites. "Sing us one of those songs of Zion," they cry. The Israelites lash out at their tormentors. The psalm ends with these bloodcurdling words:

Fair Babylon, you predator,
a blessing on him who repays you in kind
what you have inflicted on us;
a blessing on him who seizes your babies
and dashes them against the rocks!

The Israelites, so exasperated by the cruelty they perceive in the Babylonians, want to repay their captors with cruelty of their own.

Why did a psalm with such an ignominious final outburst become so popular in Judaism and Christianity? Perhaps because it represents a fundamental truth. In moments of testing, humans will act like humans, complete with pettiness, vengeance, and bile. The Bible does not whitewash this struggle. And in presenting this blunt portrait, the text poses a challenge for each of us: When faced with unimaginable trials, will we weep for what we have lost or rise up and build something new? When faced with evil in others, will we treat our tormentors with violence or compassion?

One surprising theme of the prophets is that humans don't get off easy. The prophets don't preach that God is omnipotent and humans mere pawns. Everything on earth does not reflect divine will. God may be able to control foreign leaders, as he does upon summoning Nebuchadnezzar to destroy Jerusalem, but he can't control his own people. For that he has given humans a will of their own. The relationship between heaven and earth is one in which humans constantly disappoint God and God prods them to accept his wisdom. "Now are you ready to accept me?"

In that way, John Russell was right. At the bottom of Babylon I did find a question, and it was not one I expected. It was a voice, deep in the past, wondering: Will you remember Babylon? Will you remember that you once were hopeless here? Will you recall that in that moment of helplessness you finally reached the point where you came face-to-face with your own inhumanity and realized that the only way to ensure your survival was to call out to God?

What's startling about Psalm 137 is God's response. When the Israelites beg for permission to destroy their enemy, God does not reply. With his silence, he answers. They must decide for themselves.

The surprising lesson of the Exile is that God does not abandon us in moments of despair, nor does he save us. He gives us the freedom to choose for ourselves. As history suggests, in moments of chaos, some people will flee God, some will try to smash babies against rocks, some will loot the treasuries of our past. But others will find new ways to reach out to the divine, will cradle the youths of their enemies; will hold out their arms to stop the destruction. Some will find hope among the ruins.

Psalm 137 endures precisely because it captures this essential truth of Western faith. In the relationship between humans and God, humans actually have enormous power. We are the ones who control our own behavior. Only we can save ourselves from exile. By the rivers of Babylon, we should not weep for Zion. We should not seek vengeance on our enemies.

We should redeem ourselves.

. 4 .

CITY OF PEACE

I knew my heart had warmed to Iraq when we motored back into Baghdad, and without thinking, I exclaimed, "It's nice to be home." After the pirate-infested roads of the south, Baghdad felt almost safe, even indulgent. The hot-and-cold running water in the Flowers Land Hotel felt like a luxury after so many icy showers. The generator that kept me awake at night seemed like a godsend after terrifying nights spent shivering in darkness once the daily allotment of electricity had expired. The fried rice with canned chow-mein sauce tasted like peach pie in August after only chicken and bread. I attended a party where more than one hundred foreign correspondents traded war stories and lascivious glances, and I even ran into several people I know, including a reporter for *The New York Times* who had written an announcement about my wedding. We embraced.

I never would have believed it, but Baghdad in wartime felt like the center of the world, a status the storied "City of Peace" had not enjoyed for almost eight hundred years.

As I set out to explore the Iraq National Museum, the lone synagogue, and an underground effort by a U.S. soldier to kindle interfaith relations in the capital, I wondered if Iraq would yield to the demons of religion—civil war, sectarian violence, and terror—or rise to the higher angels of faith—tolerance, compassion, and peace. Once again, what happened in Mesopotamia would define the future of the Middle East.

Baghdad was still tense. Large portions of the city were no-go zones for foreigners. The streets were littered with roadblocks, as well as the remains of vehicles, buildings, or trees that had been singed by suicide bombs. Hikmat, our fixer, showed up at the hotel one day to announce that the previous evening a car appeared in front of his neighbor's house, the driver asked the neighbor whether he was so-and-so, who once worked at the Interior Ministry, then the driver assassinated the man with two gunshots to the head. The neighbor's young children were watching from the window.

But I was equally startled to realize how much of the city continued to function. The streets neither teem like those of Cairo nor gleam like those of Kuwait City, but they do stretch in stately fashion from the banks of the Tigris, which wends it way through upscale shopping neighborhoods and a leafy embassy quarter like the Thames through London. Baghdad is hardly flush with parks; precast cement is more common. But shops were open; air conditioners and satellite dishes bloomed from every corner; and money changers sat every ten feet trading the old Saddam-faced currency for new tender honoring the country's history, including Hammurabi.

Maybe it comes from enduring three wars in twenty-five years, sanctions, and an unpredictable homicidal dictator, but Iraqis I met were inveterate problem solvers. My tape recorder broke, and within an hour I had found a replacement, a Sony, of higher quality. I dropped my camera while being searched one morning, and

Hikmat easily found a vendor who specialized in fixing Nikon lenses. Iraq may be the only place I've ever been that didn't have Coca-Cola, but nearly everything else seemed available, for a price. Everything, that is, except peace of mind.

"Is your life better or worse today?" I asked Ghaleb Nicolas, the electronics shopkeeper who sold me a tape recorder for forty U.S. dollars. He was a Catholic who had a postcard of the Virgin Mary taped over his cash register. He attended church twice a year.

"For me, no different," he said. "There are good things. I have a mobile." He reached into his blue jeans and showed me his Nokia cell phone. "But we lose something, also. Security." He reached into his other pocket and pulled out a pistol. "My neighbor had his daughter kidnapped. They asked for $25,000."

"Did they pay it?"

"They had no choice. Now she doesn't go to school. I have a family. I can't go to a restaurant. In a few minutes we close. I will go to my house and stay, until tomorrow."

"So what is your dream?" I asked.

"The same as yours."

Baghdad has faint roots in antiquity; a legal document from Hammurabi mentions a city called Bagdadu. But the city did not flower until the spread of Islam, following the death of Mohammed in 632 C.E. The Umayyad dynasty, founded in Damascus soon after the Prophet's death, made Arabic the official language and built monuments across the region, including the Dome of the Rock. Plagued by internal rivalry, the Umayyads were toppled by the Abbasids, descendants of Mohammed's uncle, who in 762 moved the capital to Baghdad. A meeting place of rivers and caravan routes, Baghdad had the added benefit of fertile land and no malaria. Its name comes either from the Aramaic term for "sheep enclosure" or the Persian phrase for "gift of God."

Built in a circle—yet another carefully planned city—Baghdad quickly became the cultural center of the medieval world. It's often hard to remember today, when Middle Eastern capitals are riddled with backwardness and rife with anti-Western rage, that cities like Baghdad were once bastions of science, philosophy, and medicine, centuries ahead of their European counterparts, which were still mired in the Dark Ages. The Abbasid caliph Mamun imported texts by Plato, Aristotle, Hippocrates, and others, which he had translated into Arabic. The Koran, he declared, could be interpreted for contemporary lives. The Baghdad Renaissance, at least half a millennium before a similar flowering in Italy, contributed to the collection of Indian, Persian, and Arab folktales known as *The Thousand and One Nights*. These stories introduced Sinbad the Sailor, based on Muslim traders; Aladdin, the Chinese boy who summons a genie from an oil lamp; and Ali Baba and the Forty Thieves. The tales continue to influence life today: the thugs who troll the streets of modern-day Iraq are called *ali baba*.

Baghdad remained a cultural and commercial hub until 1258, when it was sacked by the Mongols, who killed 800,000 people, a blow from which Arab civilization has never recovered. Osama bin Laden, among others, has looked to this moment for inspiration. In 2003, on the eve of Operation Iraqi Freedom, he quoted Ibn Taymiyya, a forerunner of extremist Islam, who in the thirteenth century exhorted Muslims to fight the infidels. "To fight in the defense of religion and belief is a collective duty," Ibn Taymiyya said. "There is no other duty after belief than fighting, the enemy who is corrupting the life and the religion." The Mongols were led by Hulagu Khan, the grandson of Genghis Khan. After the American-led invasion of Iraq, bin Laden issued another statement, saying, "Cheney and Powell killed and destroyed in Baghdad more than Hulagu of the Mongols." One difference in the worldviews of the West and Islamic extremists is that some fundamentalist Christians viewed the war in Iraq as a replay of the fall of Babylon, which they believe God prophesied in the Bible, while some fundamentalist Muslims viewed it as a replay of the fall of Baghdad, which they believe God promised to avoid in the Koran. Few on either side seem aware of the other view.

The Mongols were not empire builders, and eventually they left the region to the Ottomans. Baghdad was a backwater capital in the Turkish realm until the British took control in 1917. The British imagined they would be welcomed as liberators but ran headfirst into nascent Iraqi nationalism and were perceived as occupiers. They quickly granted the country independence and appointed a king, but successive governments proved too weak. The Arab Baath (or Renaissance) Socialist Party stepped in to fill the void, executing a coup in 1963. Saddam Hussein, from the northern town of Tikrit, became president in 1979. Secularism seemed ascendant in Iraq.

Iraq's back-and-forth between Western-inspired secularism and Islamic-based theocracy is evident in its streets. Baghdad in the 1950s was a fertile testing ground for Modernist architecture, with designs by Walter Gropius and Frank Lloyd Wright. Wright conceived an elaborate island compound in the middle of the Tigris and dubbed it Edena. Complete with a circular opera house capped by a statue of Aladdin, as well as a three-hundred-foot spiral tower adorned with camels, his design was abandoned as an embarrassment of Western chauvinism.

Saddam at first tried to strengthen ties to the West, sending architects to view St. Paul's Cathedral in London, the Alhambra in Spain, and I. M. Pei's glass pyramid at the Louvre, the last two being creative bridges between East and West. But chastened by his foray into Iran, Saddam was forced to curry loyalty from the people by building more mosques, including the "Mother of All Battles" Mosque, with four minarets shaped like Kalashnikovs and four like Scud missiles. By century's end, militant Islam was ascendant in Iraq.

But militancy has a cost. The single most striking thing about driving around Baghdad was seeing the impact of U.S. bombs. Nearly every government building was charred, its innards a tangle of twisted steel, its floors collapsed like a sad, discarded accordion. Yet in most cases, the buildings next door, the shops around the corner, the apartments just behind, were operating as if nothing had happened. Baghdad made me a believer in smart bombs. More poignant, in front of these office buildings and in the center of traffic circles were an endless number of shoulder-high concrete platforms with nothing on top. At first I didn't even notice them, but then I realized: They once held statues of Saddam Hussein. The man who deemed himself the heir to Nebuchadnezzar II was reduced to ruins as forlorn as the crumbled walls of Babylon.

Statues were not the only place where Saddam trumpeted his face. The dour visage with charcoal mustache appeared on brick billboards in front of many buildings, on posters on many lampposts, and in windows of many shops. Most of these images were defaced in some way, though few were erased entirely, leaving hints of a cold stare to peer through the destruction like blinking eyes in a rat hole, threatening to scurry back into the room and spoil the party. One missing image gave me chills. On the west bank of the Tigris, not far from the Central Rail Station, another replica of an ancient gate rises at the end of a small street. This gate was from Nineveh and has two bulls with human heads at its base. On top, where a carving of the king should have been, was a black hole that, until recently, had held the bust of Saddam. This gate marks the entrance to the Iraq National Museum.

Founded in 1923, the Iraq National Museum has always been entangled with politics. The museum was the brainchild of Gertrude Bell, the "Uncrowned Queen of Mesopotamia," the Victorian-born, Oxford-educated English explorer who was among the most influential Westerners in the twentieth-century Middle East. After traveling around Persia, photographing Jerusalem, and learning Arabic, Bell was recruited to serve under T. E. Lawrence in British intelligence during World War I. When the war ended, she became Oriental secretary in Iraq and personally drew the somewhat nonsensical borders the country has today, including Basra to the south and Mosul to the north, the latter of which had not previously been connected to the rest of the country. Her goal was to make the country an asset for Britain. "It's an amusing game when you know the country intimately," she wrote her parents. "I feel at times like the Creator about the middle of the week. He must have wondered what it was going to be like, as I do."

Bell decorated the new palace of King Faisal, whom the British appointed in 1921, and set aside a room for antiquities. In return, the king appointed her director of antiquities, a thankless job she quickly turned into a powerhouse. Iraq was rife with foreign excavators who wanted to expand their digs and, like Koldewey with the Ishtar Gate, cart their finds back home. Bell had other ideas. In a precursor to Saddam, she believed that promoting Mesopotamian history in Iraq would help persuade the Arabs they once dominated the region and could do so again (with the help from British minders, of course). She demanded that archaeologists like Woolley, whom she tagged a "tired, little man" but a "first class digger," leave 50 percent of their findings in country. She personally traveled to Ur to pick out the objects she wanted.

In Baghdad she went even further. "I've been spending most of the morning at the Ministry of Works," she wrote her father, "where we are starting—what do you think? The Iraq Museum! It will be a modest beginning, but it is a beginning." In June 1926, King Faisal dedicated the first room. One month later, suffering from depression and pushed aside by London, who found her an apologist for the Iraqi king, Gertrude Bell took an overdose of sleeping pills. She was two days shy of fifty-eight years old. In her will she left fifty thousand pounds sterling to the museum. A bronze bust was placed in its entrance in her honor.

An expanded complex, which still stands today, opened in 1966. We approached one morning. The compound is the size and style of a small American high school from the same period, with a one-story red-brick building for administration and an adjacent two-story white-brick building that housed the galleries. Palm trees dotted the courtyard, along with a statue of Hammurabi. We were greeted outside by two cordons of Iraqi security, who searched every pocket of my bag and patted down my entire body. A U.S. armored personnel carrier was stationed in front of the door, and a handful of Marines patrolled the roof. The black iron fence was being reinforced. "Better late than never," Hikmat said.

Or maybe not.

Inside we were met by the new Iraqi director of the museum, who was appointed after the war. Donny George is a gregarious roly-poly of a man, with a buoyant, gray, curly hairdo, and a tidy gray mustache. He is the spitting image of Buddy Hackett. Dr. George invited us into the galleries and explained how he became an archaeologist. "I always loved the outdoor life," he said. "As a boy I was a fisherman and enjoyed hunting with my father. I was offered a slot in college in the French Department. But I didn't want to spend four years studying French, so I said to the dean, 'What else do you have?' He said, 'Theology, Arabic literature, and archaeology.' I said, 'Just a moment, are those people who go outside, make excavations, and stay in tents?' He said, 'Yes.' I said, 'I love that.'"

"So did you get to spend a lot of time in tents?"

"Oh, yes. My Ph.D. was in a prehistoric site from the sixth millennium B.C.E. I supervised the reconstruction in Babylon, and my last excavation was a Sumerian site in the south."

We arrived at the museum's foyer. The front door was barricaded with wood; plaster littered the floor, along with broken glass and overturned display cases. The room had natural light from an internal courtyard but still seemed sad, even bereft. It felt like a movie set after the big action sequence had been filmed and the crew had gone home without cleaning up. "So what exactly happened here?" I asked.

The U.S. government has a legacy of being sensitive to history in wartime. During World War II, Washington intentionally did not bomb the ancient Japanese capital of Kyoto and took it off the list of possible targets for the atomic bomb. In January 2003, McGuire Gibson, the dean of American Mesopotamia specialists, gave the Pentagon a no-strike list of five thousand sites in Iraq, which the Defense Department posted on an internal website for commanders. Baghdad effectively fell on April 9, 2003, with the symbolic tearing down of Saddam's statue in Firdos Square. The following day, a Thursday, looters penetrated the museum.

"They came through two places," Dr. George said. "One is that window." He pointed next to the front door. "The other is the back door, in the administration area, where we just were. I myself believe they were not normal looters. We did have some hooligans who took all the computers, the desks, and any furniture they could find. But there were other people who came intentionally with the idea of stealing artifacts."

"Who would have had the motivation?" I asked.

"We don't know exactly, but people who came into the galleries knew what they wanted. They broke into a vault in the administration area and got keys to every storeroom. They brought glass cutters. Every single case that was smashed had one masterpiece in it. The cases that were untouched had nothing of significance." I was at first surprised to see the eight-foot-high Code of Hammurabi, one of the most valuable things ever pulled from these sands. Then Dr. George explained: It was a replica.

For three days—the tenth, eleventh, and twelfth—the looting went unchecked. "On the twelfth I heard the news that the museum was being robbed," Dr. George said, "and went to Marine headquarters in the Palestine Hotel and begged for help. They promised they would send immediate help to protect the museum. Unfortunately, they did not." For the next three days, Dr. George and several staffers tried to hold off the increasing crowds. "We just had clubs in our hands. There were hundreds of looters running through the building. Some of them were waving Kalashnikovs. We were afraid they were going to set fire to the entire building."

"On Tuesday, the fifteenth, some journalists from Channel 4 in Britain were here," he continued, "and they offered me the use of their Thuraya phone. It was the first time for me to use that kind of telephone. I telephoned the director of the British Museum. He sent someone to Number 10 Downing Street, and the next morning we had American tanks on the premises."

What happened afterward only inflamed the situation. The press reported that all 170,000 objects in the museum were destroyed. "Nothing remained," the *New York Times* quoted museum officials as saying, "at least nothing of real value." Reacting to the news reports, archaeologists and commentators flooded the airwaves to decry the loss. I was among them, appearing on CNN. The American Schools of Oriental Research called the episode the most severe blow to cultural heritage in modern history, comparable to the sack of Constantinople, the burning of the library at Alexandria, and the Mongol invasion of Baghdad. Stung, U.S. officials snapped back. General Richard Myers, chairman of the Joint Chiefs of Staff, said the decision was a matter of priorities. "If you remember, when some of that looting was going on, people were being killed." Secretary of Defense Donald Rumsfeld said, "Trying to pass off the fact of that unfortunate activity as a deficit in the war plan strikes me as a stretch."

Months later the story proved to be much grayer. The 170,000 figure was grossly exaggerated. "It was kind of a mistake, taken from me," Dr. George said. We had moved upstairs to one of the showrooms, which was filled with empty cases and holes in the wall. "Some journalists asked me the number of objects we had in the museum, and I said over 170,000. That was taken to be the number of objects missing, which was obviously not true. I said we had to check." The number of objects stolen was later put at 14,000. Some of those were taken by supporters of the museum, who stored them in their homes and returned them when security was restored. Through aggressive policing and international cooperation, a total of 5,000 objects were recovered in the coming months. The rest remained at large.

Some believe museum officials may have purposely cooked the numbers to stoke sympathy. "Most people I know share my relief that so much of the collection survived," John Russell said that June. "Yet many also feel that their noble instincts were manipulated not only to produce shock and grief at a loss of such unprecedented magnitude but also to provoke rage at the cultural callousness of the United States in failing to prevent this predictable tragedy. I can sympathize with those who feel conned. For two weeks after the looting I must have been known as the weeping archaeologist."

One positive outcome of Dr. Russell's weeping, along with the rest of the agitation, is that millions of dollars were raised for reconstruction. On this morning, new bookcases and computer equipment filled the halls, waiting to be unwrapped. Dr. George said he hoped to reopen the museum within three years of its stripping. Mesopotamian archaeology had once more been lifted to the front page of the world's consciousness.

"So now that the world has been wakened to the importance of Mesopotamia," I said, "what can we learn from that time that is relevant to today?"

"First we have to know our ancestors. If you want to go further into the future, you have to know your background, exactly as, if you want to shoot an arrow as far forward as possible, you have to first bring the string back as far as you can. Pottery, mining, time, geometry, astronomy, writing. They all started here. That's why I say the heritage of humankind was born here. And that heritage belongs to every single Iraqi.

"I myself am an Assyrian," he continued. "A Christian. The Assyrians are the first people to bring Christianity to this country, in the first century after Christ. But generally speaking, I feel so much like an Iraqi. Most of my relatives are in Chicago and Australia. But I am still here. I do not want to leave."

"And do you feel confident that you will be able to practice your religion openly in the future?"

"For twenty centuries we have lived together in this country," he said. "I don't think we will have problems. I have Muslim neighbors, Shias and Sunnis. We go to their houses, they come to our houses, we dine together, like good Iraqi friends. All my staff are Muslims. They love me, I love them. We don't have this kind of separation."

"So you believe the culture of Mesopotamia will continue to be available to everyone, not just one party, or one religion?"

"Of course. People make history, not leaders. People produce artists, people produce historians, people produce songs."

"So now the leader is gone."

"Exactly. But the people continue, and they are looking for a better future now."

He calls himself the last rabbi of Baghdad.

On a bright sunny morning, Hikmat and I were driving for the fifth time around Al Wahad circle looking for what Emad Levy, in an e-mail, had assured me was known by everyone as the

"Jewish church." But no one seemed to know the Jewish church, or the Jewish synagogue, or the Jewish rabbi. Al Wahad circle is fairly typical; it has a hotel, which was bombed after the war because it housed foreign aid workers; a shop run by Christians that sells beer and wine, which was also bombed because alcohol is forbidden by Islam; and a working flower shop. It also has impenetrable traffic. By informal estimates, the number of cars doubled in the months after the war, as junk models flooded in from neighboring countries. The traffic cops were helpless: poorly trained men in brand-new uniforms who stared a lot at the sky. On our final trudge, a teenage boy jumped from his car and began to direct traffic. At that instant, he could have been elected councilman.

In time we found the proper address, a single-story brick home with an overgrown garden and a swing on the front porch. I rang the bell alongside the white metal fence. No answer. I rang again. A man came hurrying from the front door, tucking on slippers. He was dressed in the same polyester brown slacks that many Iraqis seem to wear, a dark shirt, and a tie. He had a thinning widow's peak, was several days unshaven, and wore a thick, Saddam-style mustache that I was beginning to think had been requisite for survival in the old regime. In his late thirties and almost handsome, Emad was agitated. "You're an hour late," he said.

Scolded for being tardy in a war. I knew I must be in the right place.

Emad invited us into his home, which was dark because of the lack of electricity. Photographs of his family lined the walls, along with faded prints of Moses and embroideries of Hebrew prayers. Several carpets lay rolled up on the floor; he was hoping to sell them to raise enough money to emigrate. Iraq has had a continual presence of Jews since the birth of Judaism here almost 2,600 years ago. But the Jewish population, which was almost 150,000 at the end of World War II, was now down to 22. Emad hoped to shrink the number even further.

"People are crazy here," he said. "Last month someone poisoned my dog, and it died. Maybe they try to intimidate me. But I am not shamed. I am proud to be Jewish."

Emad spoke quickly, in slightly crazed but still impressive English. He sat down next to me but did not stop moving. He acted as if he was being watched.

"For ten years Saddam sent intelligence to follow me," he said. "They listen to my phone. They do everything. Believe me, they send lots of girls to sleep with me."

"They sent girls?" I said. "I don't understand."

"They make love with you and then get you to talk."

My eyes widened. "So what did you *do*?" I asked.

He looked at me as if I would not survive one week in a dictatorship. "I made love with them and kept my mouth shut."

Once the Israelites established themselves in Babylon during the Exile and became Jews, they never really left. As power shifted across the Fertile Crescent from the Babylonians to the Persians to the Greeks to the Romans, some Jews returned to the Promised Land and attempted to reestablish their lives, but an even larger number of them chose not to. These Jews became less and less dependent on their physical connection to Jerusalem and more and more attached to a series of laws that allowed them to function in what amounted to permanent exile. Babylon, for all its natural amenities, proved particularly attractive to these Jews, especially after the destruction of the Second Temple in 70 C.E. In the centuries that followed, Jewish learning thrived in Mesopotamia and gave birth to a book that in many ways would overshadow the Torah as the core text of Judaism.

The Talmud, or "learning," is an authoritative record of rabbinic discussion about Jewish law, ethics, rituals, customs, and history.

The Talmud comprises two main parts: the Mishnah, a compilation of Jewish law that dates from 200 C.E., and the Gemara, which are commentaries on those laws. There is only one Mishnah, but there are two Gemaras. The first was compiled near the Sea of Galilee around 400 C.E. and is known as the Palestinian (or Jerusalem) Talmud; the second was compiled in Babylon around 550 C.E. The Babylonian Talmud, which totals 2.5 million words and covers 5,894 folio pages, is longer than the Palestinian Talmud, easier to read, and was studied more widely across Europe, making it the more influential text. When people today say "the Talmud," they are referring to the Babylonian Talmud.

Unlike the Torah, which offers general rules for how to live, the Talmud is filled with minute detail on how to apply those rules, covering everything from how to light candles on Shabbat to how to conduct a funeral. Beginning in Babylon and continuing through the Middle Ages, study of the Talmud superseded study of the Torah in Jewish life. The Hebrew Bible continued to be the soul of the Jewish people, but the Talmud became their bible. As Avner put it, if Jews are "People of the Book," that book is the Talmud.

In recent centuries, more liberal Jews, including Reform and some Conservative Jews, have begun to rely less heavily on the fine points of Jewish law debated in the Talmud and see it more as a source of inspiration and moral guidance. The Torah, by contrast, has gained in importance because it's more accessible. I, like many American Jews, learned about the Talmud when I was a teenager but never saw a page of its formatted text until I was an adult, and then found it antiquated and arcane. Later I recoiled when I understood how it had supplanted the Bible for many Jews. One of the most inviting parts of religion, its historical narrative, had been overtaken by one of the harshest, its legalism. Now, learning more about the Israelite experience in Babylon and the importance of law as a surrogate for living on the land, I began to appreciate the Talmud as contributing to the survival of Judaism during its many years in exile.

In Babylon, meanwhile, the arrival of Islam in the seventh century did not initially hamper Jewish life. As People of the Book, Jews were considered *dhimmi*, or protected minorities, with higher taxes, restricted clothing, and limits to the types of buildings they could construct. But Jews were allowed to observe their own laws. A Jewish traveler in the twelfth century reported that Baghdad had forty thousand Jews and twenty-eight synagogues.

As elsewhere, in Iraq Muslim attitudes toward Jews did not sour fully until the twentieth century, with the rise of Zionism. In 1941 radical Muslims funded by the German embassy tried to establish a pro-Nazi regime, and a resulting pogrom killed at least 180 Iraqi Jews; more outbreaks followed the founding of Israel in 1948. In 1950 Iraqi Jews were permitted to leave the country. Israel openly encouraged the emigration: "O Zion, flee," came the cry. "Israel is calling you—come out of Babylon!" Within six months more than 100,000 Jews were airlifted to Israel under a program called Operation Ezra and Nehemiah, a reference to two prominent Babylonian Jews who returned to Jerusalem at the conclusion of the Exile. Both have biblical books named after them. Twenty thousand more Jews were smuggled through Iran.

For the 6,000 or so Jews who opted to stay in Iraq, life darkened. Following the Baath party takeover in 1963, Jews were forced to carry yellow identity cards, and they had property and bank accounts seized after the Six-Day War. In 1968 scores were arrested in an alleged spy ring; eleven were sentenced to be hanged in public squares in Baghdad. On January 27, 1969, Baghdad Radio called on all Iraqis to "come and enjoy the feast"; fifty thousand visitors attended public spectacles in front of the scaffolding holding the dead bodies. In response to an international outcry, official radio declared, "We hanged spies, but the Jews crucified Christ." In subsequent months most remaining Jews were allowed to emigrate, leaving about 150 when Saddam took power.

Though Emad Levy was born in 1965, he has memories of the day all Baghdad showed up to watch the Jews being hanged. "They invited all Muslims and Christians to come and eat lunch," he said. "Believe me, they were jealous of the Jews."

As a child, Emad observed Jewish holidays, and he became a Bar Mitzvah in 1979. He learned Hebrew and fasted on the Day of Atonement. "When I was nine years old I started fasting," he said. "Believe me, I try to fast for three days, not one day." Why? "That's the religion, if you love it." His mother died in 1981, and his father began working as a caretaker in the synagogue. Emad got a job selling cars. When the last rabbi left the country in 1999, Emad became acting head of the community. So was he happy when the Americans invaded? "Happy for what?" he said. "Because the rockets can hit us?"

"You weren't happy when Saddam fell?"

"I was very happy about that, because now I am free. Believe me, during the regime of Saddam Hussein I could not meet you. Now you are my brother."

In the first weeks after the fall of Baghdad, Jewish aid workers made a secret mission to Iraq and identified six elderly Jews who wanted to leave. One of them was eighty-two-year-old Ezra Levy, Emad's father. A charter plane was sent from Tel Aviv. A front-page picture in Israel's leading daily showed Levy, a thin-cheeked man with white stubble, arriving at the airport and kissing his sister, whom he had not seen in more than fifty years. "I am a Jew," he said in halting Hebrew. "I feel very happy and privileged that I am in this place." He then recited part of Hayim Bialik's poem "The Bird," which he had learned in Hebrew as a boy.

Do you bring me friendly greetings
From my brothers there in Zion,
Brothers far yet near?
O the happy! O the blessed!
Do they guess what heavy sorrows
I must suffer here?

I asked Emad whether he was happy or sad the day his father left. "I was very happy," he said. "Now he will get fat."

But to me the story held sadness, too. After twenty-six centuries, the Jewish population in Mesopotamia was fading to black. Jews have roots in this soil going back to Abraham, but those roots will almost surely never again bear fruit. Worse, one dream of both supporters and opponents of invading Iraq was that the fall of Saddam might help transform the country into a much-needed bulwark of religious tolerance in the Arab world. Of the country's 23 million people, roughly two-thirds are Shia Muslims, a quarter are Sunnis, and five percent are Christians, mostly Chaldean Catholics and Assyrian Christians. I certainly wouldn't wish for Emad Levy or anyone else to remain in a country where they feel threatened. Still, the absence of Jews from a pluralist conversation in Iraq would make that conversation less rich, and maybe less successful. Jews, as a minority with centuries of experience surviving alongside often intolerant majorities, could set a powerful example for Christians and Sunnis in particular, both minorities in Iraq.

Emad, for all his Borscht Belt theatrics, embodied the self-respect that comes from perseverance through hardship. I asked him what lessons he drew from the exiled Israelites who lived in Babylon under Nebuchadnezzar II. "You must keep your religion," he said. "Even though we are now twenty-two and cannot use the synagogue because it's too dangerous, we still say our prayers in my house."

"But isn't it easier to convert?"

"If you believe in God, it is not easy to convert."

"When you don't have electricity, when the police are chasing you, when your family is gone and your friends are dead, aren't you angry at God?"

"Of course not. Believe me, I have a lot of problems in my life because God exacts hardships from my people, but you must be patient. I learned that lesson long ago."

I pulled out my Bible. "I would like to read you something from Jeremiah 50," I said. "In it, God promises to overthrow the Babylonians and send Israel back to its home. 'Flee from Babylon,' God says.

Leave the land of the Chaldeans,
And be like he-goats that flee the flock!
For see, I am rousing and leading
An assemblage of great nations against Babylon
From the lands of the north.

I looked at him. "Do you feel God has set you free?"

"Yes," Emad Levy said. "God helps us in everything we do. Believe me, the most important thing right now is for me to get a better life. I have no future here. There are no women here. I must get a wife."

"You're attractive," I said. "You speak English. You like women. I'll make you a promise. If you come to New York, I'll find you a wife in three months."

"But that will be one of those American wives," he said. "I'm afraid I need an Iraqi wife, someone who will do what I say."

"In that case," I said, "it will take me four months."

He laughed and held my hand. For a second we sat quietly, brothers. I gestured toward the bundles in the corner.

"So soon you're going to sell your carpets," I said. "You're going to sell your house. And you're going to get on an airplane."

"And I will fly first to Jerusalem," he said. "I want to see the Western Wall. Then maybe I will go visit my brother in Holland."

"And after 2,600 years—"

"I will be the last Jew," he said.

"And how will you feel when that plane takes off?"

"I will feel happy," he said, "because I'm leaving Iraq. Believe me."

About six months after the war began, I received an e-mail. "Hello," it began.

I'm an Army Chaplain stationed in Baghdad, and I have just completed your book about Abraham. This is really encouraging, and I am hoping to obtain access to this book in bulk in order to accomplish the following missions:

1. Make this book available to our soldiers here in Baghdad.
2. Have a keepsake gift to give to the local religious leaders, interpreters, and other significant members of the Baghdad community as a parting gift of thanks when we finally leave.

The writer went on to discuss how learning about Abraham had deepened his faith and informed his mission in Iraq, then signed his name, Chaplain Lew Messenger, Battalion Chaplain, Task Force 1-36 IN, 1st Armored Division. Within several weeks, working with my publisher and an old friend, Congressman Jack Kingston of Georgia, I shipped several cases of books to Chaplain Messenger. And on a Saturday morning, two days after meeting Emad Levy, I went to visit Chaplain Messenger at Firebase Melody in the Rusafa district in northern Baghdad, not far from the museum.

One of over 150 Coalition bases in Iraq, Firebase Melody, "Home of the Toughest Infantry in the World," was built on the grounds of a dormitory at Mustansiriya University. The Army surrounded the facility with a ten-foot-high brick wall, installed a retractable steel gate, and painted the entire complex the color of pale bananas. A metal sign welcomed visitors to the "Winter Home of the New York Yankees." A homemade sign invited soldiers to an interfaith conversation that afternoon with a local imam and a visitor from the United States.

Chaplain Messenger looked like Radar from *M*A*S*H*. He wore a floppy desert camouflage hat with a brown cross insignia, had large, clear-rimmed glasses, and rarely managed more than a flat grin. He was soft-spoken and serious. He showed me around the facility, with green military vehicles that had been shipped from Germany before even being repainted. Some soldiers were working on the engines; others were reading *Stars & Stripes* and drinking Coca-Cola. The Army had managed to ship in American soft drinks, though most of their food was locally bought. The soggy bologna and canned baked beans in the mess had none of the opulence of Camp Doha.

Chaplain Messenger was thirty-five years old and had been born, raised, educated, ordained, married, and assigned to serve a Lutheran church in the state of Pennsylvania. Yet since he was a boy, he was drawn to the military. "From a Christian perspective, military personnel seem to have a more mature sense of duty," he said. "They honor obligations. On the civilian side, people seem to pick and choose what aspects of religion they like. If they don't like certain things, they can always go to Jim Bob's church down the street that's tailor-made to their needs."

Assigned to the 1st Armored Division in 2003, he swept into Baghdad soon after Saddam's fall and settled in for what proved to be a brutal summer, with a wave of unexpected casualties. I asked what was his toughest moment. "The hardest time for me was standing over this fellow, who was my age, from my state, who was hit by an IED," he said, using military lingo for improvised explosive device, or roadside bomb. "He came in and half his arm was gone, one side was all laid open. I didn't recognize him at first. He looked up and said, 'Hi, sir.' The medics tried to stabilize him, and in those couple of minutes I was telling him I would take him to a Phillies game after the deployment and so forth. And just like that, he went under."

"How did you feel?"

"Maybe I was detached from my feelings. Your primary effort at that moment is to help prepare that person for dying, for embracing their savior. I assumed he could hear me, because supposedly hearing is one of the last faculties to leave a person. So I read him a psalm."

"Twenty-three?" I said.

"No, ninety." We pulled out our Bibles. "You see that line about being angry at the Lord?" Chaplain Messenger asked. "I skipped over that. I began with verse 13:

"*Show mercy to your servants.*
Satisfy us at daybreak with your steadfast love
that we may sing for you all our days.
Give us joy for as long as you have afflicted us,
for the years we have suffered misfortune.
Let your deeds be seen by your servants,
Your glory by their children.
May the favor of the Lord, our God, be upon us;
let the work of our hands prosper,
O prosper the work of our hands!"

He closed his book. "Then I pretty much stood there and watched him die."

I asked Chaplain Messenger how living in Iraq had affected his faith, and he practically gushed with his answer.

"Hey, I'm just amazed at how much of the Christian Old Testament—oops, I mean the Jewish scripture—is influenced by the Babylonian Exile," he said. "Gee whiz! If you take the exile out of the Jewish experience, I would say half of Jewish scripture would lose its meaning. For Jewish people, it was a major shift. But as a Christian, I realized my faith was changed there as well. God was not just in the Temple. He was everywhere. He is wherever you happen to be." He paused. "I wish I could say I learned as much from the Koran."

"Why, did you read the Koran while you were here?"

"Roger."

"And what did you learn?"

"I have to say, most of what I know about Islam I learned from living here," he said. "I had opportunities to learn before, but frankly I didn't give a rip. My lasting impression is 'Don't accept at face value when someone says that all Muslims are the same.' They are not. There is a difference between Shia and Sunni; there is a difference between moderate and fundamentalist. I've come to understand that the Koran can be interpreted in different ways. There are factions that will interpret it to support *jihad*, just as some will interpret the Bible to support Holy War."

"So do you fear Islam?"

He thought for a second. "I have seen people celebrate in the streets every time there's a car bomb, or a foreign national is beheaded. These kinds of things do not make me want to embrace Islam. But I do not fear it. And I don't think that means the religions cannot get along here. In fact, they already are."

He led me outside to a wooden deck with picnic tables and umbrellas, where we were met by a visitor. Soon after arriving in Baghdad, Chaplain Messenger began going door-to-door in the

Rusafa district, introducing himself to local religious leaders. Did they need a generator? Would they be interested in dialogue? A few resisted, but more were welcoming. He quickly developed relationships with the heads of the Chaldean Catholic Church, the Armenian Orthodox Church, and the Sufi, Shia, and Sunni branches of Islam. The only community who shunned his advances were the Jews, who were afraid of appearing to cooperate with the Americans. He had invited a number of his fellow religious leaders to this meeting; one was able to accept.

Imam Mohammad Saleh al-Ubaidy was a mesmerizing sight: a short, seventy-four-year-old man with mocha-colored skin, a bushy gray beard like that of some nineteenth-century German philosopher, thick-rimmed black Persol glasses, and a white turban with red trim. He wore a floor-length robe the color of pewter and carried a wooden cane. He could have been a wizard in a Harry Potter novel. Imam al-Ubaidy was the spiritual leader of the 14th of Ramadan Mosque, the blue-domed building on Firdos Square that was often used as the backdrop to reports on CNN and Fox News. The front door of the mosque is not ten yards from where the statue of Saddam was pulled down by American soldiers on April 9, 2003, with help from local Iraqis. I asked the imam if he was present on that day, and he said he was in hiding.

We were joined this afternoon by about a dozen U.S. soldiers and a few Iraqi workers from the base, as well as the imam's son. Over the next half hour different strands of conversation took hold. *Islam is a religion of peace. America is a country of diversity. Abraham was born in Iraq.* Over several years I had participated in dozens of discussions like this, as people of different faiths grappled head-on with the increase of religious violence. Though typical, this conversation was also extraordinary. Imam al-Ubaidy had risked his life by coming to a U.S. military base. The American soldiers, by serving in Iraq, were risking their lives as well. Chaplain

Messenger had organized this event entirely out of his own restless desire to forge a spiritual benefit from the war.

Yet I was frustrated. "I hate to ruin this party," I said. "But everyone is getting along too well." I believe in dialogue. I have committed myself to the idea that by going back to our common ancestor—Abraham—Jews, Christians, and Muslims can build a foundation of mutual trust. I am convinced that exploring how these religions have reinterpreted our shared heritage can shed light on how we can coexist today. But I've also come to believe something else: Unless we focus on our differences—and how to accommodate them—interfaith dialogue can become bland and directionless.

I turned to Chaplain Messenger. "With everyone's permission, I'd like to invite you to ask the toughest question you can think of to the imam." Chaplain Messenger took a breath and sat forward. "You're talking about how we can all get along," he said, "but has Islam been taken over by violent extremists?"

The imam leaned forward, too. "God never instructed his people to be violent," he said. His voice was slow and confident. "Some leaders say this because war suits their purposes, but that is not in the Koran." He continued for several minutes, talking about the peacefulness of the Prophet Mohammed and the different factions of Islam, and when he finished, I asked him if he would like to ask the toughest question he could think of to the chaplain. "I congratulate you as a man of peace," he said, "but what about the violence Christians have perpetrated against Muslims over the years?"

"I think the problem is the same with the Muslims," the chaplain said. "Not all Christians practice what they say they believe. We can't even keep churches together because we fight amongst ourselves." He continued, talking about the peaceful ministry of Jesus and the violent nature of some Christians, and when he finished I did something that I had not previously done in Iraq. I said, in public, that I am Jewish.

I have pushed myself further than I ever could have imagined in recent years to speak openly about my faith. I believe deeply that one key to addressing the problems in the world is getting over the notion our mothers all taught us: "Don't talk about politics and religion in public." The extremists talk openly about religion; those of us who believe in mutual respect and tolerance must speak as well. But the one piece of advice I heard most often before coming to Iraq was not to tell anyone my religion. The experience of Danny Pearl—an American, a Jew, a reporter—has haunted every journey I have taken since he was beheaded while reporting a story in Pakistan in 2002. In the Middle East, what you believe can still get you killed.

Yet at this moment, sitting at Firebase Melody, I felt both safe and compelled. I invited the imam to ask me the toughest question he could think of. He seemed surprised by my admission and said he admired how Jews did not abandon their faith over the centuries. Then he took up my challenge: "You talk about openness," he said, "but what about the fact that in the time of the Prophet, Jews embraced Muslims, but now they prevent them from praying freely in Jerusalem?" I tried to answer the question. "Muslims are allowed to worship more freely in Jerusalem under Jews than when it was the other way around," I said. "Still, I don't condone every action the Israeli government takes." I continued, talking about how Jews got along better with Muslims than with Christians for many centuries until the rise of Israel, and then, for a second, there was silence.

What would happen now?

One premise of my journeys across the Middle East was that traveling through the land where God was born and discussing the Bible along the way would change how I feel about the Bible, about the land, and about myself. But on this particular trip I wanted more: I wanted to know if the Bible could elucidate the spiritual crisis we all face today. In Iraq, that question drew me back repeatedly to the foundation story of the Bible.

Creation is the story in the Hebrew Bible that shows its greatest debt to Mesopotamia. In the Babylonian creation story, Enuma Elish, the world begins with the mingling of two great bodies of water, Apsu, freshwater, and Tiamat, saline water. Apsu is killed by one of their offspring, Ea, prompting Tiamat to wage war with her descendants. In the ensuing struggle, Ea's son Marduk creates the world by taming Tiamat and splitting her body in two.

The Genesis story has clear echoes of its Babylonian forebear. When God begins to create heaven and earth, the earth is "unformed and void, with darkness over the surface of the deep, and a wind from God sweeping over the water." Before God does anything, the world is covered with a dark, watery chaos. The Hebrew word for "deep" in this verse, *tehom*, is the root word for *Tiamat*. God then splits these waters in two, exactly as happens in Enuma Elish. Part of the waters are tucked above the sky; the rest become the seas. Water and darkness precede God's Creation, and they succeed it as well, just more confined. The earliest verses of the Bible introduce the notion that order is not the natural state of the world; chaos is. Before there was good—to use God's phrase—there was evil.

Before there was peace, there was war.

The rest of the Hebrew Bible seems to support the idea that God is constantly struggling against forces of chaos, disorder, and disrespect. He boots Adam and Eve from his garden after they disobey his order; he destroys the world with a flood after the people act sinfully; he lashes out at his freshly liberated people after they build a golden calf at Mount Sinai; he summons Nebuchadnezzar to wipe out Jerusalem after the people despoil the Promised Land with debauchery. His chosen people, too, struggle against waves of evil enemies—the Egyptians, Philistines, Assyrians, Babylonians. The idea that the Bible represents some halcyon time that if we only get back to we could all live happily ever after is absurd. The Bible suggests there never were good ole days. Every day is a struggle. The Bible is neither conservative, in that it recommends returning to a better time, nor is it optimistic that a better time lies ahead. The Bible is redemptive, in that it gives humans the ability to save themselves.

And how should they do this? How should humans re-create themselves in a manner that will stanch the lingering waters of evil and summon the tides of good? They should do what God does at the start of Creation in the face of chaos. They should use the only force the Bible shows will quell the deep and fill the darkness with light. They should use words. "And God said." They should use ideas, prayers, pleas, complaints, lamentations, and psalms. God, at the end of Creation, commands humans to be his partners. "Be fertile and increase," God tells humans. "Fill the earth and master it." Created in God's image, humans now have the ability to create on his behalf. They also have the ability to lord over God's other creations. They can't make evil go away, but they can speak truths to control it. They may not be able to eliminate chaos, but they can use words to calm it.

But what words should humans use? What words are left that don't divide, alienate, or disunite? I was struck by a pattern that recurred during my travels in Iraq. What inspired Chaplain Munson on the eve of war? Jeremiah 29 and Psalm 91. What inspired the rabbi to emigrate to Israel? The prophets' vow to uplift the children of exile. What inspired Chaplain Messenger to extend his hand to the enemy during war? The lesson of Babylon is that God belongs everywhere, to everyone.

The Torah is central to Judaism, the Gospels to Christianity, the Koran to Islam. But I was beginning to wonder if the second half of the Hebrew Bible, precisely because it is oft overlooked, and precisely because these stories are shared by all but claimed by none, might offer fertile, common ground. The figure of the prophet transcends the Abrahamic faiths. Christianity embraces the Hebrew prophets; in the Gospels, Jesus even refers to himself as a prophet. Islam believes there are 124,000 prophets, and the Koran lists by name 25, including David, Solomon, Elijah, Ezekiel, Jonah, and Zechariah. Both Christianity and Islam quote the Hebrew psalms. War fills the second half of the Hebrew Bible, as does chaos and depravity. But the enduring images from these books come from their call to justice, their direct expression of the human need for God, their vision of a world with freedom for all where, as Psalm 104 declares, "the sinners disappear from the earth, / and the wicked be no more."

Sure enough, this dream is how Imam al-Ubaidy broke the silence at our Abraham discussion in Baghdad. "If Jews, Christians, and Muslims go back to our roots, we will be in peace," he said. "We don't need to find one person. We don't need to agree on everything. We need to find our principles—peace, love, justice, and tolerance. We need to realize the future belongs to God, not to us."

And just like that, the tension eased. Nothing was resolved in our encounter. No treaties were signed. But just for an instant, in the middle of a war, the sound heard coming from northern Baghdad was not bullets.

It was words.

. 5 .

A FUTURE WITH HOPE

I would leave Baghdad with one regret: I didn't get to see Uday's disco. During my time in the capital, titillating news swept through the expat community. The Al-Rashid hotel, famous as the location where CNN broadcast the opening nights of the first Gulf War, was reopening its nightclub. The disco had been carefully modeled after the one where John Travolta danced in *Saturday Night Fever*, complete with lighted floor and a mirrored ball. Uday, Saddam's elder son and prospective heir until he beat his father's favorite servant to death, apparently kept a private room in the back. The Al-Rashid hotel was inside the heavily fortified Green Zone, so only select individuals had access. One invited me for a beer. Prudence, for once, overcame my curiosity.

But I wasn't able to resist entering one of Saddam's plushest lairs. The Republican Palace is the political epicenter of Iraq. Tucked behind three layers of checkpoints on the banks of the Tigris, the palace looks like the kind of building a ten-year-old boy would construct if you gave him all the money in the world and invited him to build a mansion in honor of himself. The 270,000-square-foot monstrosity sits on a manicured plot covering forty-one acres; two wings flank a central foyer. The front consists of a stately colonnade, once topped by four bronze heads of Saddam, each weighing three tons.

Once Saddam's chief residence, the Republican Palace had been bombed during the first Gulf War, then it was rebuilt. After Operation Iraqi Freedom, it became the headquarters for the Coalition. I was invited to meet Ambassador L. Paul Bremer, Jerry to his friends.

If the outside of the Republican Palace was a testament to megalomania, the inside was an expression of how far the mighty can fall. A Marine stood in the front door; over his head was a poster of the fifty-two most-wanted Iraqis, each face on a playing card. Red Xs covered the faces of those who had already been caught, including the ace of spades, SADDAM HUSAYN AL-TIKRITI, President. The ten-foot-wide marble halls reminded me of the Pentagon; they teemed with U.S. service personnel and preppily dressed staffers from Washington. The bathrooms had bidets and gold-plated faucets. In the opulent throne room, just above the seat of power, a mural showed Scud missiles soaring skyward; on the opposite wall was a mural of their presumed destination—Jerusalem. The room now served as an interfaith chapel.

"So what does it feel like to come to work here every day?" I asked Kristi Clemens, my American escort.

"It's like *Groundhog Day*," she said. "Every day the same thing. We're here fighting terrorism, yet we come to work in a palace. Standing here on Christmas Eve, having Catholic mass in Saddam's throne room, it was surreal."

Paul Bremer's office was located in Saddam's former reception room. A walk-through metal detector stood in front of the entrance, followed by two men with machine guns. In the antechamber, a dozen desks were buzzing with aides. Books were scattered every-where: a Kurdish-English dictionary, *A History of Islamic Societies*, *The Constitution of the United States: Its Sources and Applications*. Bremer's office was small, and the curtains were drawn, presumably to shield him from attack. His desk had a laptop computer, a Koran, and a wooden sign: SUCCESS HAS A THOUSAND FATHERS. The book-shelves were mostly empty, save for a box of bran flakes, an espresso maker, and a photograph of him with Dick Cheney and one with George W. Bush. The latter was signed, "To Jerry, the right man for a big job."

Ambassador Bremer was gracious and surprisingly relaxed, given how pressured his time was and how little sleep he was said to receive. He seemed thinned by the job, with a blue-and-white striped shirt, blue trousers, and his trademark desert combat boots. We may have been in Baghdad, but the man who had served six secretaries of state had the air of a Yale-bred diplomat at home in any throne room in the world.

We talked about food; Bremer complained about not being able to indulge his love of French cooking. We talked about ar-chaeology. I asked him if the past seemed more present here. "The lawyers take you to Hammurabi," he said. "And the Christians will talk about the Assyrians. Saddam used to invoke the Mongol inva-sion. History in this part of the world is more alive than it is in the United States."

But in the few minutes allowed to me, I wanted to talk most about religion. Raised a Protestant in WASP Connecticut, Bremer served in U.S. embassies in Afghanistan and Malawi before being named ambassador to the Netherlands in 1983. While serving in Europe, Bremer and his college-sweetheart wife, Francine, were inspired by the legacy of the Catholic Church, with its saints, shrines, and prayer. In 1993 Bremer became visibly moved watch-ing television coverage of Pope John Paul II connect with young people on World Youth Day. The following year, he and his wife converted to Catholicism. Prayer became central to his life, and before leaving for Iraq, he sent his wife scurrying around Washington for the one thing he refused to leave without: a finger rosary to keep in his pocket.

"There is no doubt in my mind that I cannot succeed in this mission without the help of God," he told the *Catholic Standard* soon after arriving. "The job is simply too big and complex for any one person."

"Would you say religion in Iraq is a greater or lesser force than you expected?" I asked.

"I would say it's about what I expected. Islam, of course, doesn't make the kinds of distinctions that Judaism and Christianity make between the political side of life and the religious side of life. There is less separation between church and state."

"One of the goals in coming here was to make an example of democracy in this part of the world," I said, "but Iran is in flux. Egypt, Syria, Saudi Arabia are not great examples. Can Islam and democracy coexist?"

"I think they can," he said. "They have for almost a century in Turkey. And in various forms in other countries, Jordan and Morocco. And I think people who say it can't be done are essentially guilty of a form of cultural imperialism, saying only the West knows how to do democracy. I spent most of the 1990s working in China, and I can remember people saying Chinese culture is incompatible with democracy. But we have democracy in Taiwan. People said that Korean culture was incompatible with democracy. None of those democracies look exactly like ours, and that's not surprising. French democracy is different from American democracy. But it's democracy. I think there's no reason to assume that the Iraqis are incapable of governing themselves."

"But Christian churches have been attacked," I said. "The Jews are fleeing. And some fear the Shias would like to set up an Islamic theocracy, like Iran."

"My view is that probably less than 10 percent of Iraqis favor a theocratic government. A huge majority want a democratic government. Now they still have to learn what that means."

"The larger question in the world today is, Can the religions get along?" I started to say.

He got my point and interrupted. "Certainly in Iraq during the last few years, religion was a weapon," he said. "You had a dictatorship that stirred up sectarian disagreements with the Shia. The hopeful sign here is that since the liberation we have not seen the kind of retributive violence we might have expected. Nothing compared to what happened in France and Italy after World War II. There have been some isolated revenge killings, but even in the face of great provocations, like the bombing in the Shia capital of Najaf, we have not seen the kind of religious violence that the terrorists want to happen."

"I would like to turn, for a second, to a personal matter," I said. "In some of your speeches you quote Jeremiah."

"Jeremiah 29, verse 11," he said. " 'For surely I know the plans I have for you, says the Lord, plans for your welfare and not for harm, to give you a future with hope.' " This was the same verse Chaplain Munson had cited to me in Ur. "I actually use that verse in all my speeches," Ambassador Bremer continued. "And it resonates with Iraqis, because they've had a rough couple of decades. They have embraced the concept of a future of hope. I like to invoke it because they have a rich country. It's rich in land, water, and tourist possibilities. It is rich obviously in oil revenues, but it is richest of all in its people. If they can retain a hope about the future, they will achieve it."

"And how has this experience affected you personally?"

"As a young boy—" he started to say, then he cut himself off.

He paused for a second, then snapped back into diplomatic mode. "I don't confuse my own beliefs with my job. My job is to try to realize the hope that I think most Iraqis have."

But in that instant, I felt I gleaned a truth about America's foray in Iraq. Paul Bremer was a man of faith. His nickname, Jerry, came from his patron saint, Jerome, the man who translated the Bible into Latin. A framed sign on his desk contained a Latin inscription that he says is his guiding principle, NON SUM DIGNUS, "I am not worthy." Catholics utter this phrase at mass before receiving the host, the manifestation of Christ. "What is significant about it is that every Catholic says it," he later said, "even the pope."

In the same way that many Iraqis see their lives through the prism of religion, many Americans, including the ones most associated with the war in Iraq, do. This association clearly gave them strength and purpose, but it holds dangers as well. Jeremiah is a prophet and his message of hope universal, but he is not quoted in the Koran. Neither is Isaiah, whose invocation in chapter 49, "To the captives, 'come out'—and to those in darkness, 'be free,'" President Bush invoked at the close of his "Mission Accomplished" speech on the USS *Abraham Lincoln*.

The beliefs in freedom, social justice, law, and God are the creations of Mesopotamia that live on most strongly in American life. The United States embodies those ideals today in ways that the heirs of Babylon have not for some time. But as much as the religious mind-set informs the heroic service of many Americans, it risks coloring our every action by imposing our biblical view of the world onto geopolitical situations where it may not belong. Sitting in Ambassador Bremer's office, I had no way of foretelling the future of Iraq, though my experience watching nascent pluralism take hold left me more hopeful than I had expected. But I also believed that when the history of American intervention in Iraq is written, the religious motivations of U.S. leaders would prove to be equal to—if not stronger than—those of the enemies we were fighting.

"So Sumer, gone," I said to Ambassador Bremer. "Nebuchadnezzar, gone. The British, gone. Saddam, gone. And now Bremer . . ."

"I'm not sure I want to be on the same list as Nebuchadnezzar," he said, and we both chuckled. "But of course this is the oldest question in history. Empires come and go. I think the American experience shows that if you can create a government that rules with the consent of the people, it has a lot of staying power. We've been through a lot, including civil war. We're still at it. So I think our system has a lot of stability. And it's certainly the case that democracies are less likely to go to war with each other than non-democracies. So if you want to think about a more stable international system, it is in our interest that this should be a more open and representative government. I'm optimistic about Iraq."

Hikmat, Bijar, and I stepped up our precautions for the last leg of our trip. We left before dawn so we could pass through the perilous Sunni triangle before daybreak. We tinted our windows, so no one could eye my foreign features. And Hikmat brought a red-and-white checkered kaffiyah to wrap around my head. The comfort I felt in Baghdad slipped away as we edged north, toward Mosul, and two of the richest biblical sites in Iraq, Nimrud and Nineveh.

We passed by Saddam's hometown of Tikrit without incident and made a brief detour to Hatra, a well-preserved temple compound from the first century B.C.E. Sheep wandered in the Temple of the Sun. Originally an Assyrian settlement, Hatra grew to stature under Arab rulers who controlled the area in the centuries around the time of Jesus. Along with Palmyra in Syria and Petra in Jordan, Hatra was a rest stop on the famed Silk Road from China.

After a while I began to notice a certain insignia carved into many of the walls. At first the curlicue letters, like Victorian monograms the size of my hand, reminded me of the carvings I had seen in Babylon, only smaller and more ubiquitous. Some of the walls had just a few, but more had a huge rash, sometimes hundreds on a thirty-foot span, like chicken pox on a five-year-old. I asked Hikmat if he knew what they meant.

"They're from Saddam," he said.

I didn't understand.

"The first letter is Sad," he explained, "that means 'Saddam'; the second is Ha, that means 'Hussein.' Saddam Hussein had his initials carved on this monument. He did it all over Iraq."

I was flabbergasted. "You mean nobody said, 'You can't put your name here'?" I asked.

"Nobody can say that. They will be hanged."

I noticed that he still spoke in the present.

The farther north we drove, the greener the scenery became. Hills began to undulate up from the flats, sheep grew plumper, ravens plucked at fields brimming with vegetables. Iraq may not be Eden, but it has epic geographic diversity.

By late morning we arrived at the outskirts of the third great Mesopotamian seat of power, Nimrud, capital of ancient Assyria. If Sumer was the first city-state in the region and Babylon the first nation-state, Assyria was the first empire. Once again, a ziggurat stood proudly at the entrance, though this one was covered with grass, a Green Monster on the banks of the Tigris. Nearby, two eight-foot statues with the bodies of lions, wings of eagles, and faces of kings stood guard at the Northwest Palace. These griffin-like creatures designed to scare away evil spirits and thieves may be the most visible face of Mesopotamia in the West.

Though this area was populated in the third millennium B.C.E., Assyria, named after the Akkadian city of Ashur, did not come to prominence until the thirteenth century B.C.E. It reached its apogee with King Ashurnasirpal II, who in 833 B.C.E. began leading military expeditions every spring. Ashurnasirpal boasted of his torture. "I flayed all the chiefs who had revolted," he wrote of one battle, "and I covered the pillar with their skin." Of the captives, he said, "From some I cut off their noses, their ears, and their fingers, of many I put out the eyes." But he brought some of these captives back to Nimrud, which he called Kalhu, and constructed one of the most spectacular cities ever built.

For the next two hundred years, Assyria dominated the Fertile Crescent, extending its influence from Persia to Egypt. This reign of terror coincided with the internal decay of the Northern Kingdom of Israel. Around 733 B.C.E., Israel pleaded with Assyria to protect it from Egypt. The Assyrians responded by sacking Israel and dispersing its population across the region. Some people refer to these vanished Israelites as the lost tribes of Israel. "Ha! Assyria, rod of my anger," God says in Isaiah.

In whose hand, as a staff, is my fury!
I send him against an ungodly nation,
I charge him against a people that provokes me.

The walls of Ashurnasirpal's palace have been mostly reconstructed with brick. Henry Layard excavated here in 1845, but the bulk of the work was done by Max Mallowan after he was kicked out of Ur. Inside, Sakina Welly, an Iraqi conservator at the museum in Mosul, was inspecting the head of a bas-relief of the king that some looters had attempted to chisel off during the war. Welly is a short, stout woman who was wearing a red dress and spectacles; she had to stand on the toes of her practical shoes to survey the damage.

Like their Mesopotamian forebears, the Assyrians were

extremely sophisticated. They used the first known lock and key, and Ashurnasirpal II's palace had an air-conditioning system of vents cut into the walls. But the Assyrians were also brutal. Unlike the Babylonians, who drew most of their wealth from agriculture and trade, the Assyrians used wars to fatten their coffers. Alabaster reliefs depict slaves in handcuffs offering tribute. Also, the Assyrian kings elevated themselves over the gods. Few carvings depict them interacting with the deities; more show them indulging in secular activities, like picking fruit or hunting. The Assyrian kings were indulging in profane arts at the same time the kings of Israel and Judah were presiding over the moral breakdown of their realms, which suggests a growing tension in the early first millennium B.C.E. between secular and religious worldviews.

Finally, the Assyrians loved money. Sakina led me into a darkened room and the mouth of a tomb, about the size of a coffin. "Do you have any paper?" she asked. I ripped out a piece from my notebook. With admirable pluck, she lowered herself through the opening into a small chamber below. I followed, and she let me into a second chamber, no bigger than a bathroom stall. She lit the paper and held it against the stone ceiling. "This was Ashurnasirpal's tomb," she said. "This is where we found the crown jewels."

In 1988 Sakina Welly was part of the team that discovered a trove of Assyrian royal jewelry, including bracelets, rings, and necklaces made of gold and semiprecious stones. To protect them from bombing during the first Gulf War, the jewels were hidden in the basement of the Iraq National Bank, where they remained for the next decade. But the bank was bombed during the second Gulf War, and the fate of the jewels was for a time unknown. A conspiracy theory circulated that Saddam's younger son, Qusay, had lifted the jewels when he purloined a rumored $900 million from the bank. Looters didn't buy this account and tried to crack the vault. One man was killed when he fired a rocket-propelled grenade at the door from less than ten feet away. In early June 2003, U.S. personnel arrived and discovered that the vault was flooded. They drained 640,000 gallons of water, removed five waterlogged crates, and recovered all 613 pieces of jewelry.

Sakina confessed that she had tried on some of the jewelry. So how did it make her feel?

"Like one of his wives." She giggled.

"One of?" I said.

"Oh, he had many wives. I think the jewelry was for whichever one would join his celebrations."

I mentioned that many of the most treasured items from Nimrud, including a number of the human-headed lions, had been transported to museums across Europe and America. "Part of me feels sad that they are not in Iraq, for Iraqi scholars to study them and the Iraqi people to enjoy them," I said. "But another part of me is relieved that at least they are safe."

She nodded for a second as if to agree, then smiled. "So when our new Iraqi government will be formed in Baghdad, they can ask American troops to bring these things back home?"

I bowed at her expert parry. "Maybe if they put you in charge," I said.

Mosul was a lawless, scary place. Iraq's second-largest city was never fully secured during the war, in part because the Coalition was not allowed to bring in troops from nearby Turkey. Uday and Qusay sought refuge here, where they were eventually killed. Today, vehicles swarmed around traffic circles, honking and butting against one another like bumper cars. Fistfights erupted on street corners. A foot patrol of U.S. forces closed off the main thoroughfare. "There was an explosion," an officer explained, "but no one was hurt. We get mortared all the time, but nothing comes of it. They don't have good aim." In coming weeks their aim would improve and dozens of U.S. troops would be killed.

The one oasis of calm was a huge, green void in the middle of town, the tell of Nineveh. Built on the banks of the Tigris, ancient Nineveh was an enormous city, covering eighteen hundred acres, seven times larger than the Old City of Jerusalem. It reached its apogee with Sennacherib, who assumed control of the Assyrian empire around 705 B.C.E. Sennacherib reinforced the city walls, constructed a palace, and built what he called "paradise," a huge park in the center of town where he grew trees, plants, and flowers from all over his empire.

Sakina Welly led me up a grassy incline to Sennacherib's "palace without rival." Its eighty rooms were mostly in ruins now, their treasures long since shipped off to the West. Only one winged bull was discernible, and its head was lopped off and its body decomposed, like a melted ice sculpture. Sakina pointed out the doorpost where Henry Layard found an inscription detailing Sennacherib's sacking of Judah and his siege of Jerusalem, events described in II Kings. Though the Assyrian account differs from the biblical one, the similarities suggest that the Israelites' fear of their northern neighbors was well founded.

This fear is encapsulated by the most dominant structure visible from the palace. On the far bank of the Tigris, on the highest hill in Mosul, sits an enormous white stone building with a minaret. The mound once held an Assyrian temple, later a Christian church, and now a Muslim shrine. Inside is a whalebone and a tomb that Muslims and Christians still visit. "It's my favorite place in Mosul," Sakina said. The site is even referenced in chapter 83 of *Moby-Dick*. It's called Masjod Jami Nebi Yunus, the Great Mosque of the Prophet Jonah.

I pulled out my Bible. With only four chapters, Jonah is the fourth-shortest book in the Hebrew Bible, totaling 48 verses, compared with 1,292 for Isaiah, 1,533 for Genesis, and a whopping 2,461 for the Psalms. But the book, which scholars believe was one of the last to be written, contains many references to other biblical events. Jonah is a mini-Deuteronomy, or repetition, a retelling of many stories from Creation to the Exile.

The book opens with an immediate echo of Abraham, as God, unintroduced, calls out to Jonah, the son of Amittai: "Go at once to Nineveh, that great city, and proclaim judgment upon it; for their wickedness has come before me." Though Nineveh's link to the destruction of Jerusalem is not articulated, biblical ears would have recognized it. But Jonah, for no discernible reason, refuses and flees to Tarshish, in Spain. He boards a ship, prompting God, in an echo of Creation, to send a mighty wind over the sea. Jonah's shipmates jettison their cargo while Jonah goes into the hold to sleep. The men cast lots to assign blame for the storm and settle on Jonah. "I am a Hebrew," Jonah declares. "I worship the Lord, the God of Heaven, who made both sea and land." Showing sudden confidence in God, Jonah recommends that his shipmates toss him overboard. Though pagans, they pray to God, "Oh, please, Lord, do not let us perish," and heave Jonah into the water. The sea calms.

In the story's most famous scene, the Lord then provides a "huge fish" to swallow Jonah. The Hebrew term for the beast, *dag gadol*, literally means "huge fish" and not whale. Modern science considers a whale to be a mammal, of course, and not a fish, though that distinction was not known in biblical times. The usage of *whale* today comes from the King James Bible, which properly translates the references in the Book of Jonah as "huge fish" but translates a reference to Jonah's captor in the Gospel of Matthew as "whale." This reference was adopted by popular culture. The Greek term used in Matthew, *ketos*, actually means "sea monster."

Whatever the beast, Jonah remains in its belly for three days and three nights, during which he prays to God.

In my trouble I called to the Lord,
And he answered me;
From the belly of Sheol I cried out,
And you heard my voice.

The use of the word *Sheol*, which means "hell" or "pit," echoes the way Joseph is thrown into a pit before being transported down to Egypt. Later, when Jonah wails, "The waters closed in over me, / The deep engulfed me," he uses the word *deep*, an echo of the Babylonian story of Enuma Elish. These similarities are hardly accidental. Jonah has gone back to the depths of Creation, to a time when a watery chaos covered the earth. And what he discovers is a central lesson of the Bible. In moments of personal turmoil, a person no longer wants to be alone. He no longer wants independence. He wants dependence. The only answer to chaos is God. So Jonah, now that he has reached the darkest depths, calls out. Originally called to cry out against Nineveh, he now cries out for God: "When my life was ebbing away, I called the Lord to mind." And God, as he does time and again, answers. He brings Jonah "up from the pit." He allows him to be re-created. He commands the fish to spew Jonah onto dry land.

Now the story resumes where it started. God once again orders Jonah to go to Nineveh, and this time Jonah obeys. "Forty days more, and Nineveh shall be overthrown!" Jonah tells the Ninevites. His declaration appears to leave no room for negotiation, but the people change their ways anyway, fasting and dressing in sackcloth. "Let everyone turn back from his evil ways and from the injustice of which he is guilty," the king says, in a direct echo of Jeremiah. The Israelites, warned of their misbehavior for centuries by earlier prophets, consistently failed to make amends. The Ninevites make immediate adjustments and prove that God responds to changed behavior. God sees their actions and withdraws his punishment. Nineveh is saved.

But Jonah, who should be happy that he helped save the city, is disconsolate that the hated Nineveh has been spared. "Please, Lord, take my life," he cries, "for I would rather die than live." God is flabbergasted. "Are you that deeply grieved?" In an apparent attempt to test God, Jonah then flees the city and settles on a hill. God originally provides a plant to protect Jonah but then destroys the plant and leaves Jonah exposed. God seems determined to impress upon Jonah that he controls all things, even nature, even him.

But Jonah can express his sadness only at losing the plant. Again God is boggled. "Are you so deeply grieved about the plant?" "Yes," Jonah replies, "so deeply that I want to die." The book ends with a rhetorical question from God, a statement of his commitment to provide succor for anyone who promises to embrace his moral vision, no matter where they live. "You cared about the plant, which you did not work for and which you did not grow," God says to Jonah. "And should not I care about Nineveh, that great city, in which there are more than a hundred and twenty thousand persons who do not yet know their right hand from their left, and many beasts as well!" As long as humans can still learn to live righteously, God says, he will protect them.

On its surface, the Book of Jonah would seem to be a perfect candidate to slide into obscurity, like plenty of other prophetic books. (Heard any references to Obadiah, Nahum, or Habakkuk lately?) The narrative is not particularly believable. The hero is not particularly heroic. The evil enemy doesn't exactly get punished. At the climactic moment, the blubbery antagonist, having dined on the hero, actually "vomits" him onto the beach. And at the end, the regurgitated hero is chastised by God, and God's sworn enemy is redeemed. By all rightful measures, the son of Amittai is a failure and an ingrate. He should be known as Jonah Who?

Instead he's one of the most famous figures in the Bible.

Part of this has to do with the sheer fascination of a man getting swallowed by a fish. But more has to do with how the religious mind can find meaning in the least likely places and, in particular, how the religions that grew out of the Hebrew Bible—Judaism, Christianity, and Islam—have reinterpreted the same stories to extract similar but slightly different messages.

Jews attached themselves to Jonah because of the powerful message of repentance the story provides. The first repenter is Jonah. The rabbis viewed Jonah's descent into the fish as a simile for the Israelites' descent into exile. They pointed out that Hosea says Israel will be "swallowed" by Assyria, and Jeremiah says Israel will be "devoured" by Babylon. The message of Jonah echoes the message of exile: God meets you most intimately in your moments of darkness. "When you pass through the waters, I will be with you," God says in Isaiah. (Talmudic rabbis tried to make the *dag gadol* more contemporary, saying the inside of the fish was like a large synagogue, in which the fish's eyes were windows and lamps lit its stomach. The message here was hardly subtle: Come to services. We won't eat you alive!)

The even bigger repenter, the rabbis said, was Nineveh. For Jewish populations, trapped for generations in gentile empires, the story of Jonah held a powerful message. Be patient. God has larger goals in mind. You may be enraged at your tormentors, but God is postponing his judgment to give them time to accept his moral vision. Trust God. And in the meantime, attend to your own moral well-being. This message is considered so central to Jewish identity that the Book of Jonah is read annually in synagogues around the world on the holiest day of the year, Yom Kippur, the Day of Repentance.

Muslims also embraced Jonah, or Yunus in Arabic, though the Islamic version of the story differs somewhat from the biblical version. In keeping with the notion that a Muslim is "one who submits," Yunus actually does go to Nineveh upon receiving his initial call, only to have the Ninevites reject his pleas. Yunus then flees. His sin is not disobeying God; it is not trusting God to fulfill his promise eventually. But repentance echoes through the Muslim version as well, as Jonah realizes his sin while alive in the fish. The fish eventually coughs him onto the shore, whereupon he returns to Nineveh and the people embrace his call to God. Yunus is so central to Islam that an entire chapter in the Koran bears his name, an honor bestowed on only five other biblical figures: Abraham, Noah, Joseph, Mary, and the Queen of Sheba.

But the religion that most embraced Jonah was Christianity. The association began with the Gospels, which saw deep parallels between Jonah and Jesus. The most obvious connection was the amount of time both spent interred. Matthew quotes Jesus as saying, "Just as Jonah was three days and three nights in the belly of the sea monster, so for three days and three nights the Son of Man will be in the heart of the earth." Luke broadens the connection. "Just as Jonah became a sign to the people of Nineveh, so the Son of Man will be to this generation." Later interpreters read the prefigurement of Jesus across the entire narrative. Jonah descends into darkness on the ship before the nonbelievers lift him up and sacrifice him to the sea. Jesus passes through darkness at Gethsemane before being lifted up by nonbelievers and sacrificed. Just before the sacrifice, the sailors cry, "Do not hold us guilty of killing an innocent person!" Just before Jesus is killed, Judas cries, "I have sinned by betraying innocent blood."

The story of Jonah holds a special place among Assyrian Christians, who once dominated the East. As Donny George mentioned, Assyrians consider themselves the first converts to Christianity. This claim is based on the tradition that the apostle Thomas converted the town of Edessa, in Turkey, around 100 C.E. The Assyrian Church split from the Roman Catholic and Eastern Orthodox churches in 431 after it refused to accept that Nestorianism—the belief that Christ was two persons, one human and one divine—was heresy. Largely forgotten in the West, Assyrian Christians evangelized across the Silk Road to Afghanistan, India, China, and Korea. By 1200, Assyrians boasted their church was bigger than its European counterparts combined. As much as half of Genghis Khan's army was said to be Assyrian Christians, and when Marco Polo visited China in the thirteenth century, he was astonished to find Assyrian priests in the royal court.

The church later suffered under the Turks and today numbers only a few million, with an estimated several hundred thousand still in Iraq. Sakina Welly is one of them. She told me that the holiest days of her year are a three-day fast, just before Lent, called the Rogation of the Ninevites, which commemorates the town's redemption after Jonah's threat. "I remember as a girl," she said, "how scary it was to read about God calling for the destruction of my town. I had nightmares about my house catching on fire." And now, as an adult? "I have to cook during the entire fast!" she said, laughing. "On the last night we eat cakes and a special kind of bread made with seven types of grain. It represents the sand that Jonah landed on when he was spit up from the fish. It would be a lot easier to cook fish."

One surprise of my trip to Iraq was discovering these differing interpretations of Jonah. He's almost like a second Abraham, a figure from Mesopotamia who shows the common roots of Judaism, Christianity, and Islam yet also exemplifies the spiritual biases that divide them. But sitting in Nineveh, I felt that looking primarily at Jonah misses the larger meaning of the story. The principal message is that morality is the central quality God seeks in humans. He doesn't care about your status in life, he doesn't care where you live, he doesn't care what you believed in the past. He doesn't even care if, like Nineveh, you once destroyed his chosen people.

God cares only that you conduct yourself in a moral way, even if you have to repent to do so. This message reinforces the theme that has been building throughout the prophets. First, beginning with Joshua, God shows that behavior is more important than land. Later, beginning with David, God shows that behavior is more important than power. Here, with the Ninevites, he shows that behavior is more important than nationality. Moral conduct is so important to God that he's even prepared to rebuke Jonah by sending a whale to swallow him, just as he admonished his chosen people by sending them into exile.

Despite his repeated criticism of Jonah, God's final note toward him is one of compassion. By ignoring Jonah's request to die, God shows forgiveness toward him as he did toward the Ninevites. God's mercy is universal. "I am ready to respond to those who do not ask," God says in Isaiah. "I am available to those who do not seek me. I tell a nation that does not invoke my name, 'Here I am; here I am.'" In Genesis 22, God calls out to his chosen partner, Abraham, who responds, "Here I am." After the Exile, in Isaiah 65, it is God who reaches out, this time to his unchosen ones. "Here I am; here I am."

This call represents the highest cry of the prophets: God belongs to everyone, even if his universality offends some people who might want to keep him all to themselves.

B ijar drove Sakina home, leaving me alone atop the tell. Hikmat, concerned about aggravating his heart, remained at the bottom. Some children were playing with a dog. From here I could see over the edgy city. To my left was the shrine of Jonah. Directly below me was a giant mosque under construction, part of Saddam's late-term Islamification, now stopped in its tracks. Lights were beginning to flicker on in some neighborhoods;

others remained in the dark. Later the entire city suffered a black-out, and I spent my final night in Iraq sitting upright in bed, gripping my satellite telephone, staring at the bolted door, and listening to the explosions outside my window.

Before she left, Sakina asked me a question. Her tone was mothering. She knew I was leaving the country the next day. "Did you get what you came for?"

Her question lingered in my mind.

On an immediate level, one reason I came to Iraq was to understand its role in the roots of religion and the formation of Western civilization. On that front, the country surpassed my expectations. From the elemental notion that humans were made in God's image, through the revolutionary idea that God is everywhere, to the radical concept that God embraces his enemies, many of the most transformative concepts of biblical religion were born on this land. For that reason, Iraq felt very comfortable. As a teenager visiting Los Angeles for the first time, I was struck by how much of its terrain and how many of its streets I already knew, from watching television and movies. I had the same feeling in Iraq. More than in any country I'd visited in the Muslim world, life in Iraq seemed instantly familiar to me because we learn about these places in second grade and read about them in the Bible.

This sense of kinship was the revelation of this place: Iraq was more dangerous than it appeared on television, but it felt more like home.

But I came for other reasons, too, among them to search for clues into the georeligious tumult of today. There, my experience was more bracing. The most immediate lesson of Iraq at the start of its eighth millennium is that political power is fleeting. The greatest empires in the world once stood here. Today they are in ruins. Yet every empire left behind some contribution—writing from Sumer, astronomy from Babylon, the cult of personality in

Assyria—that embedded themselves in the larger evolution of civilization. Saddam perfectly illustrated this enduringness of the past. He understood he couldn't erase Iraq's past glory, so he decided to join it, which explains why he rebuilt Babylon, scripted his name across Hatra, and erected statues to himself throughout the land, like the Assyrians. His insight is telling: Just as the Israelis cling to King David, the Italians adore the Renaissance, and the British wax nostalgic about the Empire, Muslims romanticize the Baghdad caliphate, and Iraqis boast about Nebuchadnezzar. This national pride was most evident in the lingering resistance to foreign occupation. The most avoidable mistake war planners made in Iraq was underestimating Iraqis' pride in their history, their land, and themselves.

The second lesson I learned seems directly related. No civilization has exclusive claim to truth. The bromide I learned in college, "History is written by the winners," turns out to be wrong. History is written by winners *and* losers. The grandeur of Babylon suggests Nebuchadnezzar was a daring commander with an appreciation of science; the Bible presents him as a villain and a sot. The point is not that one is right and the other wrong; it's that both are right to those who believe them. I was startled to realize how many Jews and Christians look at events in the Middle East as conforming to some preordained prophetic vision of history, while many Muslims view the same events as pointing to an opposing preordained conclusion. If we look at Babylon only as a place against which God wreaks judgment in the Bible, we miss seeing the Muslim nationalist view that it's also a place that once wrought judgment on Jerusalem—and might do so again. We will only understand the threat that religious fundamentalism poses to the world if we understand that those fundamentalists read different versions of history.

The third lesson I took away from Iraq is that the roots of

religious violence in this soil are inextricable from the roots of religion itself. From the opening chapters of Genesis, in which Cain murders Abel, to the vengeful cries of Psalm 137, in which bloodthirsty Israelites imagine bludgeoning their enemies, chaos lives alongside these rivers just as much as order. Every day I felt the underlying sense that civilization could give way to inhumanity at any moment. As a result, everyone I met in Iraq, both locals and foreigners, had one thing in common: They wrapped themselves in emotional body armor. And I did, too. It's the only way to survive in an environment where anarchy and death are icy realities.

Still, I came away convinced that the triumph of violence is not precast in these stones. They tell a different story, too. They tell of the most humane things ever invented: writing, mathematics, time, the calendar, the plow, the garden. Imagination was kindled here, as was freedom. Above all, what emerged from Mesopotamia was the simple idea that humans can control our environment rather than let it control us. We could see the chaos and re-render it as order.

Before I came to Iraq, my sense of Mesopotamia was somewhat muddled. I had a hard time distinguishing among the many civilizations that seemed to jostle one another on these shores. Sumer bled into Babylon, gave way to Assyria, back to Babylon. That mix of cultures continues today. Iraq is still one of the most heterogeneous countries in the Muslim world, with an ever-shifting balance of influence among Sunnis, Shias, Kurds, and their various outside supporters.

But having traveled from one end of the country to the other, I was struck that one iconic image links all three ancient cultures I visited—Sumer, Babylon, and Assyria—the ziggurat. Yet each was built to a different god. The Bible casts this structure as the Tower of Babel, a ziggurat leading humans closer to the one God. The story of Babel has traditionally been viewed as God's punishment against humans for encroaching on his authority. "If, as one peo-ple with one language for all, this is how they have begun to act," God says, "then nothing that they may propose to do will be out of their reach. Let us, then"—note again the plural—"go down and confound their speech there, so that they shall not understand one another's speech."

But rereading the story in Iraq, I came to view it somewhat dif-ferently. In the episode that precedes Babel, the Flood, God is so angry at humans' lawlessness that he opts to wipe out all of hu-manity, "to put an end to all the flesh." Five chapters later, after humans build the Tower of Babel, God no longer seeks to annihi-late humans; he merely scatters them over the face of the earth. His leniency is telling. God is not threatened by humans' industry; he is threatened by their unity. Specifically, he worries that if hu-mans put aside their differences and act as one, they will think of themselves as more powerful than God. To reinforce his view, God's response to homogeneity is instructive: He re-creates hu-mans in heterogeneous groups, forcing them to live as distinct cul-tures, speaking multiple languages.

The message here is unexpected but powerfully relevant today. When humans try to create one language—when one group of people tries to impose an artificial order on the world—God views this as a hubristic attempt to usurp his powers and slaps down the arrogation. God insists on diversity. He demands that humans ac-cept their differences. In rejecting the Tower of Babel, God rejects fundamentalism, the idea that one way of speaking is the only way of speaking and can be imposed on others at will.

God's solution is a cacophony of voices, living side by side.

On the afternoon I left for Iraq, I called to say good-bye to my parents. In the spirit of my farewell note to my wife, I wanted to leave nothing unsaid to anyone I loved. Each conversation had been more difficult than the last. I told my parents that the most important thing they had taught me and my siblings was to engage life fully, to be ourselves. To live. "If something happens to me," I said, "I would like my journey to be remembered as an act of living." An hour later, my mother called back. She was still crying. "Do you know that when a Jewish person dies," she said, "the last words he or she is supposed to say are the *Shema*?"

I hadn't known this.

"I don't mean to hurt you," I said. "I love you."

But hearing this had a curious effect on my trip, as day after day I reflected on those words: *Shema Yisrael Adonai Elohaynu Adonai Echad.* "Hear, O Israel, the Lord is our God, the Lord is one." When I was a boy, that prayer was a source of comfort to me, a simple yet elegant exhortation, chanted in the elegiac way favored at my childhood synagogue. Life could splinter; those words never did. Coming to Iraq was an exercise in human splintering. I chose to come, and risk hurting my family, in part to look at a fractured world directly along the cut line. And what I witnessed in the face of war was the face of God, in the dreams of the people, in the fears of the participants, and in the vastly different visions that motivated each side.

Still, being surrounded by war did not make me want to blame God; it made me want to find *in* God the source of our discord and perhaps the path to our salvation, or at least our peaceful reconciliation. "Let us make man in our image," God says in Genesis 1. And later, "Let us, then, go down and confound their speech." In the verses of the Hebrew Bible most inspired by Mesopotamia, God clearly speaks of himself in the plural. Perhaps this language helps explain why, in the face of the Tower of Babel, God forces humans to live in a pluralist world. By becoming pluralistic, we become most like God.

Out of many, we are made one with God.

I had been thinking about this idea and how it relates to the

Shema when suddenly I stumbled upon its words, written down, in Baghdad. As I was leaving Firebase Melody, Chaplain Messenger showed me his chaplain's kit, a small nylon bag containing all the accoutrements needed to tend wounded soldiers on the battlefield. The kit had a crucifix, a screw-together chalice, communion wine and wafers, a rosary, a *kippah*, *teffilin* (Jewish prayer boxes), and Muslim prayer beads. Tucked into the bottom of the kit was a mimeographed booklet, "Prayers for Iron Soldiers," with the red-yellow-and-blue insignia of the 1st Armored Division, "Old Ironsides," on the cover. Inside was a list of prayers: The Prayer Before Battle; the Apostles' Creed; For One's Sweetheart, Wife, or Husband.

The last pages were entitled "When Facing Death." For Protestants the book advised saying the Lord's Prayer or reading a commendation that began "Depart, O Christian soul, out of this world of pain and suffering." For Catholics it counseled asking the person to make an Act of Perfect Contrition or repeat the Twenty-third Psalm. For Muslims it suggested saying the Prayer for the Dying that begins "Allah is great!" And for Jews it said to read a prayer that ends "O God of Abraham, Isaac, and Jacob, O God of redemption, accept me into thy everlasting presence." "And when the end is near," the book said, "one can say the *Shema*."

As I said good-bye to Chaplain Messenger, he gave me his booklet. I started to choke up. I came to Iraq, above all, to look for the prophets, to learn how the greatest religious minds of antiquity coped with pain, disappointment, and fear. I came away with a babel of prayers. And in my imagination, when I think back on Mesopotamia, before Babylon and Assyria, before Sumer and Ur, before Abraham, I see God having wiped out the Tower of One, leaving behind the blessing of many. And maybe it's out of my feeling of desperation, or maybe out of hope, but I see those many people, in those many kingdoms, not sitting by their rivers but climbing their many ziggurats. God may have demolished the Tower of Babel, but he didn't destroy the human desire to touch God. And perhaps that's why, sitting alone atop my tell, looking out across Iraq, I imagined a forest of towers, and atop each one a union of people reaching out with anguished hearts and out-stretched hands. Not to challenge God. But to join him.

BOOK THREE

DIASPORA

· 1 ·

LET THERE BE LIGHT

L anding after an overnight, international flight has a certain ritual to it—the tucking in of clothes, the resetting of watches, the twittle twittle twittle of cell phones being turned on. But on this particular flight, it comes with another ritual, as all the women on British Airways Flight 6633 from Heathrow reach into their satchels, pull out scarves—mostly black, some mottled brown, none in color—and wrap them around their heads. I see a man take a swig from a flask. We have arrived at the dead end of freedom, the largest religious dictatorship in the world, the shining city on a hill for many Islamic extremists around the globe.

The agonies of traveling to Iran are quite different from those of traveling to Iraq. For starters, the war with the West is cold here, not hot. I have returned my body armor, left behind my combat helmet. I am not carrying a satellite phone, PowerBars, or "accidental death and dismemberment" insurance. I am not worried about being beheaded.

But that doesn't mean coming here is without anxiety. I was

fifteen years old when militants stormed the U.S. embassy in Tehran on November 4, 1979, held approximately seventy Americans hostage for 444 days, and sent legions of teenagers into the streets to chant "Death to America." In many ways, my visceral fear of Iranians was greater than my instinctual fear of, say, Russians. The Cold War was waning by the time I came of age politically; the war with Islamic extremists was just getting started. Ask people of my generation to picture the face of evil, and a majority, I daresay, would pick Ayatollah Ruhollah Khomeini. For me, that dense white beard, forbidding black turban, and deep, angry crosshatch of eyebrows is the haunting insignia of America-hating, Jew-hating, freedom-hating terror.

On a sheer practical level, Iran has few of the fallback conveniences of other places. With relations with the United States never restored, credit cards do not work, getting a visa is a near impossibility, doing anything without being monitored is unthinkable. The Islamic Republic of Iran represents everything I had learned to decry: religion, elevated to political power, using its authority to impose dictatorial control over every aspect of the daily lives of 70 million people, then exporting its brand of revolutionary extremism to terrorists around the world.

Yet the Bible presents a vastly different picture of ancient Iran. Persia, or Trans-Euphrates as it's called in the Book of Ezra, is portrayed as a valiant and tolerant place that destroys Babylon in 536 B.C.E., frees the Israelites, and encourages them to return to Jerusalem and rebuild the Temple. Persia is the savior of monotheism. The Great Satan of today was the Great Messiah of antiquity.

Coming here meant confronting this odd circumstance: First, why did the prophets suddenly glorify a place previously unmentioned in the story? Second, does a place the Bible holds dear now threaten to undermine everything the Bible holds dear? And finally, in my ongoing evaluation of religious conflict today, would Iran squash any fledgling cause for hope?

I had one more reason to be cautious this morning. I wasn't just putting my own fears to the test. One of the women reaching into her bag and wrapping her head in Islamic law was not a stranger to me.

She was my wife.

Some cities bustle; Tehran stands still. Built in a natural amphitheater, with a ring of the Alborz Mountains to the north that descend into the desert to the south, Tehran doesn't have a natural, geographic raison d'être, like a river, bay, or mountain pass. It wasn't even the capital until 1789, when it replaced Shiraz, in the south. But since then it has grown exponentially, particularly under the reign of Reza Shah, the army colonel who executed a coup in 1925, and his son, Mohammad Reza, the heavy-handed secular autocrat ultimately toppled by Khomeini in 1979. At the beginning of Reza Shah's reign, Tehran's population was 210,000; it increased tenfold by 1966, and quintupled, to 10 million, by 2000.

The terrain simply can't handle this many people. Smog hangs over the city like dirt around the *Peanuts* character Pigpen. The water that flows in open canals through the streets begins as melted snow in the mountains and ends as raw sewage in the slums. Cars are everywhere. The Iranian government doesn't import cars; it brings in parts from foreign makers and assembles the final vehicles in the country, taking a cut from every unit. For a cash-strapped regime, selling cars has become a rare source of profit and triggers endless hours of immovable traffic.

Not only does the city not move now but it hasn't really moved, economically, since 1979. Tehran is a time warp for 1970s architecture. Precast concrete is everywhere—museums, flats, sidewalks, curbs, monuments, and especially office buildings, many of which are painted with murals the size of Macy's Parade balloons, all of them depicting Ayatollah Khomeini; his successor, Ayatollah Khamenei; martyrs who committed terrorist acts around the world; and slogans hailing death to Israel. Beside these, the Shia portraits I saw in southern Iraq pale in size, color, and ubiquity. The Iranian Revolution was inspired—and funded—in part by the Soviet Union; its leaders clearly took pointers from the socialist realist portraits of the 1930s. Stalin would have been proud.

He might have liked the Laleh Hotel, too. Its drab furniture, lack of air-conditioning, and general brown demeanor reminded me of hotels I visited in Moscow in the 1980s, which were untouched by decades of modernity and countless bookshelves on customer service. Linda balked at leaving her passport at the desk. She insisted on whispering, assuming our room was bugged. And, at a nearby kebab house, she promptly dripped yogurt with shallots on her *hijab*, or head covering. Discovery: Iranian restaurants don't have napkins.

The truth is, I was a little nervous about bringing Linda on this trip. Born in Newton, Massachusetts, and educated at Harvard and Yale, she embodies everything that frustrated female pacesetters like my mother dreamed the women's movement would produce. With huge black eyes, wavy brown hair, and caramel skin that makes her look almost Latin, as well as a beaming, lighthouse white smile that has been known to wile a billionaire or Third World potentate or two into donating money, she's a pioneer by nature. Three years out of law school, she began a nonprofit organization designed to promote entrepreneurship in emerging markets; less than a decade later, Endeavor operated in seven countries on three continents.

Linda achieved her improbable dream through a combination of vision, passion, and wearing down people who told her she couldn't just change the economies of countries on the other side of the world. But she conducts herself as if she just might do it anyway, and most people, including me, soon learn not to deny her. Still, for all her travels, she had never been to Asia, where muteness sometimes serves, and except for our honeymoon in Morocco, she'd never been to the Muslim world, where women aren't accustomed to getting their way. When I pressed her to buy some understated, long-sleeved clothing to wear during our trip, she came back with two outfits—one white cotton with elaborate embroidery, the other tangerine orange. I could only shake my head. "It's my goal to teach you Muslim modesty," I said.

Though maybe I didn't need to. We were struck at once that daily life was not as draconian as we had expected. The talk of Tehran was a satiric film, breaking box office records, about a petty thief who dresses as a mullah, or cleric, in order to escape prison. He ends up revitalizing Islam in the town where he hides. A woman next to me at an Internet café was using her fake fingernails to type instant messages to her lover across the country in hunt-and-peck English. Even on the streets, women of all ages seemed to test the limits of Muslim regulations and the patience of the social police, inching their *hijab* farther back on their hairlines and brushing makeup around their eyes. As we crossed the street one night to dinner, Linda grabbed my hand. I slapped it away. "We can be arrested!" On the way home, we saw several sets of lovers holding hands nonetheless. Linda grinned as only a vindicated wife can, then pecked me on the cheek.

In Israel, because of the country's existential uncertainty, talk often falls into a dialectic: Israeli versus Palestinian, land versus peace. In Iraq, perhaps because of its pall of dictatorship and war, conversations I had often veered toward the doomsday: O angel of the Lord, protect us; O religious conflagration, avoid us. In Iran, the constant threat of eavesdropping and tattletales make even the most intimate exchanges favor allegory.

On our second afternoon, we drove to the foothills of the

northern suburbs, in the shadow of the shah's former palace, where pricey pistachio shops and French bakeries hint at the country's onetime European-style sophistication. Behind a high stone wall, in the garden of a slightly crumbling estate, we were welcomed by a man whom a mutual friend described as "a grand member of the Iranian literati and a Socratic sage with more than forty books to his credit." If possible, Dr. Fereydoon Forouzan exceeded his billing. In his seventies, he was built like an old oak bookcase, with broad shoulders and thick hands. He wore a Harris tweed blazer with elbow patches, a brown wool vest, and slacks. I checked but saw no pocket watch. His eyes exhibited an air of supreme confidence yet were tinged with defeat. Linda asked him to recommend a restaurant. "My wife and I just mostly eat at home now," he said, forlorn.

Dr. Forouzan was an aristocrat on the wrong side of history. Raised in Tehran, he was educated in France and the United States, receiving a B.A. and Ph.D. in philosophy from Columbia University. He wrote his dissertation on the tension between politics and morality in Kant. I asked him if, as a young man in Iran, he felt the presence of religion.

"The same, I would say, as an American or French or anybody living in a secular country would feel about religion," he said. "My mother was a religious Muslim. She said prayers three times a day. My father was not." His accent was a rich baritone suitable for an English baron.

"I had friends in Paris and New York," he continued, "and our feeling was that religion was something that minded its own business. And coming back to this country, I had exactly the same feeling. That's why, when the revolution came, it took almost everybody like myself by surprise. Even the religious intellectuals were surprised that they succeeded so easily."

The roots of the Iranian Revolution went back at least a century, to the Tobacco Protests of 1891, when Shiite clergy objected to the selling of the country's rich tobacco stock to the British. Since then, the voices of the mullahs had steadily grown. They never warmed to Mohammad Reza Shah, in part because he refused to ban alcohol, gambling, or premarital sex. In 1963, under pressure from the United States, the shah announced a six-point reform plan called the White Revolution that stripped rich landholders of their property, gave women more power, and poured money into rural education. Among his innovations was to remove sworn allegiance to the Koran as a condition of public office.

Ayatollah Khomeini, then a sixty-year-old senior cleric in the religious capital of Qom, south of Tehran, attacked the plans as anti-Muslim. Two days later the shah took a column of soldiers to Qom, and Khomeini was soon arrested. The following year Khomeini was exiled and ended up in Najaf, the Shiite holy city in Iraq, where he lived for the next thirteen years, issuing provocative sermons attacking the shah and the moral depravity of the West. By the mid-seventies, Muslim clerics across Iran canceled Friday services in protest of the government and smuggled in cassette recordings of Khomeini's remarks, which they spread across the country.

But the religious hierarchy wasn't alone in its unhappiness with the shah. Rising oil prices exacerbated the gap between rich and poor, and both Marxists and pro-Westerners were horrified by the shah's increasing brutality. His secret police, SAVAK, tortured dissidents and engaged in widespread secret executions. Under pressure from President Jimmy Carter, the shah released three hundred political prisoners in 1977, but that hardly quelled the anger. Massive protests broke out in September 1978, and the shah called in tanks and helicopter gunships, killing hundreds. On December 12, two million people filled the streets, and one month later the shah fled to Egypt. Dozens of revolutionary groups claimed victory, but Khomeini moved quickest. He arrived in the country on February 1 and promptly announced a replacement prime minister.

A referendum in March endorsed the formation of an Islamic republic, and on April 1, 1979, Khomeini proclaimed the "first day of God's government."

Dr. Forouzan had been working for the shah in the final years and found himself suddenly out of a job, confused, and more or less expatriated within his own country. "Especially the first year," he said, "when all the fighting was going on, I felt the loneliest in my life," he said. "Almost everybody I knew felt the same way. Of course I was highly critical of the shah. But I told all my friends we had to fight for reform, not revolution.

"There was a mania in Iranian society," he continued. "Everyone—the young, the old, the middle class—felt that they had somehow been left behind by history because they had not had a revolution. They envied all the countries that had one, from the French in 1789 to the Russians in 1917. It was madness, really. Just intuitively, I didn't believe a revolution would do anybody any good."

"Were you right?"

"In most ways, yes. The only thing I can say in favor of the revolution is that it started a process that, once we pass this stage, will take us to a better life. I'm impressed by the tremendous boost it's given to people's social and political consciousness. Everybody is concerned about what's happening, and this was not the case before. Many throughout society were sort of slumbering."

Since the revolution Dr. Forouzan had turned his attention to writing about art, history, and politics. "So," I said, "as somebody who analyzed societies, how would you analyze the experiment of taking religion and using it as a basis of law?"

"Oh, it's disastrous. I can't say anything in favor of it. Besides, experience has proven that this sort of union between religion and politics is most harmful to religion itself. Though we had a secular society, I think that people here were actually more religious before the revolution. And this worries me. Because especially for the younger generation, the turning away from religion with bitterness, leaving no hope for coming back, is a big threat to society. Government can be remedied quickly, but when something happens to the faith of the people, to their basic beliefs, it's not corrected very easily."

"But you said you weren't that religious. What are you worried about?"

"Moral chaos. Because if you can't have a just, credible system of administering justice, then the only guarantee you have that people will respect one another's rights and refrain from harming one another is religion. Once that is destroyed, what are you left with? What's interesting now is that religious intellectuals are advocating more and more separation of church and state, having in mind the interests of religion more than state."

"Might this be a harbinger for Islam in general?"

"I believe so, because Iran has been on the leading edge of the Islamic resurgence in recent decades. If you look back to 1979, the kind of fundamentalist revolution that took place here was unheard of. And it's clear that the revolution in Iran played a great part in inaugurating a renewed self-confidence among other Muslims." The Iranian example, led by Shias, was so powerful, he said, that even Sunnis like Osama bin Laden were influenced by it.

"It helped Muslims throughout the world gain a certain consciousness," he explained, "making them combative and willing to fight for their place in the world. Muslims felt they had been treated unjustly by the West for several centuries, but they had always blamed European colonialism. After the Iranian Revolution, Muslims started viewing their situation more as a war between Christianity and Islam."

Given this open hostility to the West, I asked him if he believed Islam and democracy could coexist.

"In this country, yes. But the prospects in other parts of the Muslim world are rather slim, because they haven't had the experience we've had here."

"And will it happen in Iran in your lifetime?"

"It won't be a counterrevolution, certainly. Nobody has the appetite for that. Most people are hoping that this change will be gradual and nonviolent. And I don't think it will take that long, really, because even the people in power are feeling extremely insecure, despite their shows of strength."

"And if that change happens, will your pain have been worth it?"

"Historically, yes. Besides, anybody taking after Kant, like myself, can't separate politics from morality."

Though perhaps his dream might not happen quite yet. The next day Dr. Forouzan telephoned. He hoped I would understand the sensitivity of his situation and not use his name. Our meeting was an allegory for Iran today; Dr. Forouzan exists, but he has another name.

L eaving Tehran made Linda very happy; in a place with less smog she could finally breathe. But it also raised a challenge, because Muslim law is more strictly enforced in the provinces. Our first stop would be Qom, the political capital of Shia Islam and possibly the most conservative city in the Middle East.

We set off southward, past a string of roadside vendors hawking watermelons, into the desert flats. A salt lake, with turquoise water ringed by white deposits, appeared to our west. Low mountains began to rise. We were traveling in a Toyota four-wheeler, stuffed with water and pistachio nuts, driven by Kamran, a wry, fifty-something bookshop owner from Tehran who satisfied his penchant for the wilderness by leading occasional expeditions. He called himself "Strong Man of the Desert." He called Linda "Khanoom," or madame, and brought along for a chador a single piece of black cloth that ran from her head to the ground. "I don't like Qom," he said. "It's too religious for me. The women are all closed up."

The veil was the first symbol I encountered in Iran that began to reshape my religious geography. Before coming on this trip, I'd viewed the history of Islam as a relatively straightforward narrative. Mohammed was born in the small oasis town of Mecca in 571 C.E., received the dictated Koran, and established the Islamic religion before his death in 632. Over the next century, Islam spread rapidly from Arabia east across Asia as far as India and China, west across the Mediterranean as far as modern-day Morocco, south into sub-Saharan Africa, and north into eastern Europe. Islam was not always unified; a violent disagreement over who would succeed the Prophet—an appointed caliph or his nearest relative—divided the religion into Sunni and Shiite sects. But Islam, at its core, was still an Arabian faith; Arabic was its lingua franca, and nomadic life was its chief cultural influence. The lingering importance of the desert was most visible in its use of carpets for praying (no wood is required) and in the presence of green in so many of its decorations (the enduring hope of an oasis to a people trapped in sand).

Persia tells a different story, beginning with the veil. The idea of covering women when they went outdoors in order to shield their sexuality predates Islam by almost two millennia. The custom was first recorded by the Assyrians in the thirteenth century B.C.E. Brutal by nature, the Assyrians undid many of the more enlightened laws toward women that Hammurabi had put in place. It became harder for a woman to get a divorce, and a man could offer his daughters or his wives as temporary slaves to his creditors until he repaid his debts. Assyrian laws also contained regulations on which women could wear a veil. The custom was limited to upper-class women and was used to indicate they were respectable. Prostitutes were expressly excluded.

Veiling spread around the world via the Greeks and Romans and became particularly common with Byzantine Christians and with Zoroastrians in Persia and India. But the custom was not adapted by the Arab world until Islam reached these countries. Arabian women were at first eager to adopt the veil as a sign that they were as sophisticated as the rest of the world. The Koran advises modesty for men and women but specifically orders women to cast garments over their bodies when they go outside. The custom of wearing a veil was widely adopted in the early centuries of Islam, but it became less popular during the Ottoman Empire and under the shahs. Ayatollah Khomeini reinvigorated veil wearing, in part to distinguish Islam from the profanity of the West. After the revolution, he originally wanted to require the full chador, or tent, but accepted the lesser version of a scarf along with loose clothing and nontransparent stockings.

Qom was full of chadors, as well as almost every other kind of traditional clothing. Mullahs in brown cloaks strolled the narrow streets, some in black turbans, indicating they were descended from Mohammed; others in white turbans were ordinary clerics. The city is a bastion of religious schools, libraries, and sanctuaries, with a population of 750,000, though it feels more intimate, with most people coming for the same purpose: to study Shia Islam. The combination of bookshops on every block and students from around the world in national garb made the community feel like Oxford or Cambridge, industry towns where the industry is ideas.

The centerpiece of the city is an elaborate shrine built to honor Fatima, the sister of the eighth of twelve imams honored by most Shiites. Fatima died here in 816, and the golden-domed shrine was constructed over her tomb in the seventeenth century. Non-Muslims are forced to stop at the entrance, but Kamran tipped the guard to let us enter. Linda tightened the chador under her chin, and I bowed slightly. A policeman shadowed us.

The front of the three-story shrine, with its enormous arched entrance, was covered in a mosaic of thousands of mirrored tiles that reflected the sun in every direction, filling the courtyard with a transcendental, disorienting light. Men washed their feet in a line of low faucets. Families held picnics. A lone woman, draped in black, sat yoga-style, with her hands on her knees, praying in the direction of the shrine. I raised my camera to snap a photograph, and an angry man approached. "He's taking pictures of our women," the man said in Arabic. "No, he's not," Kamran said. "He's taking pictures of the men washing their feet." Within seconds we were on our way.

Qom was a bastion of Shiism long before Iran formally adopted the religion in the sixteenth century. Influenced by the spirituality of the imams, Shiism became a more mystical, meditative branch of Islam, in which politics were mostly kept separate from spiritual matters. Feeding off Christianity, the twelfth and final imam was said to have disappeared and would return at the Last Judgment to battle the forces of good and evil and inaugurate a reign of justice. Outside the shrine a billboard reads, in English, SOMEDAY HE WILL COME. It could easily have fit in many parts of America.

Ayatollah Khomeini bucked this tradition by returning Shiism to a proactive role in civic life. But as soon as he assumed power, he became as autocratic as his predecessor, insisting on a uniformity of belief (a position counter to Islamic tradition) and calling for the death of anyone who threatened Islam. In a move that would eventually backfire, he also ordered families to have more children for God. Two decades later, nearly 60 percent of the population was under twenty-five, a population time bomb that the underperforming economy could barely control. Reform seemed to flower with the landslide election of Mohammad Khatami in 1996, but he soon bowed to the lingering grip of hard-liners. Iran was at a standstill.

Though not entirely. On the outskirts of town, we parked our vehicle in front of a modest two-story building, left our shoes at the door, and were ushered into a small library. Three women soon strode through the door. Two were in pants with long-sleeved coats; one was in the most elegant chador I had ever seen. Fahimeh Moussavi-nejad is a vision of religion at the start of a new millennium. The wife of one of Iran's vice presidents and a distant relative of Khomeini, Mrs. Moussavi-nejad took Islamic law seriously. She wore not one modest garment but three: a long-sleeved shirt, covered by a lightweight tan chador, on top of which was a thick, beautifully made raven-colored chador, which hung down over her eyebrows and inched halfway up her chin. Under-neath, she had one scarf wrapped around her hair and another around her neck. The only things visible on her entire body were her eyes, nose, and mouth, as well as her hands, which she used constantly to wrap the yards of fabric over her face.

But boy, did those eyes shine. They leapt from the blackness like diamonds from velvet and, along with her big-toothed grin, emit-ted as much wattage as the mirrored front of Fatima's shrine. Any-one who says a chador conceals a woman's personality has never seen my wife and Fahimeh Moussavi-nejad beaming at each other through impenetrable fabric like two sixteen-year-olds showing off their brand-new bikinis. At least one other person might have un-derstood the feeling I had watching them. Mrs. Moussavi-nejad's husband, an Islamic cleric imprisoned by the shah who became vice president under Khatami, kept an English-language blog on the In-ternet, in which he detailed everything from his dabbling in Super 8 filmmaking to his service in the diplomatic corps. In a revelation of his private life unheard of in Iranian politics, his online bio ends: "I married Mrs. Fahimeh Moussavi-nejad in 1980. We have three issues. They are all girls—Faezeh, Fatemeh, and Farideh. I am happy with my marital life and have no complaint whatsoever."

After his election, the vice president began the Institute for In-terreligious Dialogue, an unrivaled step in the Islamic Republic.

He appointed his wife president, an even more stunning move. "Our goal was to provide some information for the public," she said, "promote a culture of dialogue, and publish books."

"Has the work been easier or harder than you expected?" I asked.

"Rather than say it was harder or easier, I would say some care should be taken in this work. I have been satisfied. Conditions are good for this kind of dialogue, but we have to view the situation realistically." In their first five years, they opened a library, began issuing a journal, and held the first-ever conference of religious minorities in Iran, including Assyrian and Armenian Christians, Zoroastrians, and Jews. Perhaps most astounding, they published a book on the rise of anti-Semitism in Europe.

"Twenty-five years ago, everything in Iran was going to be Islamic," I said. "Now you are holding meetings with religious minorities. What happened?"

She laughed and pulled her chador over her face. "I was a child then," she demurred.

I had no intention of letting her off that easily. "But you are a student of history."

She relented. "After the revolution, our society was involved in some internal problems. A big revolution had occurred, and the society was not that . . . firm, shall we say. It was not stable enough to get involved in ideological debates. After a while, the society turned normal again. This dialogue became possible because spirituality had earned a special place in society, whether it was Jewish people, Armenians, Assyrians, or Muslims."

"Many people around the world wonder whether an Islamic country can be open to different religions," I said. "You're suggesting it took twenty years but that the answer is yes."

"I think Iran is a good example of this. Different religions are living here with much respect. We have religious minorities in parliament."

"But until recently, Islamic law said a Jew, Christian, or Assyrian was worth only one-eighth of a Muslim."

"You're talking about blood money," she said, "which says the compensation a minority can receive from a Muslim in the case of murder is equal to one-eighth of that which would be paid if the victim was Muslim. Our constitution says our country should be based on Muslim law but that we can change it. We just eliminated that law, so now all people are equal."

"If you excuse me for being direct," I said, "I notice in this conversation that all of you are women."

She laughed again and clutched her chador. "It's a coincidence," she said.

"I don't believe you," I said.

"Well, you can say that, in the university, more than 70 percent of religion majors are women."

"I look at you," I said, "and I see a woman in a chador. But your smile and your eyes burst with light. In ten years, which side will win? The chador or your sense of hope?"

"I see no conflict between these two things," she quickly shot back. "What's wrong with a chador? I believe in Islamic covering, which is law in my religion. I like it. And since I obey all my religious laws, I like this one as well. Wherever I go, even in Europe, I wear this chador. I drive with this, and I climb mountains in this."

"But you said you have to take care in these matters," I said. "You said your work is difficult. Will you prevail?"

"There is no definite answer to this question, but I believe that whatever happens in the world will happen in Iran as well. Like everywhere, there are fundamentalists here, as well as open-minded people. Some may prevail at one time, but then others will succeed, just like in American elections."

"So when I read in the paper that the conservatives have prevailed in parliament . . . ?"

She chortled. "Why should you be so disappointed? Nothing happened when the reformers were in power."

"But wasn't your husband one of those reformers?"

Now she laughed. "I believe this movement will be better if we separate the spiritual aspects of religion from the political aspects of religion. It's good for Islam to do that, and good for other religions as well. If you read history, whenever religion has been used as an instrument for government, the religion has been destroyed. Religion is too important for a few men to destroy."

We got up to say good-bye, and suddenly a moment of awkwardness arose. Mrs. Moussavi-nejad stared at the table where we'd been sitting. A cup of coffee, one of tea, a piece of chocolate cake, and some cookies had been served during our conversation. I had touched none of them. "You must eat something," Kamran whispered. "She thinks you don't like her food." I sat down and hurriedly took a few bites of cake and a few sips of tea. This was the allegory of Qom: Even among those committed to sweeping change, small gestures still matter.

We headed south, farther into the hinterlands and even deeper into the spiritual roots of the Ancient Near East. Our destination was Yazd, a wilderness city on the main road to Afghanistan that is the de facto geographic center of Iran. Known for its textiles, Yazd is perched halfway between the northern and southern deserts, in the foothills of the mountains that divide the country between east and west. When Marco Polo came here in 1272, he called it a "good and noble city." Then, as now, it was known as the home of a religion whose leader is a shadowy gleam but whose ideas played a much bigger role in the history of Judaism, Christianity, and Islam than I had ever fathomed.

If Iraq had felt more familiar than I'd expected, Iran, at first blush, seemed more exotic. To begin, it's huge. At 636,000 square miles, Iran is six times larger than the United Kingdom and three times larger than France. It's larger than Iraq, Syria, Lebanon, Israel, and Egypt combined, which means the newest force to enter Near Eastern geopolitics during the latter half of the Hebrew Bible had more land than the entire Fertile Crescent put together. It's also lofty, surrounded by mountains and built on an elevated plateau set between two depressions, the Caspian Sea and the Persian Gulf. Two-thirds of Iran gets snow in the winter.

Closer to India than to Israel, Iran is part of a different ecosystem than much of the Middle East and a different cultural tradition as well, with a language unrelated to the Semitic tongues, closer to Sanskrit, Greek, Latin, and English. The first Iranian cities were set up in the Susa plain, on the western border with Iraq. The Elamites, as they were called, had a tug-of-war with Mesopotamia in the third millennium B.C.E., linked by trade but also by rivalry. During the tumultuous twelfth century B.C.E., while the Sea Peoples were invading the Fertile Crescent from the west, the Elamites were attacking from the east, defeating Babylon and Assyria and bringing back the copy of the Code of Hammurabi that eventually ended up in the Louvre.

In the late second millennium B.C.E., two new Indo-European tribes, the Medes and the Parsuas, infiltrated the Iranian highlands from the north, most likely from the Austro-Hungarian plain. The former set up an empire in the northern part of the country and were the ones to sack Nineveh in the seventh century B.C.E. The latter set up a rival region in the south, called Pars, which became the root for the term *Persia* when Cyrus the Great merged the two regions in the middle of the first millennium B.C.E. Under Cyrus, Persia became the dominant player in the Ancient Near East and the newest, least understood major influence on the Bible.

From their earliest days, the Indo-Europeans had a different religious tradition from the Mesopotamians', mostly localized polytheistic beliefs brought to the region by the nomadic tribes. By the first millennium B.C.E., these were folded into the most mysterious religion to emerge in the Axial Age. In some ways, Zoroastrianism has striking parallels with Judaism. Its central figures (Moses for Judaism, Zoroaster for his faith) left behind no archaeological traces; its canonical texts (the Torah for Judaism, the Avesta for Zoroastrianism) were not written down until hundreds of years after their events took place. The Avesta, recorded in the sixth century C.E., is so fragmentary one scholar has compared writing about Zoroastrianism from its stories to writing about Judaism based only on a few psalms and fragments from the Talmud.

Also like Judaism's, Zoroastrianism's influence on world affairs has been disproportionate to its size—both then and now. Thomas Hyde, the Oxford don who coined the word *cuneiform*, claimed in 1700 that Zoroaster taught Pythagoras and prophesied about Jesus. Voltaire, writing in the mid–eighteenth century, used Zoroastrianism to prove that truth existed outside Christianity. Mozart based a central character in *The Magic Flute*, Sorastro, the benevolent priest of sun and light, on Zoroaster. And a century later, Friedrich Nietzsche used Zoroaster as the mouthpiece for his effort to emancipate humanity from the grip of religion. In *Thus Spake Zarathustra*, Nietzsche, using the original version of the prophet's name, said the Iranian sage was the source of the most profound error in human history, the invention of morality. As a result, Nietzsche argued, Zarathustra himself must reverse that mistake and inspire humans to think beyond traditional Christian morality.

In many ways, Nietzsche's anti-Zarathustra tract became a sort of anti-Bible, a canonical text for those skeptical of religion. During World War I, the German government printed 150,000 copies of the book and distributed them to conscripts along with the Bible. Freud praised Nietzsche's self-awareness, and in the 1930s

Carl Jung held weekly seminars on the meaning of *Thus Spake Zarathustra* with the Zurich Psychological Club. Both Gustav Mahler and Richard Strauss set Nietzsche's work to music. The fanfare to Strauss's *Also sprach Zarathustra* was used as the theme in Stanley Kubrick's *2001: A Space Odyssey*. An ancient Persian prophet who left behind no historical record had suddenly become the spiritual guru of the iconic science-fiction film of the 1960s.

How did this happen?

Zoroaster, from the Greek translation of Zarathustra, meaning "he who can manage camels," lived as early as 1500 B.C.E., scholars estimate, or as late as 600 B.C.E. Everything known about him comes from oral tradition or texts written down centuries later. These stories tell of a man, like Moses, Jesus, and Mohammed, who came from a desert background, perhaps an animal herder. Married three times, with six children, he was harassed by nomads and fled into the wilderness. There he communicated with Ahuramazda, the Wise Lord and the chief deity of the faith that would grow out of their partnership.

Ahuramazda's chief teaching was that life consists of a duality between good and bad. God is wholly good, but he is not wholly powerful. Only with the help of humans will God triumph over evil. Aligned with good are light, fire, summer, water, fertility, and health. Aligned with evil are darkness, cold, winter, drought, sickness, and death. As the ideas of Zoroaster moved from their shadowy beginnings to become the leading religion of Persia in the sixth century B.C.E., one revolution in Zoroastrian thought brought it into line with Judaism, the Pythagorean philosophers of Greece, and Buddhism, the other prominent belief systems of the Axial Age. Zoroaster stressed that all humans, not just the elite, must live an ethical life in order to save the world, and themselves. Even the humble could achieve redemption; even the mighty could fall. The chief way goodness was achieved was by living a life based on "good thoughts, good words, and good deeds."

Zoroastrianism became the dominant religion of Persia at exactly the moment that Persia became the dominant player in the Ancient Near East. Not surprisingly, Zoroastrian ideas began to infiltrate other belief systems of the region, including Judaism. Zoroastrianism, for instance, stressed that life had not just a beginning but an ending, at which point one's deeds were judged and one's soul sent to a heavenly paradise or an underworld hell. In biblical writings before the Babylonian Exile, the word *heaven* was used as a synonym for *firmament* and a vague description of where God resided.

After the Exile, heaven began to be a place where certain humans could visit during their lives and everyone might have a chance to live after death. The idea of hell as a place of punishment also deepened at this time, as did the notion of Satan, one of the angels sent by God to obstruct good human behavior. Though scholars dispute the origin of these ideas, most agree they began to enter Western religion during the years when Persia stood astride the Near East. It seems safe to conclude that in the same way Mesopotamian ideas crept into the biblical notion of Creation, Persian (read: Zoroastrian) ideas crept into the Jewish and later Christian notions of afterlife.

The world's preeminent Zoroastrian Fire Temple is located just off a major thoroughfare in the middle of the urban clutter of Yazd. Though Iran's Zoroastrian population numbered in the millions before the rise of Islam, it has dwindled to less than 100,000 today. (A similar number live in India and are called Parsees.) Owing to their limited numbers, the grounds of the temple in Yazd are small, about an acre. The two-story tan-brick building, built in 1940, is modest, about the size of a small-town public library, with white stone stairs leading up to a four-column porch. Over the door is the symbol of Zoroaster, a spread eagle bird with the head of a bearded man. The bird is similar to the one used in the seal of the United States, though its wings are stretched straight. The image is designed to show humans using their good qualities to triumph over evil and soar into union with Ahuramazda.

Inside the marble foyer, a handful of worshipers were milling about under a chandelier. The room was largely empty, except for a giant portrait of bearded Zoroaster in a toga, painted in an animated, soft-focus style that made it seem almost airbrushed. The centerpiece of the temple, behind a tinted glass, was a foot-tall brass urn with a fire said to have been burning for three thousand years. "Zoroastrians are theists and do not worship the fire," a plaque explained in English. "Rather they regard it as a symbol of purity. Only the unique God, Ahuramazda, deserves to be worshiped. The fire of this temple has been kept burning from the past until now by a special responsible person, a priest, by adding dry wood, such as almond or apricot, several times a day."

Behind the fire, through a small door, we were welcomed into the office of the president of the Iranian Zoroastrian Association. Dr. Kasra Vafadari was decorating. He was placing bowls of fruit on an antique table, with pieces of warm bread and small cups of tea. He was nipping off leaves and pouring water from a copper jug into houseplants on the windowsill. He was arranging the kilim cushions on upright chairs with mumbled excitement. Dressed in an expensive gray-and-white-checked suit and constantly tugging his fashionably floppy black hair from his eyes, he had the I-know-you're-watching-me-and-I'm-slightly-crazed-yet-you-still-find-me-charming-don't-you look of a movie diva before a photo shoot.

"Okay, shall we start?" he said, and we sat down. "I think it's important for you to know who's talking. I'm Kasra Vafadari. I have a doctorate in Anglo-American modern history, and then I got another doctorate in ancient Iranian studies, both from Paris University. I taught in Tehran before the revolution, but the mullahs asked me not to teach because I didn't pray to their god. So I went to Paris. I only came back in the last few years to become head of the Zoroastrian community, but the government does not like me, so they harass me and sometimes arrest me. But now I'm getting lost in my conversation, because I don't know what—"

"How about I start asking questions?" I said.

"Good," he said, and put his hands on his lap like a schoolboy. He looked to Linda for approval.

"Question one: Do you think Zarathustra existed, and do you care?"

"You obviously are a well-matured writer," he said, "because outside this, I might be tempted to accept your provocation, which is very, very below the belt, and say no. But I do care, because I don't think there's smoke without fire. I do think the hymns that make up the Avesta were said by somebody. So I would say yes, but obviously it's not a scientific answer."

"You say it's a below-the-belt question," I said. "I think it's an above-the-neck question. I think in biblical religion we are too obsessed with the question Did Noah exist? or Did Abraham exist? One of the appealing things about Zoroastrianism is that its origin is so vague it seems freed from this question."

"In that case I appreciate the question," he said. "But you have to understand, in Iran for the past fourteen hundred years, if our god isn't Allah, people will say we don't believe in a real god. If we say our god is Ahuramazda and that we try to balance the twin forces of good and evil, then they say we're dualistic. We experienced genocides in the past, so we are very sensitive."

I asked him about the moment when Zoroastrianism first took hold in Iran, and he stressed that the religion arose out of a merger of different traditions, including shamanism and Mithraism. "The only god who could satisfy all these different movements had to be a wishy-washy god," he said. "I'm making fun, but the point is serious. The idea of having an open, universal god, who values wisdom above all else, allowed society to function more successfully. This is why Zoroastrianism still has appeal. It respects people. I love being a Zoroastrian. I get to interact with this modern god based on my own intelligence. *Transfigurating* is the most beautiful word I learned in English for my religion, because it means God can never do anything without me. For the world to get better, we must work together."

"I'm beginning to think this is the great contribution of this moment in religious history," I said. "The Buddha made similar points, as well as the prophets. They moved the central relationship away from god and king, to god and individual. The prophets say it's not about the powerful, it's about the people. All humans deserve justice, and they must act justly in order to achieve it."

"Perfectly put," he said. "The people become co-workers of God's. You have a responsibility to make life better."

I asked him what Zoroastrian ideas he saw echoed in Judaism, Christianity, and Islam. He talked about the idea of the messiah and candlelight in Judaism, the notion of resurrection and the halo in Christianity, and the respect for fire in certain communities of Muslims. "But many Iranians have the tendency to say that everything is from Iran," he said. "The reason is that you, the West, do the opposite. You talk about the Cradle of Civilization being Mesopotamia, and you forget Persia. We have become a little defensive."

"So all of this is leading to a big question," I said. "We live in a world where religion has become more important than it was at any time in the last century. If we go back to the moment when all these religions came into being, and we see how Zoroastrianism and its wishy-washy god influenced other faiths, what can we learn from that moment that will help us today?"

"I honestly believe that the most important thing to remember from Zoroastrianism is that man is free to choose. We are our own masters, and we must respect nature, not kill animals, keep the air and water clean. I can't find a better philosophy of life than that, and it was invented more than 2,500 years ago. The most beautiful thing about Zoroastrianism is that it's not moralistic—do this and don't do that—it's moral. And there's a big difference."

"So if you were to choose a motto for our time to take away from your faith, what would it be?"

"'You are free to choose, choose well.' God is in your brain. You must educate that part of you, you must read, you must help others. A Muslim can remain a Muslim. A Christian can remain a Christian. A Jew can remain a Jew. But think independently. Be calm. Be beautiful. And above all, be good."

A few miles outside Yazd is one of the more unusual religious structures I have ever seen. At the edge of the desert, two reddish brown hilltops with no vegetation rise like sentries. On top of each hill is a squat, round structure about fifty feet in diameter and thirty feet tall that looks like the watch tower of a medieval fort cut off at the knees. These buildings, called *dakhmas*, or silence towers, were built by Zoroastrians as places to bring their dead to be eaten by birds.

Dusk was settling by the time we arrived, so we hurried to climb the narrow path. Linda was wearing sandals and her chador. From behind, silhouetted against the shadowy mountains, she looked like a bat. We were accompanied by Pallan, a Zoroastrian graduate student and friend of Kamran's. I asked him if it was difficult being Zoroastrian in Iran. "All Iranians, in their heart, love Zoroastrians," he said. "They think it's cool. They think we are the pure Iranians."

In the battle of good and evil, Zoroastrians view death as a temporary triumph of evil, so any contact with a dead object can taint the forces of good. As a result, humans were not cremated, because burning the body would defile the fire. Bodies were not buried, because they would defile the earth. Bodies were left exposed in the open air, where they could be decomposed by the sun and devoured by vultures. This public exposure had the added benefit of reinforcing the religion's egalitarian principles, as rich and poor were disposed of in the same manner.

After about twenty minutes, we arrived at the entrance to the silence tower. A small doorway about chest-high was cut into the side of the circular building. I boosted Linda and Pallan, then climbed through myself. The interior was covered in small pebbles and was about the size of a circus ring. Until the Iranian government outlawed the practice in 1978, bodies were laid out with heads facing the perimeter, like spokes on a wheel. After three days, the remaining bones were swept into an internal pit, then dissolved with chemicals. Though the Iranian government banned the custom, some Zoroastrians in India still practice it. I asked Pallan what he'd thought of the idea when he learned about it as a boy.

"I heard it had some advantages," he said. "It's neat, it doesn't take up too much land, it doesn't pollute. Also, it feeds the birds. My grandmother had it done."

"So if the custom were permitted again, would you do it?"

"Maybe. It really doesn't matter to me what happens to my body. What really matters is my soul, and it's going to heaven."

As we walked down the hill, the sun was setting behind the central mountains, creating a vivid tableau, with a jagged line of black peaks followed by a similar line in chocolate brown, both backed by a nectarine sky. The sun was the color of fire. I had proposed we come to Yazd on something of a whim, knowing it was the heart-beat of Zoroastrianism but understanding little about what that meant. Now I could see the flame of Zoroaster burning behind some of the most familiar icons in Western faith—good and evil, heaven and hell—and I could see its tensions flickering in the shadows of Judaism, Christianity, and Islam. As we were saying good-bye to Kasra Vafadari, I mentioned that Linda and I had begun lighting candles on Friday nights to celebrate Shabbat. "When we look into the light, should we think of Zoroastrianism?" I asked.

"No," he said. "The goal is not to replace one religion with an-other. It's to realize that we all grew out of a similar time and place, and share similar dreams. When you look at that light, you should think higher thoughts, and dedicate yourself to making them come true."

Zoroastrianism, I was beginning to think, may be the first light unto the nations, a religion so tiny that its contributions to West-ern religion have long since been consumed by other traditions, their origins long since forgotten. And yet those contributions are testament to the rich foundry of faith that characterized the An-cient Near East in the first millennium B.C.E., when religions viewed the spiritual ideas of other faiths not as threatening their existence but as enhancing their appreciation of a complex, multi-faceted world. The Zoroastrian contribution to that moment is that life is not about hewing to one invariable truth; it's about per-severing through the tension of light and dark, achieving the vic-tory of good over evil, and ending life not with trumpets of noise but on towers of quiet. This may be the greatest allegory of Iran: The most influential ideas in the history of religion were not all made with proclamations.

Some were made in silence.

· 2 ·

His Anointed One

When I was a freshman in high school, a man came to Ms. Arden's ancient history class one day when we were studying Greek and Roman mythology. I remember that course so fondly that the textbook we used, *Myths and Their Meaning*, by Max J. Herzberg, still sits on my bookshelf, its spine mended with masking tape. The man was hawking a summer trip and showed us slides from Greece with white cliffs, green hills, and the most mesmerizing marble ruins sticking up from the ground. That afternoon I went home and talked with my mother.

"I fell in love today," I said.

"With whom?" she said.

"With travel."

We couldn't afford that trip, she explained, and twenty-five years later I've still not been to Greece. In fact, I'd mostly forgotten about that afternoon until Kamran turned our vehicle into a site in south-eastern Iran, just outside Shiraz, whose grounds were as plush and ruins as ethereal as those images I saw more than two decades earlier.

Pasargadae is the forgotten face of Persia, overshadowed by its larger, more famous cousin Persepolis, fifty miles to the south and west. Built on the fertile Plain of the Water Bird, six thousand feet above sea level, Pasargadae is greener than any site I had visited in the Middle East, with hilly grasslands reminiscent of Switzerland, interrupted occasionally by ruins. The grounds were blanketed with newly blossomed red poppies and dotted with petite yellow daisies. The limestone columns that poked up from the greenery had the look and color of classroom chalk. The idea of gardens as paradise seems to have originated in Iran, and likely reached its apotheosis in Pasargadae, the personal creation of Cyrus the Great.

The man the Bible would ultimately hail as God's "anointed one" rose to power in cloudy circumstances, shaded by legend. Born around 590 B.C.E., Cyrus II was said to be the son of an Iranian prince of the Achaemenid dynasty and his wife, the daughter of the prince's rival, the king of Medes. A Delphic oracle purportedly warned the Median monarch that his grandson would threaten his realm. After becoming king of Pars in 559, Cyrus defeated the Medes and forged an unprecedented alliance with his former enemy. In an echo of David, he constructed a new capital for the united monarchy in a neutral place, the site of their final battle, Pasargadae. One account described the city as a large park, filled with wild animals, which the king used to hunt on horseback.

Cyrus's ascendancy changed the world. For the first time in history, the Iranian plateau was unified under one leader, who quickly asserted his power over previously unimaginable spans, from the Mediterranean to the Indian Ocean. Two hundred years before Alexander, Cyrus defined the nickname Great. He first moved west, barreling through a panic-driven alliance formed by Egypt, Mesopotamia, and Sparta, to capture Lydia, on the coast of Turkey. His triumph was reportedly advanced when Lydian horses became unsettled by the odor of the camels ridden by Persian soldiers into battle. His western flank secure, Cyrus moved east, into Afghanistan and India.

But his most consequential feat was to strike at the heart of Mesopotamia's two-millennium-old dominance of world affairs. Babylon, which had sacked Jerusalem at the start of the sixth century B.C.E., was already in decline half a century later under King Nabonidus, who had relocated to Arabia. Nabonidus returned to Babylon in 539 B.C.E. to confront the gathering threat from Persia, but he was too late. Cyrus crossed the Tigris and, according to Herodotus, dammed the Euphrates to parch the city. The Persians then entered without a battle, and local residents greeted Cyrus by spreading green branches before him. Cyrus was so confident of his control over the region that he flung open the city gates and told captives, including the Jews, they could return to their homelands.

Cyrus's victory over Babylon forever reshaped the political geography of the Ancient Near East. Since starting my explorations of the Bible, I had been fond of describing the Fertile Crescent in the second millennium B.C.E. as being like a modern American shopping mall, with an anchor store—Egypt and Mesopotamia—on each end, and smaller, more vulnerable boutique stores—Canaan, Edom, Philistia, Israel, Judah—in between. By the middle of the first millennium B.C.E., this situation had changed irrevocably. Persia was rising to the east, Greece to the west. To overstretch my analogy, it was as if the Fertile Crescent Mall suddenly got a Target across the street on one side and a Wal-Mart across the street on the other. Whereas the anchor stores once competed only with each other, now they had to wrestle with their big-box rivals. To the boutique stores, like Israel and Judah, the new reality meant even more trouble competing and confinement to permanent second-tier status. It may be sacrilege to suggest it, but Jerusalem, capital of the mini-empire of David around 1000 B.C.E., by the mid–first millennium B.C.E. had become little more than a Gap store.

More significant was how the new political reality of the Ancient Near East quickly produced a new cultural reality. Simply put, Cyrus conducted himself with more compassion toward his subjects, more respect toward his victims, and more tolerance toward other faiths than any leader before him in history. He instituted a policy of placating the gods of his subjects rather than carting off their statues, as the Elamites, Hittites, Assyrians, and Babylonians had done. He rebuilt temples in his colonies. And in Babylon he actually celebrated the New Year's rite of Marduk, the chief deity. In 1879 a cylinder was unearthed in Babylon that articulated Cyrus's worldview, the most sweeping declaration of human rights ever found in the Ancient Near East. Cyrus couched his vision in the name of Ahuramazda, the god of Zoroastrianism.

> Now that I put the crown of the kingdom of Iran, Babylon, and the nations of the four directions on the head with the help of Ahuramazda, I announce that I will respect the traditions, customs, and religions of the nations of my empire and never let any of my governors and subordinates look down on or insult them as long as I am alive. From now on, till Ahuramazda grants me the kingdom favor, I will impose my monarchy on no nation. Each is free to accept it, and if any one of them rejects it, I never resolve on war to reign.

Part of this reads like propaganda, for sure; Cyrus never hesitated to use war to advance his realm. But in matters of culture, his actions backed up his words.

No group benefited more from Cyrus's magnanimity than the Jews, and no document heralds his greatness more than the Bible. Cyrus is mentioned by name twenty-five times in the Hebrew Bible and is alluded to many times more. The Book of Ezra is dedicated almost entirely to trumpeting his patronage. It opens with

Cyrus announcing that in addition to sending the Jews back to Jerusalem, he will *pay* to rebuild the Temple. "The Lord God of Heaven has given me all the kingdoms of the earth and has charged me with building him a house in Jerusalem."

The irony is sharp: David, perceived as the great hero of the Bible, is denied the right to build the First Temple; Cyrus, an alien, is credited with building the Second. Even when the residents of Jerusalem object to a new House of God, the Israelites cite Cyrus's edict to his eventual successor, Darius I. Darius endorses the construction. The era of Achaemenid tolerance would last for the next two hundred years, reshaping the world in its wake.

The world, in turn, reshaped Persia. On the far southern edge of Pasargadae sits a curious structure. A stone hut with a gabled roof, about the size of a doghouse, rests atop a six-level base modeled on the ziggurat. From top to bottom, the structure measures thirty-six feet. For centuries local Muslims referred to this building as the Tomb of the Mother of Solomon. Unclear on its origin, they credited this and other ruins around Pasargadae to Solomon, because the Koran, cognizant of his construction of the Temple, presents him as a great builder.

In reality, this tomb was built for Cyrus. He died in battle in 530 B.C.E. near modern-day Kazakhstan and was buried in Pasargadae in a gold sarcophagus, surrounded by his weapons, jewelry, and a cloak. The tomb today is enclosed by a fence, but I was able to bribe the gatekeeper and scurried to its top. Inside the vacant chamber, a graduate student from Shiraz was inspecting an inscription. "O mortal, I am Cyrus the son of Cambyses, who founded the empire of Persia, and was king of Asia. Grudge me not therefore this monument." Two centuries later, Alexander the Great was so impressed that Cyrus had made such a humble plea to posterity that he ordered the burned and looted tomb restored.

But Ali Khazaee said the inscription was probably ordered not by Cyrus but by Darius. The same mix-up applies to a nearby bas-relief, he said, showing a man with an Egyptian crown, Assyrian wings, and an Elamite garment. Though it was once labeled Cyrus, Ali believed it was Darius but stressed that its significance lay in its amalgamation of styles.

"Art has no boundary," he said. "Some scholars believe Achaemenid art is a complete imitation of others, because they took elements from here and there. I believe the Achaemenids' talent was to take all different forms and combine them to produce something entirely new."

Before coming to Iran, I went back and flipped through *Myths and Their Meaning* to see if the book mentioned Persia. It did not, even though Persia dominated the eastern Mediterranean for almost a century during the heyday of ancient mythology. Next I flipped through the prayer book I used as a child to see if it had anything about Persia. It, too, did not, even though the Bible credits Persia with liberating the Israelites from their national humiliation.

My journey had shattered that silence. Here, on the eastern flank of the Fertile Crescent, unmentioned in the story of Western civilization, barely uttered in the religious dialogue of today, is a culture whose lessons for our time may be the most relevant of the entire Ancient Near East. One city, above all, tells that tale.

In a region of breathtaking archaeological sites, Persepolis may take the prize. Poised on an elevated plateau at the base of Koh-E-Rahmat, the Mountain of Mercy, Persepolis exudes an air of regal isolation and opulence, as if the walls of Versailles had been flattened in a tornado and left hundreds of inner columns still standing, along with the occasional statue from the king's private bath. Though Persians called it Parsa, from the tribe that dominated the region, the city was known in Greek by the contraction of *Persia* and *polis*, Persepolis. At thirty-five acres, Persepolis is the same size as Herod's Temple Mount compound, and, at 5,800 feet, it's the original mile-high city. The Roman writer Augustus described it as "the most beautifully constructed city."

Darius I began building Persepolis sometime after 520 B.C.E., and work continued for the next sixty years, under the reigns of Xerxes and Artaxerxes I. The entire complex was built over three levels on an enormous raised terrace that included fortifications, a monumental stairway, a palace, and a ninety-three-room treasury. Alexander the Great burned the city in 330 B.C.E. Plutarch wrote that it took ten thousand mules and five thousand camels to carry off the booty.

Because it's built on a platform, thirty miles from modern-day Shiraz, Persepolis still reveals itself to the visitor with levitating charm, a magic carpet over the green hills of Pars. "The important thing about Persepolis is the location," Kamran said as we approached. "The temperature here is just right. They have four seasons. The underground aqueduct is perfect. The climate is so good the fields in this area have two, sometimes three crops a year."

Through a glass gate, we were led into a laboratory, covered with tablets, dusty language books, and antiquated computers, where we met the chief of Achaemenid research at the Iran National Museum and the startling new face of Persian archaeology. Almost exactly my age, Shahrokh Razmjou was taller, darker, better looking, thinner, gentler, more learned, and even more articulate than I, though he was speaking his seventh language and I was speaking my first. He had a boyish smile, huge, frameless glasses, and an aw-shucks demeanor that seemed more like Christopher Robin than Indiana Jones. Linda squirmed on meeting him, choked up when we left, and for months afterward I referred to him simply as "your boyfriend."

"My *Iranian* boyfriend," she corrected, to separate him from the myriad others.

Above all, he inspired in me a passion and intimacy with the ancient world unrivaled since I'd first met Avner. One of the cruelties of Middle Eastern politics is that, because Shahrokh and Avner come from countries that don't speak to each other, it would take a feat of diplomatic strength worthy of Hercules for them to meet.

Shahrokh Razmjou fell in love with archaeology when he was seven years old, but his dream was nearly stymied by the revolution, when the mullahs asserted that anything that occurred before Mohammed was *jahiliyyah*, ignorance. Overnight, undergraduate ancient history classes were canceled, teachers reassigned. Shahrokh began buying up textbooks from rare book markets to teach himself the necessary language skills, including cuneiform.

"Didn't the library have them?"

"Yes, but I wanted to continue my studies at night."

His first day of university, he talked his way into a master's program in archaeology whose enrollment was a mere ten people. Twenty years later, in another sign of the dwindling zeal of the revolution, enrollment had climbed to one hundred. I asked if that pleased him.

"Why not? We need an army of archaeologists. Even if we had a hundred people working on the same topic, that would be brilliant, we'd have a hundred different opinions."

I picked a piece of paper off his desk and sketched a map of the Ancient Near East, with the Fertile Crescent at its heart. "Ten thousand years ago people began to take these rivers and create civilization. That happened first in Sumer, then Babylon, then Assyria. There are rivers in Iran. Why did it not happen here?"

"We don't know if it happened here or not," he said. "One problem is that we don't have enough information about Iran, because Iran is an almost unexcavated country. During the nineteenth century, Europeans were more interested in sites that were mentioned in the Bible, especially Mesopotamia and Egypt.

According to the latest reports, we have half a million known sites in this country that are not dug."

"Half a million?"

"That's why I say we need an army of archaeologists. Take Sumer; in the third millennium B.C.E. it had one of the most famous civilizations in history. Recent excavations in Jiroft, in southeast Iran, show a huge civilization at the same time, unfortunately unknown until today. Jiroft had a very strong trade system with other countries, and one of their roads went directly to Mesopotamia. The writing and engraving in Jiroft seems to have influenced that in Sumer."

"So you think Jiroft should get more attention, like Ur?"

"Not more than Ur, but something equal to Ur. You can't ignore one and say, 'Okay, civilization began in one and not the other.' Until three years ago, nobody had heard about Jiroft. Now we have to rewrite our history books."

"There's one thing I've always wondered about that period," I said. "The Bible has Abraham living in Ur around 2000 B.C.E. When he leaves, why does he go west, toward Harran, and not east, toward Iran?"

"It is very difficult to speak about that period. We don't know the precise relations between Elam and Mesopotamia. The two traded, but somehow they were always fighting. Even today, there is an unseen border between these two areas. Not just a geographical-political border but a cultural one as well. On one side were the Elamites, on the other the Mesopotamians. The same with the Qajars in Iran and the Ottoman Empire. And more recently, the Iran-Iraq war."

"What would explain such a line?"

"I don't know exactly. You can see such borders in other places. The Great Wall of China was to protect the Chinese from the northern people. Between Iran and Iraq we have an invisible wall.

Even if the two sides are living in peace, there is always something to keep them separated."

We stepped into the blazing sun and proceeded up the monumental staircase at the entrance to the compound. Labeled "perhaps the most perfect flight of steps ever built," by Ernst Herzfeld, the excavator of Persepolis in 1920s, the 111 steps have a height of only five inches each, compared with seven and a half inches for a normal stair. The low rise was designed for horses or nobles in long cloaks to ascend more easily.

Unlike Pasargadae, with its scattered remains, the buildings at Persepolis are concentrated on a great terrace, fourteen hundred by one thousand feet, as long as the Acropolis but five times as wide. Arriving at the plateau, we were greeted by a forest of columns, slabs, and statues. Most of the excavation of Persepolis was completed in the 1930s by the Oriental Institute of Chicago. As a sign of Iran's cultural warming with the West, the institute had just returned three hundred tablets, which Shahrokh received to much fanfare.

The entrance to the city is the stately Gate of All Nations, with sixty-foot columns flanked by two standing bulls with wings and human heads, as in Assyria. Muslim observers in the twelfth century likened them to Buraq, the winged horse on which Mohammed made his night journey to heaven. The capitals have back-to-back bird heads that look like the pushmi-pullyu llamas from *Doctor Dolittle*. The gate boasts graffiti going back nearly two centuries, including "STANLEY, NEW YORK HERALD, 1870" and "F. W. Graf Schulenberg, 1931." Sir Henry Morton Stanley was the Welsh-born reporter who tracked down the missing Scottish missionary David Livingstone in Africa in 1871 and introduced himself by saying, "Dr. Livingstone, I presume?" Schulenberg was the Nazi ambassador to Russia in the 1930s who was executed in 1944 after trying to execute a coup against Hitler. Persepolis's status as a crossroads of the world clearly did not end with Alexander's sacking.

But why was Persepolis so prominent? The Achaemenids had a summer residence in Susa and a winter residence in Hamadan, both to the northwest. Persepolis had no discernible raison d'être. For most of the last century, the leading explanation held that the city was a ceremonial center, used for the New Year's festival of No Ruz. But Shahrokh disagreed. Persepolis, he said, was more likely a dynastic residence, a showplace for the grandeur of the Persian empire. And how would he characterize that empire?

"Some aspects show that they were a very open people," he said. We were walking through the main courtyard, where visitors once waited to enter one of the ceremonial buildings. Dwarfed by the columns, dressed in rumpled khakis and a blue jean shirt, Shahrokh Razmjou looked like a fourteen-year-old boy on a school field trip.

"Until the Achaemenids," he continued, "the tradition with leaders like Ashurnasirpal was to destroy your enemy and burn them to the ground. But the Persians introduced a different way. Darius began with violence, but afterwards he gave his subjects freedom, as Cyrus had done. We have inscriptions from Asia Minor and Egypt that show Darius saying, 'Ahuramazda gave this land to me, and there was chaos here. So I put everyone in their place and didn't let them beat one another.' There were periods of hostility, but for two hundred years there was largely peace among these countries called the Pax Persica."

"So if everybody before them wiped out the gods of their enemies, why were the Achaemenids suddenly so open-minded?"

"Very good question. I think one reason was their religion. I don't believe, according to the documents, that they were pure

Zoroastrians. I think it was a broader, Iranian ideology, though Zoroastrianism gave them clear ideas about peace and friendship, goodwill and good thoughts. They had a religion based on respect. We have receipts from annual payments they made to gods other than their own. We have reliefs of them giving rations to other gods. And we have the best evidence of all, right here."

Shahrokh brought us to a stop at the Great Audience Hall, the largest building on the site, measuring four hundred feet along each side. Of the original seventy-two columns, thirteen are still standing. At its peak, the hall could accommodate ten thousand people and was called the most magnificent room in the world. The most stirring feature of the building, though, is not its inner chamber but its external staircase. On the northeast corner sits an enormous stairwell, called the Apadana staircase, with two wings the length of a football field. The stairs are protected by a decorative front, like the pediment on a Greek temple, which displays more than eight hundred miniature carvings—each about three feet tall—of subjects from twenty-three countries bearing tribute to the king. The cavalcade reminded me of the parade of nations from the opening ceremony of the Olympic Games.

The carvings celebrate the stunning diversity of the empire and the individuality of each culture. The Ethiopians march with a giraffe, the Libyans with an antelope, the Assyrians with sheep, the Arabs with a camel. The Indians wear saris and lead an ass, the Ionians hold honeycombs and skeins of yarn, the Babylonians carry textiles and tug along a bull. In a sense, these delegations are the depiction of the post-Babel world, with twenty-three cultures expressing themselves in twenty-three different idioms. Although Jews were too insignificant to be included in the parade, a number of Jewish names do appear in tablets found in Persepolis, including Zechariah, Hezekiah, and Shabbatay, "born of the Sabbath."

"If you look at this staircase, you can see that the main idea for the Achaemenids was unification," Shahrokh said. "Theirs was the earliest united kingdom. And their iconography demonstrates this. Mesopotamian sculpture was very violent. In Assyrian carvings the subjects were often bound in chains. Here, everyone is smiling. They're walking. They're holding hands. This one is holding that one's beer. This one is gently pushing the other. It's a pretty friendly group.

"And here's the most amazing thing," he said. "Many of them have swords. That means they were allowed to go armed in front of the king. It's against all logic. If your subjects hated you, you would never allow them to bring weapons into a meeting with you."

"When most people think of Persepolis, they think of the power of Darius," I said. "But when you think of Persepolis, you think of the positive relations among the people?"

"I do think of the Achaemenids' power," he said. "They created a vast empire, with a canal in Egypt, as well as a huge road system. Darius invented the world's first postal system, for getting news to people in the provinces. Men would ride horses to appointed spots, hop off one horse and onto another, then ride on. The horse would then receive rations. Postal carriers had regular horses and fast horses, and could travel from here to the Mediterranean in seven days.

"But their biggest innovation," he continued, "was their emphasis on personal happiness, which they believed was the fourth creation of the gods. In their inscriptions, their god created heaven, he created earth, he created man, and he created happiness for man. I found a name in one of the treasury tablets that says, 'The Gate of Happiness.' They named gates to happiness! And they were happy people. They had so many celebrations every month I don't know how they could work."

"I think of personal happiness entering the idea of statehood thousands of years later," I said, "like the Declaration of

Independence promising 'life, liberty, and the pursuit of happiness.' It's almost mind-blowing to think that even that idea started here, 2,500 years ago."

"And like the United States, the Achaemenids believed they could draw strength from their diversity. When they designed Persepolis, they invited different artists from different countries to put different elements into the buildings. They wanted an international style. You see all these lotus flowers on the walls? They came from Egypt. They took the winged bulls from Assyria, and so on.

"So just imagine when people walked through the main palaces," he continued. "They would say, 'Oh, that's an arch from Ionia, that's a rose from Babylon. Those bricks look very Elamite.' Everyone would find something that reflected themselves, so they automatically felt a part of the place. Persepolis was not only a palace to show power. It was a palace designed to keep the whole empire together in peace and happiness."

Something unusual happened during my conversation with Shahrokh. Linda grabbed my notebook and began jotting notes. She had never done this before, on this trip or any other trip we'd taken. By the time Shahrokh and I finished, she was sitting on the stairs, cuddling the notebook. I went over to see her.

"Is everything okay?"

"Yes. I'm sorry."

"Why?"

"It's very emotional."

"Emotional?"

"This experience. Being here, feeling the places, breathing the air." She began to cry. "I thought I understood what happens to you on these trips," she said. "But being here, seeing all this . . . It's so much more powerful than I imagined."

We sat quietly for a moment. I wanted to touch her but felt restricted by Muslim dictates.

"Iran is supposed to be a pariah," she continued. "But now that I'm here, I've never had this feeling of wanting to go deeper in a society. The fact that 95 percent of Pasargadae is unexcavated, and that every Iranian we've met keeps bringing up Cyrus and the idea of mingling of cultures. It's just so untapped. It saddens me."

"But we're Americans. Aren't we taught to love everything new?"

"That's the point. In America we pride ourselves on being innovative. We're entrepreneurs. I love that, but being here makes me believe that we're missing out on something." She looked at me with her big, open brown eyes. The tears had smeared around them. "I just wish we weren't so cut off from this place. For the first time in a long time, I can see a source of hope."

The four of us—Kamran, Shahrokh, Linda, and I—set out for a small cliff on the Mountain of Mercy where several Achaemenid kings were buried. The tombs, carved directly into the mountain, reminded me of similar graves in Petra, in Jordan. From the perch, Persepolis looked like a train set laid out beneath us. Past the ruins, Kamran pointed out the skeletal shell of a tent, large enough to hold a one-ring circus. I could see shreds of blue and pink fabric flapping in the wind. These remains, scarcely thirty-five years old, come from what many observers have called the grandest party of the twentieth century, and what I now realized was the ongoing struggle to define the legacy of Cyrus.

By October 1971, the shah of Iran was already losing his grip on authority. To bolster his image, he announced that he would hold a celebration marking the 2,500th anniversary of Cyrus's rise. Though pedants pointed out that 2,500 years from 559 B.C.E. was actually 1941, the shah pushed forward, stuffing his chandeliered big top with Limoges china, Baccarat crystal, and what he called the greatest gathering of heads of state in history. Sixty-nine countries sent representatives, including twenty kings, five queens, twenty-one princes and princesses, sixteen presidents, four vice presidents, three prime ministers, and two foreign ministers. The guest list reads, in part, like a rogues' gallery of the late twentieth century, including Haile Selassie, Nicolae Ceausescu, and Imelda Marcos. President Nixon sent Spiro Agnew.

At the start of the three-day event, the shah stood before Cyrus's tomb in Pasargadae. "Cyrus, great king of kings," he orated, "noblest of the noble, hero of the history of Iran and of the world, rest in peace. For we are awake. We will always stay awake." At the closing gala, guests were treated to a meal airlifted from Maxim's in Paris that was so lavish the restaurant was forced to close for fifteen days to prepare it. Courses included quail eggs topped with caviar, crayfish mousse, roast lamb with truffles, and roast peacock stuffed with foie gras. Dessert was port-glazed figs with raspberries served with Dom Pérignon rosé 1959. In an homage to the Apadana staircase, guests witnessed phalanx after phalanx of soldiers dressed as Iranian figures from history. Afterward, the dignitaries traipsed to Persepolis in the suddenly freezing temperature and watched a sound and light show on the ruins, the women wrapped in blankets. When a fireworks show was delayed by an explosion on the launching pad, many thought they were victims of a terrorist attack.

"It was really a terrible embarrassment," Kamran said. "I remember watching on television. They said the party cost $120 million. And Iran was such a poor country. It was the beginning of the end of the shah."

After the revolution, Khomeini's infamous "hanging judge," Ayatollah Sadegh Khalkhali, went to the other extreme and proposed destroying Persepolis as a symbol of pre-Islamic ignorance. (Khalkhali later went on Iranian television to poke the charred bodies of U.S. military personnel killed in the failed mission to free the hostages in the U.S. embassy.) The ayatollah's plan to dynamite Persepolis sounds similar to what the Taliban carried out against two Buddhist statues in Afghanistan in 2001, calling them "un-Islamic idols." But just before Khalkhali's scheme was carried out, local Shirazis, led by the governor, stood in front of the bulldozers, prompting Ayatollah Khomeini to nix the plan, though he still eliminated Cyrus's name from street signs across the country.

In the back-and-forth between Cyrus the Wonderful and Cyrus the Apostate, the most rousing amicus brief in support of the king does not come from Persepolis, Pasargadae, or any of the inscriptions stored in museums across the West. It comes from an unnamed Hebrew prophet writing in the late sixth century B.C.E.

We pulled out our Bibles. The Book of Isaiah is the longest, some say the most beautiful, and certainly the most influential of the twenty-one books of the Hebrew prophets. It contains sixty-six chapters, but for several hundred years scholars, clergy, and lay readers alike have agreed that the prophesies should be divided into two, three, or even more sections. The first thirty-nine chapters belong to the self-identified "Isaiah of Jerusalem," who was called to be a prophet in 739 B.C.E. The next sixteen chapters, 40 through 55, appear to belong to an unnamed prophet who lived in exile and was part of an Isaian school, in the same way that Greek philosophers or Renaissance painters were later surrounded by schools of disciples, some of whose work was occasionally assigned to their master. The last eleven chapters, 56 through 66, are sometimes assigned to this prophet, sometimes to a third, other times to a redactor, living in Jerusalem, who merged the two voices into a unified whole. The prophet of the middle verses arose around 540 B.C.E., on the eve of Cyrus's conquest of Babylon, and is commonly called Second Isaiah or Deutero-Isaiah.

Second Isaiah appears at yet another moment of transition for the children of Israel and casts the events of history as a tale of redemption. His primary goal is to comfort Israel, whose sons are "like an antelope caught in a net." The prophet pleads with God to forgive the sins of the past. "You have hidden your face from us, / And made us melt because of our iniquities," he cries.

We are the clay, and you are the potter,
We are all the work of your hands.
Be not implacably angry, O Lord,
Do not remember iniquity forever.

God responds with some of the most compassionate words in prophetic literature:

Comfort, oh comfort my people,
Says your God.
Speak tenderly to Jerusalem,
And declare to her
That her term of service is over,
That her iniquity is expiated;
For she has received at the hand of the Lord
Double for all her sins.

God, the prophet suggests, feels pain at how he has treated the Israelites. "I was angry at my people," he says. "I defiled my heritage." God and humans, searching for each other since the first light of Creation, finally find each other in grief.

And God, once again, reaches out. He promises to rescue humans, and thus rescue himself. "I am about to do something new," he declares. This new thing, he says, will produce a new Eden. "You shall be like a watered garden, / Like a spring whose waters do not fail." This new thing will be a new flood.

As I swore that the waters of Noah
Nevermore would flood the earth,
So I swear that I will not
Be angry with you or rebuke you.

This new thing will be a new exodus. It was the Lord, after all, "who made a road through the sea / And a path through mighty waters." This new thing will be another expression of the cycle of creation, destruction, and re-creation. The rivers of Babylon have become the latest waters God will split, allowing the Israelites to pass on to dry land.

So what does God do? He summons a "swooping bird from the East / From a distant land, the man for my purpose." He delivers nations to this savior and renders their swords into dust. God earlier did something similar with Nebuchadnezzar, but this time he goes further. He says of his new deliverer, "He is my shepherd, / He shall fulfill my purposes!" And then, in Isaiah 45, he calls out to this figure directly.

Thus said the Lord to Cyrus, his anointed one—
Whose right hand he has grasped,
Treading down nations before him,
Ungirding the loins of king . . .
I will give you treasures concealed in the dark
And secret hoards—
So that you may know that it is I the Lord,
The God of Israel, who calls you by name.
For the sake of my servant Jacob,
Israel my chosen one,
I call you by name,
I hail you by title, though you have not known me.

Few passages in the Prophets echo with such epoch-making fanfare. The God of the Hebrew Bible, longing since the Garden of Eden for an everlasting relationship with humans, following a history of being thwarted by nearly every human he tapped to be his personal envoy, after yet another seismic exile of his stiff-necked people, extends his sacred blessing to a king who *doesn't even know him*. And he terms that man his *anointed one*.

The appellation *anointed one* is the common translation for the Hebrew word *mashiah*, which is also rendered in English as *messiah*. *Mashiah* comes from the verb *mashah*, which indicates the applying of oil to an object or person by rubbing, pouring, or smearing. In the Hebrew Bible, Saul, David, Solomon, and several other kings were called "the Lord's anointed," as were priests and at least one prophet, Elisha. The word *mashiah* as a noun, applied to a specific person, implying that this person receives a divine commission to secure peace and freedom for God's chosen people, is used only once in the Hebrew Bible, here, and it's in reference to Cyrus.

Messiah is a loaded word today, because of its association with Jesus and the disagreement among members of different faiths over whether Jesus was the Jewish messiah. The Greek translation for *mashiah*, for instance, is *kristos*, the root for *Christ*. But *mashiah* to mean a transcendent individual, the future son of David, who would appear at the end of time and introduce a new age of peace for Israel and the nations, was not widely used in the Ancient Near East in the middle of the first millennium B.C.E. That idea came during the last centuries of that millennium. That notion of the messiah bears striking similarities to the Zoroastrian belief in a series of saviors, or "bringers of benefit," as the Avesta calls them, who will heal the world and brighten existence. No matter the interpretation, the idea of the messiah in Ancient Near East religion shows intriguing connections to Persia.

Still, even if Second Isaiah does not use the word *mashiah* as it would come to mean, he does use the word for Cyrus, augmenting it by calling the Persian king God's "shepherd," whose "right hand he has grasped." Collectively, these terms represent an unprecedented expression of respect in the Hebrew Bible. Second Isaiah considers Cyrus a vessel for good so transformative that what follows his liberating Israel from Babylon will be a new era in God's dominion over the earth. God vows to raise up the tribes of Jacob and "make you a light of nations."

> *Kings shall tend your children,*
> *Their queens shall serve you as nurses.*
> *They shall bow to you, face to the ground,*
> *And lick the dust of your feet.*
> *And you shall know that I am the Lord—*
> *Those who trust in me shall not be shamed.*

Many scholars regard the vision of a God-centered world in Second Isaiah as the most universal expression of God's glory in the Hebrew Bible. The time has come, God says in Isaiah 66, "to gather all the nations and tongues; they shall come and behold my glory." Having dispersed the tongues after the Tower of Babel, now he aspires to unite them in his honor.

At first glance, the vivid universalism of Second Isaiah would seem to make the anonymous prophet an ideal candidate to bring together all believers of God. Second Isaiah could be the unifying vessel so desperately needed among rival monotheists. Instead his words rub at the sensitive division that rends Jews and Christians in particular. The focus of dispute lies in a series of verses known as the Servant Songs (42:1–4, 49:1–6, 50:4–11, 52:13–53:12). In these passages, God promises to choose a servant who will teach his true way to the nations. This servant shall not shout aloud nor make his voice heard in the streets. "He shall not grow dim or be bruised / Till he has established the true way on earth." In some verses, the servant appears to be a person, in others a group, in some a real figure, in others imaginary.

More than half a millennium after these verses were recorded, early Christians began seeing in them a prophecy of Jesus. They pointed to parts of the second Servant Song, "The Lord appointed me before I was born, / He named me while I was in my mother's womb," and especially the fourth.

> *He was despised, we held him of no account.*
> *Yet it was our sickness that he was bearing,*
> *Our suffering that he endured.*
> *We accounted him plagued,*
> *Smitten and afflicted by God;*
> *But he was wounded because of our sins . . .*
> *He shall receive the multitude as his spoil.*
> *For he exposed himself to death,*
> *And was numbered among the sinners,*
> *Whereas he bore the guilt of the many.*

For thousands of years, many Christians have fervently believed that these verses are predictions of Jesus Christ. The universalism of Second Isaiah, in this view, applies less to a general time of God's kingdom and more to the specific dominion of Christ Almighty.

Jews, not surprisingly, have viewed these verses differently. Some do see the servant as an individual, with Abraham, Moses, or Second Isaiah having been proposed. But more see the servant not as the messiah but as an ideal that reflects the innate character of the entire people. The only time the servant is named, for example, in the second song, the reference is to Israel, "You are my servant,

Israel in whom I glory." In this view, the righteous of Israel were sent into exile, suffered in silence, were smitten and afflicted by God, and bore the guilt of the many residents of Israel and Judah who had sinned over the centuries. By rewarding the moral conduct of the Israelites in exile and lifting them out of Babylon, God turned Israel into a light to the nations.

Sitting in Persepolis, I couldn't help viewing these passages differently. One overriding challenge of my journeys across the Middle East was trying to remove the stories of the Bible from the gilt-edged pages that sometimes ossify them today, as well as the rigid, sectarian interpretations that have come to define them over the centuries. My goal was to replant those stories into the ground from which they sprang and see if viewing them in the context of their time changed the lessons I gleaned from them. In the case of the Prophets, that meant viewing them not through the prism of the New Testament or the Talmud, both of which were colored by the already boiling rivalry between Jews and Christians in the early centuries of the first millennium C.E. Instead, I wanted to view them in light of the mid–first millennium B.C.E.

In the case of the Servant Songs, that meant understanding that they were written during a period ripe with Persian influence. The songs cry out to be interpreted in a broad context. Considering that they are dispersed over five chapters, it seems fair to assume that the compiler of Isaiah viewed them as part of the larger book. The servant, after all, was not an end unto himself but a means to a world in which *all* humans work to fulfill God's mission. "Observe what is right and do what is just," God commands.

> For soon my salvation shall come.
> Happy is the man who does this . . .
> Who keeps the sabbath and does not profane it,
> And stays his hand from doing evil.

The message here is that each person who follows God's laws and acts morally can help bring about God's ultimate triumph. And by working toward this end, humans will be "happy."

If this philosophy sounds familiar, it is: The grand idea at the heart of Second Isaiah bears striking similarity to the grand idea introduced by the Persian kings of the sixth century B.C.E. Morality is the highest calling of human conduct, and happiness the ultimate reward. And while these ideas may be practiced differently by different peoples, they ultimately transcend national borders and religious boundaries. They are universal.

This type of overarching, all-inclusive value system—especially one based on justice for all and happiness for every individual—was not widespread before the mid–first millennium B.C.E. The premise of the Pentateuch is finding a piece of land for God's chosen people so they can live a God-centered life. Universality is hinted at in the story of Abraham—"all the families of the earth shall bless themselves by you"—but the idea that his life would lead to righteousness and contentedness for everyone would have been far-fetched to him, as well as to Moses, Joshua, David, and almost any other Israelite leader.

By the sixth century B.C.E., this idea was no longer absurd. The epoch of rival nation-states had given way to one of sprawling empires. A unified world was now imaginable. The vision of unity advanced by the Achaemenids allowed Jews and others to maintain their cultural identity as part of a new enlightened empire. The Bible pays tribute to that policy of tolerance in the Book of Ezra. Given that acknowledgment, it seems reasonable to conclude that God in Isaiah knows of Cyrus's respect for different faiths when he chooses him to be his anointed one. The lesson here is transcendent: *Even those who believe in other gods can still, by acting morally, be part of God's world*. In a moving confluence of scripture and history, one figure embodies this ideal more than any other, both in the real world of the Ancient Near East and in the verses of Second Isaiah. Cyrus may not be the messiah as the term would later come to mean, but he was the messiah as it was understood at the time.

He was a shepherd who inaugurated a radical era of peace.

So do you agree?" Linda said to Shahrokh. We were sitting on a rock overlooking the ruins. Only a handful of visitors were wandering the grounds. I found it amusing, but ultimately touching, that Linda had all but taken over our outing. Her visceral reaction to being in Persepolis reminded me why I had embarked on a journey of visiting biblical places to begin with—and why I had married her.

"Does history confirm that Cyrus was a messianic figure?" she said.

"I think so," he said. "In archaeology we have to use all categories of sources—texts, remains, classical sources. We need first to see the physical context, then check sources like the Bible and other texts. But this is an example where the written text, the Bible, captures the greatness of Cyrus that we see evidence of in other places."

"But few people know this story," she said. "We know about Rome and Athens and Jerusalem. Do you think Persepolis was as important as the other great cities of antiquity?"

He smiled. "At that time, yes. But the problem with Persepolis is that it wasn't the only major city of the Achaemenids. The king was itinerant and traveled between residences, so no one city rose to the level of Athens or Rome."

Linda touched my arm. "So, as my husband would say," she began, but paused when I glared at her hand for flouting Muslim law. She kept talking. "As my husband would say, the big question in the world today is Can the religions get along? It sounds like the

Achaemenid empire may be the first example where this actually happened."

"They began this idea, actually. And they showed that they could provide a space for different people to believe in their own gods and follow their own religion. We have tablets in which a Babylonian priest received a tribute for an Iranian god. This would be like a Christian priest participating in a Jewish ceremony, and a Jewish priest in a Muslim ceremony."

"I love it! I wish everybody could hear your story." Now she touched his arm. "You make me feel hope."

For a second Shahrokh paused, unsure what to do. Would Kamran point out this violation of Muslim law? Would he? And in that instant, I realized that this innocent pose—one visitor lightly touching another—was the exact same one carved on the outer walls of the Great Audience Hall: a small gesture of happiness in a forbidding world.

"Khanoom Linda," Kamran said, shaking his head in exasperation. Now Shahrokh was free to speak from his heart.

"I've always believed that archaeology is not just something for archaeologists," he said. "We are doing archaeology for the people. If we just say, 'This pot is from 669 B.C.E.,' that means nothing. We have to go through the entire ancient culture and say, 'This was the idea of that time, and this is how it's relevant today.' We are building lots of roads today. But if we don't follow the old roads, we are wasting lots of time and energy. If we do follow the old road, we can see that others may already have chosen the best way to go, the best passes, the best part of the mountain to cross. If everything we create is new, we are ignoring six thousand years of experience."

"So the road to peace begins here?" Linda asked.

"I don't think it's the only one," he said. "But I do think it's one. Maybe even the anointed one."

. 3 .

A CROWN OF BEAUTY

Linda was the first to notice: No cops were standing guard in front of the building on Palestine Street. Nor were there security guards stationed in front of the door. There were no metal detectors, either. The Abrishami Synagogue in downtown Tehran, the largest of the capital's twenty-three shuls, was the only big-city synagogue either of us had visited in more than a decade without visible police protection.

Even more shocking: the place was overflowing. On a ho-hum Friday night, more than eight hundred Jews had shown up to attend Shabbat services in the capital of one of Israel's most vocal critics. As we stepped through the door, Linda was escorted to the women's section, and I was shown to the men's. Once I was seated, the president of Iran's Jewish Federation, Harun Yesha'ya, legendary for befriending Ayatollah Khomeini when the two were imprisoned together in the 1960s, leaned over. "We don't get many visitors from America," he said. "Would you say a few words to the congregation?"

Jews have a slightly self-mocking, slightly self-congratulatory way of expressing their feeling that they live in a small, beleaguered community, scattered around the globe. The term *Jewish Geography* is often used when two Jews meet and want to determine whom they know in common—not *if* they know people in common but *how many*.

In many ways, the idea of Jewish Geography began in Iran. When Cyrus swept into Babylon in 539 B.C.E., the expatriated Jewish community appeared to get its dreams fulfilled. They could return to Jerusalem, rebuild the Temple, and begin to restore God's kingdom on earth. Exile was finally over. But in yet another twist in their national epic, the Jews did not react as expected. Some did rush back to Jerusalem, where they began drawing up plans for a new Temple. But in the most vivid evidence yet that exile was not as weepy as believed, many chose to stay by the rivers of Babylon. Others went to Egypt, and still more burst through the invisible wall between Mesopotamia and Persia and followed their unlikely savior back home. Faced with God-given freedom, some Israelites chose to be landed, but more chose to be landless.

Exile was so good for some Jews that they now opted to exile themselves.

The consequence of these migrations cannot be overstated. In Babylon, early Jews had shifted the definition of God from being a deity attached to a specific piece of geography to one universal in his reach. But that change, in many ways, was forced on them. This new shift was voluntary. With their dreams of empire lost, Jews took Cyrus up on his promise that they could worship freely in other people's land. While Second Isaiah stressed to Jews that their God was strong enough to control foreign leaders, the newly liberated people adopted a more humble approach. Instead of being triumphalist and forcing others to lick their feet, as Isaiah had prophesied, Jews would become pluralists, content to live as religious minorities in others' kingdoms. Being a light to the nations did not mean imposing their will on others; it meant, among other things, being a shining example of coexistence.

This new pan-national approach to Judaism has come to be known by the Greek word *diaspora*, meaning "disperse" or "scatter about," from *dia*, meaning "about," and *speirein*, "scatter." The term was adopted from the Greek translation of Deuteronomy 28:25, "thou shalt be a diaspora in all the kingdoms of the earth." Begun in the sixth century B.C.E., the diaspora widened under Persian, then Hellenistic control over the Ancient Near East. By 200 B.C.E. Jews were living and worshiping in the ancient equivalents of Afghanistan, Iran, Iraq, Phoenicia, Turkey, Cyprus, Crete, Greece, Italy, Libya, Egypt, and Ethiopia. Diaspora was central to the future of Western religion first because it broadened the popularity of the God of the Israelites, ensuring that his influence would survive even after his new home in Jerusalem was again destroyed. Second, the diaspora provided a broad-based population familiar with the Hebrew scripture, which later facilitated the lightning spread of Christianity.

Life in Iran proved particularly welcoming for Jews, first under the Pax Persica, then under successive regimes, especially the Sassanians in the third century C.E., who made Zoroastrianism the official state religion. It was during these years that the Babylonian Talmud was compiled under Persian hegemony in Iraq. Even the arrival of Islam in Persia in the seventh century was not initially bad for the Jewish community.

The souring for Iranian Jews began with the Safavid dynasty, who converted the country to Shiism in the sixteenth century, plunging the Jews into a 350-year bog of marginalization, hardship, and alienation. Jews were not the only abused minority, as Sunnis and Sufis were also forced to convert to Shiism. But Jews were singled out for their religious impurity and forbidden from coming into contact with Muslims or touching food in Muslim shops. White was a symbol of cleanliness, and Jews were not allowed to paint the insides of their homes white or to ride white donkeys. With germs thought to be passed through water, Jews were not allowed to use public baths, drink from public wells, or walk in the streets on rainy days. The penalty for not complying was death.

Jews were slowly reintegrated into Iranian society in the twentieth century, as they left the ghettos and were even invited into government service. A new Golden Age of Iranian Jewry arrived with Reza Shah and his son, who allowed Jews to enter the arts, banking, insurance, and manufacturing. But their new high profile brought problems, too. A controversy erupted in 1974, when a new two-hundred-rial banknote was issued and had a six-pointed star on the back. Though the hexagram was often used in Muslim mosaics, its appearance on the currency flamed rumors that the shah was being secretly financed by Israel. The scandal was so great that the note was withdrawn from circulation by the end of business on its first day of distribution.

The Iranian Revolution at first devastated local Jews. For years Khomeini had blamed Jews for spreading anti-Islamic propaganda, mistranslating the Koran, and taking over Iran's economy. In 1979 the Israeli consulate was seized along with the American embassy, and the head of the Jewish community was executed. Of the 100,000 Jews in the country, 25,000 fled to Israel, 40,000 to the United States, and 10,000 to the rest of the world. As revolutionary embers cooled, Khomeini backtracked, saying, "We distinguish between Jews and Zionists." Those Jews who stayed in the country were surprised by the freedom of worship they found in the Islamic republic. The result was a curious dynamic: At the start of the twenty-fifth century of Judaism in diaspora, Iran still had the largest Jewish population of any country in the Middle

East outside Israel even as the Iranian government proclaimed its mortal hostility to the Jewish state.

One advantage of Jewish Geography is that just a few in-quiries can give one access to the Jewish community any-where in the world. In the case of Iran, that meant my making a few telephone calls around Beverly Hills (nickname: Tehran-geles), where an enormous concentration of wealthy Iranians fled around the time of the revolution. In no time I had a notebook full of names and an earful of advice. "You're going to where?" one ex-pat exclaimed. "I hope you like prison." "You're taking your wife?" another questioned. "Are you insane?"

"It's a second honeymoon," I said.

By consensus, the first person I had to call in Tehran was Yesha'ya—"He has the heart of a lion," I was told—a film pro-ducer who serves as the chief liaison between the Jewish commu-nity and the Islamic republic. If a Jew is harassed, Yesha'ya knows which mullah to call to have it stopped, I was told. If a family needs wine for a bris, Yesha'ya can garner special permission. A soft-spoken man who looks like an aging Omar Sharif, he struck me as someone who could fight with his guile, his charm, or his hands, depending on the need. He had a callous demeanor that in-dicated he didn't win all of his battles, but an ease of manner that suggested he won enough. He arrived at our hotel along with his thirty-eight-year-old daughter and drove us to synagogue.

Abrishami Synagogue looked more like an overgrown Sunday school classroom than a house of worship. Barely one story high, it had white tile on the floor and ceiling, brown vinyl chairs, and fourteen chandeliers. Persian influences were everywhere. Persian carpets lined the floor of the central pulpit; a glass of mint and a pitcher of rose water were on the lectern. In deference to traditional

Jewish laws, which forbid the use of electricity on Shabbat, the rabbi did not use a microphone. "We used to have a microphone," Yesha'ya explained. "But after the revolution, as Muslims became more traditional, we become more traditional, too. I think it's ridiculous. Nobody can hear."

Most striking was the sheer sense of joy that permeated the room. Children ran up and down the aisles. Worshipers chatted with one another as if at a picnic. There was no sense of fear or cowering. "Synagogue is not just a place for praying," Yesha'ya explained. "It's also a place for connecting. Boys and girls who want to marry must come here." The reason for the crowds, he noted, was that Friday is the Muslim Sabbath, so Saturday is a workday. It may seem like a rabbinic fantasy, but the most happening place for Jewish singles in Iran is Friday night services.

"But what about security?" I said. "Even most synagogues in America have guards."

"Security in Iran is hidden," he said. "The religious police have control over everything. You don't see it, but they control the streets. And they have decided that we can pray freely."

"So many Jews have left, though. Why not you?"

"Many Iranians see a nice life in the U.S. and Israel," he said. "And it's true, many of their problems are solved, but others are created—financial, cultural. I have many relatives who left but can't find work. You have no property. Here I have a middle-class life."

"And you don't feel afraid?"

"Safety is a big problem in Iran no matter who you are," he said. "I am sure that if a major earthquake came, 50 percent of the buildings in this country would collapse. But I live here, I deal with it."

"Wait. You're saying that being Jewish in Iran is like living on a geological fault—you just have to live with the fear?"

"I have been to many countries across Europe, and the fear there is greater than here. In Sweden they told men not to wear *kippahs*. Here we wear black *kippahs* on the streets. Every country has its advantages."

Iranian Jews are so eager to prove that their plight is no worse than that of other Jews in the world, he explained, that when expat Iranians in Los Angeles began sending back videos of their lavish weddings, their relatives in the homeland started aping them. The custom of fathers walking their daughters down the aisle, unknown among Iranian Jews, is now widely used, as is the fashion of brides wearing their hair swept up in buns. Bat Mitzvahs, in which thirteen-year-old girls read the Torah as boys have done for generations, are also now popular. "We are not Third World Jews," Yesha'ya told me.

The time had come for me to address the congregation. Yesha'ya introduced me and served as translator. For the first time all night, the room was silent. I began by saying that my family had lived for 150 years as Jews in America, and that recently I had been married in my childhood synagogue. I introduced Linda. I mentioned my years of visiting biblical sites and said that I had come here because Iran had been the savior of the Jews since the time of Cyrus. "For that reason, American Jews are very grateful to Iranian Jews," I said. "We will never forget you. And even though I have been here for only a brief time, I already feel at home." There was some murmuring, followed by applause.

As I sat down, my heart was throbbing. For most of my life, I had gone out of my way to avoid talking about being Jewish. In Iraq, I had actively concealed my identity. Here, having come to the country convinced that the religious police would trail us, I stood in front of a roomful of Jews and openly proclaimed my Jewishness. This tiny gesture felt like an affirmation, a stroke of confidence against the cowering so common for Jews in this part of the world. And doing so in front of people for whom anxiety is a daily

reality made me appreciate the gift of religious tolerance first prof-
fered by this land. It also made me grateful for the sacrifices these
particular Jews made to maintain a presence large enough to protect such proclamations—mine, and especially theirs.

And finally I learned that small gestures do have unexpected
consequences. As we were leaving the synagogue, Linda told me
that the murmuring that followed my remarks had nothing to do
with my attempted eloquence and everything to do with the fact
that I had introduced her. "All the women were talking about it,"
she said. "They were very impressed. They said, 'We wish our
husbands would do the same!'"

Located three hundred miles south of Tehran, Esfahan is Iran's
third-largest city and certainly its most beautiful. Shah Abbas
the Great made this trading outpost his capital in 1598 and transformed it into one of the most exquisite cities in the Muslim
world, the rival of Kyoto or Florence, with gardens, bridges, tree-
lined boulevards, and a resplendent skyline of cobalt blue tiles. By
1660 Esfahan had 162 mosques, 1,802 caravansaries, 48 colleges,
and 273 baths to serve a population of 600,000, the size of London
at the time.

Like many places in Iran, Esfahan has a checkered history of
interreligious relations, with periods of openness followed by long
stretches of bloody rivalries. In the early seventeenth century,
Shah Abbas imported large numbers of Armenian Christians and
gave them virtual autonomy on the south bank of the Zayandeh
River, where they thrived for over a century. A spectacular cathedral still stands there today.

The Jewish presence in Esfahan dates back earlier, perhaps even
before the Exile. Some reports claim that after Assyria overran the
kingdom of Israel in the eighth century B.C.E., a number of Israelites

were deported to as far away as here. Jews almost definitely settled in Esfahan following Nebuchadnezzar II's conquest of Babylon. Later, during the Sassanian dynasty in the fifth century C.E., a Jewish ghetto was established to the north of town. And recently, Esfahan and nearby Shiraz became the epicenter of an international uproar about the fate of Jews in the Muslim world.

In early 1999, thirteen Jews in Shiraz and Esfahan were arrested by Iranian authorities. The jailed included a rabbi, a kosher butcher, several Hebrew teachers, merchants, and a sixteen-year-old boy. While the Shiraz Thirteen, as they came to be called, were not charged for more than a year, the government accused them of spying for "the Zionist regime" and "world arrogance"— code words for supporting the State of Israel. The defendants went on trial on May 1, 2000. They were forbidden from hiring their own lawyers, and the court was closed to observers, including families and human rights groups. The prosecution said nine of the thirteen confessed to espionage. A tenth defendant was also convicted, while three, including the boy, were acquitted. Sentences ranged from four to thirteen years in prison.

The case of the Shiraz Thirteen inflamed emotions. Across Iran, Jewish homes were vandalized and schoolchildren were harassed. "The trial has created problems for the whole Jewish community," Yesha'ya said, noting that several shops were attacked and one was set on fire. Iranian expatriates in the United States and elsewhere brought enormous pressure on the Iranian government, which many believed contributed to a lessening of the sentences. In February 2003, the last five prisoners were released.

Before coming to Esfahan, I asked about meeting some of the convicted spies but was told by their advocates in Los Angeles and Tehran that they would not speak. Yesha'ya did introduce me to the head of Esfahan's Jewish community, Mah Gerefteh, a soft-spoken businessman who gave us a tour of the largest of the city's thirteen synagogues. The room was compact, and we were asked to remove our shoes, as in a mosque. The architecture was similar to that of the synagogue in Tehran, with a central platform and plain seating. The Torah scrolls in the Ark were kept inside rigid cylindrical containers, called *tiqs*, a common practice in the Middle East. Also as in Tehran, the road outside the synagogue had been named Palestine, and I asked Mr. Gerefteh if the name was trying to send a signal. "Since the revolution, this has been the trend," he said.

Mr. Gerefteh was clearly circumspect in our conversation and refused to acknowledge that life was harsh for Jews in central Iran. Kosher food was a little difficult to come by, he noted; otherwise life was pretty much as it was before the revolution. "But many Iranian Jews who have left the country say conditions here are very difficult," I said. He countered: "It's best for them to have a little trip to Iran and see for themselves."

"But what about the Jews from Esfahan and Shiraz who were sent to prison?"

"Now they are all out," he said. "In fact, one of them is upstairs. Would you like to meet him?"

My heart leapt. *"Here?"* I said. He nodded and without hesitation led us up a dark set of stairs to a small classroom on the second floor. My hands were trembling. A handful of men in their twenties were sitting at miniature desks studying pages of the Talmud. The instructor was seated at the front of the room. Mr. Gerefteh indicated he was one of the Shiraz Thirteen. He appeared to be in his mid-thirties, short, healthily plump, with a trim beard and *kippah*. The man shook my hand but was clearly reluctant to talk and kept his back toward me. He was a textile merchant during the day and a Hebrew instructor at night, he said, and on this night they were studying rituals before prayers. He was curious if I was Jewish.

"Do you know why you were arrested?" I asked.

"I don't want to answer that," he said.

"Will you tell me how long you were in prison?"

He thought for a second. "Four years. But I don't really want to talk about those things. It's something that happened. It's over and done with."

"But there are many people in America and around the world who prayed for you," I said. "What would you like to say to all those people who worked hard for your release?"

For the first time he turned his body toward me, and his face flushed with emotion. "I would like to thank them for all their efforts," he said.

"Some people in your position would have turned their back on their religion," I said. "Did you ever want to leave Judaism?"

"Just the opposite. It actually made me more anxious to be Jewish. I became more into my faith than before."

"More?"

"Look, I made a mistake," he said, "and got what I deserved. And I learned the meaning of what I heard from God. I know now that if I do something wrong, I will pay the consequences."

His language startled me. None of the accounts of the trial I had read gave me the impression that there might be some truth behind the charges. Now this man, who introduced himself only with the Hebrew name Binyomin, seemed to drop that hint. His words could easily have been a sort of semiconfession he had honed in prison to get himself out of danger and preserve his life. They could have been a deft expression of piousness designed to appease the religious police. But something about his tone told me that this allegory of Iran was far more complicated than I could easily untangle.

Either way, one thing I knew for sure: The lesson he wanted me to take from his experience was that religious freedom is fragile and I should renew my devotion to my own faith.

"I think you should stop being a Reform Jew," he said, "and start being an Orthodox Jew, the way you were supposed to be."

"Why?" I said. "I think I'm a very good Jew. I write books about faith. I talk about Judaism. I married a Jew."

"Being a good writer is fine," he said, "but being a good Jew would be better."

The last stop of our trip was Hamadan, the summer capital of the Achaemenid empire two hundred miles northwest of Esfahan. Located in the foothills of the Zagros Mountains, in the plateau that divides Iraq and Iran, Hamadan became a Persian stronghold under Cyrus the Great. But because of its prime location on the Indo-European highway, Hamadan later became one of the first Persian cities battered by foreign leaders, from Alexander the Great to Genghis Khan. It's also long been home to one of the larger Jewish communities in Persia, in part because of its identification with one of the most beloved—and reviled—stories in the Hebrew Bible.

The Book of Esther appears near the close of the Hebrew Bible and is part of the third major section of biblical texts, the Writings, which includes Psalms and Proverbs. Jews refer to the book as the *megillah*, or scroll, of Esther, and celebrate its story as part of the springtime festival of Purim. Esther tells the story of the salvation of Persia's Jewish community and may be the greatest endorsement of the idea of Jews living in diaspora to appear in the Bible.

The story opens at a lavish party thrown by King Ahasuerus of Persia in Susa, the winter capital of the Achaemenids, not far from Hamadan. Ahasuerus asks his wife, Vashti, to dress up so he can show her off, but she refuses and Ahasuerus banishes her from his presence and strips her of her title. Among the "beautiful young virgins" brought to the palace as possible replacements is Esther, or Hadassah in Hebrew, the cousin and adopted daughter of Mordecai the Jew. At Mordecai's advice, Esther does not reveal her Jewishness to the king. After a yearlong tryout, with all the prospective queens living in one house in the manner of a modern reality television show, Esther is chosen.

Mordecai, who seems to be a member of the king's court, soon uncovers a plot to kill the king, and Esther informs her husband. Mordecai's service is recorded, but the king is not told who saved his life. For unspecified reasons, Mordecai then refuses to bow down to the new prime minister, Haman, who retaliates by saying he will have all the Jews in Persia killed. Haman tells Ahasuerus that a certain people in the kingdom, who refuse to obey the king's laws, threaten his reign and should be destroyed. Ahasuerus agrees (though he doesn't know the order refers to Jews) and sends out postal couriers to spread word of the genocide to be held eleven months later, on the thirteenth of Adar.

Mordecai pleads with Esther to intervene. After initially refusing, she invites the king and Haman to a private party. Haman is flattered by the attention and, feeling cocky, decides to build a special stake to impale Mordecai. That night the king cannot sleep and decides to look through his records, where he discovers that Mordecai saved his life. "How should a devoted subject be honored?" the king asks Haman. Thinking the king must be referring to himself, Haman says, "Ride him through town on special steeds." Haman is then asked to lead Mordecai on such a journey.

The next night Esther again invites the king and Haman to a private party, where she reveals her identity to the king and begs for the life of her people. Horrified by the realization that he ordered the killing of the Jews, Ahasuerus sentences Haman to be impaled on the stake he built for Mordecai. Mordecai is elevated to prime minister and is invited to issue a new edict in the king's name, delivered again by postal couriers. Unable to overturn the irrevocable command, Mordecai orders the Jews to defend themselves from attack and *massacre any people* who assault them, including women and children.

When the thirteenth of Adar arrives, the Jews fight back, slaying more than 500 people in Susa. The king asks Esther what else she would like. If it please Your Majesty, Esther replies, please allow the Jews to kill for a second day. By the time the fighting ends, the Jews have slain more than 75,000 people. Mordecai orders Jews to celebrate a festival of Purim, from the word *pur*, the lot that Haman cast to determine the date for the genocide. The festival, on the fourteenth and fifteenth days of Adar, is regarded as a period of deliverance, a second Exodus, and is observed around the world with feasting, joy, and elaborate costumes children wear while acting out the story.

So is the Book of Esther an allegory, too, or is it based on historical events in ancient Persia?

We arrived in Hamadan, a city that today holds more than a million people. At an altitude higher than a mile, Hamadan was dramatically colder than Esfahan. As a medieval Arab poet wrote, "Even the heat of the fire becomes frozen in Hamadan / And the cold there is a chronic evil." The modern city is built around a giant circular plaza named after Ayatollah Khomeini, with six streets radiating out from it like sun rays. Just off one of those streets, in an alley dedicated to electronic products, is a mausoleum said to house the tombs of Esther and Mordecai.

The squat, square shrine is medieval in origin, lined with brick, and topped with a small domed tower that looks like a wasps' nest. The shrine is surrounded by an overgrown garden. The locked metal gate was opened by a Dickensian figure, a gaunt, bug-eyed man in a brown suit and white, prickly stubble. He didn't request an entrance fee but asked in simple English if I would give him a pen. I brightened. "I have the perfect one!" I said, and pulled out a pen I had been given that was emblazoned with the logo of the Jewish Federation of Kansas City. He took it, snapped it open and closed a few times, then unscrewed it to see how much ink was in the cartridge. Then he handed it back to me. "Mister, do you have a Parker?" he said.

"A Parker?" I exclaimed. "I haven't had one of those since receiving ten for my Bar Mitzvah."

He seemed dejected and reclaimed the inferior model from my hand.

Moving toward the shrine, we took off our shoes and passed through a stone doorway so low I had to duck my head. Inside were two rooms lined with Persian carpets. The first was a chapel, large enough for about twenty people, decorated with the names of local Jews, a sign that said "Love your neighbor" in Persian, and a verse from Psalm 42, "Like a hind crying for water, / my soul cries for you, O God." Down several stairs, in an arched room directly under the dome, were two dark wooden cenotaphs. The left is labeled Mordecai, the right Esther. The graves themselves are said to be under the earth. Are they real?

In part because the Book of Esther contains no sea-splitting miracles or supernatural foliage, the story seems believable enough. Many Bible commentaries observe that Ahasuerus is likely the Hebraicized version of King Xerxes, the Achaemenid leader who ruled from 486 to 465 B.C.E. But fundamental problems in the story call into question its status as a historical annal. Mordecai is identified as having been sent into exile by Nebuchadnezzar, an event that took place over a century before Xerxes assumed power. Esther is even less likely to have been Xerxes' wife, because his only known wife, Amestris, continued in her role well beyond his third year as king (the date the text suggests Vashti was deposed).

Whatever its origin, the story shows deep familiarity with the Persian court, which suggests it emerged out of the eastern Jewish diaspora in the late first millennium B.C.E. The opening sentence of Esther says Ahasuerus reigned over 127 provinces from India to Ethiopia, which is more than the twenty-three countries represented on the staircase at Persepolis but still reflects the range of the Pax Persica. The real Persian king may not have had parties that lasted 180 days, as the text suggests, but the eating, drinking, and court activities reflect reality. Even the names—Esther, which is likely derived from that of the Babylonian god Ishtar; and Mordecai, derived from that of the Babylonian God Marduk—seem to reflect Jewish life outside the land of Israel. The Book of Esther represents the high point of Persian influence on the Hebrew Bible and is additional testimony to the diverse range of cultures—Mesopotamian, Egyptian, Philistine, Babylonian—that echo in the foundation text for Western faith.

While the connection between Esther and Persia is profound, the connection between Esther and Hamadan is not. An inscription in the shrine, believed to date from its construction in the Middle Ages, suggests it was built in honor of Elias and Samuel, sons of Ismail Karlan. That suggests the building was later converted to its present function. However it came to be associated with Esther and Mordecai, the mausoleum eventually became an icon for Iranian Jews and the site of an annual three-day fast in honor of Purim. In 1950 Hamadan had a Jewish population of sixty thousand. Today, the gatekeeper said, the number was twenty-eight. I asked him the reasons for the decline.

"There are not enough universities," he said. "Many people moved to bigger cities. Some went out of Iran. I don't know why. I like this country very much, and I live here freely."

And what lessons should be taken from the story of Esther?

"The best way for Jews to survive in other lands is to adopt local customs but still maintain their Jewish ways. We can live with other people, but we shouldn't become them."

In my conversations with the Iranian Jews of Los Angeles, I had learned that Hamadan once had a sprawling Jewish cemetery that had purportedly been relocated to build a public park. They wanted me to scope it out. For religious Jews, moving graves is a grievous sin. The guardian directed us to the other side of town, where a circular park, lined with flagstones and recently planted oak and pistachio trees, was filling with late-afternoon visitors. Some boys kicked a soccer ball. Women in chadors huddled around a picnic blanket. A gaggle of aging men played chess on a bench. In the center of the park were about a dozen graves covered in Hebrew lettering.

As we eyed the stones, a man came over to see us. He was bald and had a few missing teeth. He began pointing out various tombstones and exclaiming the virtues of the deceased. This one was a doctor, that one a schoolteacher. Many graves had been relocated outside town, he said, but those were all older than thirty-six years, as Muslim law allows. The few graves left behind were more recent. I asked him how he knew so much about the departed. "I was a postman," he said.

"A postman!" Linda said. "Do you know about the story of Esther?"

"Sure," he said, bursting with pride. "The postmen saved the Jews in ancient times. They used the postal road built by Darius."

Linda applauded, and the man beamed at the attention. "God be with you," he said.

We continued perusing the stones, then settled on a bench. Our trip would end here, overlooking half a graveyard, in a half-erased community.

We pulled out our Bibles. Long before we came to Iran, Linda knew that one central idea of my travels was reading the stories of the Bible in the places where they occurred. In Hamadan, that meant Esther. In the days leading up to our visit, I noticed that she had tucked away her guidebook and begun leafing through the Bible. I would step out of the shower or roll over in the middle of the night and find her frantically scribbling notes on a piece of paper or stuffing bookmarks next to notable passages. By the time we sat down for our supposedly impromptu reading, Linda had enough notes for a Yom Kippur sermon.

And enough insights to earn her a Ph.D.

The first thing she told me, which surprised me, was that she had grown up idolizing Esther. "Long before I wanted to be a Moroccan princess at my wedding," she said, "I wanted to be a Persian princess, and I dressed up as Queen Esther on Halloween. Not Purim, Halloween. I wore a green dress with a crown and dangly earrings. I think my mother still has a picture of it."

"How come you never mentioned this before?"

"I had forgotten about it until now. But the truth is, now that I've read the real story, I'm realizing that we must have gotten the sanitized version in Sunday school."

For both of us, reading the Book of Esther in Iran was unnerving. From its opening, in which the king throws a party that lasts half a year, to its closing, in which the Jews throw a festival to celebrate their slaughter of 75,500 people, the story reeks of moral depravity. The narrative revolves around parties—ten in all. The king, who is portrayed as an impulsive drunk, deposes his first queen at a banquet, enthrones Esther at another, celebrates with Haman at one gala, then sends him to death at another. The Jews celebrate their edict to fight back at one party, then their bloody victory at two more. Considering that the Bible is so interested in morality, this open ribaldry is surprising.

In part for this reason, the Book of Esther has come under withering attack since antiquity. Critics have lambasted its debauchery, the cruelty of its characters, and the fact that none of the central figures shows any kindness or forgiveness. More important, nowhere in the story is there a mention of God. Ancient Jewish sages argued against its inclusion in the Hebrew Bible. Martin Luther said he wished it did not exist at all, arguing that it lionized Jews too much. Some contemporary polemicists used it as the basis for anti-Semitism, pointing out that once the Jews assume power they massacre their neighbors.

I asked Linda how she felt the Jews came across.

"Horribly. When the Jews are oppressed, they're generous, but once they get power, they're vengeful. It reminds me—" She started to talk about contemporary Israeli politics but caught herself. An obliterated Jewish cemetery in Iran was hardly the place to discuss the merits of land distribution in the West Bank.

"But you know what it really reminded me of?" she continued. "David and Solomon. I guess the Bible doesn't like kings very much. Once Esther and Mordecai join the royal court, they also behave poorly. I think Jews are best as the moral minority. And when we get power, we're not immune to the fact that power corrupts."

"So wait, now you don't even like Esther anymore?"

"Well, at the beginning she's really passive. But after a while, I do think she begins to understand that as a woman she has more influence than she thinks. One line in the first chapter seemed comical." Linda flipped through her Bible until she found the reference, Esther 1:20. "When Queen Vashti refuses to attend the king's party, Ahasuerus is so embarrassed that he issues an edict that 'all wives will treat their husbands with respect.'"

"And what's wrong with that!"

She looked at me pityingly. "Later, Ahasuerus bows to every wish that Esther has," she said, "and even Haman is constantly told what to do by his wife. So clearly it's farcical, this bureaucratic attempt to keep women down."

"But look around you," I said. "Seems to work."

"No, and that's the point," she said. "I think many Westerners think the veil is similar to that edict. That it's meant to keep women subservient in some way. Yet being here, meeting influential women like Mrs. Moussavi-nejad, and going to the gym, where all the women wear skimpy outfits and makeup, I began to think that maybe this modern decree to have women in the veil and chador isn't being any more successful in holding women down."

Despite its moral ambiguity, the Book of Esther has remained popular, especially among Jews, in part for its positive vision of diaspora life. The Jews are perfectly content to live in Persia and not return to the Promised Land. Plus, they use their proximity to power to protect their coreligionists. As Mordecai says to Esther: "Do not imagine that you, of all the Jews, will escape with your life by being in the king's palace." Total assimilation is not good, the story suggests; Jews should identify with their faith no matter how prominent in Gentile society they become.

This message was particularly poignant to me. As a Jew growing up in Georgia, I felt my minority status as a burden. My parents were deeply devoted to their Jewish life and served their community in numerous ways, yet they still tugged at the gossamers of assimilation. They were driven to overcome the anti-Semitism of the past, yet secretly believed they never would. I remember a particularly anguished conversation with my dad when I was a teenager in which he said that, despite his professional success, he would always feel a degree of insecurity, with that proverbial packed suitcase tucked under his bed in the event he needed to flee.

I could not live that way, I said. Perhaps I was the naïve beneficiary of their sacrifices, but I refused to see myself as restricted by my Judaism. Two decades later, I still didn't feel confined by my faith, but I no longer tried to shutter my Judaism away. For me, learning to talk openly about religion was a way of toppling the past and standing, knock-kneed yet proudly, in the light. For me, and Linda as well, assimilation was not the goal. Acceptance was. We dreamed of succeeding in the world not in spite of our faith but, in part, because of it. Being in Iran, I was reminded that this idea was hardly new.

It found eloquent expression in the Book of Esther.

I asked Linda if she felt Jews in the story were oppressed.

"No," she said. "I'm amazed how much they seem integrated into the community." She pointed to Esther 3:15, after the king issues his initial order to kill the Jews: "The couriers went out posthaste on the royal mission, and the decree was proclaimed in the fortress Susa. The king and Haman sat down to feast, but Susa was dumbfounded."

"I read that to mean that the Susans liked their Jewish neighbors," Linda said, "and were confused about why the king would suddenly order the Jews to be annihilated."

That sense of acceptance is reinforced when the order for the Jews to defend themselves is again sent by mounted courier, this time on the king's own steeds. "First of all," Linda said, "I'm thinking absolutely of Darius's postal system and the fact that they have two types of horses, the regular and the fast. The first order, to kill the Jews, goes out on regular horses, but the second goes out on the FedEx horses because the king is more anxious to counteract that order. And again, the order goes out in the script of each province, even the Jewish script. They don't have to assimilate. They're allowed to keep their own language."

"So do you think the story is an ode to the diaspora?"

"In some ways. It's striking that nowhere do the Jews ask to be returned to Jerusalem, or to rebuild the Temple. They're happy to be living side by side with their Persian neighbors, drinking in their own way, worshiping in their own language. It's exactly like Persepolis, with all these different people talking with one another, being happy. It's not that diaspora is necessarily good, it's that diaspora works if there are certain conditions under which the Jews are able to live in peaceful coexistence."

"What I love about what you're saying is that we never would have made that connection unless we came here."

"No way. All my life, Iran was the epitome of darkness. And I came here really concerned. Would I wear the right veil? Would it be dangerous? And instead I've come away realizing how much we have to learn from this place. As Shahrokh said, we're paving new roads, yet we're not trying to see if some previous roads may be able to take us to where we want to go even faster."

As she spoke, I was struck by the tone in Linda's voice. Despite all the external pressures she faced—the black head covering she could never quite master, the dangers of being in a totalitarian regime, the fear of being a Jew in a fundamentalist Muslim state—she had completely succumbed to the spirit of the place. She had stopped thinking of Iran and started feeling it.

She had stopped reading the Bible and started becoming a part of its ongoing story.

Near the end of the Book of Esther, Mordecai charges the Jews to celebrate the feast of Purim in the month that had been transformed "from one of grief and mourning to one of festive joy." This shift embodies what happens to the Jews in diaspora, as they move out of exile into freedom. Rereading the story, I began to think that maybe God is present during this time. Maybe God is there when Mordecai overhears the plot to kill the king and when the king discovers that Mordecai saved his life. Maybe God is there when Esther overcomes her instinct to save herself and instead saves her people. Maybe God is even there when the Jews succumb to their baser instincts and attack the Persians. And maybe God is there when Mordecai, understanding that vindictiveness, declares that Jews should observe Purim by "sending gifts to one another and presents to the poor." In the unshackled possibility of diaspora, God is everywhere orphans and courtiers, prime ministers and little girls believe in the possibility of redemption.

This is the gift of the prophets: the belief that out of grief can come joy.

I reached for Linda's hands. "And if we were lucky enough to have a child someday, and that child wanted to dress up like Esther, what would you tell her?"

"I would tell her to dig deeper," Linda said. "I would tell her to go beyond the differences we're told exist between us and other cultures. I would tell her to uncover a piece of herself in a land that may seem alien. And I would tell her, as a Jew growing up in the diaspora, that a piece of herself lies dormant in all these places . . ." Linda looked at me. "Why are you crying?"

"Because what you're saying is so beautiful."

We sat facing each other, alone in the hills of western Iran, in a place that as a child I had doubted would ever be possible: Jews at home in the world.

"And I would tell our daughter, 'Wherever you go, first you will find some commonality with the Jews of these different places. In each of these lands, you can find shards of your own culture, your own history. Your own self.

"And finally," Linda said, "I would say to her, 'Wherever you go, you'll find remnants of our family's home, too: African masks, Persian carpets, nomadic necklaces. So wherever you travel, your father and I will always be there. You can feel at peace. Because you'll be at home.'"

CONCLUSION

WITH GLADNESS AND JOY

Avner's father died on Friday morning, and I arrived in Jerusalem that Sunday afternoon. A few hours later, about three dozen friends and family gathered at a small cemetery at Kibbutz Gezer, halfway between Jerusalem and Tel Aviv, not far from Tel Gezer, where the biblical-era battle in which Canaanite kings stand up to Joshua took place. Avner chose this site because it accommodates nontraditional burials. His father, a fifth-generation native of the land of Israel, a pioneer in Israel's fight for independence, and a schoolteacher, was fiercely secular and wanted a nonreligious funeral.

The guests gathered on folded chairs in a small grove of pine, carob, and hawthorn trees. The plain wooden coffin, draped in black fabric, was poised above a grave in front of a giant yucca. The kibbutz had tucked several hand-painted signs into the ground quoting biblical passages about ancient foods:

Your limbs are an orchard of pomegranates
And of all luscious fruits,
Of henna and of nard,
The Song of Songs.

Avner's thirty-year-old daughter, Smadar, was the first to speak. *"Saba,"* she said, using the Hebrew word for "grandfather," "you said you didn't want a religious burial and we'll do as you ask, but we think there is a place to talk about your life." Yair Goren was born in Rosh Pina, in the Galilee, in 1923 and left home at sixteen to join the Jewish Underground, bicycling around the Dead Sea buying up weapons. He later led the Jewish invasion of the Jerusalem neighborhood of Catamon during the War of Independence, helped open the Mount Scopus campus of Hebrew University, and pioneered relations with the bedouin of the Sinai.

Yair was a gigantic man, outsize in personality and disposition, who could quote the Bible by heart. The last time I saw him, while Avner and I were searching for King David in Jerusalem, I mentioned that I was put off by David's behavior. Yair scolded me. "Nobody said we have to be like David," he said. "And compared with Rameses II"—the brutal pharaoh of the late second millennium B.C.E.—"he was an angel."

At the funeral, Smadar poked fun at his towering presence. *"Saba,* you always knew what you wanted to teach," she said, "even if we didn't want to learn. You had a huge belly we could jump on. You were the world for us."

Avner spoke next. Like most guests, he was dressed casually, in black pants, a white cotton shirt, and sandals. His squiggly hair seemed more gray than usual. Like other men I have known at the time of their fathers' deaths, he seemed to age as a result of the event, assuming the mantle of patriarch. He talked about how his father used to take him on biblical walking tours of Jerusalem. "I grew up with great openness," he said. "Humanity was the most important value. Like a lot of founders of the state, my father's values were so obvious he didn't have to communicate them: to belong to a society; to contribute. I do what I do now because of him."

Avner choked up once, as he spoke of his new wife, Asnat, and how she had helped make his father's last years more enjoyable. Avner and Asnat stood hand in hand as the coffin was lowered into the ground and guests helped shovel dirt on top. One by one, each mourner lay a rose on the small mound of earth. A few, in deference to Jewish custom, placed a stone. Then Avner, in a move that amused the guests and surely would have made his father proud, delivered a short lecture about the history of Tel Gezer. Avner's gesture ensured that the final sound was one of laughter.

A few days later, we drove past Tel Gezer on our way to the Tomb of the Maccabees, shrine to one of the seminal events in the late first millennium B.C.E., the Jewish uprising against Greek hegemony. Two thousand years after Abraham first heard the call of God, a small band of Abraham's descendants stood up to the leading superpower of the day and declared their right to worship freely. This event, coming at the end of the biblical era, became the centerpiece of the Jewish festival of Hanukkah and the backdrop to one of the most beloved rituals of my childhood.

But recently I had begun to view Hanukkah differently. The bloody mix of politics, violence, and faith that forms the core of the story is an uncanny prism through which to view the struggles of today. Were the Maccabees pioneers for religious freedom or terrorists imposing their faith on others? To answer that, I returned to Israel in time for the festival. I came to end my journey where it began, to walk the final steps of the birth of Western faith with Avner, and finally to confront my ambiguities about the role of religion in my life.

I pulled out my Bible. The end of the Exile in Babylon introduces an unexpected dimension to Israel's national story. The debate revolves around a simple question: Who is a Jew? The Israelites who remained in exile after the fall of Babylon and practiced a lifestyle based on worshiping Yahweh, keeping the Sabbath, and marrying only within the faith believed that they were the real Jews. Religion, they maintained, did not need a political entity to survive.

But for the Israelites who did return to the Promised Land, the dream of re-creating God's kingdom *on his chosen land* was still central. Judah, however, was in tatters. The population of native Israelites in the Promised Land was scarcely more than twenty thousand, confined to an area of less than twenty-five square miles. Israel was a speck of a nation, with hostile neighbors, limited arable land, and harsh weather. Worse, the remnants of Judah who had stayed behind had intermarried with locals and abandoned the rituals associated with the Temple. They knew little of the sacral observances introduced in Babylon. To the returnees, these natives were hardly Jews at all.

To reduce tensions, a group of returnees set about rebuilding the Temple, a project that took eighteen years. According to the Book of Ezra, the Temple was ultimately rededicated with an elaborate celebration in which locals and returnees together sacrificed one hundred bulls, two hundred rams, four hundred lambs, and twelve goats, one for each of the tribes of Israel. But the Temple hardly heralded the return of a Jewish state. If anything, since it was paid for by the Achaemenids, the Temple epitomized how Israel was a third-tier precinct under Persian hegemony. If Jews were going to survive, they needed more than a house of stones. They needed a way to remain intimate with the universal, nonterritorial God they had embraced in Babylon. They needed to elevate a new centerpiece of national identity, with an epic backstory and a code of values broad enough to serve both those living in diaspora *and* those living on the land.

They needed the Bible.

Sometime around 450 B.C.E., King Artaxerxes of Persia dispatched a Jewish scribe named Ezra to Jerusalem to instruct Jews in the teaching of Moses. Artaxerxes cared about the strength of the Jewish community because he needed their allegiance in his ongoing struggle with Egypt. Earlier, Artaxerxes had appointed a eunuch, Nehemiah, as governor of Judah. Nehemiah rebuilt the city walls, slashed taxes, and toughened laws on intermarriage. But while Nehemiah focused largely on the political life of the community, Ezra concentrated on the spiritual life. He was so disturbed by the Jews' lack of faithfulness that he rent his garments and tore out his hair. In a manner prescient of modern American televangelists, Ezra held huge outdoor rallies where he read the Pentateuch from dawn to noon and exhorted Jews to divorce their pagan wives and tithe to assuage their sins. Jews stood in the rain to hear his rebuke.

Ezra's innovation was profound. For the first time, he seized control of the sprawling Jewish community and began to regulate its internal affairs. With the dream of monarchical power collapsed, he shifted the organizing principle of the Jews away from being a nation and toward being a community of law, away from being a political entity and toward being an ism. "Ezra is the epitome of a new kind of leader," Avner said. "He's a priest, but he's also a teacher. He's everything but a king."

By focusing on an increasingly canonized written text and encouraging others to read, reproduce, and study it, Ezra secured the place of the Bible in Jewish life. From then on, the distinguishing characteristic of being a Jew would be not membership in a state or observance of Temple rituals. It would be following the Laws of Moses as outlined in the Bible. Values had become the chief characteristic of the people.

The story of these years is presented in the books of Ezra and Nehemiah, the last two narrative books of the Hebrew Bible. At the end of Nehemiah, the story abruptly stops, practically in mid-sentence, as the Jews have gathered to listen to the law being read out loud and realize how far they have fallen. The chapter concludes, "O my God, remember it to my credit!" Why does the Bible, which has such a dazzling opening, have such a lifeless close?

"That has everything to do with canonization," Avner said, referring to the process by which the rabbis decided which books would be included in the final Bible. "And we know *nothing* about those conversations." The Bibles we use today are based on the Masoretic text, which was completed in the early centuries after Christ. But the version used by Greeks in the late first millennium B.C.E. contains books not in the Masoretic text. Many of these, including the four books of the Maccabees, outline the epic clash between the Jews and the Greeks, which helped define Western civilization.

No sooner did Judaism reach maturity under Ezra than it came under assault from the West. In 334 B.C.E., Alexander of Macedon, having inherited the remnants of Greece from his father, set out to liberate the Ancient Near East from the Persians. Crossing the Hellespont, he cut the legendary Gordian knot in Turkey, indicating he would conquer Asia. He promptly did, darting first into Egypt, where he was declared a god, then into Mesopotamia, where he faced Darius north of Baghdad. Using his versatile phalanx army, Alexander's force of 40,000 defeated Darius's 200,000. He then marched through Babylon, Susa, and Persepolis. He made it all the way to India before retreating to Babylon, where he became ill and died on June 13, 323, in a room within eyeshot of where Saddam later built his palace.

Tutored by Aristotle, Alexander set the goal of uniting East and West under the aegis of Greek civilization. He ended the multiculturalism of the Pax Persica and replaced it with one universal, cosmopolitan culture, which other nations were allowed to embrace but not improve. Greek became the lingua franca, Greek sports became the leading cultural activity, Greek gods became the primary deities. Even after Alexander died and his political empire collapsed, his cultural legacy thrived. The Hellenists told local populations across Asia they could keep their barbarian religions if they wished, but if they wanted to join the West they should give their gods Greek names, give themselves Greek names, and intermarry with Greeks.

Jews, in particular, embraced Hellenism. Adopting a pattern that would continue through today, many Jews chose assimilation over confrontation. Hellenism, they felt, not only didn't threaten their faith but provided many benefits, including a shared love of intellectual pursuits, wider career opportunities, and more fun, especially with athletics. For nearly two centuries Judaism and Hellenism thrived side by side. But confrontation seemed inevitable in the early second century B.C.E., when Hellenist rulers began pressuring Jews to abandon the Torah.

The resulting clash produced one of the most controversial holidays of the Jewish calendar.

W
e arrived in Modiin, a thriving settlement begun in 1996 that bills itself as the fastest-growing city in the world other than Las Vegas. After seven years it had a population of 50,000, with 10,000 people moving in every year. A map in the town showed an ambitious plan to expand to 250,000. As part of that dream, the mayor passed a ruling declaring Hanukkah the official holiday.

On the outskirts of town, at the crest of a mostly barren hill, with scattered pistachio and cypress trees nestled into cracks, is a small park. Peeking out of the bedrock were a dozen man-made caverns large enough to hold two corpses. Nearby were large boulders that Avner said would have been rolled over the pits, both to protect the dead from wild animals and to serve as tombstones. "Like the Church of the Holy Sepulcher," Avner said, speaking of where Jesus is said to have been buried, "this was once a quarry that was later converted into a cemetery."

I lowered myself into a pit, which was about eight feet deep. No writing was visible, because families wealthy enough to afford such tombs would not have wanted robbers to identify them. These graves are reputed to have held the most famous residents of Hellenistic Israel, the Maccabees, heroes of the Hanukkah story. "There is no evidence to support that claim," Avner said, "and most probably they are from later. Archaeologically speaking, they do not fit the Maccabean period."

"Then why the tradition?"

"Ancient Modiin was known to be in this area, and the Maccabees were from Modiin. For early Zionists looking for heroes, the Maccabees seemed a good fit: they were young, they were bold, they fought for what they believed in."

The death of Alexander the Great in 323 B.C.E. quickly tore his kingdom in two, as his successors divided the world between the Ptolemies in Egypt and the Seleucids in Syria. But the Seleucids struggled to maintain power from Persia to Palestine and fought off rebellions from their subjects. Antiochus IV, who seized the Seleucid throne in a coup in 175 B.C.E., faced hostility on all fronts. A lavish despot nicknamed "the maniac," Antiochus did what many leaders before and since have done in times of crisis: He used religion to unify the public. He issued edicts enforcing the status of Zeus as the common god of his heterogeneous people.

Many citizens, including wealthy, well-educated, urban Jews in Jerusalem who enjoyed their association with Hellenism, welcomed his moves. Some Jews were so desperate to join the ultimate Hellenist club, the gymnasium, which promised exclusive access to the Olympic Games, that they submitted themselves to an unimaginable procedure. Since athletes competed in the nude, Jewish men who hoped to participate had to undergo a reverse circumcision, or epispasm, to stretch their foreskin to cover their penises. The surgery became so widespread that the Talmud was later forced to condemn it as being so sinful that it could not be tolerated, even by praying for forgiveness on Yom Kippur, the Day of Atonement.

Buoyed by the rapid Hellenization of the Jews and needing funds, Antiochus stormed Jerusalem and, on the twenty-fifth of Kislev 167 B.C.E. (roughly December), plundered the Temple, removed its sacred furniture, and stripped the gold leaf from the façade. Further, he burned the Bible, ended circumcision, and converted the Temple into a shrine of Zeus, in front of which Jews were required to sacrifice pigs. The date, the twenty-fifth of Kislev, was likely chosen because it was a pagan holiday, immediately following the winter solstice, celebrating the rebirth of the sun.

As forced Hellenization spread, the policy reached Modiin, where a priest, Mattathias, lived with his sons: John, Simon, Judah, Eleazar, and Jonathan. Asked to lead a sacrifice to Zeus, Mattathias refused and fled with his sons and supporters to the hills. "Why was I born to witness the ruin of my people and the ruin of the Holy City?" he asked. The family began a stealth campaign, attacking Hellenists and their Jewish sympathizers, burning altars to Zeus, and forcibly circumcising children. When Mattathias died, leadership passed to Judah, nicknamed Maccabeus, or "the Hammer," likely from his mallet-shaped head, who turned the guerrilla war into a full-scale fight for independence.

Antiochus, bogged down in Persia, sent only minimal forces to squash the revolt. Judah eluded them and marched into Jerusalem, shuttered the gymnasium, and cleansed the Temple. On the twenty-fifth of Kislev 164, three years after the original desecration, the Temple was rededicated. The Book of Maccabees says the Jews celebrated for eight days, a number chosen because the new holiday made up for the eight-day holiday of Sukkot (designed to mark the dedication of the First Temple), which had not been held while the Temple was under pagan control. The Maccabees ordained that the dedication be honored each year "with gladness and joy."

Later the rabbis named the holiday Hanukkah, or "Dedication," and began the annual festivities on the twenty-fifth of Kislev. Similarly, in the third century C.E., church officials transferred the date of Christmas from the sixth of January to the twenty-fifth of December in what some suggested was a move to appropriate the still-popular pagan practice of celebrating the passing of the darkest days of the year. Long before twentieth-century consumerism brought them into union once again, Hanukkah and Christmas shared one theme in common: both were crafted in part to move the world from paganism to monotheism.

By the time I emerged from the cavern, a stirring scene had unfolded on the hilltop. At least three extended families had swarmed over the tombs, spilling forth with squealing children, parents carrying cookies and juice cartons, grandmothers toting babies. A father struggled to rouse more enthusiasm from a group of eight-year-olds apathetically singing a holiday song. A mother retold the Maccabees story as she lit the candles on a tin menorah, the nine-branch candelabra in which each arm represents a different night and the ninth is the master that lights the others.

As I watched, a woman invited me to join her party. She had curly blond hair with a hint of gray and was wearing a lavender T-shirt and matching eye makeup. She carried a two-year-old girl.

The forty-eight-year-old Yael Simckes was born on Long Island. She had first visited Israel in 1973. A second visit, in 1981, inspired her to move. She married an expatriated American, and the two live with four children in a settlement called Elazar, named after the fourth Maccabee, who was trampled by an elephant. I asked her why she had brought her children here.

"My kids know this is where the Maccabees are from," she said, "and that they were buried here—" A sound caught her attention, and she turned toward the tomb. "Watch out for the scorpions and snakes!" she cried. She turned back and apologized.

"I find the story of Hanukkah is more complicated than the version I grew up with," I said. "I never realized the Jews were fighting other Jews as well as the Greeks. Forced circumcision seems pretty brutal. Is the story you tell your kids different from the story you were told growing up?"

"No. I'm a schoolteacher, and what I tell my kids has more to do with the fact that the Greeks came and said, 'You can't be Jewish anymore. Be like us.' And a few Jews were courageous enough to say, 'No, we want our freedom.' Being Jewish is being different. It's standing up to that pressure, which has always been around us, and saying, 'We don't bow down to idols. We have Jewish values. We dress differently. We eat different foods.'"

"So the message is self-confidence."

"It's confidence in your own identity, no matter how difficult it may be. There's real pressure, even in Israel, to conform. All the young people want to look like they're on MTV. They go to extremes, with the piercings, the tattoos, trying to be like everyone else.

"I thank God I came here and didn't assimilate," she continued. "I went to Vassar College, and I was like a Jew turning into a WASP. And I didn't know until I came to Israel and saw proud, normal people who were Jewish that I didn't have to be ashamed. I didn't realize until I came to Israel that every time we'd be in a restaurant and a Jewish subject would come up I kind of lowered my voice. It's not that we were afraid, but that we felt we had to keep quiet. We were hiding. Three-quarters of the people I grew up with did assimilate in the end."

"One thing about Israel," I said. "Here you can speak as loudly as you want."

"Absolutely!" she said, beaming. "That's what everyone does!"

We said good-bye, and Avner and I made our way back toward Jerusalem, where we had been invited to join the lighting of Israel's equivalent of the National Christmas Tree, the menorah at the Western Wall. The elevation of Hanukkah to a focal point in contemporary Judaism was by no means guaranteed. If anything, the story of the Maccabees was almost erased from Jewish history.

The Jews gained nominal independence from the Seleucids in 142 B.C.E. But once the heirs to the Maccabees, known as the Hasmoneans, became leaders of the Jewish nation, they quickly descended into tyranny, ransacking the countryside for mistresses, hiring mercenaries, and plundering David's tombs to fund foolish military excursions. The Jewish values that had inspired the original revolt were subverted to vulgar corruption. By the time they lost power in the first century B.C.E., the Hasmoneans represented yet another failed experiment in political leadership in a line that stretched across the entire biblical era.

Perhaps for this reason, the books of the Maccabees have a curious relationship with the Bible. Two of the four books were included in the Greek Bible, which Christians adopted from the Jews of Egypt. The rabbis, though, excluded them from the Jewish canon, perhaps because they didn't approve of the Hasmoneans, or perhaps because the story glorifies a war begun by humans, not God. We don't know. As Avner notes, scholars have unearthed little about the process of canonization.

The church eventually dropped the Maccabees from its canon, too, though Christians continued to embrace the story, in part because Judah Maccabee embodies the believer who is willing to use violence to defend his faith. Pope Urban II, when he called for the Crusades in the eleventh century, brandished the sword of the Maccabees. Judah Maccabee is one of "nine worthies" carved into the doors of medieval churches; the other two Old Testament figures on the doors are also warriors: Joshua and David.

Jews also continued to love the story, despite its noncanonical status. Josephus notes that in the first century C.E. the holiday was being called the Festival of Lights, "I think from the fact that the right to worship appeared to us like a flash of light at a time when we hardly dared hope for it." The Talmud downplays the holiday, but the rabbis, convinced it would endure anyway, introduced a divine spin. When the Maccabees entered the Temple, the Talmud says, they found only one cruse of olive oil to light the seven-branch menorah that had stood in the Temple since the time of Solomon. With no time to make more oil, they lit the menorah, and it burned for eight days. This story, unmentioned in the books of the Maccabees, brought the Hanukkah tale in line with other biblical stories, including Moses' dedication of the tabernacle and Solomon's construction of the First Temple, both of which were accompanied by fire miracles.

Hanukkah remained a minor holiday through the Middle Ages, with no respite from work and no gift giving. Jewish families would light eight oil lamps to commemorate the miracle, but in the sixteenth century families began to replace the oil with tallow and wax candles. Menorahs were placed outside, to the left of the door, to be visible to neighbors returning home after sunset.

Hanukkah began to emerge as a major holiday in the late nineteenth century, on the backs of the two new forces in world Jewry: Zionists and Americans. Early Zionists latched onto the story because it showed the power of Jews seizing independence through military action. Zionists renamed the festival the Holiday of the Maccabees and wrote a popular song that boasted, "No miracle happened here." Jews *won* this victory, they insisted.

In the United States, meanwhile, Hanukkah was elevated as a counterpart to Christmas and a way for Jews to participate in the American winter sport of competitive consumption. This Christianized Hanukkah is the one I grew up with, and I loved it. My family lit candles every night, and my mother, who believed all gifts had to be earned, hid presents and made my siblings and me find them before we could open them.

Rereading the story of Hanukkah now, I was frustrated to learn how whitewashed our version had been. I was also disappointed that American Jews had pumped up Hanukkah to mimic one of the least spiritual sides of Christmas. Hanukkah fit a pattern consistent with the way many in my generation were raised to be Jewish. Judaism was cherished in my home for its values of self-reliance, community service, and education. Still, many parents, rabbis, and teachers I knew couldn't help dwelling on the negative reasons to be Jewish—Jews can be wiped out at any moment; Israel is imperiled; you face discrimination, so you better stick together—as well as reactive reasons: We're just like Christians, only better.

Recently I had begun to wonder if Jews might find a way to stress the more affirmative reasons for their faith.

Just above the Western Wall, we stopped off to meet Noam Zion, a philosopher from Minneapolis who now heads the Center for Jewish Continuity at the Shalom Hartman Institute and has become one of the world's leading experts on Jewish holidays, including Hanukkah. He is a passionate advocate for what he calls "Home-made Judaism." The future of Judaism (and perhaps religion in general), he believes, depends on turning away from the professionalization of faith that has occurred in recent centuries, which overemphasized soaring buildings, stern public rituals, and passive congregants, and rediscovering a more familial, do-it-yourself tradition of creatively celebrating holidays at home. "This change fits other aspects of modern living," he said, "in which people say, 'I'm taking back control over my life. I exercise, I eat healthily. Why can't I do the same thing with the way I shape my home time?'"

I asked him if the struggle to redefine Hanukkah worried him.

"I find it a very exciting battle," he said. "The celebration of holidays has always been based on creating collective identities, and Hanukkah fits that perfectly. It's a home holiday, but it's different from most home holidays because it's a liminal holiday—it's about putting the menorah in the window. It's about a public statement of what I believe in. With Passover, the mitzvah is to publicize the miracle to the next generation of your family. With Hanukkah, the mitzvah is to publicize the miracle to the outside world."

For that reason, he continued, "Hanukkah is the perfect holiday for a multicultural world. It's a statement that I want to preserve my values and trumpet my beliefs—not that other people have to adopt them, but that other people accept them. And I think each home has to be the center of those values, so that instead of the light coming from the outside world, which is what television is, ultimately dissolving everybody into their own rooms, the light comes from inside the family and illuminates the neighborhood."

I mentioned my frustration that Hanukkah had become too reactive to Christmas.

"I faced the same thing growing up in Minnesota," he said. "The Christmas tree was always in the background, even if we didn't have one ourselves. But I'm trying to make you more appreciative of your parents. Understand that all cultures, at all periods in human history, have been in dialogue with others. Early Christians adopted customs from Judaism in the way that Judaism later adopted customs from Christianity. The question should be whether your parents used the competitive religious environment to spur you to retrieve your Judaism."

"That raises my big question," I said. "If my wife and I are lucky enough to have children, what narrative should we tell them?"

"For me, I think the narrative is of personal courage. In the darkest month of the year, in a dark time for Jews in the world, Hanukkah was the first piece of light. But I think it's important to remember that the Maccabees' struggle for independence lasted another twenty-five years. Hanukkah does not celebrate the final victory. It's not the Exodus from Egypt. It's the first victory in a long struggle against the Greco-Roman empire.

"And I want to celebrate beginnings," he continued. "As my teacher, David Hartman, says, the miracle is not that one vessel of oil lasted for eight days but that the community was willing to light one vessel not knowing whether it would last. The true miracle is daring to dream. And that's the key to Jewish life. Any realistic analysis says, 'Forget it! You'll never succeed.' But if you say I believe in the power of a little bit of light, and I believe in the kinds of things that aren't codified, then I believe that this little tiny flicker of faith I have can produce an enormous transformation, so that somehow I'll have a greater and greater effect on the world."

The winter light on the Western Wall becomes dull and gray by the middle of the afternoon, as the sun dips behind the crest of Mount Zion. Though the sky is still blue at 4:00 P.M. and the last rays of sun are just glinting off the Dome of the Rock, the limestone blocks of Herod's retaining wall have already descended into shadow. On this afternoon, a ten-foot span to the far right of the men's praying area had been illuminated with stage lights. A small dais had been erected, covered in a black velvet mantle, embroidered with the name of its maker, www.rikmatova.com.

On top of the stage was a protective glass box about seven feet high, and inside it stood a giant sterling-silver menorah. The menorah had nine glass containers for oil, each the size of a shot glass, and elaborate silver arabesques that connected the arms to the trunk. If Louis XIV had needed a menorah, this one would have fit perfectly at Versailles. It, too, boasted a sign at its base, perfectly positioned for news cameras, sporting the name of its manufacturer, Hazorfim. Americans are clearly not the only ones who understand marketing.

We arrived just as afternoon prayers were beginning, and were ushered onto the dais. About a hundred people were praying. The only other person on the stage was the chief of police of Jerusalem. He was a gruff man, with eyes darting anxiously about, but when I asked him if he looked forward to Hanukkah, he brightened. "Doesn't every Jew?"

At that moment, the crowd of onlookers parted, and a broad-shouldered man in a perfectly pressed black cape with gold embroidery on the shoulders strode into view. He had a white beard that reminded me of Santa Claus, spectacles, and a mesmerizing black satin hat, in the shape of a turban, that indicated he was the spiritual leader of the Sephardic Jewish community. Shlomo Amar, a native of Morocco, was also a chief rabbi of Israel. As he moved toward the stage, worshipers took their prayer shawls and kissed his cape, as if he were a Torah being paraded through a synagogue.

Arriving on the stage, he greeted each of us warmly and stood to my right, in front of the menorah. While a men's chorus began to sing, Rabbi Amar struck up a conversation. "Forget the outside world," he said to me. "Assume you're on an empty planet. What's the meaning of Hanukkah? If you take the rabbinic story of the oil, it shows there is something that makes things go beyond their natural limit. I want to connect myself to that ultimate fire.

"Look at these stones," he continued, gesturing to the Wall. "When you stare at them, you see just stones. But if you're connected to a higher power, they are so much more."

The time had come to light the menorah. Rabbi Amar took a braided candle, lit it, and began chanting the prayer: *"Baruch ata Adonai, Eloheinu melech ha-olam . . ."* "Blessed are you, Adonai, our God, ruler of the world . . ." As he did, the crowd, which had swelled to four hundred, chanted with him. Then he began lighting the cups of oil, and when he finished, he did something I didn't expect: He took the few steps to the Wall, bent at the waist, and kissed it. I froze.

The last time I had stood in this spot, I had recoiled. I was fed up with religious extremists who seemed to place the physical symbols of religion over the spiritual message. The Wall had become for me an example of this kind of religious fervor. More than a summons to elevation, it had become a rallying point for radical fantasies of Armageddon.

Now I felt somewhat differently. One gift of my journey was discovering that the Hebrew Bible tells a more subtle story of the origins of monotheism than I had been led to expect. Land is not the focal point of that story; walls are not its core. At the center of the biblical model is a moral relationship between humans and God. Land is important to that relationship. From the moment God calls Abraham to set out to the Promised Land, through the Exodus, through Joshua's conquest, humans and God dream of a home where they can realize their relationship in freedom. But from the Exodus, through the Exile, to the diaspora, humans and God reach their most intimate moments when they are *not* on the land.

If anything, Jewish life finally seems to achieve a working equilibrium near the end of the biblical era, when some people live on the land and some people live off it. The ideal condition for a fully realized relationship between humans and God may be this period, the late first millennium B.C.E., when land-based monotheism and landless monotheism exist in a state of creative tension. It was during this era that the returnees from Babylon restored faith to the land, and when Ezra and Nehemiah infused the fractured Jerusalem community with a stronger, text-based faith. They are the final heroes of the Bible. And as an American Jew, I found their story revolutionary, even freeing. Diaspora Judaism is not secondary Judaism.

It is coequal.

Particularly in the pluralist world of today, the example of these latter biblical years is resonant, and even uplifting. They show that in the birth moment of Western religion, Judaism pioneered the idea that religion need not be imperial, ever-expanding, and intolerant. From Persia to Babylon to Egypt, Judaism thrived as a minority faith in the late first millennium B.C.E., living alongside much stronger, majority faiths. Through a combination of historical circumstance and the tutelage of at least some of the prophets, the first great monotheistic religion began its existence in a posture of humility.

As a Jew, I take from the final books of the prophets the positive message I had been craving in my upbringing. Judaism can be a living alternative to triumphalism. After centuries in which many Christians and Muslims tried to assert themselves as the universal religion; at a time when violent fundamentalists of all Abrahamic faiths try to impose their views on rivals; Jews, and non-Jews, can reach back to the base text for all three traditions and declare, "There's another way." Faith in God does not depend on size. As lovers of the Bible, we fulfill our relationship with God by upholding his values, and we define our relationship with others not by thrusting our ways onto them but by asserting our willingness to be vulnerable in the face of dominant cultures.

And in this new, affirmative worldview, Hanukkah is uniquely positioned as a shining example. Like the Bible, the Maccabees' story contains sickening undercurrents of extremism. But Hanukkah endures because it's a tribute to the absurd idea that even something tiny can outshine its potential. Not until I reexamined the holiday as an adult did I realize that one is not supposed to light the candles in private, then move them to the door. One is supposed to light them in the threshold. The blessing comes from willingly asserting your faith in public, not with raging fire but with a single, quiet flame.

And by reaching this belief, I had arrived at an unexpected destination in my journey. As Rabbi Amar leaned up from the Wall, the crowd behind him began to sing *Maoz Tzur*, "Rock of Ages," the traditional hymn of Hanukkah. I was transported back to my childhood home, my family awkwardly holding hands, butchering this beautiful melody. My throat caught. My eyes welled. I had finally broken through my hostility. I bent toward the Wall, smiled, and kissed the stones.

And when I turned around, the rabbi had lifted his hands in the air, the five hundred people now gathered before him bowed their heads, and he offered a blessing. When he finished, what seemed like half the crowd retrieved cameras, raised them to their eyes, and flashed. The explosion of white was unlike anything I'd ever seen. A paparazzi scrum in the holiest place on earth. Modernity bowing down to tradition. And looking up, I saw the most magical constellation. In every window, in every doorway, an infinite galaxy of light.

W‌ithin half an hour, the lighting ceremony had ended, and Avner and I made our way around the southern perimeter of the Temple Mount to the base of the Mount of Olives. We planned to spend the final night of our travels in a place intimately connected to the end of the first millennium B.C.E. and to a revolutionary new phenomenon in Western religious life. From the remnants of the biblical era, the dream of the messiah would rise.

The Mount of Olives is actually three mountains in one, a two-mile-long ridge of Israel's central mountains that contains three separate summits. At 3,000 feet above sea level, the highest peak is the tallest mountain in Jerusalem, 230 feet taller than the Temple Mount. During the Second Temple period, Olives, named for the abundant trees that once lined its slopes, was the first in the chain of peaks throughout the countryside where bonfires were lit at the start of each month. The Talmud says the chain of bonfires continued all the way to Babylon.

As early as the time of the prophets, the Mount of Olives had been associated with divine redemption. Jewish tradition held that the Shechina, or Divine Presence, left the First Temple after its destruction and hovered over Olives for three and a half years, waiting for Israel to repent. When it did not, the Shechina ascended to heaven on the footstool of God. During the Second Temple period, many Jews wanted to be buried on the mountain because God, when he returned to earth, would descend the same footstool and stand here first.

But late in the first millennium B.C.E., Jews began associating Olives with an even more supernatural notion. The dream of a messiah, evolving for centuries, erupted into a full-scale societal frenzy following the collapse of the Hasmonean empire. The idea of an anointed savior took two forms. The first was restorative and political: The day would come when a militaristic leader from the House of David would rise up, restore Israel to its rightful place, and redistribute the land to the twelve tribes. The second was futuristic and utopian: The day would come when a spiritual figure would arise, remake the cosmic order, and deliver the world into salvation.

"The utopian movement was really something unique," Avner said. "The messiah it imagines has no political power to speak of. Instead he remakes the laws of nature, so that the wolf and the lamb will live together."

I asked him what happened between the middle of the first millennium B.C.E. and the late first millennium that allowed this idea to take hold.

"A lot of it has to do with the Maccabees," he said. "Many people were uncomfortable with the Hasmonean kings because they weren't from the House of David. So they went back to the Davidic image but updated it with a more complete purpose and aura."

"So after two thousand years of failed leaders, the people finally get the hint that profane leadership is not going to work," I said. "They need a miracle."

"With good reason," Avner said. "The Romans conquered Israel, and the Hasmoneans failed. Sure enough, soon you begin to encounter self-proclaimed saviors, somewhere between prophets and messiahs, who are roaming the countryside making promises. 'My breath will bring about the fall of the walls of Jerusalem.' 'I will part the seas of the Jordan.' 'Let's go back to the desert and establish God's kingdom.'"

"So it's in the air."

"Yes, and what happens is that people take ideas that have been percolating for centuries, like resurrection of the dead and life after death, and combine them with this new ideal of messiah."

"So if we were standing on this mountain at the end of the first millennium B.C.E.," I said, "and I said to you that a figure was going to emerge—"

"Yes . . ."

"—who was going to husband all the people who believe in the utopian, end-of-days, nonphysical, cosmological messiah, that would not have shocked you."

"No. That's what was happening." He paused. "And we certainly know one messianic figure—or at least one messianic movement—who did just that."

Beaming our flashlights, we reached the halfway point of the mountain and the crowded huddle of churches, shrines, and monasteries. The narrow streets were mostly empty at this hour, but I could smell incense. The New Testament overflows with references to the Mount of Olives, which played a central role in the last week of Jesus' life. Olivet, as Luke calls it, is where Jesus liked to meet his disciples, where he wept for the Jewish nation, and where he began his walk into Jerusalem on Palm Sunday. As a result, the western slope today contains three triumphal entry trails, three Gardens of Gethsemane, three sites for Jesus' ascension, and a shrine to the supposed last footprints of Christ.

By far the most visually arresting facility is the Russian Orthodox Compound of St. Mary Magdalene, the centerpiece of which is a two-story white sandstone church built in 1888 by Czar Alexander III with seven gilded, bulbous domes that look like a bouquet of giant garlic cloves. Nearing six o'clock, the street in front of the compound was dark and spooky. We rang the bell, and a nun opened a window in the door and told us that the monastery was closed. "But you invited us," Avner said.

"Oh, we invited *you*," she said, opening the door. "I'm sorry. Evening prayers are under way. Ask for Sister Xenia."

The interior of the church was dim, illuminated by a half dozen candles placed in front of icons. We sat alongside one of the columns. The squarish nave was largely empty, with smaller alcoves along each side. The entire facility was painted in shades of brown, red, and gold. The centerpiece was a giant iconostasis, a white marble and bronze screen that shielded a private sanctuary and was painted with the four evangelists—Matthew, Mark, Luke, and John. Above the screen was a painting depicting Mary Magdalene, one of Jesus' followers and the first to see him after the Resurrection, standing before Emperor Tiberius in Rome. In the painting, she is holding a red egg. Tradition says she brought a regular egg to the emperor and declared, "Christ has risen!" "How could anyone rise from the dead?" he said. "It is as impossible as that egg turning red!" As the emperor spoke, the egg turned crimson, a symbol of Jesus' blood. Some believe the custom of dyeing eggs on Easter came from this story.

The only other people in the church were about a dozen nuns in black habits and head scarves, as well as a bishop who emerged from behind the screen waving an incense holder, giving the room the mesmerizing smell of allspice and cinnamon. The service was conducted by a nun chanting in Slavonic, the ancient Slavic liturgical language that sounds Russian, only sweeter. The sweetness was enhanced by three sisters standing behind her, singing magically harmonic tunes that seemed like a combination of Mozart sonatas and Appalachian folk melodies. Their voices were plaintive, as if coming through a gramophone.

Sister Xenia turned out to be an American, who had been raised Catholic in Northern California. When the service ended, she shyly but warmly invited us to dinner in an underground hall. We sat in silence as the sisters prayed, and ate boiled potatoes and pasta, sliced tomato, and a persimmon. Avner advised me to leave some food on my plate, as nuns adopted this custom to indicate they are eating only for survival, not pleasure. When we finished, Sister Xenia led us up the hill to a small, whitewashed room for pilgrims.

As a teenager, Catherine, as she was known, grew disillusioned with her faith and went seeking other truths. At sixteen she was hit by a car and flew forty feet, smashing her pelvis. Doctors told her she would never walk again. When she did, she went on to study medicine at Berkeley, working as a maid to pay the bills, until she nearly lost her life in the Loma Prieta earthquake in 1989. Penniless, she moved in temporarily with a friend in a Russian Orthodox monastery. "I had only one dress I could wear," she said. "I was very fashionable and into boys. I said, 'Just for a few months.'" But when one of the sisters got cancer, Catherine began attending morning services to help with the singing. "And I began to notice: If I got up to say morning prayers, my day was brighter. If I slept in, my day was more pressured."

She never left.

She moved to the Mount of Olives in 1994 and nearly lost her life again, in Jericho in 2000, when Palestinian gunmen held her captive in a Russian Orthodox monastery for forty-five nights in a precursor to the second Intifada. "I felt so free, even though I was so captive," she said. "It's like a curtain opened, and I saw something. I felt Christ."

"You remind me of someone I met, not far from here, over a year ago," I said. "Her name was Tzippy Cohen, and she was nearly killed twice. First in New York on 9/11, and then here, in the bombing at Café Hillel."

"I always say, 'Living here, we have orchestra seats on history.'"

"So what have you learned from your front-row seat about the relationship between faith and violence?"

"I think the violence we have developed as humans is a very negative violence," Sister Xenia said, and I was struck by how beautiful her face became when she spoke about faith. "The violence we should use in religion is the violence of commitment: Using every means you have as a creative being to bring yourself closer to God. The violence out there"—she gestured toward the Temple Mount—"is a repellent thing. But the violence in here"—she gestured to the compound—"is of people coming together."

"So the answer to violence in the name of God is violence in the service of God?"

"Sort of, but it's not the violence people know. It's destroying the culture in which people put themselves at the center of everything. And putting God at the center. The day will come, Isaiah said, when 'the haughtiness of man shall be humbled, and the pride of men shall be brought low; and the Lord alone will be exalted.'"

"And do you believe that will happen? Do you believe the religions will get along?"

"Look, I'm a nun in the Orthodox Church. I believe that Orthodoxy is the truth. I believe that Christ is the messiah. But I also believe that everybody on earth was created in God's image. We are all related in being created. So I, as a created, have to respect other created things. That's what I mean when I say putting God at the center. He created us this way. We have to learn to live together."

In front of our room was a large stone patio with palm trees that looked west over the Old City. Directly in front of the patio, at eye level, was the Dome of the Rock, almost hovering in the air, illuminated by the moon.

Avner and I began talking about his father. I mentioned that there was one thing about his dad I had never understood. "There would seem to be a contradiction in his feeling this personal connection to the land and to the Bible yet being openly hostile to religion."

"I don't think he considered it a tension," Avner said. "I think one of the things that bothered him most was religion being used for politics. That's what he fought against. His idea was that religion should be a private belief. He even tried to get a bill introduced into parliament."

"So do you think his resistance mirrored what was going on in the world at that time, with the Holocaust, socialism, et cetera? In the mid–twentieth century, God seemed to be dead."

"Very much so. A big part of secular Zionism was turning against the ghetto mentality of Judaism and reconnecting to the land. I felt the same attachment. And I loved the Bible, but not necessarily religion."

"So what happened? When we met in the mid-1990s, religion and God were not part of our conversation. Now we talk about them all the time. Obviously part of that's the world, but part of it is us, too."

"A lot of it has to do with our travels," he said. "We've met so many people who are believers but who are also committed to peace. I've come to appreciate the more generous side of faith. And I've also come to realize that so many people who are fighting in the name of religion actually lack an identity, so they cling to things that are physical, like land. I really believe now that religion is central to helping people develop an identity that is more mature, having to do with morals and ways of living."

"So you're saying that in this part of the world, where religion seems to be the motivation for many of the problems, you believe that religion can actually be part of the solution?"

"I think that's true for all parties. Once you are mature enough, and have self-confidence, you can talk better with others, be more open, and give up your convictions for things that might be more important, like peace."

It took a second for this idea to settle over me, yet I knew it mirrored my own journey, in which knowledge of matters of faith had helped buttress my self-confidence. Only when I became confident in myself as a Jew could I safely reach out to others.

"When I met you, I would have described you as an archaeologist and an adventurer. Maybe even a humanist," I said. "But I'm not sure I would have described you as a Jew. Are you a Jew now?"

"I'm quite sure that the answer is yes. One reason is that I've learned a lot more. As we know from Babylon and elsewhere, the power of Judaism is its openness to change, to answering the needs of a new world. There's always been change, but the twentieth century, the State of Israel, and 9/11 pushed these changes even faster. I'm proud to be a part of that."

"Does that mean wanting a relationship with God?"

"You can call it God. You can call it values. You can call it heritage."

"And would your father approve of that relationship?"

"I think so, because whatever it is, it brings me closer to other humans, and that's what he really wanted out of life."

Avner went off to bed, and I decided to stroll down the stairs to see the view from in front of the church. Pine trees mostly blocked the light on the path, and I was startled to hear in the bushes a hound, geese, and several cats. My heart lurched with each sound. I realized my hands were trembling. The Mount of Olives at midnight seemed like an eerie menagerie. Reaching the wall, I sat beneath an olive tree and peered out at the Eye of the World.

When I made my first journey retracing the Pentateuch through the desert, I was struck by how linear the biblical narrative was—the Israelites begin in Mesopotamia with Abraham, travel down to the Promised Land, descend into Egypt, then cross the Red Sea into the wilderness. The story gallops along like one of those moving red lines on a map in a 1950s movie. The second half of the Hebrew Bible begins with that momentum with Joshua, David, and Solomon. But around the time of the Exile, the story line shifts. Gone is the linear drive, replaced with a diffusion, as if the straight red line on the map got wet and the color began to seep across the region.

This diffusion is one of the reasons the second half of the Bible is less appreciated; there's simply less action. But it's also why the themes from this period have endured across so many cultures. If the Pentateuch is the story of a nation coming of age, the prophets tell what happened when that nation left home and interacted with the world. The prophets are mediators who spread the message of God to the ages.

This difference between the first and second halves of the narrative reflects what happened to me on my journeys. On my first trek, I was focused more on my personal relation to the story—whether it was fact or fiction, science or myth; whether something that happened thirty centuries ago could still speak to me today. Looking back, I see that that journey occurred at a time when it may have been easier to indulge in those private questions. That time seems far away now. The second Intifada, September 11, Afghanistan, Iraq, the growing divide between secular-minded Western Europeans and faith-based Americans, have all changed the global reality. Closer to home, gay marriage, the Ten Commandments, moral values in Washington, God in Hollywood, suddenly dominated nearly every conversation. Sorry, Ma, we have no choice: We have to talk about religion and politics in public.

As a teenager and young adult, I, like many Jews, cheered what appeared to be the receding of faith from everyday life. The further religion got from our lives the better our lives would become, I thought, because persecution had been such a burden to our parents, and to Jewish families for generations. But the older I get, the more I realize that religion is not going to be easily marginalized by one of its wannabe successors—science, capitalism, communism, consumerism. The last thirty years witnessed what George Weigel called the desecularization of the world, a resurgence of faith in part as a counter to the impersonalization of modernity.

Religion surged also because it offered a counterweight to the searing speed of contemporary life and to the burden of national rivalries that have dragged the world through war after war. Religion is broader than nationalism. It addresses the dignity of all human beings, not just those in one geographic area. It is universal. "Politicians have power," says Jonathan Sacks, the chief rabbi of Britain, "but religions have something stronger: They have influence. Politics moves the pieces on the chessboard. Religion changes lives." Religion also breeds overconfidence, and one challenge for today's believers is to rediscover in the fire of faith the source of warmth that can overpower the flames of destruction. This change can be achieved only by fellow believers, I think. The first conviction I took from my journey is that the only force strong enough to take on religious extremism is religious moderation.

Religion can be saved only by religion.

And in that battle, one of the greatest weapons of all may be the Bible.

For all its singularity, the Hebrew Bible can still be seen as a product of the Axial Age, that several-century span in the middle of the first millennium B.C.E. when great belief systems emerged across the world to answer the most profound questions of the human spirit. Religions, as those systems came to be called, are what Rabbi Sacks calls "sustained reflections on humanity's place in nature and what constitutes the proper goals of society and an individual life." My experience traveling and exploring this period reinforced the logical-yet-unprovable notion lingering behind the idea of an Axial Age: It's no coincidence that so many great religions evolved around the same time.

Religion is not a single red line. It's not a private universe in which each of us can look only at our own past, read only our own version of history, and talk only to our coreligionists. Religion began as a complex, interdependent web, in which people took ideas from other cultures, rituals from rival faiths, and even notions about their deities from competing gods. If religion is to be preserved as a moral force in the multifarious world of today, I believe, we must rediscover the legacy of interaction and accommodation. The great religions were not born in isolation from one another; they cannot survive in isolation from one another.

One reason that organized religions emerged as human societies became more complex is that they build community. The name of the other great force of community building, politics, comes from the Greek *polis*, or "city," and refers to the governing of civic affairs through the mediation of power. The word *religion* comes from the Latin *religare*, "to bind," and religion sets out to fuse people to one another and to God through rituals, narratives, symbols, and ceremonies.

These two colossal human creations—politics and religion, state and church—arose nearly simultaneously in antiquity and, through their fertile and sometimes tense interaction, created the twin pillars of contemporary civilization. In the West, those two pillars were defined by two cultures. "No two people have set such a mark upon the world as the Greeks and the Jews," Winston Churchill once said. "Each of them from angles so different, have left us with the inheritance of its genius and wisdom. No two cities have counted more with humankind than Athens and Jerusalem. Their messages in religion, philosophy and art have been the main guiding light in modern faith and culture. Personally, I have always been on the side of both."

At its core, Greek philosophy revolves around the individual and focuses on intellectual achievement, autonomy, and self-sufficiency. In Greek politics, as in Plato's *Republic*, the philosopher has to be persuaded to go back to the community. In Greek religion, the God of Aristotle is a perfect being, rapt in thought, whom humans contemplate and want to emulate but don't necessarily interact with. In the Bible, by contrast, God and humans have a relationship with one another. God seeks partnership with humans. He speaks through human agents. He cannot achieve his vision of a moral universe unless he acts in concert with humans. The Bible, at its heart, is an ode to interdependency. In the biblical view, God is born not in any particular place but anyplace where humans and the divine act in the service of a righteous world.

And nowhere in the Bible is this vision of interdependency expressed with more eloquence and passion than in the Prophets. Any effort to celebrate moderation in the text rightfully focuses on them. Working in intimate contact with God and speaking in sometimes abstruse, highly stylized rhetoric, the Hebrew prophets burst from the ashes of monarchy and the squalor of exile to persuade the Israelites—and the world—that when human beings act as part of a community, they fully realize their God-given powers. The Hebrew prophets were the first spiritual leaders to think globally, to conceive of God as transcending national borders and of humanity as a single moral entity. The idea of a global village began in Babylon.

The notion of universal values has deep roots in the Bible, especially in the stories of Abraham and Moses. But the prophets take these rudimentary ideas and amplify them into an all-embracing vision of humanity, in which, as Amos says, "justice rolls down like water and righteousness like a never-ending stream." God knows what he requires of humans, Micah declares: "Only to do justice and to love goodness, and to walk humbly with your God." In presenting this new ideal, the prophets show that the relationship between God and humans is not static; it evolves. As Avner put it, "The earlier laws were created because these values existed, but the values were not presented specifically. The prophets articulate the values themselves."

The heart of the prophets' philosophy of humane values relies on one of the oldest ideas in the text, the story of Creation. In going back to the Garden of Eden, the prophets alight on God's deepest desires for humans: that they live alongside other humans. In Genesis 2, after God has created Adam and placed him in the Garden of Eden, he looks at Adam and declares, "It is not good for man to be alone." Humans, God insists, must be in relationship with others.

And the foundation of all human relationships rests on an even earlier notion: "And God said, 'Let us make man in our image, after our likeness.'" All humans are created in God's image, so disrespecting another human is disrespecting God. From the earliest days of human existence, God compels us to honor his creation by respecting its diversity. As Rabbi Sacks put it in his seminal book *The Dignity of Difference*, "The challenge to the religious imagination is to see God's image in one who is not in our image." The Bible answers this challenge and clears the path to a pluralist world. It shows that all humans, at one time or another, are strangers. "You shall not oppress the stranger for you know the heart of a stranger," says Exodus 23:9, "you yourselves were strangers in the land of Egypt."

The early religious showdowns of the early twenty-first century have made one thing clear: In the battle for the soul of Western religion, it is scripture—whether the Hebrew Bible, the New Testament, or the Koran—that is ground zero. Fundamentalists of all stripes cite text as the inerrant foundation of their convictions. After more than a year of traveling through some of the most extreme places of religious fundamentalism, I determined that the Hebrew Bible, at least, cannot be read as endorsing the idea that one group of people has exclusive claim to God. In fact, from Creation to Jonah to Second Isaiah, the text explicitly endorses the opposite idea, that God embraces any people who share his moral vision, no matter their identity.

Religious extremists cite the Bible continuously as advocating their beliefs. Religious moderates can, and must, do the same. Just as flamethrowers lift the text and say, "It says this," progressives can lift the same text and say, "But it also says something else." The Bible simply is too central to the history of Western civilization—and too vital to its future—to be ceded to one side in the biggest struggle of our time, the quest to define the nature of God.

And in that struggle, as it has done so many times before, the Bible summons us to act. Before setting out on my journey, I viewed the prophets as giant nags, disembodied hands of God, suspended in the air, wagging their fingers. "I'm going to count to three, and if you don't start behaving, I'm going to send you to your room . . . in Babylon!" Now, I view them as open hands, beckoning us to take responsibility, reminding us that God can't do it alone and that each of us must help create a just and moral world. The prophets' chief legacy is an ecology of change. They locate within each individual the power to influence the community as a whole. They evangelize initiative.

The most surprising part of my trip was arriving at this destination: realizing that even though God created the world, he wants each of us to re-create it. The creator God seeks creativity in humans. This idea, so pronounced in the Prophets, is what allowed me to change my view of religion, from one of reaction to one of pro-action. At the end of my travels, I came to view my relationship with religion as I do my relationship with God. I can no longer be a passive recipient. I must be an active partner. Just as Abraham, Moses, and Isaiah talk back to God, I can talk back to religion. I don't have to blindly accept what my tradition hands down to me. I can go back to the text and make my own interpretation. I can make my own faith, grounded in the moral clarity and human dignity of the oldest source of all.

As liberating as this realization was, it did give me pause: Is there a danger in placing too much trust in a more independent, autonomous relationship with God? "But that's what believers do," said David Hartman when I went to see him in his office in Jerusalem, the day before embarking on this final leg. One of the leading philosophers of religion in the world, the Montreal-born Hartman has bushy white hair and wore hikers' fleece and tennis shoes behind his enormous oak desk. "You can't get rid of the tradition, so you re-create it. The burden is to reinterpret. We have to find where in our traditions are alternative melodies that allow us to coexist as human beings."

"Does that mean you have five million theologians in this country, three hundred million in the U.S., and five billion around the world . . . ?"

"But you do it in community. You don't do it in isolation. You deal with it in discussion with the other."

"So after all these years, we've finally merged Athens and Jerusalem," I said. "We've blended the individualistic, self-sufficient streak of the Greeks with the interdependent, communal streak of Judaism."

"You could see it that way," he said. "But you have to remember, most human beings don't have the desire to reinterpret. To them it's a burden. They have the desire to be safe. 'But you're making religion too hard,' they say. 'Just give me the truth. Tell me what to do in the morning, in the afternoon, and at night.' They want to sit down at the table and eat, but they don't want to cook the meal."

"So what's your response?"

"I say, 'What can I do?' Religion is not for the weak and the sick. It's for the healthy. If you want to have a mature life, you're going to have to take responsibility. Rabbi Akiva, in the second century, taught that God deliberately left the world unfinished so it would be completed by the work of human beings."

"That brings me to a question I've been wondering about for a long time," I said. "Why does the Hebrew Bible not really end?"

He smiled. "Because each of us has to write our own ending," he said. "The question is, Are we going to write a new chapter, or a new book? If we're going to write a new chapter, then we have to read the earlier stuff first, to see if what we're writing fits into the book."

"So at the end of my journey, there is no end."

"There is just a beginning. You may end your traveling, but if you enter the Bible, you have to keep on living, keep on thinking, keep on choosing. Keep on walking."

During all the years I had been coming to Jerusalem, I had longed to do one thing: View the sunrise over the city from the Mount of Olives. Avner and I got up at 5:00 A.M. and attended morning services in the church, which were even more ethereal than evening prayers and ended with the gentlest recitation, "Lord have mercy. Lord have mercy. Lord have mercy."

The sky began to lighten around six o'clock, and I hurried to the garden to wait for the golden halo of pink, lavender, and rose. It never came. Because the Mount of Olives is so much higher than the Temple Mount, I realized, the sun had lost its gentleness by the time the rays reached the Dome of the Rock. I could only chuckle. Even dawn relinquishes its gentleness in the face of such contention.

After breakfast, Avner said he had something to show me, and we set out through the Garden of Gethsemane, over the long slope of the mountain, toward the southwest corner of the Mount of Olives. The Old City was to our right. Avner led us upward through terrace after terrace of one of the oldest cemeteries in the country. At the highest tier, we stopped along a wall where several Hasidic men had removed two stone tablets, each about four feet high, that had been carved with the Ten Commandments. Behind the tablets was a cave.

"Shall we?" Avner said. I was a little confused but stepped forward. We were just about to enter the cave when I noticed a commotion at the bottom of the hill. Two royal blue hearses appeared around the corner. They were inching along at a mourners' crawl and were followed by a throng of men in black coats and hats that, once it rounded the bend, proved to be nearly three hundred strong. The men were chanting and swaying back and forth. "Who died?" I said to Avner.

"Nobody," he said. "They're carrying Torah scrolls and Bibles that were damaged in a fire. They can't be used anymore. But since these are holy books, you can't throw them away. The custom is to bury them in a cave or building. It's called a *geniza*."

I had never heard of this custom. "But why not bury them in the ground?"

"They would absorb water and rot too quickly. Also, people might step on them, because you don't put tombstones on *geniza*s."

The hearses came to a stop, and several of the older men retrieved around half a dozen clay canisters, each about ten inches in diameter and three feet tall, along with a plain brown coffin. The canisters contained Torahs; the coffin was for Bibles. A few of the men carried the vessels up the two tiers to where we were standing and handed them, one by one, into the cave. The handlers cradled the canisters as they might a wounded child. The chanting stopped, and the crowd peered on in silence. A few lit candles. The feeling wasn't sorrow exactly. It was awe. A funeral for a book. Here was an ending worthy of the Bible. These words, which had sprung from the Fertile Crescent more than five thousand years ago, would end their lives near the soil from which they came. "From dust you are," God says to Adam, "to dust you shall return."

Avner put his hand on my shoulder. "I know you have a deep love of the book," he said, "but I brought you here to remind you what Jeremiah said: By now you have the story inscribed in your heart. You don't necessarily need the book anymore."

I pulled out my Bible. Its cover was warped, its pages stained. From all the wear, it had actually expanded over the years. I raised my eyebrows. "Should I bury it?"

He grinned. "No, keep it and give it to your children someday. Maybe they'll bring it back here."

Once the canisters and coffin were in place, several men returned the stone tablets to the entrance and began mixing mortar to seal the *geniza*. A rabbi chanted Psalm 121.

I turn my eyes to the mountains;
From where will my help come?
My help comes from the Lord.

As the praying stopped, I noticed a woman standing off to one side, almost hiding behind one of the tombstones. She was holding the hands of her two young children, a boy and a girl. Chani Fischer works for the Funeral Society of Jerusalem and had helped organize this ceremony. She was dressed modestly, in the manner of a deeply religious woman, in a long black skirt and maroon sweater.

"The rabbi called for everyone to witness this occasion," she said. "He said we should bring our children. When I was making the arrangements, the idea of burying books didn't really affect me. But when I came out here, seeing all these people, it did something to me. It tore my heart."

"What would you like your children to learn?" I asked.

"Respect," she said. "Respect for God. For the Bible." She started to cry. "I'm sorry, it's just so sad."

"I understand," I said.

"I just love these words so much."

I struggled for something to say that might comfort her. "But don't you feel that even though the books are in the ground, their message will live on?"

Suddenly her back straightened. She wiped a tear from her cheek. And she looked at me with a gaze filled with serenity, trust, and total, utter confidence. "Forever," she said.

O Give Thanks

Avner Goren helped imagine, design, and execute this journey, and his wisdom and humanity inform every step. I am ennobled by his continued presence in my life.

I am deeply grateful to the dozens of people who appear by name in these pages, many of whom took personal risks to speak with me and who freely discussed sometimes intimate details of their private and spiritual lives. In addition I would like to thank the even greater number of people who helped arrange the logistics of this adventure, the introductions that brought it to life, and the safety precautions that were sometimes necessary. These friends, new and old, include the following: Mehdi Agha, Maziar Bahari, Arnold Belzer, Dean Bonura, Asnat Cohen, Catherine Collins and Doug Frantz, Simon Ebrahimi, Hamid Ebrahami, Marjan Eghbali, Dariush Fakheri, Israel Finkelstein, Isaiah Gafni, Wes Gardenswartz, Sam Gordon and Patty Gerstenblith, Ido Goren, Wayne Green, Matthew Gutman, Jessica Harani, Bill Hamilton, Robert Hormats, Avraham Infeld, Jack Kingston, Steve

Leder, Bijar Munib, Gina Nahai, Amnon Netzer, Evan Osnos, Guy Raz, Alyssa Rubin, Jeff Salkin, Houman Sarshar, Parveneh Sattari, Barnea Selavan, and Barry Shrage.

David Black is my friend, partner, confidant, and agent, as well as the bedrock of my professional life. I am indebted to Ken Weinrib; the team at Royce Carlton; and, for keeping things going, Jazie Ingram, Charlotte Malot, Gary Morris, Trish Potts, and especially Greg Takoudes.

Jane Friedman is fearless, visionary, and bold. I am humbled by her support. Michael Morrison has built a powerhouse at William Morrow that I am honored to be a part of. Lisa Gallagher is the hardest-working woman in publishing, as well as one of the smartest and most delightful. Henry Ferris has reminded me every day of the values of a keen eye and a big heart. And Sharyn Rosenblum teaches everyone she meets the meaning of dedication and joy. These people, along with Debbie Stier and many others, have given me a home. Everlasting thanks to Trish Grader, who believed before anyone else.

I can hardly convey the depth of commitment and total confidence that the editors and staff at *Parade* magazine displayed in sending me to Iraq in the middle of a war. I am forever beholden to Lee Kravitz for his passion, trust, and friendship. Gwendolen Cates and I are forever bonded by our experience. Walter Anderson, Lamar Graham, Dakila Divina, and many others worked exhaustively for months to ensure our safety. Thank you.

I am blessed to be surrounded by a wide circle of creative friends and colleagues never far with support and opinions. Ben Sherwood continues to inspire and push me with his rigorous mind and Olympian commitment to friendship. Jane Lear is a woman of faith, grace, and an effortless gift with words. Karen Lehrman and Joe Weisberg are daily fonts of invigorating ideas and emotional strength. Beth Middleworth is a quiet genius.

Thanks always to Lynn Cohen, Karen Essex, Karen Kehela-Sherwood, Jessica Liebowitz, Lauren Schneider, Chip Seelig, Jeff Shumlin, Max Stier, Jane von Mehren, and the incomparable Bob Wunsch.

I am fortunate to have picked up another family in the last few years who have retaught me everything wonderful about generosity, unconditional love, and blunt editing. In return they're stuck with an insufferable seder guest for life. I am thrilled to include Debbie and Alan Rottenberg; Dan, Elissa, and Nathan Rottenberg; and Becky Rottenberg in my life.

My natural-born family continues to redefine the boundaries of love and support, even as I continue to throw more painful obstacles in their way. My work is informed and shaped by a lifetime of engaging the world alongside Jane and Ed Feiler. My brother, Andrew, is a beacon of humanity and exacting thought who improved every sentence in this book—many more than once. Cari Feiler Bender has shown us all the way to balance life, work, and family.

One person, above all, helped nurture the ideas and deepen the emotion that transformed this journey into such an enriching experience. Linda Rottenberg is a woman of passion, courage, and vivid color, who manages to find time to improve me and my work, even while devoting herself to serving so many around the globe. Her heart beats in these pages. During our trip to Iran, as we were leaving the Shrine to Fatima, a crow deposited its noontime droppings on my back. An elderly woman in a chador was the first to point out the rather large despoiling. "You will be very lucky," she said. "Then we will have a good trip," I replied. "Oh, no," she said, remarking on the size, "much luckier than that!" "In that case," I said, "my wife will get pregnant."

Well the stain must have been larger than we had realized.

A year later, just days after I completed my manuscript, Linda gave birth to two healthy, hearty, heaven-sent identical girls, Eden Elenor Feiler and Tybee Rose Feiler. God willing, they will find in these pages someday the dreams their mother had for them and find out anew the inconceivable blessing they enjoy of carrying her around in their hearts. This book is dedicated to their mom.

WORDS OF PEACE
AND TRUTH

I have come to relish the research part of my travels as much as the travels themselves. I have tried to read as widely as possible in the academic and popular literature on these subjects, while understanding that my efforts will never be definitive. In lieu of a formal bibliography, I have included an annotated list of books that have been particularly helpful, with an eye toward directing those who might wish to explore further a particular area.

First, a few words on fundamentals. Bible translations vary in style and emphasis. For the sake of consistency, all quotations from the Hebrew Bible, unless otherwise noted, come from the new Jewish Publication Society translation, *Tanakh: The Holy Scriptures* (JPS, Philadelphia). Quotations from the New Testament are taken from *The Holy Bible, with Apocrypha*, New Revised Standard Version (Oxford University Press, New York).

In keeping with long-standing academic custom and recent trends in popular writing, the nonsectarian terms B.C.E. (Before the Common Era) and c.e. (Common Era) are used throughout the book in place of the terms b.c. and a.d.

When disputes of fact arose, I relied on *The Anchor Bible Dictionary* (New York, 1992), a six-volume reference book that sits alongside my desk. I have also consulted *The Oxford Companion to the Bible*, *The Cambridge Companion to the Bible*, and *Lutterworth Dictionary of the Bible*.

Book I: Land

In studying the history of the Ancient Near East, I benefited from *Ancient Israel* by Roland DeVaux, *Axial Age Civilizations*, edited by S.N. Eisenstadt, *The Bible Unearthed* by Israel Finkelstein and Neil Asher Silberman, *A History of Israel* by John Bright, and *Memory and the Mediterranean* by Fernand Braudel.

The story of King David is teased out in penetrating ways in Robert Alter's *The David Story*, Baruch Halpern's *David's Secret Demons*, Jonathan Kirsch's *King David*, Yael Lotan's novel *Avishag*, and Steven L. McKenzie's *King David*.

Gershom Gorenberg has written an illuminating study of the contemporary battle over the Temple Mount called *The End of Days*.

Book II: Exile

A number of fascinating books explore the history of the Israelites in exile, including *Exile and Restoration* by Peter Ackroyd, *A History of Prophecy in Israel* and *Prophecy and Canon*, both by Joseph Blenkinsopp, and *Israel in Exile* by Ralph Klein.

The phenomenon of prophecy is explored in *Hopeful Imagination*, *The Land*, and *The Prophetic Imagination*, all by Walter Brueggemann, *The Prophets* by Abraham Joshua Heschel, *God* by Jack Miles, and *The Prophets* by Norman Podhoretz.

A number of wonderful books delve into the theology and impact of the Garden of Eden story, most notably *Adam, Eve, and the Serpent* by Elaine Pagels and *History of Paradise* by Jean Delumeau. I will read anything by Jon Levenson and was both awed and educated by *Creation and the Persistence of Evil*, *Sinai and Zion*, and *Esther*.

Ancient Iraq by George Roux is an extremely well-written general history of the area. I also drew from *Babylon* by Albert Champdor, *The Sumerians* by Samuel Noah Kramer, and *Return to Babylon* by Brian Fagan.

Penguin publishes an edition of *Tales from the Thousand and One Nights*, and the Anchor Bible edition of *Jonah* by Jack Sasson is also helpful.

On the subject of war, I was entranced by *War Is a Force That Gives Us Meaning* by Chris Hedges and learned from *Just and Unjust Wars* by Michael Walzer.

Book III: Diaspora

Mary Boyce's *Zoroastrians* is still definitive in its field; Paul Kriwaczek has written a wonderful contemporary travel book, *In Search of Zarathustra*. Houman Sarshar is the editor of a beautiful book on the Jews of Iran called *Esther's Children*. Michael Fox's study *Esther* was helpful.

The rise of Judaism in the ancient world is discussed in *The God of the Maccabees* by Elias Bickerman, *Between Athens and Jerusalem* by John J. Collins, *Religions of the Hellenistic-Roman Age* by Antonia Tripolitis, and *Hellenistic Civilization and the Jews* by Victor Tcherikover.

General

A number of books enhanced my study of Judaism, both past and present: *On Judaism* by Martin Buber, *A Heart of Many Rooms* and

A Living Covenant by David Hartman, *The Jewish Way* by Irving Greenberg, *The Jews in America* by Arthur Hertzberg, *The Jewish Way of Life and Thought* by Abraham Karp, *The Messiah Texts* by Raphael Patai, and *A Different Light*, edited by Noam Zion and Barbara Spectre.

On the history and philosophy of religion, I enjoyed Mircea Eliade's *The Sacred and the Profane*, John Hick's *Philosophy of Religion*, Harold Kushner's *Who Needs God*, Rudolf Otto's *The Idea of the Holy*, and Huston Smith's *Why Religion Matters*.

I would especially like to recommend three sensational books that speak to the larger themes of our time: *The Battle for God* by Karen Armstrong, which explores the rise of fundamentalism in the three Abrahamic faiths; *Islam Under Seige* by my friend Akbar Ahmed, which illuminates the challenges facing Islam today; and *The Dignity of Difference* by Jonathan Sacks, the best book I know that lays out a realistic vision of interfaith harmony.

Finally, after *Walking the Bible* was published, I set up a website, www.brucefeiler.com, and encouraged readers to share their thoughts. I have been overwhelmed and deeply moved by the outpouring of honest, intimate, heartfelt letters. I am hard-pressed to convey how life affirming—and life changing—these exchanges have been. From the beginning I have tried to answer every letter I receive (even the occasional grumbling ones), and have added more features in response to requests. I invite you to visit the site, where you'll find photographs of some places along my journey, resources for interfaith activities, and discussion questions for reading groups. The best way to uphold the values in the Bible, I believe, is to find a way to keep talking about them today.

INDEX

Aaron (biblical figure), 131
Abbasids, 212, 213
Abraham (biblical figure), 17, 52–53, 55, 75, 86, 130, 131, 194, 255, 257
 Mesopotamian origins of, 126, 153, 159, 160, 162–64, 166, 171, 175, 193, 197, 200, 227, 233, 256, 302
Abrishami Synagogue, 320, 324–25
Achaemenid dynasty, 295, 298, 299, 300, 304–7, 308, 317, 318, 319, 331, 334, 346
 see also Persia; *specific Achaemenid kings*
Afghanistan, Buddhist statues defaced in, 310
afterlife, 287, 292
Agnew, Spiro, 309
agriculture, 189–90
Ahasuerus (biblical figure), 331, 332, 334, 335, 337, 338
Ahuramazda, 286, 288, 289, 297, 304
Ai, Israelite attack on, 12–13
Air Force, U.S., 157

Akiva ben Joseph, 377
Akkadian language, 159, 185, 246
Al Aqsa mosque, 66, 91, 101–2
Alexander III, Czar of Russia, 365
Alexander III (the Great), King of Macedon, 295, 298, 300, 304, 331, 348–49, 350
Al-Rashid hotel, 239
al-Ubaidy, Mohammad Saleh, 233, 238
Alwash, Azzam, 144–46, 147, 155
Amar, Shlomo, 359–60, 362
Amos (biblical figure), 134, 374
Antiochus IV, King of Syria, 350–51
Antipater of Sidon, 201
anti-Semitism, 281, 326, 338, 339
Apadana staircase, 305, 309
Applebaum, David, 29, 30
Applebaum, Nava, 29, 30
Arabic language, 212, 213, 277
Arafat, Yasser, 112
Aramaic language, 212
Aristotle, 348, 373
Ark of the Covenant, 76–77, 98, 113

About the author

About the book

Insights,
Interviews
& More...

Read on

Meet Bruce Feiler

Jim Coane

BRUCE FEILER is the *New York Times* bestselling author of nine books, an award-winning journalist, and the writer-presenter of PBS miniseries. He has traveled to more than sixty countries, on six continents, immersing himself in different cultures and bringing other worlds vividly to life.

Learning to Bow, published in 1991, is his humorous account of the year he spent teaching in a small Japanese town. *Looking for Class* describes life inside the world's most prestigious academic institutions, Oxford and Cambridge. *Under the Big Top* depicts the turbulent, engrossing year he spent performing as a clown in the Clyde Beatty–Cole Bros. Circus. And *Dreaming Out Loud* relates his all-access adventures on the road with Garth Brooks, Wynonna Judd, and other top stars in country music.

> 66 [Feiler] has traveled to more than sixty countries, on six continents, immersing himself in different cultures and bringing other worlds vividly to life. 99

His most recent work explores the parallels between religion, geography, and the emotional issues of our time. *Walking the Bible* describes his perilous, ten-thousand-mile journey through the desert retracing the greatest stories ever told. Named one of the best books of the year by the *Los Angeles Times,* it spent more than a year on the *New York Times* bestseller list and has been translated into fifteen languages. *Walking the Bible* was the subject of a three-part PBS series presented by Feiler.

Recounting Feiler's personal search for the shared ancestor of Jews, Christians, and Muslims, *Abraham* was featured on the cover of *Time,* became a runaway *New York Times* bestseller, and was named one of the best books of the year by the *Christian Science Monitor, St. Louis Post-Dispatch,* Amazon.com, Barnes & Noble, Borders, and *Publishers Weekly.*

A native of Savannah, Georgia, Bruce Feiler writes for numerous publications and is a contributing editor for *Gourmet* and *Parade.* He is a frequent contributor to National Public Radio. He has received the ASCAP Deems Taylor Award for Excellence in Music Journalism and three James Beard Awards for writing about food and restaurants. ∾

A Conversation with Bruce Feiler

Near the start of Where God Was Born, *you recall feeling a unique sense of urgency to write this particular book. "I had wanted to go on my first journeys back to the Bible. I needed to go on this one." Tell us a little more about this. Why Israel, Iraq, and Iran? Why now?*

A few years ago, I went to the library and retrieved the April 16, 1966, cover story in *Time* magazine entitled "Is God Dead?" The article suggested that God had retreated forever from public life and that religion was dead as a matter of influence in world affairs and would never return again. What a difference a generation makes. Today, the biggest news stories include terrorism, the Middle East, the Ten Commandments, and gay marriage. The biggest movie of recent years: *The Passion of the Christ.* The biggest book: *The Da Vinci Code.* Religion is bigger today than at any time in the last century. I realized that if I wanted to make sense of this situation I should go back to the origins of religion itself. I had to go back to the place where God was born to figure out: Is religion tearing us apart, or can it

> 66 I had to go back to the place where God was born to figure out: Is religion tearing us apart, or can it bring us back together? 99

bring us back together? That journey led me to the second half of the Hebrew Bible, which takes place in Israel, Iraq, and Iran.

As a Jew growing up in Georgia, you witnessed your parents' ambivalent relationship with their heritage and faith—at one point, you describe the way they "tugged at the gossamers of assimilation." In what ways do you feel these memories inform—or possibly belie—the religious, political, and historical concerns in your writing today?

When I was growing up, I, like many Jews, cheered what appeared to be the receding of faith from everyday life. The further religion got from our lives the better our lives would get, I thought, because persecution had been such a burden to Jewish families for generations. But the older I get, the more I realize that religion is not going to be easily marginalized by one of its wannabe successors—science, capitalism, consumerism. Religion has grown stronger in the last thirty years because it's broader than any country. It addresses the dignity of all human beings. It is universal. Religion also breeds overconfidence, and one challenge for today's believers is to rediscover in the ▶

A Conversation with Bruce Feiler *(continued)*

fire of faith the source of warmth that can overpower the flames of destruction.

One of the most striking passages in the book finds you engaged in a freely associative conversation with your wife, Linda: the two of you parse the Book of Esther, assess the state of women's rights in contemporary Iran, and explore the consequences of Jewish assimilation around the world. This portrait of a marriage rooted in intellectual exploration, emotional generosity, and mutual discovery is deeply affecting—and it also powerfully underscores the larger themes of your book. What were your intentions in adding such a personal dimension to your narrative?

First, you should know that my wife reads most things that I write, and it turns out she LOVES this question! When I set out to write *Walking the Bible* nearly ten years ago I insisted that it would not be personal. It would be about archaeology, not me and my own search for God. What a fool I was. The longer I have traveled on this road the more personal my travels have become and the more willing I have become to probe those parts of the experience. The way to tell a really big

66 When I set out to write *Walking the Bible* nearly ten years ago I insisted that it would not be personal. It would be about archaeology, not me and my own search for God. What a fool I was. 99

story, I think, is to tell a really small story. Also, while writing about the raw emotion of *Walking the Bible* was difficult, it was, inevitably, the part of the book that people appreciated the most. So this time I went even further. Linda is a central part of my emotional life, and my work life, and I thought putting that story on paper was the most honest way to convey what happened to me.

Where God Was Born is being published at a time of great tumult and uncertainty in the Middle East—to say nothing of the perpetual, low-flying dread afflicting life in the United States and Western Europe. Tell us about your hopes and expectations for human civilization in the coming decade. What success might Bible-rooted, interfaith dialogue have in providing consolation— or at least perspective—in this so-called age of terror?

I think it's safe to say that the biggest question in the world today is, "Can the religions figure out a way to relate to one another that is not by killing one another?" I think the answer is pretty much up in the air—and definitely up to us. It's either open warfare among ▶

the faiths, or it's some alternative. And the only path to alternative is some kind of dialogue. I think the Bible can play an important role in this conversation because, from its opening verses, it suggests that chaos is a natural state in the world, and the only force strong enough to calm the chaos is words. Don't forget, God uses words to create the world. Words! Words are our only hope.

Tell us about your travels and experiences since finishing Where God Was Born. *What can we look forward to reading next?*

I spent half of every month, for six months, back in the Middle East— in Turkey, Israel, Egypt, and Jordan— shooting a three-hour documentary for PBS based on *Walking the Bible*. It was a challenging and, at times, dangerous experience, but the footage is spectacular, high-definition camera work shot by a British crew of exceptional talent. Then, a few weeks after we finished filming and a few days after turning in the manuscript for *Where God Was Born,* my wife gave birth to two healthy, hearty, heaven-sent identical girls. Since then, I've been doing a lot of traveling between my bedroom and theirs in the wee hours of the morning. I hope they make this journey in peace sometime in their lives. ∽

66 A few days after turning in the manuscript for *Where God Was Born,* my wife gave birth to two healthy, hearty, heaven-sent identical girls. I hope they make this journey in peace sometime in their lives. 99

Photographs from
Bruce Feiler's Journey

Bruce Feiler

The Dome of the Rock atop the Temple Mount
in Jerusalem

Bruce Feiler

Aerial view of the Old City and the Temple Mount with the Mount of
Olives (upper right) and City of David (lower right)

An olive tree in the "Garden of Eden"
in Qurnah, Iraq

The confluence of the Tigris and Euphrates Rivers north of Basra, Iraq

Bruce Feiler

U.S. soldiers from the 607th MP Battalion read the Bible on the steps of the ziggurat in Ur, southern Iraq

Bruce Feiler

Saddam's palace, built above the ruins of Nebuchadnezzar II's palace, in Babylon, Iraq

Ruins of Cyrus the Great's palace in Pasagardae, Iran

Close-up of the staircase with Achaemenid carvings in Persepolis, Iran

Topics and Questions
for Discussion

*The following are intended to enrich your
conversation and help your group find
new and interesting topics and angles for
approaching this book.*

1. Of all the destinations illuminated over
   the course of *Where God Was Born*—
   from modern-day Israel, Iran, and Iraq
   to ancient Babylon and Persia—which
   did you find the most compelling?
   In what specific ways have your
   perceptions of each of these places
   been enriched, challenged, or even
   transformed altogether by the portraits
   in this book?

2. Consider Feiler's own perceptions with
   regard to the places listed above. How
   do his feelings, fears, and/or passions
   shift and evolve as he moves from city
   to city, nation to nation?

3. An abiding question throughout *Where
   God Was Born* concerns the historical
   accuracy of the Hebrew Bible. At one
   point, Feiler calls it "the tantalizing,
   tender relationship between the details
   in the text and the facts in the ground."
   Discuss Feiler's treatment of this

relationship at different points in the book, beginning with his theorizing on the viability of Joshua's lightning conquest of Canaan and continuing through his ruminations on Esther's power plays in Persia.

4. Why did Karl Jaspers term the years 800 to 200 B.C.E. the Axial Age? What happened in the span of these centuries? And what is it about our own era that has led some scholars to argue that we are in the midst of a new Axial Age? What parallels exist between then and now?

5. Discuss Feiler's writing voice and the lucid structure of his travel narrative. What role does dialogue play in the narrative? What words would you use to characterize his style?

6. What kind of person is Avner Goren? What do we learn about the nature of his passions and beliefs, and how do these beliefs inform his work as an archaeologist? How does Goren's voice and presence color the action and tone of *Where God Was Born*?

7. Consider the diverse ideologies and personalities of the people with whom Feiler dialogues in this book, including the staunchly Zionist General Yoram "Yaya" Yair in "Be Strong and Very Courageous"; the ▶

Topics and Questions for Discussion
(continued)

activist/archaeologist John Malcolm
Russell in Iraq in "By the Rivers of
Babylon"; Chaplain Lew Messenger,
the impassioned seeker of interfaith
dialogue in "City of Peace"; and Pallan,
the Zoroastrian graduate student in
Iran in "Let There Be Light." How do
these—and so very many others—
inform Feiler's own reflections about
the journey he has undertaken?

8. Discuss *Where God Was Born* in the
context of Feiler's previous Bible-
themed books, *Abraham* and *Walking
the Bible*. What themes link the three
works? And how have Feiler's
perceptions evolved and shifted over
the course of the three narratives—
whether regarding the notion of land,
the idea of Diaspora, or the prospects
for the interfaith movement?

*For more discussion questions
relating to* Where God Was Born
*and Bruce Feiler's other books,
visit www.brucefeiler.com.* ⌒

Have You Read?

**WALKING THE BIBLE:
A PHOTOGRAPHIC JOURNEY**

Featuring Bruce Feiler's own photography as well as his selections from professional collections, *Walking the Bible: A Photographic Journey* brings together breathtaking vistas, intimate portraits, and fascinating panoramas, providing firsthand access to the inscrutable land where three of the world's great religions were born—and finally puts a face on the stories that have long inspired the human spirit.

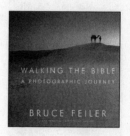

"Beautifully depicts the dramatic land that gave birth to three of the world's great religions."   —*USA Today*

ABRAHAM: A JOURNEY TO THE HEART OF THREE FAITHS

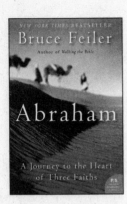

Both immediate and timeless, *Abraham* tells the powerful story of one man's search for the shared ancestor of Judaism, Christianity, and Islam. Traveling through war zones, braving violence at religious sites, and seeking out faith leaders, Bruce Feiler uncovers the defining yet divisive role that Abraham plays for half the world's believers. Provocative and uplifting, *Abraham* offers a thoughtful and inspiring vision of unity that redefines what we think about our neighbors, our future, and ourselves.

"An exquisitely written journey."
—*Boston Globe*

"Feiler's combination of journalism, commentary, and self-discovery tells the reader volumes about humankind."
—*Atlanta Journal-Constitution*

WALKING THE BIBLE: A JOURNEY BY LAND THROUGH THE FIVE BOOKS OF MOSES

Feeling disconnected from the religious community he had known as a child, Bruce Feiler set out on a perilous, ten-thousand-mile journey across the Middle East to discover the roots of the Bible. Traveling through three continents, five countries, and four war zones, Feiler is the first person ever to complete such an adventure in an attempt to answer the question, Is the Bible just an abstraction, some book gathering dust, or is it a living, breathing entity with relevance to contemporary life? From Turkey to Israel, the Sinai to Egypt, Feiler explores how geography affects the larger narrative of the Bible and ultimately realizes how much these places—and his experience— have affected his faith.

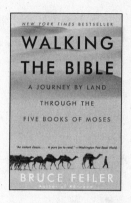

"Ranks among the great spiritual autobiographies."
> —*Washington Post Book World*

"Smart and savvy, insightful and illuminating." —*Los Angeles Times*

DREAMING OUT LOUD: GARTH BROOKS, WYNONNA JUDD, WADE HAYES, AND THE CHANGING FACE OF NASHVILLE

Country music has exploded across the United States and undergone a sweeping revolution, transforming the once ridiculed world of Nashville into an unlikely focal point of American pop culture. In writing this fascinating book, Feiler was granted unprecedented access to the private moments of the revolution. Here is the acclaimed report: a chronicle of the genre's biggest stars as they changed the face of American music. With intimate portraits of Garth Brooks, Wynonna Judd, and Wade Hayes, Feiler has written the defining book on the new Nashville.

"Penetrating and insightful."
　　　　　—Elvis Mitchell, *New York Times*

"Essential reading for anyone who cares about American music."
　　　　　—*Washington Post*

UNDER THE BIG TOP:
A SEASON WITH THE CIRCUS

It's every child's dream: to run away and
join the circus. Feiler did just that, joining
the Clyde Beatty–Cole Bros. Circus as a
clown for one year. This is the story of that
crazy, chaotic, heartbreaking ride, a book
that will remind you of how dreams
can go horribly wrong—and then
miraculously come true."

"A stunning collective portrait."

—*The New Yorker*

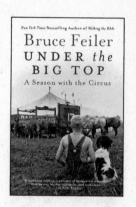

LOOKING FOR CLASS: DAYS AND NIGHTS
AT OXFORD AND CAMBRIDGE

An irresistible, entertaining peek into the
privileged realm of Wordsworth and
Wodehouse, Chelsea Clinton and Hugh
Grant, *Looking for Class* offers a hilarious
account of Feiler's year at Britain's most
exclusive universities, Oxford and
Cambridge—the garden parties and
formal balls, the high-minded debates
and drinking Olympics—and gives
us an eye-opening view of the often
romanticized but rarely seen British
upper class. ▶

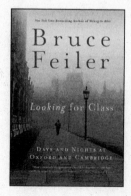

Have You Read? *(continued)*

"[A] trenchant, witty, and engaging critique of the English establishment."
—*San Francisco Chronicle*

LEARNING TO BOW:
INSIDE THE HEART OF JAPAN

Feiler's first book, *Learning to Bow,* is one of the funniest, liveliest, and most insightful books ever written about the clash of cultures between America and Japan. With warmth and candor, Feiler recounts the year he spent as a teacher in a small rural Japanese town. Beginning with a ritual outdoor bath and culminating in an all-night trek to the top of Mount Fuji, Feiler teaches his students about American culture, while they teach him everything from how to properly address an envelope to how to date a Japanese girl.

"Incisive, often hilarious, and presents a rounded portrait of the modern Japanese."
—*USA Today*